Jesus, the Temple, and Early Christian Memory

Jesus, the Temple, and Early Christian Memory

—— Scott K. Brevard ——

◦PICKWICK *Publications* · Eugene, Oregon

JESUS, THE TEMPLE, AND EARLY CHRISTIAN MEMORY

Copyright © 2025 Scott K. Brevard. All rights reserved. Except for brief quotations in critical publications or reviews, no part of this book may be reproduced in any manner without prior written permission from the publisher. Write: Permissions, Wipf and Stock Publishers, 199 W. 8th Ave., Suite 3, Eugene, OR 97401.

Pickwick Publications
An Imprint of Wipf and Stock Publishers
199 W. 8th Ave., Suite 3
Eugene, OR 97401

www.wipfandstock.com

PAPERBACK ISBN: 979-8-3852-5027-1
HARDCOVER ISBN: 979-8-3852-5028-8
EBOOK ISBN: 979-8-3852-5029-5

Cataloguing-in-Publication data:

Names: Brevard, Scott K., author.

Title: Jesus, the temple, and early Christian memory / Scott K. Brevard.

Description: Eugene, OR: Pickwick Publications, 2025. | Includes bibliographical references and indexes.

Identifiers: ISBN 979-8-3852-5027-1 (paperback). | ISBN 979-8-3852-5028-8 (hardcover). | ISBN 979-8-3852-5029-5 (ebook)

Subjects: LCSH: Jesus Christ—Historicity. | Temple of Jerusalem (Jerusalem). | Memory—Social aspects—History. | Collective memory—History.

Classification: BM620 B75 2025 (print). | BM620 (ebook).

VERSION NUMBER 08/05/25

All Bible translations are my own.

For Aubrey and Laine.

Words cannot contain the love
I have for you all.

Contents

Acknowledgments | ix
Introduction | xi
List of Abbreviations | xv

1 Social Memory Theory: What We Remember and How | 1
2 Memory Theory in New Testament Research | 47
3 Jewish Attitudes Toward the Jerusalem Temple
   in the Second Temple Period (540 BCE–70 CE) | 110
4 Jesus and the Temple | 172
5 Jesus, the Temple, and Early Christian Memory | 234

Bibliography | 249

Acknowledgments

French composer Claude Debussy once said, "Music is the space between the notes." The same can be said about the production of this dissertation, as much of the "music" of this study—if any exists at all—is thanks to the "space" of the conversations, interactions, and relationships that have formed my thought and made my writing possible. For that, there are several people that deserve immense gratitude.

First and foremost, I am grateful for the patience, wisdom, guidance, and compassion of my dissertation committee: Christopher W. Skinner, Olivia Stewart Lester, and Rafael Rodríguez. Each of you have played an integral role not only in the content of this study, but in the context of its production, and your willingness and flexibility in working with me over the years has meant the world to me. The constant effort and support you all offered me truly made a difference, and I hope seeing this in print is another way I can thank you for your investment in my life.

I am especially grateful to the faculty, staff, and students of the Theology Department at Loyola University Chicago. As professors, colleagues, and friends, you all created an environment in which the pursuit of knowledge was not a competition of ego, but a celebration of learning from one another. In particular, I am grateful to Edmondo Lupieri for including me in an international colloquium that morphed into a publication; it has taken many years, but I am happy to see my name in print alongside so many distinguished scholars. I am also grateful for my fellow students in the New Testament/Early Christianity program, and I want to give particular thanks to Shane Gormley, Jon Hatter, Josh King, Paul Adaja, Scott Harris, Megan Wines, Eric Zito, and the rest of the graduate students whose participation in classes, colloquia, and conversations made me a better thinker and communicator.

To my friends Zach Eberhart, Tyler Kelley, and Raleigh Heth: from our early days at the University of Georgia, you all have consistently inspired and supported me, and your friendship has been a major part of why I continued to pursue a doctoral program. You all are brilliant, original thinkers, thorough conversation partners, but most importantly, you are the best friends that I could ever have asked for as I set out on my initial journey in the field of biblical studies. As much as I think you all will be (and already are) fantastic scholars, I am so grateful that you are even better friends.

The folks at Wipf and Stock Publishers were not only exceedingly kind, but also made the publication process a breeze. In particular, I am grateful for the guidance of Michael Thomson, Matt Wimer, George Callihan, and Dr. K. C. Hanson.

Finally, there is no way I would be where I am without the love and support of my family. In particular, the one person who deserves the most gratitude is my wife, Aubrey. Without her support, I would not be—and not want to be—where I am today. You encouraged me through every unproductive day, cared for me through every moment I wanted to quit, and loved me through all the chaos and unknowns of the journey. Inasmuch as you would not describe yourself as a "patient person," you have been endlessly patient with me as I pursued this dream, and I owe every single page (that I hope you never have to read) to you. You made the dream of completing a doctoral program come true, pushed me to dream bigger and publish my work, but most of all, you continually make the dream of living a life full of love and joy come true every single day, and for that I am and will always be eternally grateful.

Introduction

I am faced with the appalling fact that I don't know anything.
—Paul Newman[1]

In the late second century CE, Irenaeus attacked Marcion, Valentinus, and their followers for their rejection of the prophets, pointing to the imagery shared between Daniel and John the revelator as evidence of the continuity of scriptural authority. Irenaeus's interpretation of the apocalyptic imagery of Revelation focuses specifically on identifying the rise of the antichrist, and while he declines to put forth an interpretation as to the name (Rev 13:18), he makes the interesting claim that the antichrist would "sit in the temple in Jerusalem" (*sedebit in templo Hierosolymis*, *Haer.* 5.30.4). The big problem for Irenaeus, however, was that this expectation was impossible: the temple had been destroyed about a century prior to his writing and continued to lie in waste.

Irenaeus was not alone, however, as other second-century Christians wrestled with this same conviction about the status and place of the temple. Justin Martyr doubled down on his belief that Jerusalem and its temple would be restored (*Dial.* 80). On the other hand, Tertullian reinterpreted the temple to be Christ, where God dwelled, and the church, then, was the natural successor of the temple (*Marc.* 3.20–23).[2] Early Christian texts also follow this same hermeneutic of spiritualizing

1. Itzkoff, "Posthumous Memoir."
2. "While some early Christian writers continued to see Palestine as the locus of the parousia of Christ and of his eschatological kingdom . . . they stood in continuity with the traditions reflected in Hebrews 12–13 and Revelation 21 and claimed gentile Christian supercession of the historical Israel" (Taylor, "Jerusalem and the Temple," 447).

(as a form of superseding) the temple. For instance, 1 Clem. 40–42 views the temple as a positive model for the priesthood, Barn. 16 rejects the physical structure of the temple in favor of repentance, and Ps.-Cl. *Recognitions* 1.39 understands sacrifice to have been replaced by water baptism. Even after its destruction in 70 CE, the temple remained a complex, meaningful, relevant symbol.

One potential reason for the continued relevance of the Jerusalem temple is its status in first- and second-century Jesus traditions. As early Christians commemorated, constructed, transmitted, and received traditions about Jesus's life, ministry, and death, they found significance in Jesus's miracles, teachings, dialogues, conflicts, and the interactions between Jesus and his setting in first-century Roman Judaea. Within this world, the Jerusalem temple was a dominant political, social, cultural, economic, and religious force for life in Second Temple Judaea.

Based on the importance of temple for daily life in and around Judaea and its continued significance in the late second century, it is seemingly odd to find Jesus tradition commemorating his relationship with the temple in an antagonistic manner. For instance, in Mark 15:29–30, Jesus is mocked during the crucifixion for supposedly claiming to destroy and rebuild the temple.[3] This scene conflicts with Jesus's trial, where this claim is outright rejected as false witness and inconsistent with other claims against him.[4] Earlier in the narrative, however, Jesus did prophesy the destruction of the temple in such a catastrophic manner that "a stone upon a stone" would not be left (οὐ μὴ ἀφεθῇ ὧδε λίθος ἐπὶ λίθον, Mark 13:2). Furthermore, when other early Christians engaged and retold these traditions, they also constructed Jesus's attitude in conflicting ways. For example, the Gospel of John (2:19) and *Gospel of Thomas* (log. 71) report Jesus saying he would destroy the temple, whereas Luke only reports the reputation in light of Stephen's behavior (Acts 6:8–7:60). These traditions, then, display competing conceptions

---

3. "Ha! The one destroying the temple and building it in three days, having come down from the cross, let him save himself" (Οὐὰ ὁ καταλύων τὸν ναὸν καὶ οἰκοδομῶν ἐν τρισὶν ἡμέραις, σῶσον σεαυτὸν καταβὰς ἀπὸ τοῦ σταυροῦ). All Bible translations are my own.

4. "They were giving false witness against him, saying 'We heard him saying 'I will destroy this handmade temple and after three days I will build another not made from hands.' But even on this their testimony was not the same" (ἐψευδομαρτύρουν κατ' αὐτοῦ λέγοντες ὅτι Ἡμεῖς ἠκούσαμεν αὐτοῦ λέγοντος ὅτι Ἐγὼ καταλύσω τὸν ναὸν τοῦτον τὸν χειροποίητον καὶ διὰ τριῶν ἡμερῶν ἄλλον ἀχειροποίητον οἰκοδομήσω καὶ οὐδὲ οὕτως ἴση ἦν ἡ μαρτυρία αὐτῶν, Mark 14:57–59).

of Jesus's relationship with the Jerusalem temple and lead to a series of difficult questions. Was Jesus really against the institution of the Jerusalem temple? Do these traditions reflect later anti-Jewish attitudes? Or, put differently, do these attitudes fit within the broader world of Second Temple Judaism? And why would early Christians portray his attitude in competing, complex, and multivalent ways?

To answer these questions, this study examines the relationship between Jesus and the Jerusalem temple in the first three centuries CE. By investigating the characterization of Jesus and the temple in the gospels, we are engaging in questions of tradition, history, and memory. Therefore, chapter 1 introduces the basic terms, figures, and concepts of social memory theory. Proceeding from the theoretical framework pioneered by Maurice Halbwachs and developed by later twentieth-century scholars, social memory theory contends that all memory is an active, constructive process, that memory exists within social frameworks, and that the past and the present are mutually informative. In chapter 2, I examine how the tenets of social memory theory have been introduced into New Testament studies. Scholars such as Alan Kirk and Tom Thatcher, Anthony Le Donne, Rafael Rodríguez, Chris Keith, and Sandra Huebenthal have offered instructive insights into how memory theory can reshape assumptions in New Testament studies on the historical Jesus, gospels studies, and the traditioning process in early Christianity. Because this study is concerned with attitudes about the Jerusalem temple, chapter 3 investigates the socio-historical context of Second Temple Judaism as the social, cultural, historical, political, and religious frameworks of the gospels's first-century memories of Jesus. I discuss paradigms of identity in Second Temple Judaism that allow for understanding the temple as an important, yet contested, feature of life in the Second Temple world. Chapter 4 examines the traditions of the gospels, particularly the Gospel of Mark, to understand exactly how Jesus was remembered in relation to the Jerusalem temple. Finally, chapter 5 draws together the previous chapters by proposing explanations for why Jesus's relationship to the temple was remembered in complex, contested, and multivalent ways.

The gospels are cultural, commemorative artifacts comprised of narrative traditions and memories about Jesus and imbued with meaning and formative for group identity. Previous centuries of Jesus studies have treated them as if they contained kernels of historical reality that can be mined from theological reflection. Social memory theory, however, has offered a helpful corrective: the gospels cannot be separated from the present social frameworks in which they commemorate the past. What we find within the gospels allows us to see how early Christians remembered, constructed, transmitted, and received stories about and sayings of Jesus. Within this commemorative sphere, Jesus's relationship with the temple demonstrates early Christians wrestling with a complex symbol in a contested world in the same way as Second Temple Jews, but memory theory also allows us to postulate about the historical Jesus as the past by which Christian communities were constrained in their commemorative retellings. Due to its turbulent history and place within Israel's prophetic tradition, the temple meant many things to many people. It is not surprising to see early Christians contend with the same complexities as Second Temple Jews, and this common struggle allows us to see points of unity, diversity, stability, and variability across both Second Temple Judaism and early Christianity.

Abbreviations

AASOR	Annual of the American Schools of Oriental Research
BHGNT	Baylor Handbook on the Greek New Testament
Bib	*Biblica*
BJRL	*Bulletin of the John Rylands University Library of Manchester*
BTB	*Biblical Theology Bulletin*
BZAW	Beihefte zur Zeitschrift für die alttestamentliche Wissenschaft
CBQ	*Catholic Biblical Quarterly*
CurBR	*Currents in Biblical Research*
CHANE	Culture and History of the Ancient Near East
DCLS	Deuterocanonical and Cognate Literature Studies
DSD	*Dead Sea Discoveries*
EC	*Early Christianity*
ECL	Early Christianity and Its Literature
ICC	International Critical Commentary
IEJ	*Israel Exploration Journal*
JBL	*Journal of Biblical Literature*
JRASup	Journal of Roman Architecture Supplemental Series
JRS	*Journal of Roman Studies*
JSHJ	*Journal for the Study of the Historical Jesus*
JSJ	*Journal for the Study of Judaism in the Persian, Hellenistic, and Roman Periods*

JSJSup	Journal for the Study of Judaism Supplements
JSNT	*Journal for the Study of the New Testament*
JSNTSup	Journal for the Study of the New Testament Supplement Series
JSOTSup	Journal for the Study of the Old Testament Supplement Series
JTS	*Journal of Theological Studies*
LHJS	Library of Historical Jesus Studies
LNTS	Library of New Testament Studies
Neot	*Neotestamentica*
NIGTC	New International Greek Testament Commentary
NovT	*Novum Testamentum*
NTL	New Testament Library
NTS	*New Testament Studies*
RB	*Revue biblique*
RBS	Resources for Biblical Study
SBLDS	Society of Biblical Literature Dissertation Series
SemeiaSt	Semeia Studies
SJOT	*Scandinavian Journal of the Old Testament*
SNTSMS	Society for New Testament Studies Monograph Series
SR	*Studies in Religion*
SSEJC	Studies in Scripture in Early Judaism and Christianity
STK	*Svensk teologisk kvartalskrift*
TBN	Themes in Biblical Narrative
TENTS	Texts and Editions for New Testament Study
TSAJ	Texts and Studies in Ancient Judaism
VC	*Vigiliae Christianae*
VT	*Vetus Testamentum*
WMANT	Wissenschaftliche Monographien zum Alten und Neuen Testament
WUNT	Wissenschaftliche Untersuchungen zum Neuen Testament
ZAC	*Zeitschrift für Antikes Christentum*
ZNW	*Zeitschrift für die neutestamentliche Wissenschaft und die Kunde der älteren Kirche*

1

Social Memory Theory

What We Remember and How

> How many people are critical enough to discern what they owe to others in their thinking and so acknowledge to themselves how small their own contribution usually is?
> —Maurice Halbwachs[1]

WHENEVER WE STUDY THE past, or the ways in which the past is represented and reconstructed, we are inevitably dancing around questions of memory: How does memory work, where is it located, and how can it be accessed? How exactly do we examine the past, and what is it that we are investigating? How is our understanding of the past shaped by our context, such as the social groups that form our identities? These are all questions that social memory theory—and the memory theorists that work from its theoretical foundations—seeks to answer. But what exactly is social memory theory, and, more importantly, how does it aid our investigation of the past? In this chapter, I will present an overview of social memory theory, drawing attention to the foundational work of Maurice Halbwachs and Frederic Bartlett, as well as Pierre Nora, Jan Assmann, and Barry Schwartz. I will discuss how we remember and reconstruct the past, the relationship of memory, tradition, and history, and how media plays a role in commemorative activity. Before discussing social memory theory, however, it is important to start with its central concept: memory.

1. Halbwachs, *Collective Memory*, 45.

What Is Memory?

Memory has been of interest for millennia: as a subject of scrutiny for intellectuals from Socrates to Freud, from rhetoricians[2] to neuroscientists; as a prominent literary theme from Hemingway to Rowling and a topic of numerous self-help books; and even as the focus of a famous showtune performed by some of the greatest voices in Broadway and Hollywood history. But what exactly *is* memory? Jacques Le Goff offers a simple definition as "the capacity for conserving certain information."[3] Barry Schwartz goes further, describing it as "an active, constructive process, not a simple matter of retrieving information. To remember is to place a part of the past in the service and conceptions and needs of the present."[4] More specifically, "memory" refers to a multitude of actions, cognitive processes, and concepts that, even though familiar, are extremely complex phenomena to study. Memory spans a vast range of activities, such as recounting, retrieving, recalling, and commemorating, and includes objective and subjective elements.[5] James Fentress and Chris Wickham sum up the difficulty in discussing the many dimensions of mnemonic activity by pointing out how "'memory' can include anything from a highly private and spontaneous, possibly wordless, mental sensation to a formalized public ceremony."[6] Further complicating the nature of memory is its spectrum of reliability. Because memory navigates a relationship between the past and the present, memories can be assessed to be "true" or "faulty" in their reflecting or distorting actual events, or even "false" if referring to events that did not happen in a

---

2. "The first basic fact which the student of the history of the classical art of memory must remember is that the art belonged to rhetoric as a technique by which the orator could improve his memory" (Yates, *Art of Memory*, 2).

3. Le Goff, *History and Memory*, 51.

4. Schwartz, "Social Context of Commemoration," 374.

5. Many scholars have attempted to systematize or categorize memory based on the type of activity associated with the act of remembering, but the ordering of "subjective" or "objective" memory activities is not always transparent. For example, Paul Connerton maps out three specific types of memory: personal memories, or "life histories," which consist of individual recollections of personal, biographical detail; cognitive memories, which recall experiences or facts that one has learned in the past; and finally, habit memories, which carry "the capacity to reproduce a certain [behavioral] performance." On the other hand, Fentress and Wickham front their discussion of the dimensions of memory in its two capacities: as an objective, passive "container of facts" and as a subjective, active "interpretation" of experiences, information, and feelings. See Connerton, *How Societies Remember*, 22–23; Fentress and Wickham, *Social Memory*, 3–4.

6. Fentress and Wickham, *Social Memory*, x.

positive manner.[7] Furthermore, memory, particularly in the transmission of tradition, can act in stable (relatively fixed) or dynamic (relatively malleable) ways.[8] Regardless of the way it acts, memory is never a substitute for an actual event; even "true" and "stable" memories must be distinguished from the past they remember.[9] Despite any notion of reliability—even in cases where we are able to check memories against historical records—Fentress and Wickham rightly note that "the question of whether *we* [figures in the present] regard these memories as historically true will often turn out to be less important than whether *they* [figures from the past] regard their memories as true."[10]

Another issue social memory theory draws attention to is the determination of where memories are located. Memory is often associated with the mind, and cognitive studies has provided significant advances for our neuro-psychological understanding of the way our minds encode habitual abilities, facts, or our past experiences.[11] Indeed, one of the most significant forms of memory is narrative memory, representations of the past fixed in story form.[12] However, memory is not merely a cognitive

---

7. Though related, the line between "faulty" and "false" memories is complex, and "false" memories should be clearly distinguished from "faulty" memories. Both are "characteristic of normal, rather than pathological, remembering," but "false" memories are attributed to "errors of commission rather than omission" (Brainerd and Reyna, *Science of False Memory*, 5). Perhaps one of the most fascinating examples of false memory from recent decades is the case of Bruno Dossekker. Writing under the pseudonym Binjamin Wilkomirski, Dossekker published a 1996 "memoir" about his experience as a child during the Holocaust, only for the story to be debunked in 1998. While it certainly could be a simple case of profiteering from tales of national trauma, Dossekker/Wilkomirski's insistence that the recollections truly are his experiences at least make it a possible case of false memory. See Schacter, *Seven Sins of Memory*, 2–3.

8. Fentress and Wickham, *Social Memory*, 97. Edward Shils's investigation of tradition included several features of stability and patterns of change traditions undergo, and many of these patterns serve as directly analogous to the way memories behave. See Shils, *Tradition*, 200–213, 273–86. One of the key dynamic features of memory is distortion, which will be covered below.

9. "Any attempt to use memory as a historical source in a sensitive way must confront the subjective, yet social, character of memory from the outset" (Fentress and Wickham, *Social Memory*, 7).

10. Fentress and Wickham, *Social Memory*, 25–26, emphasis original. Judith Redman's work on eyewitness memory has shown that memory—even eyewitness memory—can be fallible for a number of different reasons but still can be useful. After all, "[testimonies] are reliable in that they tell us *what* [those giving the testimonies] *believe to be true*. This does not necessarily make [them] true" (Redman, "How Accurate Are Eyewitnesses?," 196, emphasis original).

11. See Wexler, *Brain and Culture*.

12. Narrative memory often refers to the actions in the similar cognitive processes

phenomenon located only in the mind, and social memory theorists point to a variety of other locations where memory can be observed and studied. Fentress and Wickham argue that memory must have the capacity to be transmitted and articulated, but this does not only limit memory to the realm of speech. Memories can be articulated in ritual acts, manual skills, bodily gestures, or in a host of evolving manners and media: oral traditions, literature, inscriptions, monuments, art, institutions, dress, songs, and more.[13] Media play a key role in the transmission of memory; for instance, Fentress and Wickham argue that "freezing" narrative memories in writing is "a more convenient way of preserving the memory of detailed and specific information."[14] In addition, mnemonic "sites" allow us to locate group or national memories around or in association with geographic landmarks and physical spaces.[15] Furthermore, memory can be located within a community, which Bellah refers to as a "community of memory" that is "involved in retelling its story,

---

of episodic and autobiographical memory where the events of the past are represented in ordered story forms. See Hoerl, "Episodic Memory," 621–40. On the function of using a story form to represent memories, Fentress and Wickham argue that "stories do more than represent particular events: they connect, clarify, and interpret events in a general fashion. Stories provide us with a set of stock explanations which underlie our predispositions to interpret reality in the ways that we do" (Fentress and Wickham, *Social Memory*, 51).

13. "Individuals and cultures construct their memories interactively through communication by speech, images, and rituals. Without such representations, it is impossible to build a memory that can transcend generations and historical epochs, but this also means that with the changing nature and development of the various media, the constitution of the memory will also be continually changing" (Assmann, *Cultural Memory and Western Civilization*, 10; cf. Fentress and Wickham, *Social Memory*, 47; Connerton, *How Societies Remember*, 39–40).

14. "As long as this [written] information is available when and where it is needed, no one is going to go through the trouble of memorizing it" (Fentress and Wickham, *Social Memory*, 9; cf. Assmann, *Cultural Memory and Early Civilization*, 71–72, 108).

15. Olick and Robbins, "Social Memory Studies," 124–25; cf. Zerubavel, *Recovered Roots*. One example of memory concretized in material culture is the creation of confederate monuments, which appeared in large amounts during two general time periods: in the early decades of the twentieth century and in the middle of the twentieth century. It is rare for confederate monuments to have appeared during Reconstruction-era America; instead, the overwhelming amount were constructed and dedicated as commemorations of confederate beliefs in support of the interests of their contemporary worlds: the enactment of Jim Crow laws in the 1900s–1920s and pushback against the Civil Rights era in the 1950s–1960s. For more, see Southern Poverty Law Center, "Whose Heritage?"

its constitutive narrative."[16] Memory is pervasive, located in a variety of physical, mental, and cultural sites.

Memory is a complex subject but pertinent to our everyday lives. It is located all around us; it is central to a number of common activities; it relates to our attempts to connect the present and the past, and it shapes and defines identity. It is not solely an individual, psychological phenomenon; instead, it is a phenomenon that carries significant weight for—and is subsequently impacted by—society. A great deal is at stake in understanding the social character of memory, and social memory theorists have spent almost a century theorizing how the phenomenon works, how it impacts us, and how we can better understand it. However, before discussing the specific tenets of social memory theory and the structure of memory studies as a whole, it is useful to examine the terminology surrounding it.

Terminology

The study of social memory is not unitary, but is rather an interdisciplinary and, frankly, rather disorganized field that Jeffrey Olick and Joyce Robbins call "a nonparadigmatic, transdisciplinary, centerless enterprise."[17] This is not to deny the significant work done, but rather to remark on the diverse, yet interrelated, nature of the field. As such, the language used in social memory studies can also be disorganized, so it is helpful to begin with a brief primer on terminology in order to articulate what social memory is and, more helpfully, what it is not.

While the term "social memory" was used sparingly in Frederic Bartlett's *Remembering* (1932), Bartlett notes that the actual conversation about social memory was driven by Maurice Halbwachs's discussion of "collective memory" (*la mémoire collective*) in *Les cadres sociaux de la mémoire* (1925).[18] However, Halbwachs's use of the term was not monolithic; Jeffrey Olick notes that there are actually two phenomena

---

16. Bellah et al., *Habits of the Heart*, 153.

17. Olick and Robbins, "Social Memory Studies," 106. As such, this "enterprise" takes the observer through a variety of fields of inquiry: history and historiography (use and understanding of "the past"), neurology and psychology (cognitive processes), sociology and anthropology (public and social aspects of remembering in human culture), orality and textuality studies (transmission of tradition through media), and more.

18. It is important to note that the term "social memory" (*mémoire sociaux*) is not absent from Halbwachs's work nor was it out of reach, but he rather preferred to use the term "collective memory" (*la mémoire collective*).

connected to the term "collective memory" in Halbwachs's writings: "socially framed individual memories and collective commemorative representations and mnemonic traces."[19] Olick argues this dichotomy is reflective of Halbwachs's contemporary intellectual environment, but the unintended consequence of lumping two separate phenomena under the larger umbrella of "collective memory" has resulted in "radically distinct ontological orders . . . requir[ing] different epistemological and methodological strategies."[20] Reflecting on the status of collective memory at the end of the twentieth century, Olick writes,

> Collective memory has been used to refer to aggregated individual recollections, to official commemorations, to collective representations, and to disembodied constitutive features of shared identities; it is said to be located in dreamy reminiscence, personal testimony, oral history, tradition, myth, style, language, art, popular culture, and the built world. What is to be gained, and what is to be lost, by calling all of these "collective memory"?[21]

While Olick argues Halbwachs's use of the term was perhaps too ambivalent, another critique of "collective memory" terminology runs in the opposite direction: whether intended or not, the term seems to evoke a particular resonance of the Jungian ethereal "collective unconscious," an autonomous part of the unconscious mind tapped into the universality of human life. These resonances not only dogged Halbwachs's work in the eyes of his contemporaries—Bartlett spent considerable time discussing Jung's work immediately before discussing Halbwachs—but also in those that returned to his theoretical endeavors at the end of the twentieth century. Fentress and Wickham, opting to use the term "social memory" in order to avoid confusion with Jung, remark that one of the problems contemporary memory theorists face is "how to elaborate a

---

19. Olick separates these categories into "collected memory" and "collective memory," respectively. Olick, "Collective Memory," 336.

20. Olick, "Collective Memory," 336. Michael Schudson recognizes collective memory approaches with a slightly different taxonomy: "First, collective memory may refer to the fact that individual memory is socially organized or socially mediated. Second, collective memory may refer not to socially organized memories in individuals who experienced the past but to the socially produced artifacts that are the memory repositories for it—libraries, museums, monuments, language itself in clichés and word coinages, place names, history books, and so forth. Third, collective memory may be the image of the past held by individuals who did not themselves experience it but learned of it through cultural artifacts" (Schudson, "Dynamics of Distortion in Collective Memory," in Schacter, ed., *Memory Distortion*, 348).

21. Olick, "Collective Memory," 336.

conception of memory which, while doing full justice to the collective side of one's conscious life, does not render the individual a sort of automaton, passively obeying the interiorized collective will."[22] Noa Gedi and Yigal Elam also take umbrage with the "collective" terminology, arguing that it is problematic to discuss memory as a "collective" entity "because [entities bearing 'collective' terminology] are conceived of as having capacities that are in fact actualized only on an individual level, that is, they can only be performed by individuals."[23] This particular point is actually quietly addressed, at least tangentially, in Halbwachs's *The Collective Memory*. In this later work, Halbwachs returns to his notion of "collective memory" and emphasizes group membership and the intersectionality of individuals in multiple social groups. Halbwachs writes, "While the collective memory endures and draws strength from its base in a coherent body of people, it is individuals as group members who remember."[24] Gedi and Elam's larger point is that "collective memory" is utilized as an amorphous category that takes on the roles previously held by "real (factual) history" and "real (personal) memory."[25] The category of "collective memory" is used in place of other terms "as a general code name for something that is supposedly behind myths, traditions, customs, cults, all of which represent the 'spirit,' the 'psyche,' of a society, a tribe, a nation."[26] While Gedi and Elam are right that Halbwachs's overall body of work is loose with terms like tradition, memory, and history, later memory theorists have attempted to amend this deficiency and elicit particular nuance in their choice of terminology.[27]

22. Fentress and Wickham, *Social Memory*, ix.
23. Gedi and Elam, "Collective Memory," 34.
24. Halbwachs, *Collective Memory*, 48. Jan Assmann also supports Halbwachs on this point, arguing that it is not the fault of the terminology but rather the understanding of collective memory which causes difficulty in grasping the theory. "Neither the group, nor even culture, 'has' a memory in that sense . . . As always, man is the sole possessor of memory" (Assmann, *Religion and Cultural Memory*, 8).
25. Gedi and Elam, "Collective Memory," 40. Gedi and Elam go on to critique the way in which history is often downplayed in light of memory. For more on the discussion of memory and history, see below.
26. Gedi and Elam, "Collective Memory," 35.
27. Jan Assmann does a useful job of parsing out the function of Halbwachs's broader concepts of history and tradition and the ways in which they contrast his understanding of memory but still notes that "his terminology lacks the sharpness that would make his ideas truly communicable" (Assmann, *Cultural Memory and Early Civilization*, 31). It should be noted that much of the confusion regarding "collective" terminology may stem from Durkheim and his understanding of society (typically capitalized in his works) as an organic entity. To his credit, Halbwachs seems to have

To avoid the problems seen in Halbwachs's work, several alternatives have been used in place of "collective memory" in recent decades. Applying the same theoretical insights and building from Halbwachs's foundation, memory theorists have variously discussed the "politics of memory," "communicative memory," "cultural memory" (*kulturelle Gedächtnis*), "mnemohistory," "realms of memory" (*lieux de mémoire*), and more. In addition, there are tangential topics or terms that appear related to the issues of memory: tradition, history,[28] reputation, collective/group identity, group membership, nationalism, power, and contestation. To further complicate things, each discipline that engages memory studies has its own terminology and employs jargon decipherable to those within its own stream of scholarly tradition. With such a variable vocabulary, any attempt to create a glossary will woefully underrepresent the diversity of disciplinary conversation. Nonetheless, it is important to draw attention to this vocabulary at the outset in an attempt to highlight both how truly "nonparadigmatic" the field is and also acknowledge the limited scope of conversations and scholars appearing in this chapter. In what follows, I will attempt to unpack the nuance of these particular terms and

---

substituted Durkheim's "Society" with "groups," which tampers some of the ethereal treatment of society. See Olick, "Collective Memory," 334.

28. Both "history" and "tradition" have a complicated past in historical Jesus scholarship and carry certain conceptions in the way they have been used by New Testament scholars. Early form critics (furthered later by redaction critics) viewed the gospels as accumulations of theological material from the "life setting" (*Sitz im Leben*) of the early church. In other words, the events of Jesus's life were considered to be part of a "traditional historical core," a kernel of facts that were later interpreted, arranged, and presented to speak to the contemporary situation of the first-century church. Rudolf Bultmann articulates this idea in relation to the Gospel of Mark: "Mark is the work of an author who is steeped in the theology of the early Church, and who ordered and arranged the traditional material that he received in the light of the faith of the early Church—that was the result; and the task which follows for historical research is this: to separate the various strata in Mark and to determine which belonged to *the original historical tradition* and which derived from the work of the author" (Bultmann, *History of the Synoptic Tradition*, 1, emphasis added). On the contrary, "tradition" and "history" need not carry the baggage of a historical kernel to be stripped from later interpretations or a one-to-one correlation to the events of the past. For instance, Eric Hobsbawm and Terence Ranger's study of "invented traditions" brings the language of "tradition" to a variety of practices and institutions that are imbued with meaning and passed on as if connected to a remembered past, even though these traditions may have no real connection to actual events (the historical past). See Hobsbawm and Ranger, *Invention of Tradition*.

situate them within a representative history of what I will refer to, both as a theory and discipline, as social memory studies.[29]

What Is Social Memory Theory?

Social memory theory is an interdisciplinary[30] theory of memory that highlights the social frameworks and group identities that factor into the present-day act(s) of remembering, reconstructing, and structuring our understanding(s) of the past.[31] Social memory theory is not a methodology;[32] in other words, it does not provide a list of boxes to check or an order of operations through which a topic should be approached and investigated. Rather, it is a starting point, a set of formative assumptions drawn from socio-cultural, historical, and cognitive research, and it works in tandem with social-scientific and literary methodologies.

29. I follow Jeffrey Olick (among others) who uses the terminology of social memory studies, rather than collective memory, in order to acknowledge the field's "wide variety of mnemonic processes, practices, and outcomes, neurological, cognitive, personal, aggregated, and collective" (Olick, "Collective Memory," 346).

30. As Aleida Assmann notes, "The range of approaches alone makes it clear that memory is a phenomenon that no single discipline can call its own subject" (Assmann, *Cultural Memory and Western Civilization*, 7). While it is not necessary to engage every work in every field to have studied memory, treatments of memory often pull from or draw connections across several different fields in order to construct an application of the theory of memory.

31. In referring to the past, memory theorists understand a variety of relationships between "actual events" and "remembered events" and acknowledge that memory, as an active process of constructing "the past," is prone to simplification, transposition, schematization, and a number of other conscious and unconscious distortions in constructing past events and experiences. This is not to say that memory is inherently "unreliable," but rather that it is subjective. Memories can range along a spectrum that is reflective of a past event (i.e., "true") or unreflective of a past event (i.e., "false"), but memory can never be fully equated with the actual event itself. In other words, even if I may remember an event "as it was," my recollection of the event *is not* the event. Rather than serving as a verification process of the past "as it was," social memory theory is employed to identify social structures and contextual frameworks at play in the transmission of memories—whether they are reflective or unreflective of the past.

32. Though it is not often recognized as a proper methodology, social memory theory still offers many avenues to investigate traditions and the way(s) in which groups construct the past. Still, because it is interdisciplinary, it is often employed with the methods forged in other disciplines, such as literary, social-scientific, or historical-critical methods. In the field of New Testament Studies, Chris Keith discusses social memory theory in contradistinction to the form-critical Criteria of Authenticity, arguing that social memory theory should be understood "not as a prescriptive methodology like the criteria of authenticity, but as a general theory about the relation of the past and the present in commemorative activity" (Keith, "Yes and No," 67).

Inasmuch as it is theoretical, social memory is also epistemological in the sense that it offers and builds upon a body of knowledge concerned with how tradition and memory work.[33] It patterns our understandings of memory, tradition, and the construction of group identity.[34] Memories intertwine with culture as formative yet malleable forces, and social memory theory details this relationship through time. In addition, social memory theory highlights the dynamics of temporality, the ways that the past and the present act upon one another, and the positioning and interaction of concepts like memory, history, and tradition. As Fentress and Wickham put it, "Recalled past experiences and shared images of the historical past are kinds of memories that have particular importance for the constitution of social groups in the present."[35]

In order to grasp more fully what social memory theory is and how it works, the following section will provide a representative survey of important memory theorists and their foundational works.

A Brief History of Social Memory Theory

One of the difficulties of tracing a history of social memory studies is that the interdisciplinary nature of the field complicates any discernible starting point. A "history of social memory" stems from a larger history of memory, but it could just as well be connected to a history

---

33. "Social memory is a source of knowledge. This means that it does more than provide a set of categories through which, in an unselfconscious way, a group experiences its surroundings; it also provides the group with material for conscious reflection. This means that we must situate groups in relation to their own traditions, asking how they interpret their own 'ghosts', and how they use them as a source of knowledge" (Fentress and Wickham, *Social Memory*, 26). Le Goff also makes this point in relation to the ancient Greek goddess Mnemosyne's "possession" of poets. "When poetry is identified with memory, this makes the latter a kind of knowledge and even of wisdom, of *sophia*" (Le Goff, *History and Memory*, 64).

34. As stated above, one of the difficulties in social memory theory, as with most theoretical forms of knowledge, is utilizing a set terminology, and this difficulty is rooted even in stock words and phrases that would garner little attention in other contexts. One term Halbwachs uses without clear distinction or qualification is "tradition," which Assmann clarifies: "For [Halbwachs] tradition is not a form but a distortion of [living] memory" (Assmann, *Cultural Memory and Early Civilization*, 30). Because it can be understood in variety of ways, it seems best to set out a general understanding of the term from the outset. Thus, I will draw on Shils's definition, that the most neutral sense of tradition is "anything which is transmitted or handed down from the past to the present" (Shils, *Tradition*, 12).

35. Fentress and Wickham, *Social Memory*, xi.

of societies or even a history of history. Thus, any attempt to derive a "history of social memory" runs into several snags along the way. This is not a unique experience; Marc Bloch raised similar concerns regarding studying the history of law: "It may be that the history of law has no separate existence except as the history of jurists . . . [however,] the history of law sheds some glimmers of light upon phenomena which are extremely diversified, yet subject to a common human activity."[36] In a similar vein, the following history of social memory studies is a history of its representatives—in this case sociologists, psychologists, and historians rather than jurists—but it also offers "glimmers" into our understandings of society, memory, tradition, history, and other "common human activities" that concern the relationship between the past and the present. In just under one hundred years, social memory theory has gone from an extension of Durkheimian sociology to a major cross-disciplinary interest in history, literature, and the social sciences. To gain a better grasp of what social memory theory is and what it can do, we can investigate the insights of some of the most foundational works on social memory of the past century. The following survey will highlight the achievements of significant scholars such as Maurice Halbwachs, Frederic Bartlett, Pierre Nora, Jan Assmann, and Barry Schwartz.

Maurice Halbwachs

Maurice Halbwachs was by no means the first scholar to study the nature of memory,[37] but his work pioneered social memory theory in the early twentieth century. Halbwachs's *Les Cadres Sociaux de la Mémoire*, later translated as *On Collective Memory*, combined the influences of Emile Durkheim and Henri Bergson and pushed the thesis that social frameworks play a pivotal role in shaping, and even limiting, memory and recollection. Whereas Bergson investigated the memory of the individual,[38] a project born out of the Enlightenment's philosophical interest in introspection and individual freedom (e.g., Descartes's "I think therefore I am"),

36. Bloch, *Historian's Craft*, 149.

37. After all, Halbwachs studied under Henri Bergson, whose *Matter and Memory* (1896) argued for a new understanding of individual, psychological memory.

38. Bergson argued memory was a storehouse of "motor-mechanisms" (habits) and "personal memory-images" and believed that attention ("attentive perception") and introspection could trigger the connection of perceptions with similar stored memory-images. See Bergson, *Matter and Memory*, 123.

Halbwachs railed against the entire notion of individual memory as isolated from the influence of society. For Halbwachs, the individual's memory is spurred on and buttressed by the memories of other individuals, so much so that he argued "no memory is possible outside frameworks used by people living in society to determine and retrieve their recollections."[39] Halbwachs was very aware of the implications of this thesis on individual memory; in his later work, he further argued that all individual memory was rooted in an individual's belonging to one or more social groups, and that even "our most personal feelings and thoughts originate in definite social milieus and circumstances."[40] Memory, for Halbwachs, is inherently social. In a manner reminiscent of Ferdinand de Saussure and the lasting legacy of his structuralist thought, Halbwachs argued that language, as the most foundational social phenomenon, "allows us at every moment to reconstruct our past."[41] The core of remembering is rooted in—and only accessible through—the influence of social constructs, and because of this, Halbwachs's work emphasized and investigated the effect that social groups and social relationships like family,[42] social class,[43] and religion[44] have on the construction and recollection taking place in what we would normally typify as individual memories. For Halbwachs, these various

39. Halbwachs, *On Collective Memory*, 43.

40. Halbwachs, *Collective Memory*, 33. While he did not deny that individuals do remember, it is their belonging to different social groups which forms and shapes memory. The interplay between individual group members and the larger body of collective memory varies in how strong the group member's relationship is to different social milieus, but Halbwachs argued that the complex web of interconnecting groups—and the individual's positioning in relation to these groups—can always explain an individual's remembrances.

41. Halbwachs, *On Collective Memory*, 173.

42. "Each family has its proper mentality, its memories which it alone commemorates, and its secrets that are revealed only to its members. But these memories . . . consist not only of a series of individual images of the past. They are at the same time models, examples, and elements of teaching. They express the general attitude of the group; they not only reproduce its history but also define its nature and its qualities and weaknesses" (Halbwachs, *On Collective Memory*, 59).

43. "While a society may be broken down into a number of groups of people serving a variety of functions, we can also find in it a narrower society whose role, it may be said, is to preserve and maintain the living force of tradition" (Halbwachs, *On Collective Memory*, 129).

44. "Although religious memory attempts to isolate itself from temporal society, it obeys the same laws as every collective memory: it does not preserve the past but reconstructs it with the aid of the material traces, rites, texts, and traditions left behind by that past, and with the aid moreover of recent psychological and social data, that is to say, with the present" (Halbwachs, *On Collective Memory*, 119).

social groups play a key role in the present "reshaping" the past.[45] Simply put, Halbwachs believed that all individual memory is dependent upon social frameworks, that the individual "reconstructs its memories under the pressure of society."[46]

Halbwachs's focus on the ways a social group "pressures" individual memory led him to discuss the role of "localization." For Halbwachs, localization is essentially the organization of memories based on the influence of a formative social group. Memories are not solely related by time, so recalling a significant event in the past does not automatically unearth a swath of other events—whether significant or trivial—in temporal proximity. Recounting the events of my wedding on a Sunday does not mean I can necessarily tell you what clothes I wore on Saturday, what I had for lunch on Friday, or what the weather was like on Monday.[47] Halbwachs instead argued that one of the most significant ways memories are bound together is by group interest; according to Halbwachs, the "various modes by which memories become associated result from the various ways in which people can become associated."[48] Formative social groups, such as families,[49] can tie memories together, which means that even a chain of associated or related memories may owe more to social relationships than to the individual psyche.[50] If we take the ancient mnemonic technique of the memory palace,[51] the individual may have arranged memories as objects and images, but social

45. Halbwachs strengthened this argument in *Collective Memory*.

46. Halbwachs, *On Collective Memory*, 51.

47. I am no memory savant, but even the act of calendar calculating has been identified as a form of rote or habitual memory rather than a semantic form of memory necessitating interpretation and meaning. See Dubischar-Krivec et al., "Calendar Calculating," 1355–63; Neumann et al., "Mind of the Mnemonists," 114–21.

48. Halbwachs, *On Collective Memory*, 53.

49. "Each family ends up with its own logic and traditions, which resemble those of the general society in that they derive from it and continue to regulate the family's relations with general society. But this logic and these traditions are nevertheless distinct because they are little by little pervaded by the family's particular experiences and because their role is increasingly to insure the family's cohesion and to guarantee its continuity" (Halbwachs, *On Collective Memory*, 83).

50. "It is not because memories resemble each other that several can be called to mind at the same time. It is rather because the same group is interested in them and is able to call them to mind at the same time that they resemble each other" (Halbwachs, *On Collective Memory*, 52).

51. See Fentress and Wickham, *Social Memory*, 11–12. For more on the general phenomenon of places (*loci*) of memory and the development of mnemotechnology throughout the history of Europe, see Yates, *Art of Memory*.

groups structure the building, color the walls, and organize the furniture according to the socio-historical frameworks of the contemporary world. Anthony Le Donne illustrates this process, stating, "Localization has two equally important functions: (1) to reinforce the mnemonic capacity of information, and (2) to shape and give meaning to perceived images."[52] In essence, social groups play a crucial role in how memories are bound together, imbued with meaning, and anchored.[53]

For Halbwachs, the relationship between individual and collective memory is analogous to the relationship between the past and present. In the same way that the individual cannot recollect outside of the influence of its social groups, the past cannot be perceived outside of the influence of the present situations in which the past is reconstructed. Halbwachs noted that "even at the moment of reproducing the past our imagination remains under the influence of the present social milieu."[54] The past is not an external body of objective events but is rather bound by the present and only appears if it is determined to be salient for present-day needs.[55] The past, as a collection of events or "ideas," is preserved and used by society "provided . . . [recollections of the past] have a place in its thought and that they still interest present-day people who understand them."[56] In other words, the past must be able to fit within the social frameworks of the present;[57] if not, it will not be rec-

---

52. Le Donne, "Theological Memory Distortion," in Stuckenbruck et al., eds., *Memory in the Bible and Antiquity*, 164.

53. "Objects and events become arranged in our minds in two ways: either following the chronological order of their appearance, or by the names we give them and the meaning that is attributed to them within our group" (Halbwachs, *On Collective Memory*, 175). Localization has interesting implications for the Jesus historian. As Le Donne argues, "historical interpretations do not begin with the historian, but within the perceptions, memories and articulations of the first witnesses . . . the historian's task is not simply to sift through the data looking for facts . . . but to account for these *early* interpretations by explaining the perceptions and memories that birthed them" (Le Donne, "Theological Memory Distortion," in Stuckenbruck et al., eds., *Memory in the Bible and Antiquity* 165). It is not enough to make a valuation of whether an extant (written) gospel tradition's presentation of Jesus is historical ("authentic") or fabricated; instead, it is necessary to dive into the socio-historical conditions and group identities of the first century since these not only shaped the worldview of Jesus tradents but shaped the actual tradition.

54. Halbwachs, *On Collective Memory*, 49.

55. Halbwachs's most famous and rigorous attempt at investigating this is his essay "Legendary Topography of the Gospels," in Halbwachs, *On Collective Memory*, 193–235.

56. Halbwachs, *On Collective Memory*, 188–89.

57. "It follows that social thought is essentially a memory and that its entire content

ollected and will be lost to history, which Halbwachs's *The Collective Memory* understands as an entirely separate entity from remembered tradition.[58] Whereas collective memory is the body of remembrances found in living and active groups, history is attributed to traditions or remembrances with groups from the past that have a ruptured relationship with the present; in other words, as Olick and Robbins put it, Halbwachs believed that "history is dead memory."[59]

As an important pioneer for social memory theory, Halbwachs's work opened new avenues for the study of memory, group identity, and the past. Several of his foundational ideas, such as the differences between history and memory, the shape and form of remembrances, and the relationship between the past and the present, were picked up and reworked in the latter half of the twentieth century. But he was not without critique from contemporaries, particularly from historians like Marc Bloch or psychologists like Frederic Bartlett.

Frederic Bartlett

Frederic Bartlett, a Cambridge psychologist and English contemporary of Halbwachs, is not often involved in conversations about social memory. Instead, Bartlett is often noted for his work on individual memory. To understand Bartlett's importance in this area, one needs only brief context: the standard view of memory in the late nineteenth and early twentieth centuries was shaped by Sigmund Freud, a giant in the field of psychology. Freud argued that memories are located in the unconscious mind, an archive where all of an individual's experiences, feelings, thoughts, and perceptions are stored. When an experience is painful, the mind actively works to repress that experience, overtaking the efficacy of memory; thus, it was forgetting—even in innocuous situations such as remembering a proper name or the order of words—that was an active process of the mind repressing past experiences. This became a crucial foundation for Freud's psychoanalytical practice and falls in line with many of his other

---

consists only of collective recollections or remembrances. But it also follows that, among them, only those recollections subsist that in every period society, working within its present-day frameworks, can reconstruct" (Halbwachs, *On Collective Memory*, 189).

58. "General history starts only when tradition ends and the social memory is fading or breaking up" (Halbwachs, *Collective Memory*, 78; cf. Olick and Robbins, "Social Memory Studies," 108).

59. Olick and Robbins, "Social Memory Studies," 110.

psychological arguments.[60] Bartlett's work, particularly his pioneering of the schematization[61] of memory, reversed Freud's theory and argued that memory was not a conscious process of forgetting but rather "the *construction* of psychological material and of psychological reactions into organised settings plays a leading part in perceiving, in recognising, and in remembering."[62] Bartlett partnered his individual case studies and empirical data with an interest in theorizing how memory itself was a social act. Whereas Halbwachs's work was rooted in sociology, Bartlett worked within the stream of psychology, and specifically social psychology, to investigate the ways an individual's recall is influenced by social conditions.

An important focus of Bartlett's work was not the *accuracy* of recall, but rather the "effort after meaning," a phrase used to indicate the process of connecting patterns or mental representations of the past to "schemes," which are frameworks that make sense of these representations.[63] In other words, for our minds to formulate representations of the past, these representations must be reconstructed and organized so that they hold meaning. Bartlett's study highlighted a number of interconnected "schemata" that are utilized in this organizational process, such as chronology of events, the impact of the senses/sensory material (images, sounds, etc.), spatial or temporal factors, and attitudes. Bartlett also noted that each of these schemes had the capacity to effect the different alterations he witnessed in individual memory: simplification, elaboration, invention, condensation. Though he derived his conclusions in an entirely different manner, it is important to point

---

60. See Freud, *Psychopathology of Everyday Life*.

61. On the use of "schema," which Bartlett used as an alternative to his preferred "organised setting," Bartlett writes that "'schema' refers to an active organisation of past reactions, or of past experiences, which must always be supposed to be operating in any well-adapted organic response" (Bartlett, *Remembering*, 201).

62. Bartlett, *Remembering*, 227, emphasis added. Halbwachs's approach to social memory in 1925 (eight years before Bartlett's work was published) was one of the first major critiques of Freud's theory of memory, contending that memories required meaning in social settings in order to remain preserved in the minds of individuals living in groups. Rather than emphasize internal, neurobiological factors, Halbwachs dispensed with psychology and argued that memories, when communicated, exist externally to individuals and are decipherable via the social groups in which one is located. Bartlett's contribution was to bring a similar critique and reverse Freud's theory within the field of psychology.

63. "Even when material is arranged in a short series, is small in bulk and simple in objective structure, and when it is so given that an observer knows that he will be asked to describe it later, remembering is rapidly affected by unwitting transformations: accurate recall is the exception and not the rule" (Bartlett, *Remembering*, 61).

out that Bartlett agreed with Halbwachs regarding the constructive and constructed nature of memory. For Bartlett, the act of remembering is not merely an act of reduplication or reproduction of the past, but a *reconstruction*: "Remembering appears to be far more decisively an affair of construction rather than one of mere reproduction."[64]

Bartlett emphasized that the interests governing the process of organization and meaning-making (schematization) are located in the mind of individuals rather than a collective group memory. In fact, contrary to Halbwachs, Bartlett was quite skeptical of the existence of anything like a group memory, preferring to discuss memory *in* a group, not memory *of* a particular group.[65] However, Bartlett recognized significant features of memory that put his work in a similar vein as Halbwachs. Bartlett recognized that the same interests governing individual recall tend to have "a direct social origin."[66] In analyzing these interests, Bartlett discussed the way groups handle the introduction of cultural (external) material, dubbing the process "conventionalisation." Bartlett theorized four main ways that groups change cultural material—including mental representations of the past—until it is either stable or eradicated: (1) Assimilation to existing cultural forms; (2) Simplification of material that phases out unfamiliar details; (3) Retention of peculiarities unconnected with the customs adopted; and (4) "Social Constructiveness," which Bartlett describes as the welding of disparate cultural materials together in line with the overall transformation of the group's identity "*in the direction along which the group happens to be developing* at the time at which [the cultural material is] introduced."[67] In other words, Bartlett theorized that the same schematic processes occurring in the individual's memory take place in social group organization by the processes of "social conventionalisation." Concluding his study, Bartlett offered the following summary:

---

64. Bartlett, *Remembering*, 205.

65. "Strictly speaking, a theory of social memory ought to be able to demonstrate that a group, considered as a unit, itself actually does remember, and not merely that it provides either the stimulus or the conditions under which individuals belonging to the group recall the past" (Bartlett, *Remembering*, 294). Similar to Halbwachs's interest in language, and again possibly due to the rising interest in de Saussure's work on structural linguistics, Bartlett also believed that evidence of "group memory" would require a form of "group language" in which groups could directly communicate with one another. See Bartlett, *Remembering*, 299.

66. Bartlett, *Remembering*, 257.

67. Bartlett, *Remembering*, 275, emphasis original.

It is certain that practically all the processes of individual repeated recall have their precise parallels in those of social conventionalisation. There are the same types of change in original material: of blending, condensation, omission, invention and the like. There is the same strong tendency to reduplication of detail in certain circumstances. In both cases, the final product approaches stability, that of the determined and relatively fixed individual memory in the one case, and that of the social conventionalisation in the other. *Alike with the individual and with the group, the past is being continually re-made, reconstructed in the interests of the present, and in both cases certain outstanding events or details may play a leading part in setting the course of reaction. Just as individual recall takes on a peculiar personal tinge, owing to the play of temperament and character; so that kind of recall which is directed and dominated by social conditions takes a colouring which is characteristic of the special social organisation concerned, owing to the play of preferred persistent tendencies in the group.*[68]

Despite their differences, Halbwachs and Bartlett both worked to highlight the ways in which social structures impact the memory of individuals and groups. Bartlett's emphasis on the underlying schemata of recall and the ways in which they affect and alter representations of the past will be useful in discussing how memory works below. Still, it is important to highlight Bartlett's work for its value to social memory studies, particularly his theory of "social conventionalization."

Pierre Nora

There are many differential qualities in the way that scholars have studied memory; the interdisciplinary nature of the field, as stated earlier, is central to memory studies as a whole. As such, each discussion of memory takes place within a larger context. Whereas Halbwachs worked within the field of sociology and Bartlett within psychology, Pierre Nora's magisterial work on sites or "realms" (*lieux*) of memory extended the conversation of memory into the context of French historiography. Nora's study and use of memory, then, is situated within the genre of national history in an "attempt to write a history in multiple voices . . . a history that is interested in memory not as remembrance

---

68. Bartlett, *Remembering*, 309, emphasis added.

but as the overall structure of the past within the present: history of the second degree."[69] While the two concepts of memory and history may seem synonymous at first glance, Nora, following Halbwachs, argued that there is a deep divide between history and memory:

> Memory is life, always embodied in living societies and as such in permanent evolution, subject to the dialectic of remembering and forgetting, unconscious of the distortions to which it is subject, vulnerable in various ways to appropriation and manipulation, and capable of lying dormant for long periods only to be suddenly reawakened. History, on the other hand, is the reconstruction, always problematic and incomplete, of what is no longer... Memory wells up from groups that it welds together, which is to say, as Maurice Halbwachs observed, that there are as many memories as there are groups, that memory is by nature multiple yet specific; collective and plural yet individual. By contrast, history belongs to everyone and to no one and therefore has a universal vocation.[70]

In short, Nora follows an oppositional approach to the relationship between memory and history, arguing that history's "mission is to demolish [memory], to repress it."[71] Memory, then, is always at risk of being lost to history, and in Nora's estimation, "true memory" already has been lost; what remains is "historicized memory," memory that has been altered, and left behind in the interaction of memory and history are particular *lieux de mémoire*.

Nora's work is centered on these particular *lieux de mémoire* that he and his colleagues deemed central to French national history and identity.[72] Nora defined a *lieu de mémoire* as "any significant entity, whether

69. Nora, *Realms of Memory*, 1:xxiv.
70. Nora, *Realms of Memory*, 1:3.
71. Nora, *Realms of Memory*, 1:3. Nora's oppositional approach is as much a development of Halbwachs's thought as it is a response to the approach and critical methodologies used in his contemporary French history. In critiquing the history genre, Nora presents a brief survey of several prominent historians like Michelet and Lavisse only to unite each thinker with the same goal: "Each of these historians was convinced that his task was to correct his predecessors by making memory more factual, comprehensive, and useful as an explanation of the past. The scientific arsenal with which history has equipped itself over the past century has done nothing but reinforce this view of history as a critical method whose purpose is to establish true memory" (Nora, *Realms of Memory*, 1:4). It is also important to note that Nora sees historiography as a *via media* between history and memory, but one that is looked at with suspicion in contemporary French thought.
72. Nora contrasts these *lieux* with *milieux de mémoire*, which Nora argues no

material or non-material in nature, which by dint of human will or the work of time has become a symbolic element of the memorial heritage of any community."[73] This definition is constructed broadly, leaving room for both traditional sites—the Eiffel Tower, Arc de Triomphe, Versailles, Notre Dame—as well as literature, material artifacts and objects, historical persons, organizations, and more. These *lieux* exist in three particular interlocking forms—material, symbolic, and functional—and are limited by the criterion of "a [necessary] will to remember."[74] This reconceptualization of memory and memorialized "sites" or "realms" opens the door to a number of possible *lieux*, and the voluminous collection presents a number of interesting case studies: Joan of Arc, the French Revolutionary calendar, *La Tour de la France par deux enfants*, the Rhine, Michelet's *Précis d'histoire modern*,[75] or even the funeral of Jean-Paul Sartre. For Nora, these and other *lieux de mémoire* serve an important function in the formulation of national identity and national memory "because of their capacity for change, their ability to resurrect old meanings and generate new ones along with new and unforeseeable connections."[76]

Whereas Halbwachs sought social frameworks or "foundations" for collective memory, Nora's survey of *lieux de mémoire* compiled the "scaffolding" of French collective memory, in a sense unveiling where memory—historicized memory—is located. By emphasizing the symbolic, material, and functional elements of memory, Nora's work brings together seemingly disparate subjects in a presentation of collective memory, identity, and national history. In summarizing the endeavor, Nora concludes that all of the different "realms," subjects, and identities and histories built from them, "belong to a complex network, an unconscious organization of collective memory," and it is up to the historian of memory to draw out these sites in contemporary consciousness.[77]

---

longer exist, but once served as "settings in which memory is a real part of everyday experience" (Nora, *Realms of Memory*, 1:1).

73. Nora, *Realms of Memory*, 1:xvii.

74. Nora, *Realms of Memory*, 1:14.

75. Nora limits which works of history may be classified as *lieux de mémoire*, allowing only "those that reshape memory in some fundamental way or that epitomize a revision of memory for pedagogical purposes" (Nora, *Realms of Memory*, 1:17).

76. Nora, *Realms of Memory*, 1:15.

77. Nora, *Realms of Memory*, 1:19.

Jan Assmann

As contemporaries of Nora, Jan and Aleida Assmann's work demonstrates an alternative approach to locating collective memory. Working across a range of fields in the humanities, the Assmanns built on the work of Halbwachs and Aby Warburg[78] by pioneering the idea of "cultural memory." Jan Assmann defines four types of "external," socially-influenced memory: mimetic memory of imitative behaviors and actions, the object-oriented memory of things, communicative memory, and cultural memory, and it is the latter two that take central stage in his work. First, Assmann reframes several aspects of Halbwachs's "collective memory" as "communicative memory," a type of memory resulting from everyday communication, persisting only in living memory.[79] While communicative memory is still socially-determined and group-oriented, its most defining feature is that it is temporally limited to an indeterminate period of eighty to one hundred years; to transmit memories beyond that period requires a "fixity" that, as Assmann notes, "can only be achieved through a cultural formation."[80] Whereas Halbwachs saw this concretizing transitional period—the production of a text, image, monument, city, ritual—as the site where living memory dies and history begins, Assmann finds these "forms of objectivized culture" as still formative and normative for society, reifying and reproducing group identity. For Assmann, these forms transition into what he calls "figures of memory"—texts and monuments, but also observances and practices—that mark the beginning of cultural memory, which is defined by its proximity away from the everyday.[81] Thus, there are two key qualities of cultural memory: (1) it must

---

78. Assmann credits Warburg—whose own project, *Mnemosyne*, investigated areas of objectivized culture such as art, costumes, postage stamps, and other visual representations—with "emphatically directing attention to the power of cultural objectivation in the stabilizing of cultural memory" (Assmann, "Collective Memory and Cultural Identity," 129). For more on Warburg's impact on memory studies, see Erll, *Memory in Culture*, 19–22.

79. Assmann later clarified that communicative memory, as used by both him and Aleida Assmann, takes the place of "individual memory" in the work of Halbwachs. They make this move out of the necessity of their argument that all memory is social and a truly individual memory would be something unintelligible to others, something of a "private language." Communicative memory, then, "describe[s] the social aspect of individual memory identified by Halbwachs" (Assmann, *Religion and Cultural Memory*, 3).

80. Assmann, "Collective Memory and Cultural Identity," 127.

81. Although he mentions his indebtedness to orality studies and scholars of oral history in developing the idea of communicative memory, Assmann clarifies that the

serve as an interpretive social framework for group behavior and identity; and (2) it must be passed along through intergenerational practices.[82] Assmann elaborates on these general qualities by highlighting a number of features of cultural memory, including the constitution of a collective group identity, the stabilization (what Assmann calls "*formation*") of meaning,[83] the development and practice of formulaic and specialized knowledge, and a normative set of values that serve to establish community guidelines. Cultural memory, as a binding "connective structure"[84] for society, operates by drawing the past and the present together, relating key cultural symbols to a contemporary situation. Assmann notes that he follows Halbwachs's "socio-constructivist" view of the past: "it is a social construction whose nature arises out of the needs and frames of reference of each particular present. The past is not a natural growth but a cultural creation."[85] On the dynamic between past and present, Assmann writes, "[cultural memory] is fixed in immovable figures of memory and stores of knowledge, but every contemporary context relates to these differently, sometimes by appropriation, sometimes by criticism, sometimes by preservation or by transformation."[86]

When Jan Assmann applies the principles of cultural memory to ancient religious practice, he draws on the role that significant symbols play in the construction of group identity. In *Moses the Egyptian*, Assmann discusses the "Mosaic distinction"—the cultural significance of the monotheistic tradition of Moses, which he calls "counter-religion"—by noting how and where symbols appear: "Exodus is a symbolical story, the Law is a symbolical legislation, and Moses is a symbolical figure.

---

shift from communicative to cultural memory is not one of medium, but one of stability and crystallization; in other words, "The distinction between the communicative memory and the cultural memory is *not* identical with the distinction between oral and written language" (Assmann, "Collective Memory and Cultural Identity," 131, emphasis original).

82. For Jan Assmann, cultural memory is "a collective concept for all knowledge that directs behavior and experience in the interactive framework of a society and one that obtains through generations in repeated societal practice and initiation" (Assmann, "Collective Memory and Cultural Identity," 126).

83. Astrid Erll describes cultural memory's formative quality as "the continuation of meaning through established, stable forms of expression" (Erll, *Memory in Culture*, 29–30).

84. For his use of connective structures, see Assmann, *Cultural Memory and Early Civilization*, 2–4.

85. Assmann, *Cultural Memory and Early Civilization*, 33.

86. Assmann, "Collective Memory and Cultural Identity," 130.

The whole constellation of Israel and Egypt is symbolical and comes to symbolize all kinds of opposition."[87] He continues his study on the ways that Egypt has been remembered in the Western monotheistic world by engaging in what he calls *mnemohistory*, which "is not concerned with the past as such, but only with the past as it is remembered"; in other words, "mnemohistory is reception theory applied to history."[88] But Assmann is careful not to portray "reception" as a passive vehicle from the past to the present; instead, "the present is 'haunted' by the past and the past is modeled, invented, reinvented, and reconstructed by the present."[89] Highlighting the interrelation between past and present brings Assmann to what is perhaps his most crucial point, the actual goal of "mnemohistory." This goal, for Assmann, is

> not to ascertain the possible truth of traditions . . . but to study these traditions as phenomena of collective memory . . . for the historian of memory, the "truth" of a given memory lies not so much in its "factuality" as in its "actuality." Events tend to be forgotten unless they live on in collective memory . . . There is no meaning in history unless these distinctions are remembered. The reason for this "living on" lies in the continuous relevance of these events. This relevance comes not from their historical past, but from an ever-changing present in which these events are remembered as facts of importance.[90]

It is important to note Assmann's critique of historicism, particularly in its emphatic search for "pure facts." Instead of looking to sift historical details from mythical narratives of the past, mnemohistory "consists in analyzing the mythical elements in tradition and discovering their hidden agenda."[91] Rather than categorizing tradition into piles of historical and mythical and only examining one set, Assmann's approach seeks to

---

87. Assmann, *Moses the Egyptian*, 4. Assmann goes on to highlight the opposition between the Egyptian priest Manetho and the Mosaic tradition, arguing that this opposition is actually rooted in the monotheistic religion introduced by Egyptian Pharaoh Akhenaten in the fourteenth century BCE. When Akhenaten's religious "distinction" was lost to history and forgotten in memory, the trauma of such a distinction on cultural identity was later displaced and shifted against the Jews, demonstrated by Manetho's third-century BCE critique of Judaism as a cult consisting of desolate Egyptian lepers surrounding Moses.

88. Assmann, *Moses the Egyptian*, 9.
89. Assmann, *Moses the Egyptian*, 9.
90. Assmann, *Moses the Egyptian*, 9–10.
91. Assmann, *Moses the Egyptian*, 10.

draw the two together and ask *why* and *how* particular traditions persisted.[92] His approach also does not seek to prioritize the historical over the mythical because, for Assmann, "history turns into myth as soon as it is remembered, narrated, and used, that is, woven into the fabric of the present."[93] While history and mnemohistory may be digging in the same ground,[94] they are not identical tasks; "The historical study of the events should be carefully distinguished from the study of their commemoration, tradition, and transformation in the collective memory of the people concerned."[95] Thus, in the same way that Geertz defined culture as the vehicle that offers and transmits meaning to symbols that are passed on inter-generationally,[96] Assmann takes memory as the site of meaning, shaping different symbols from the past (events, figures, practices, observations). "Mnemohistory," then, allows the historian of memory to analyze the ways that various temporal presents orient themselves toward the meaning or knowledge—the cultural memory—transmitted about symbols of the past.

Barry Schwartz

Before his untimely death, Marc Bloch's *The Historian's Craft* provided a fragmentary, but helpful, glimpse of his understanding of historical inquiry and methodology. In what was probably as much an observation about historical tradition as it was a dig at his friend and former

---

92. One particularly interesting area of Assmann's work is his concept of "countermemory." Assmann defines countermemory as "a memory that puts elements to the fore that are, or tend to be, forgotten in the official memory." Countermemories play an important role in contradicting official records, and, if countermemories are "codified in the form of a traditional story or even in a work of written historiography," they can serve as examples of what Funkestein and Biale call "counterhistory." See Assmann, *Moses the Egyptian*, 13. Assmann also discusses "contra-present memory" (drawing on Theissen) and "anachronous structures" (drawing on Erdheim) as forms of memory where meaning "takes on such a solid consistency that it can even contradict the social and political reality of the present" (Assmann, *Cultural Memory and Early Civilization*, 10).

93. Assmann, *Moses the Egyptian*, 14.

94. "Memory and history are different but inextricably related . . . Memory and history are poles of the same range of activities, some of which are closer to one pole than to the other" (Assmann, *Moses the Egyptian*, 21–22).

95. Assmann, *Moses the Egyptian*, 14.

96. For Geertz, culture "denotes an historically transmitted pattern of meanings embodied in symbols, a system of inherited conceptions expressed in symbolic forms by means of which men communicate, perpetuate, and develop their knowledge about and attitudes toward life" (Geertz, *Interpretation of Cultures*, 89).

colleague Maurice Halbwachs, Bloch wrote, "A society that could be completely molded by its immediately preceding period would have to have a structure so malleable as to be virtually invertebrate."[97] Several decades later sociologist Barry Schwartz would pick up the same line of critique against Halbwachs's present-focused theory of collective memory. Schwartz's major issue with Halbwachs's theory was that it "promotes the idea that our conception of the past is entirely at the mercy of current conditions, that there is no objectivity in events, nothing in history which transcends the peculiarities of the present."[98] Stuck between the "relativism" of Halbwachs and the "absolutism" of Eliade and Levi-Strauss, Schwartz proposed a *via media*, a more "reciprocal" relationship between the past and the present, between history and memory.[99] For Schwartz, "collective memory is based on two sources of belief about the past—*history* and *commemoration*. Collective memory is a representation of the past embodied in *both* historical evidence and commemorative symbolism."[100] Olick supports Schwartz's "both/and" reciprocal approach by arguing that the prioritization of either the past or the present in the formation of tradition does not accurately capture "the complexities of remembering, which is always a fluid negotiation between the desires of the present and the legacies of the past."[101] In other words, narratives are not anchored by the past *or* the present, but rather by the past *and* the present; past and present are wrestlers locked in battle over the way we tell our stories, and our study must account for both features, even when one is dominant over the other.

Schwartz articulates the "both/and" approach by arguing that collective memory is the construction of a fluid past.[102] This fluid past

97. Bloch, *Historian's Craft*, 40.

98. Schwartz, "Social Context of Commemoration," 376.

99. "Reduced to commemoration, collective memory becomes, for Halbwachs and Nora, a distorted version of history. They cannot see, let alone examine, collective memory as the reciprocal working of history and commemoration" (Schwartz, *Abraham Lincoln*, 11).

100. Schwartz, *Abraham Lincoln*, 9, emphasis original. Elsewhere, Schwartz discusses these two sources as "commemoration" and "chronicling," which is "the direct recording of events and their sequence" (Schwartz, "Social Context of Commemoration," 377).

101. Olick, "Products, Processes, and Practices," 13.

102. "To conceive of collective memory as a mirror of reality is to conceive a fiction, for if, independently of historical evidence, our changing understanding of the past uniquely parallels changes in our society, then the only relevant reality would be the present, and the very concept of collective memory would be meaningless. To conceive

"shape[s] reality by articulating ideals and generating the motivation to realize them."[103] On the other hand, a formative era of the past "is not a fixed entity which imposes itself on the present; it is a continuously evolving product of social definition."[104] Commemoration, then, pulls these two threads together: "While the object of commemoration is usually to be found in the *past*, the issue which motivates its selection and shaping is always to be found among the concerns of the *present*."[105]

Schwartz's early work maps this out in American political history, discussing the role of "recovered" or "rediscovered" history on the remembered past.[106] However, it is his work on the ancient Jewish fortress of Masada that most effectively demonstrates the ways that the past and the present mutually inform one another. Schwartz, Zerubavel, and Barnett question how a largely forgotten and unsuccessful incident in the history of the Jewish people became such a celebrated and commemorated event for Palestinian Jews in the early twentieth century.[107] Decades before the archaeological uncovering of the ancient fortress, Yitzhak Lamdan's bleak 1927 poem "Masada" popularly captured the sentiment of the Zionist ideology of Jewish settlers in Palestine and triggered a "recovery" of Masada in contemporary consciousness. Whereas Lamdan's poem reflects the "not dominance, but survival" attitude of his contemporary Zionist settlers,[108] Masada carries a different meaning in contemporary Israeli thought as a "symbol of military valor and national commitment," an event of honorable defeat that represents the fighting

---

the meaning of the past as fixed and steady is likewise meaningless, since any event must appear differently as perceptual circumstances change" (Schwartz, *Abraham Lincoln*, 7).

103. Schwartz, *Abraham Lincoln*, 5.

104. Schwartz, "Social Context of Commemoration," 390.

105. Schwartz, "Social Context of Commemoration," 395, emphasis added.

106. "In the antebellum Capitol, recovered history was a part of a support system which amplified remembered history" (Schwartz, "Social Context of Commemoration," 390).

107. "The battle of Masada . . . possesses no formative significance, as did the Exodus; it does not represent a political peak in Jewish history, as did the kingdoms of David and Solomon, and does not distinguish itself as a negative event. Masada fell in a mopping-up operation that followed an occasion of far greater significance: the defense, fall, and destruction of Jerusalem. Masada's loss cannot even be regarded as a last gasp in the history of ancient Israel. To the 132–135 AD revolt and defeat of Bar Kochba belongs this distinction" (Schwartz et al., "Recovery of Masada," 149).

108. This is unsurprising because Lamdan's poem is rooted in "the consciousness of a specific people living under specific social conditions. As these conditions change, his poem's affective and historical vision lose their representativeness" (Schwartz et al., "Recovery of Masada," 158).

spirit of the nation and its people, even against insurmountable odds.[109] However, the historical events of Masada are not irrelevant for the construction of that past; rather, Schwartz, Zerubavel, and Barnett argue that the events of Masada are pulled into Lamdan's present in order to shape or reflect Palestinian Jewish identity in five ways:

> (1) The settler's sense of being in a situation of "no choice"; (2) their realization that the Zionist cause was a last stand against fate; (3) their sense of isolation from the main body of the Jewish people; (4) their despair and the essential ambivalence of their commitment to one another and to their new homeland; and (5) the very real prospect that the second Masada would fall in the same manner as did the first—by self-destruction. Thus the effect of the poem was not only to make the situation in Palestine more hopeful, or to bolster the collective ego—its effect was also to make that situation meaningful.[110]

For Schwartz, there is at least some level of continuity between the past and the ways that past is (re)presented in the present. One must examine both the way the past is remembered ("how") and the reasons for the preservation of that memory ("why"). Pulling together these two functions—how societies remember and why—can determine the way(s) in which societies use collective memory to mediate meaning.[111] In some cases, such as Masada, the reason for the "why" may not be straightforward or may change through time, but it is helpful to remember that "collective memory is drawn not to that which is *useful* but to that which is *appropriate*."[112] The commemorative function of memory enacts the meaning for both society and individual in a manner appropriate with present interests, but not entirely separated from the past itself; in reference to his work on Abraham Lincoln, Schwartz writes:

> So far as commemoration selects and lifts out of Lincoln's biographical record the episodes embodying fundamental values, Americans commemorating an event in Lincoln's life connect themselves to it, identify with it, and exercise their sense of who they are collectively in terms of it. Commemoration transforms historical facts about Lincoln into objects of attachment

---

109. Schwartz et al., "Recovery of Masada," 151.

110. Schwartz et al., "Recovery of Masada," 159.

111. "How the past is symbolized and how it functions as a mediator of meaning are questions that go to the heart of collective memory" (Schwartz, *Abraham Lincoln*, 17).

112. Schwartz et al., "Recovery of Masada," 160, emphasis added.

by defining their meaning and explaining how people should feel about them.[113]

In other words, in addition to the present determining meaning and salience of past events, Schwartz argues that commemorative activities in the present can transform or affect social groups based on "historical facts." This two-way approach differs from Halbwachs's one-way approach where the salience of the past rests entirely on the circumstances (ideas, moods, moors, etc.) of society in the present.

While Schwartz's work on Lincoln, George Washington, and other American political figures offers examples of the dynamics between past and present in the construction of cultural memory, we could also consider the alternative example in the figure of Alexander Hamilton. Constructions of this historical figure have ranged far and wide in the past two and a half centuries. During his life and in the immediate aftermath of his death, his political opponents castigated him as a proponent of aristocratic authoritarianism.[114] A century later, Hamilton was a figure renowned for his political acumen. Frederick Scott Oliver's 1906 biography, *Alexander Hamilton: An Essay on the American Union*, decisively praised Hamilton's political leanings against his contemporaries and denigrated his political opposition, including Thomas Jefferson.[115] Similarly, major American politicians Theodore Roosevelt and William Howard Taft praised Hamilton as the paragon of American statesmanship and reveled in his economic genius.[116] In the twenty-first century, Hamilton has become a wildly popular cultural phenomenon after a new construction in Lin-Manuel Miranda's *Hamilton: An American Musical*. Miranda's star turn depicted the character as a sympathetic-yet-flawed, hardworking, ambitious immigrant concerned with his thumbprint on America's legacy. When we examine the reception of Alexander Hamilton in the two and a half centuries since his death, we can see the ways that his life, character, or deeds have been constructed to "stabilize and

113. Schwartz, *Abraham Lincoln*, 12.

114. According to Ron Chernow, Hamilton was "demonized as a slavish pawn to the British crown, a closet monarchist, a Machiavellian intriguer, a would-be Caesar" (Chernow, *Alexander Hamilton*, 3).

115. Charles A. Beard points to the way a construction can change within a generation. Oliver's biography was rereleased after twenty years, and Beard remarks that Oliver's general appraisal of Hamilton's aristocratic proposals feel much more at home in early twentieth-century English colonialism than it does in the post-war period. See Beard, "Review of *Alexander Hamilton*," 852–53.

116. Chernow, *Alexander Hamilton*, 4.

convey" a particular image of American life. First, his rivals portrayed him as an opponent of the popular liberal democracy of the early nineteenth century due to his desire for an expansive executive form of government. As this expansive view of government became popular in the politics of the late nineteenth and early twentieth centuries, Hamilton was looked at as a paragon of American progressivism. Finally, the contemporary examination of his legacy draws out themes that embody American ideals in the twenty-first century. In each of these representations, however, there are still core tenets, what we might call "historical facts," about Hamilton that have not been altered. For example, Hamilton is still connected to the view of expansive government; these historical representations did not (and perhaps could not) make him out in the form of an anachronistic Marxist. Furthermore, the theatrical performance of *Hamilton* best demonstrates Schwartz's emphasis on how historical facts from the past can be employed in narratives that shape the self-image of society in the present and offer a normative valuation of transcendent actions, ideals, and beliefs: the importance of immigrants ("Immigrants, we get the job done"), American opportunism ("I am not throwin' away my shot"), and the abhorrence of slavery ("We'll never be free until we end slavery").[117] When viewed in this way, Alexander Hamilton is not an American founding father lost to history, nor is he entirely a fabrication of the present; rather, he operates as a "binding and reflexive" figure of memory, a symbol from the past whose meaning is passed on to present and future generations.[118]

With an eye toward commemoration and other systems of transmitting memories between cultural groups, Schwartz's focus on a "cultural system" of memory highlights how "society changes constantly, but social memory endures because new beliefs are superimposed upon—rather than replace—old ones."[119] Representations and constructions of the

117. The impact of Lin-Manuel Miranda's brilliant musical is still being felt worldwide. Recent scholarship on *Hamilton* has demonstrated potential avenues for historians to make insights into the futures of popular history and storytelling. See Romano and Potter, *Historians on Hamilton*.

118. Note that this "construction" goes beyond a mere survey of receptions of Alexander Hamilton in order to offer insights into *why* particular historical representations were constructed. Astrid Erll offers a helpful distinction on the limitations of Assmann's theory of cultural memory, writing, "'Cultural memory' does therefore *not* describe all manifestations of 'memory in culture'; rather it represents a subset of this: the societal construction of normative and formative versions of the past" (Erll, *Memory in Culture*, 30).

119. Schwartz, "Christian Origins," in Kirk and Thatcher, eds., *Memory, Tradition,*

past are shaped by the present in important ways, but the present is also shaped by the past; social memory is not "invertebrate," but malleable and dynamic.

Summary

The scholars surveyed represent how social memory theory has developed in the past century. Halbwachs's initial thrust investigated the ways that social groups serve as frameworks of meaning that shape individual memories, and Bartlett's experiments further examined ways that memories are affected by such "social conventionalization." Nora applied Halbwachs's insights to national identity and French historiography, whereas Jan Assmann built upon Halbwachs's works to develop his theory of communicative and cultural memory. Finally, Barry Schwartz expanded Halbwachs's work while also arguing for a more robust continuity between the past and the present. While this survey offers a basic history of social memory theory by highlighting significant scholars, these scholars are by no means the only important voices in the field. In order to demonstrate how many of the basic assumptions and arguments surveyed above have been applied or furthered, we can investigate a number of important issues in memory studies.

How Does Social Memory Theory Shape Our Understanding of Memory?

Social memory theory offers an analytic framework for interpreting the data of "memory." Upon this framework one can see the interrelation of a number of different fields: of cognitive processes of memory, of sociological features of group identity, of the past and the present as categories of historical-critical inquiry, and of the processes of media and transmission. A systematic approach to social memory is doomed to fail or fall short due to the decentralized nature of the topic, and it is beyond the scope of this study to attempt such an ill-advised project. Instead, the remainder of this chapter investigates particular areas of interest for memory theorists: the use of tradition, the stability of memory, the role of distortion, the attention to media dynamics, and the relationship between history and memory.

---

and Text, 44.

Tradition[120]

"Tradition" is one of the most prominent terms in discussions of collective memory, but it can be difficult to discern the relationship between "tradition" and "memory." Both concepts deal with the past, both are vehicles of transmitting information, experiences, and perceptions, and both are shaped by social forces. Both also seem to be used in contradistinction to history, a point Jan Vansina makes when noting how dissimilarity is a shared feature of memory and tradition; Vansina writes, "Traditions in memory are only distinguished from other more recent information by the conviction that they stemmed from previous generations, just as memory itself is only distinguished from other information by the conviction that the item is remembered, not dreamt or fantasized."[121] Still, there are ways in which the two terms differ, as some scholars seem to employ the terms in technical or nuanced ways. For instance, Assmann notes how Halbwachs viewed tradition as a "distortion" of memory, a form between history (as dead memory) and collective memory (as the living memory of a community).[122] In non-technical usage, however, "tradition" can have a number of different referents. It may refer to oral traditions, behaviors, myths, beliefs, commemorative practices, skills, or any other form of information passed down from generation to generation. Traditions need not be ancient, either; Eric Hobsbawm and Terence Ranger's study details how "invented traditions"—"both 'traditions' actually invented, constructed and formally instituted and those emerging in a less easily traceable manner"—are more recent phenomena intended to convey a sense of continuity with the past through repetition and symbolic or ritual rules.[123] In this sense, tradition itself is an "invention" that serves the interests of the present in which it is conceived and invented.

---

120. Tradition, broadly conceived, may refer to a categorical concept of practices that Jeffrey Barash describes as "codified and institutionally sanctioned." In this sense of tradition, Shils notes that traditional practices must be transmissible through particular patterns that leave "conditions for subsequent actions, images in memory and documents" guiding the normative repetition of the practice. On the other hand, tradition can refer to the specific instances of customs, practices, and beliefs transmitted from one group to another. Throughout this section, I use "tradition" in a flexible manner to incorporate both intended meanings, whereas "traditions" refers specifically to the latter specific sense. See Barash, *Collective Memory and the Historical Past*, 2; Shils, *Tradition*, 12.

121. Vansina, *Oral Tradition as History*, 147.

122. Assmann, *Cultural Memory and Early Civilization*, 48.

123. Hobsbawm and Ranger, *Invention of Tradition*, 1.

Hobsbawm and Ranger's work on "invented traditions" displays remarkable similarities to how Halbwachs conceived of collective memory, and these similarities make it more clear that for all intents and purposes, "traditions concerning the past" ("invented" or actual) appear to be interchangeable with "social memory."[124] Assmann finds the attempts at drawing distinctions arbitrary and distracting from the broader connections between the two phenomena, arguing, "The borderlines between memory and tradition can be so flexible that it seems pointless to try and introduce conceptual distinctions."[125] Edward Shils's landmark study of tradition serves as a good base, offering a neutral way to understand "tradition" as "anything which is transmitted or handed down from the past to the present."[126] Shils goes on to describe the relationship between memory and tradition as two agents in the transmission process: "To become a tradition, and to remain a tradition, a pattern of assertion or action must have entered into memory."[127] While memory and tradition may not be the exact same thing, social memory and tradition are quite similar and act in interchangeable ways, offering mutually beneficial understandings for the ways groups relate the past and the present.

Stability and Change

Memory and tradition are both processes of transmission, so elements of stability and change are naturally involved. Shils's work on tradition proposes a number of reasons why the past remains "ineluctable" and traditions stay the same. Traditions may relate knowledge, so the transmission of tradition is in effect the passing on of acquired knowledge, which remains stable at its foundation as it is built upon and passed on to each subsequent generation. More generally, Shils argues that there are

---

124. "We shall find that in articulating traditions concerning the past, social memory, groups may sometimes assert very odd connections. Were we to assume that all traditions must have some real, tangible basis, we might arrive at some bizarre reconstructions of the histories of these groups" (Fentress and Wickham, *Social Memory*, 49).

125. Assmann, *Cultural Memory and Early Civilization*, 31.

126. Shils, *Tradition*, 12. Shils also includes a temporal element to his definition, stating that traditions must be passed down for at least three generations, however long a generation is decided. See Shils, *Tradition*, 15.

127. Shils links memory and tradition more directly in describing the process of social continuity and change: "It is this chain of memory and of the tradition which assimilates it that enables societies to go on reproducing themselves while also changing" (Shils, *Tradition*, 167).

two basic reasons why humans "adopt and adapt" the traditions ("practices and beliefs") of the preceding generation.[128] First, the pastness of tradition means there is little effort in receiving versus the effort required in changing a tradition or creating ("inventing") anew. In other words, it is far more convenient to treat traditions as normative, where "the given becomes the received and retained."[129] Second, stable traditions are typically efficacious because these traditions tend to "work" if they have been preserved for multiple generations.

Shils offers several examples of stability in tradition, such as the names for geographical locations or nations, the biological classification of family, or educational institutions, but we could also consider the example of rules of sport. For instance, the offside rule in English football was established as a corollary to the changing of Law Six—which had prohibited passing the ball to any teammate in a more advanced position—in 1866. When the team controlling the ball was allowed to actually pass forward, the game became much more fluid, contrasting the previous strategy of hoofing the ball down the field and having a majority of the team chase the ball, a tactic familiar to anyone playing or coaching those of a young age. Once dribbling and progressive passing became the norm, the offside rule limited positioning and passing by ruling a player "offside" if they did not have three opposing defenders ahead of them. The 1866 iteration of the rule led to a prolonged period of low-scoring games; as Jonathan Wilson puts it, "The football was boring, attendances were falling and the [ruling body, the Football Association], for once, not merely recognised that something needed to be done, but set about doing it."[130] Prior to the 1925–1926 season, the offside rule was amended to reduce the number of intervening defenders to two, and that iteration of the rule remained intact until it was amended again in the early 1990s to clarify that the most advanced offensive player must at least be level with second-to-last defender. The offside rule, despite small amendments, has remained stable since its inception; it has accomplished its purpose in maintaining fair play in the run of the game, and, because it is such an integral part of the international rules of the game, it is treated as normative for football fans across the globe.[131] Rules of sport, like other stable

---

128. Shils, *Tradition*, 205.
129. Shils, *Tradition*, 200.
130. Wilson, *Inverting the Pyramid*, 42.
131. See Wilson, *Inverting the Pyramid*, 12–13, 42–43.

forms of tradition, persist in order to maintain "sameness" and provide continuity as the game is transmitted to new audiences and players.

As seen, however, traditions—even stable traditions—also undergo changes as they are transmitted, and these changes can be subtle or more radical.[132] Fentress and Wickham argue that traditions change because of the need for reinterpretation due to recontextualization:

> Every time a tradition is articulated, it must be given a meaning appropriate to the context, or to the genre, in which it is articulated. This necessity to reinterpret often lies behind changes within the tradition itself. These changes may be small in scale, or they may be large-scale recontextualizations of the entire tradition. In whatever case, the process of reinterpretations reflects real changes in external circumstances as well.[133]

In other words, "the natural tendency of social memory is to suppress what is not meaningful or intuitively satisfying in the collective memories of the past, and interpolate or substitute what seems more appropriate or more in keeping with their particular conception of the world."[134] Shils echoes the importance of context, writing, "Traditions change because the circumstances to which they refer change. Traditions, to survive, must be fitting to the circumstances in which they operate and to which they are directed."[135] Mapping out some of the patterns of change, Shils categorizes two sets of changes: endogenous changes and exogenous changes. Both sets of changes require human action upon the potentiality for change, but endogenous changes are located within the tradition,

---

132. In his discussion of religious traditions, particularly within Islam, Talal Asad notes that the language of "tradition" often assumes a rigid and unchanging sense of pastness as opposed to an active participatory process located in the present: "Talking of tradition ... as though it was the passing on of an unchanging substance in homogenous time oversimplifies the problem of time's definition of practice, experience, and event ... We make a false assumption when we suppose that the present is merely a fleeting moment in a historical teleology connecting past to future. In tradition the 'present' is always at the center. If we attend to the way time present is separated from but also included within events and epochs, the way time past authoritatively constitutes present practices, *and the way authenticating practices invoke or distance themselves from the past (by reiterating, reinterpreting, and reconnecting textualized memory and memorialized history),* we move toward a richer understanding of tradition's temporality" (Asad, *Formations of the Secular*, 222, emphasis added).

133. Fentress and Wickham, *Social Memory*, 85–86.

134. Fentress and Wickham, *Social Memory*, 58–59.

135. Shils, *Tradition*, 258. For instance, traditions located in a particular social stratum may change if the recipient of the tradition attains a changed social status.

such as innovation and imagination, new forms of rationalization, or correction of previously held traditional knowledge.[136] Exogenous changes, on the other hand, occur due to points of contact taking place outside the tradition. For instance, the association between communities may lead to addition, amalgamation, and absorption as syncretistic changes that result in the acquisition of new traditional material, but when social groups disassociate from one another, social ramifications, conflicts, and attenuation due to irrelevance of traditional material or a lack of attention can all lead to the dissolution or death of a tradition.[137] Hobsbawm focuses on the forms that such changes take, arguing that gradual and incremental changes "can be absorbed into the formalized social past in the form of a mythologized and perhaps ritualized history, by a tacit modification of the system of beliefs, by 'stretching' the framework, or in other ways."[138] Overall, changes in context lead to changes in tradition, and although it may take time for these changes to take root, they can reshape tradition and memory in a number of ways.

Distortion

Because the process of remembering is active, there are several ways that memories are encoded and recalled, and this process is susceptible to distortion.[139] "Distortion" is not a loaded term, but rather a natural feature of both individual and collective memory; in fact, Michael Schudson has gone so far as to claim that "memory is distortion since memory is invariably and inevitably selective."[140] Distortion takes place when particular "social, psychological, and historical influences" result in effects to the overall mnemonic process of "encoding information, storing information, and strategically retrieving information."[141] In essence, memory distortion is a particular subset of changes to tradition.

---

136. Shils, *Tradition*, 213–39.
137. Shils, *Tradition*, 273–86.
138. Hobsbawm, "Social Function of the Past," 5.
139. See Schacter, *Memory Distortion*; Schacter et al., "Memory Distortion," 467–74.
140. Schudson, "Dynamics of Distortion in Collective Memory," in Schacter, ed., *Memory Distortion*, 348. Here it is again worth mentioning Bartlett's "effort after meaning," a first foray into the process of distortion by noticing the ways in which individuals "named" certain abstract images in ways that ordered, organized, and structured them into representations of concrete images. See Bartlett, *Remembering*, 20.
141. Schudson, "Dynamics of Distortion in Collective Memory," in Schacter, ed., *Memory Distortion*, 348.

There are a number of types of distortion that can occur in memory. For physical images and visual concepts, Fentress and Wickham suggest that sights are actively constructed through cognitive processes where concepts are distorted via simplification and schematization, and these processes can happen consciously or subconsciously.[142] Judith Redman's work on eyewitness memory deals with schematization and draws out several predictable patterns of memory acquisition, such as the persistence of information that matches a social schema or the aligning of missing information toward a schema.[143] Redman goes on to detail several factors that affect the ability to remember, including expectations, type of fact, event significance and detail salience or prominence,[144] personality and interests of the witness, and observational point of view and perceptual adequacy.[145] Additionally, Redman points to several ways that memories, including narrative accounts, can be concretized or distorted post-event, such as the "freezing effect" that occurs after continually reproducing past mistakes, the type of retrieval (recalling specific vs. general information), or whether the memory has been repeatedly articulated (practice makes better than *not* practicing).[146]

Processes of distortion also exist in social memory as well. Olick detects one of the key functions of narrative memory—the distortion of memory by articulating it into story form—as the construction of group

---

142. Fentress and Wickham, *Social Memory*, 31–32. Building off of Gombrich's experiment, which asked children to replicate a classic piece of art (John Constable's *Wivenhoe Park*), Fentress and Wickham note how the children's artistic copies often flatten the textures and colors, reduce the complexity of images (e.g., representing human figures in two-dimensional front portraits containing all the component parts of humans—head, hands, hair, legs, fingers, etc.—as opposed to side-profiles or other natural body contortions that obstruct or obscure such component parts), and simplify the scale of spatial dimensions.

143. Redman, "How Accurate Are Eyewitnesses?," 181.

144. "In order to remember something, a person needs to attend to it, and, since it is impossible for an individual to attend to all the stimuli in his or her environment at any given time, s/he selects those things to which s/he will attend, often unconsciously" (Redman, "How Accurate Are Eyewitnesses?," 182–83). To demonstrate the difficulty of attending to details, consider the different literary techniques of Anton Chekhov, famous for the dramatic use of every detail (i.e., "Chekhov's gun") and Ernest Hemingway, who frequently offered inconsequential details in his writing: "The chances are, gentlemen, that if it hangs upon the wall, it will not even shoot . . . Yes, the unfireable gun may be a symbol. This is true. But with a good enough writer, the chances are some jerk just hung it there to look at" (Hemingway, "Art of the Short Story," 91).

145. Redman, "How Accurate Are Eyewitnesses?," 181–85.

146. Redman, "How Accurate Are Eyewitnesses?," 186–89.

identity. For Olick, "Storytelling about the past is thus not merely something communities do; it is, in important ways, what they are. Rather than being a mechanism that underwrites cohesion, *storytelling about the past 'per-forms' the group by 're-member-ing' it.*"[147] Similar to the memory of visual images, narrative memory is most prone to simplification where inconsequential details are minimized.[148] Stories arrange memories into sequential order (plot), and the plotting of a narrative memory "permits the ordering, retention, and subsequent transmission of a vast amount of information."[149] Schudson's work addresses this and three other ways in which distortion impacts collective memory. First, *distanciation* occurs the further removed the memory is from the event, and its effects are vagueness, loss of detail, and disconnect from the initial emotion. Second, *instrumentalization* occurs in how the memory is used, and its effects are any changes that are made in order to serve the interests of the present. Third, *narrativization* (as seen above) reframes memories through literary conventions, effectively ordering and simplifying memories into narrative forms that may not be as reflective of the complexities of the events being remembered. Fourth, and finally, *conventionalization* shapes memories in order to conform them to social conventions, since memories that represent cultural norms are more likely to be collectively remembered than those that counter the culture in which they arise.[150] In short, the various processes of distortion, whether in individual or collective memory, remind us that "memory is selective . . . [and this] selection is driven by various processes, both willful and unconscious."[151]

We can use the example of movies to illustrate how even the most fixed view of memory must reckon with the dynamics of distortion. A movie is a fixed, formalized narrative presentation. Once copied onto the "reel"—as either analog or digital media—scenes are not added to the film. In other words, the film, barring any physical or digital data corruption (a different kind of "distortion"), appears to be the same exact

147. Olick, "Products, Processes, and Practices," 6, emphasis original.
148. See Fentress and Wickham, *Social Memory*, 68.
149. Fentress and Wickham, *Social Memory*, 72.
150. Schudson, "Dynamics of Distortion in Collective Memory," in Schacter, ed., *Memory Distortion*, 348–59. On the last point of conventionalization, this process does not deny that unconventional details can be remembered and transmitted in collective memory. Rather, as memories grow more distanced and vaguer, they are more likely to be represented in ways that conform to social norms rather than the alternative.
151. Schudson, "Dynamics of Distortion in Collective Memory," in Schacter, ed., *Memory Distortion*, 360.

film in each viewing. However, film, just like memory, is never truly the same because while the format may be fixed, the "viewing" takes place in another context, spatially and/or temporally, and the effects of the film are shaped by different factors at the time of the viewing. Watching (or recollecting) violence has different effects in times of peace than it does in times of war; viewing (or recalling) loss or trauma has different effects once one has experienced loss or trauma first-hand.[152] Aspects such as characterization and pop-cultural references can have different effects depending on life circumstances. Audiences may experience changes with whom they identify as they take on new social roles (single vs. spouse, childless vs. parent, employee vs. boss, etc.),[153] and cultural references may not translate into new contexts.[154] In other words, since movies still must contend with the processes of distortion and reception, then we should not expect otherwise in the ways in which memories shift and transform perceptions (people, events, things) in order to be intelligible in a different context.[155] The same argument can be

---

152. Experiences of violence or trauma can be socially-orienting, commemorated, and salient for communities of memory, and "in this way the traumatic experience of violence comes to inscribe itself upon the collective memory in the form of what George Bonanno refers to as a 'nuclear script'—that is, a cognitive schema that fundamentally organizes memory, supplies group orientation and exerts a determinative effect upon perception and interpretation of subsequent experience" (Kirk, "Violence and the Death of Jesus in Q," in Kirk and Thatcher, eds., *Memory, Tradition, and Text*, 192–93; cf. Malkki, *Purity and Exile*; James W. Pennebaker and Amy L. Gonzales, "Making History: Social and Psychological Processes Underlying Collective Memory," in Boyer and Wertsch, *Memory in Mind and Culture*, 175–78).

153. In discussing his remembrances of his father, Halbwachs notes how the image of his father changed not only due to circumstances in his father's life, but his own as well: "The image I have of my father continuously evolved over time, not only because my remembrances of him while he lived accumulated *but also because I myself changed and my perspective altered as I occupied different positions in my family and, more important, in other milieus*" (Halbwachs, *Collective Memory*, 72, emphasis added).

154. Pixar director Brad Bird notes that one of the difficulties of pop-cultural references is that they can easily lose their meaning. Bird points to an impression of Arsenio Hall in the 1992 original animated *Aladdin*, a pop-culture reference that meant more for audiences in 1992—when Hall's late night television show was in its prime—than for audiences in the early 2000s after Hall's show ended its run. See Gilbey, "Toy Story."

155. *Pace* Richard Bauckham, who argues for the "continuity of tradition before and after the resurrection" due to the "degree of stability that severely limited the degree to which [the eyewitnesses] were changed by further interpretive insight" (Bauckham, *Jesus and the Eyewitnesses*, 355). In response to Bauckham, Redman makes a similar point about the malleability of memory and how significant factors can shape postevent memory, arguing, "While eyewitness accounts provide useful information about what happened, many factors can influence both how accurate and how complete any

made for alternative types of media as well.[156] For Shils, media such as paintings or texts might remain the same given they do not deteriorate or are not defaced in some manner, a constant threat undermining the "fixity" of media, but the effects or interpretations of such media are much more fluid and subject to malleability:

> *The interpretation of the text does not remain the same equally among all the recipients at a given time or among the recipients who succeed each other in time.* A rule of conduct, explicitly articulated or implied in a pattern of conduct, or a belief about the soul, or a philosophical idea about the common good *does not remain identical through its career of transmissions over generations* . . . Constellations of symbols, clusters of images, are received and modified. They change in the process of transmission as interpretations are made of the tradition presented; they change also while they are in the possession of their recipients.[157]

Remembered events, people, and things change in the minds and commemorative practices of those that continue to remember them. Distortion is part and parcel of transmission, and it reminds us that memory is not merely a process of passively retrieving but of actively reconstructing the past. In the words of Olick and Robbins, "Memory is not an unchanging vessel for carrying the past into the present; memory is a process, not a thing, and it works differently at different points in time."[158]

Media

Media have always played a crucial role in conceptualizing the phenomenon of memory. As seen above, examples of new media can be useful in relating how memory works and revealing about the era in which the conception of memory is drawn. For instance, writing in the 1980s, Jan

---

account might be. What happens at the time of the event and afterwards can affect the accuracy and completeness of the account" (Redman, "How Accurate Are Eyewitnesses?," 190). For an early skeptical position about the reliability of the evangelists as eyewitnesses, see Stein, "'Criteria' for Authenticity," in France and Wenham, eds., *Gospel Perspectives*, 226.

156. Halbwachs uses the example of reading books from childhood, remarking how the nostalgia that we long for in actuality breeds disappointment because "we actually seem to be reading a new book, or at least an altered version" (Halbwachs, *On Collective Memory*, 46–47).

157. Shils, *Tradition*, 13, emphasis added.

158. Olick and Robbins, "Social Memory Studies," 122.

Vansina discusses memory as "not an inert storage system like a tape recorder or a computer," referring to technology that looked (and, to an extent, worked) much differently at the end of the twentieth century than it does in the early twenty-first century today.[159] Modern scholars are not alone in their attempts at conceptualizing memory in familiar ways; even ancient peoples discussed memory in terms of their own available media. Socrates conceived of memory as an internal block of wax (κήρινον ἐκμαγεῖον) upon which we imprint our perceptions of the world around us.[160] Cicero, Quintilian, and other rhetoricians conceived of the art of memory as architectural places (*loci*) where certain mental perceptions (*imagines*) could be stored for later retrieval.[161] Memory and media are bound together, and both are foundational for our understanding of ourselves, our societies, and the larger world in which we live. As Astrid Erll puts it, "Whatever we know about the world, we know through media and in dependence of media. The images of the past which circulate in memory culture are thus not extrinsic to media. They are media constructs."[162]

Media not only influence our understanding of memory, but also have direct effects on how memory works, so it is important to note how the two work together. One way scholars have noted this relationship is through a history of mediated memory, or representations of the past rooted in forms of available media. Jacques Le Goff maps the relationship between memory and media, mostly structured around literacy and orality, into four particular phases: (1) "Ethnic Memory," or predominantly oral memory of societies where writing is not as highly valued;[163] (2) societies (primarily in the medieval period) where oral memory and written memory have reached an "equilibrium"; (3) the modern period where written memory is dominant (via literacy, printing, etc.); and (4) new forms of technology that shape the future of memory (e.g., computers and new media).[164] Another way scholars approach the relationship between media and memory is via points of contact, or what Erll calls the "media

159. Vansina, *Oral Tradition as History*, 147.
160. Plato, *Theaet.* 191c–d.
161. Yates, *Art of Memory*, 2–26.
162. Erll, *Memory in Culture*, 114.
163. "Collective memory seems to function [in societies without writing that are centered around 'memory specialists'] in accordance with a 'generative reconstruction' rather than with a 'mechanical memorization'" (Le Goff, *History and Memory*, 57).
164. Le Goff, *History and Memory*, 54.

of memory." Erll notes several functions for the media of memory, such as storage through time, circulation through space, and offering cultural cues that trigger communities to make associations with formative narratives.[165] In terms of media's effect on memory, Erll argues for two major types of mediation. Following Bolter and Grusin, Erll discusses "remediation" as the way in which media interacts with and changes previous forms of media, arguing "remediation tends to solidify cultural memory, creating and stabilizing certain narratives and icons of the past."[166] Erll also discusses "premediation" as the way in which existent media provide frameworks and schemata for the preservation of future experiences. Erll pulls these two types of mediation together in order to argue for literature as a medium of cultural memory; both literature and cultural memory are active construction processes: "cultural systems of meaning, narrative operations, and reception participate equally."[167]

Due to the symbiotic relationship between media and memory, changes in media can also signify changes in memory. Erll writes that "the most significant ruptures in the history of mediated remembering appear to be the transitions" that take place between one medium to another.[168] Le Goff points to the shift from orality to literacy as a "profound transformation in collective memory" because of two "forms" of memory that appear with writing: commemorative monuments (inscriptions, epigraphs, steles) and documents, which also have "the character of the monument."[169] Assmann notes that the role of writing plays an important part in the transformation of communicative memory to cultural memory. Cultural memory is not solely located in literate societies; after all, Assmann argues that ritual is a form of cultural memory that does not rely upon literacy for its preservation or transmission to new participants. However, writing radically reshapes cultural memory, supplanting the repetition of ritual with text-centered re-presentation.[170] Not only does the shift in media change social memory, but it also has a significant impact on group identity. Assmann notes that "striking

---

165. Erll, *Memory in Culture*, 126–28.
166. Erll, *Memory in Culture*, 141.
167. Erll, *Memory in Culture*, 152.
168. Erll, *Memory in Culture*, 120.
169. Le Goff, *History and Memory*, 58–59.
170. "It is through the written element of traditions that the dominance of repetition gradually gives way to that of re-presentation—ritual gives way to textual coherence" (Assmann, *Cultural Memory and Early Civilization*, 4).

enhancements of collective identity are to be found wherever there are particular advances in cultural technology."[171]

Media and memory are mutually informative. The various forms of available media offer frameworks for conceptualizing, understanding, and tracking how social memory is preserved, transmitted, and formative for social groups. As Erll argues, mediated memory *is* cultural memory; it is essential for memory scholars to be attuned to how media dynamics work in society and operate alongside memory.

History

Halbwachs's initial work employed "history" in a less technical and more ambivalent sense, but *The Collective Memory* witnessed a more intense separation between memory and history.[172] This divide was more pronounced by Nora, whose project aimed at countering the genre of "national history" and afforded a more vigorous role for memory as "absolute" as opposed to history's "relative" role.[173] In countering the impulse of historians to use "collective memory," Gedi and Elam remark that Nora's notion "is certainly not the same memory historians since Thucydides have normally referred to. Historians' memory is a human faculty, personal and therefore fallible, yet a vital means for the reconstruction of the past."[174] For Gedi and Elam, memory is unreliable and

---

171. Assmann, *Cultural Memory and Early Civilization*, 140.

172. In *On Collective Memory*, Halbwachs appears to use "history" in the same vein as "tradition," and at times it appears to operate in the same exact way that "memory" does. For instance, when discussing the memory of family groups, Halbwachs writes, "History does not limit itself to reproducing a tale told by people contemporary with events of the past, but rather refashions it from period to period not only because of other testimony that has become available, but also to adapt it to the mental habits and the type of representation of the past common among contemporaries" (Halbwachs, *On Collective Memory*, 75).

173. See Nora, *Realms of Memory*, 1:3. Nora's dichotomy between history and memory has been critiqued more recently by other memory theorists for building on some of Halbwachs's conclusions without existing in the same intellectual sphere, particularly regarding views of contemporary historiography, as Halbwachs. "While Halbwachs's polemic needs to be understood against the backdrop of nineteenth-century historicism, blocking out the memorial function of historiography appears strange in light of the discussions among historians—beginning as early as the 1970s—regarding the constructed nature, subjectivity, and perspectivity of all history writing" (Erll, *Memory in Culture*, 25).

174. Gedi and Elam, "Collective Memory," 33–34.

in need of verification, while history is comprised of valid facts.[175] If one were only to follow this thread, it would indeed seem that memory and history are incompatible in almost every facet.[176]

On the contrary, there are many similar features between memory and history and, by extension, memory theory and historiography. Both social memory and history are interested in the act of reconstruction, and both phenomena are always subject to interpretation. In the same way that memory theorists reject notions of a "pure memory" or a total unfiltered recall of an event, historians also recognize that there is no free-floating category of "pure history," although this is not always as widely acknowledged. Edward Hallett Carr presents the "common sense view of history" in the mid-twentieth century as a repository of objective, uninterpreted facts, which in essence treats historical fact as "pure history" and the interpretation of the historian as the subjective element. However, Carr argues that this view is insufficient: "The belief in a hard core of historical facts existing objectively and independently of the interpretation of the historian is a preposterous fallacy, but one which it is very hard to eradicate."[177] The historian arranges "facts" in order to tell a coherent story, and the process of arrangement requires the historian to make certain interpretive decisions that, at the least, shape the effects these "facts" have. Hayden White discusses this as "emplotment," writing,

> No given set of casually recorded historical events can in itself constitute a story; the most it might offer to the historian are story *elements*. The events are *made* into a story by the suppression or subordination of certain of them and the highlighting of others, by characterization, motific repetition, variation of tone and point of view, alternative descriptive strategies, and the like—in short, all of the techniques we would normally expect to find in the emplotment of a novel or a play.[178]

---

175. Patrick Hutton locates the divide between history and memory in post-modern historiography's turn toward forms of the politics of commemoration, although his ultimate goal is to provide a path for post-modern historiographers to see memory and history in a new light where history mediates repetition (tradition) and recollection (memory). See Hutton, *History as an Art of Memory*, xx–xxiv, 160–68.

176. After all, as Le Goff writes, "even the greatest Greek philosophers never fully succeeded in reconciling memory and history" (Le Goff, *History and Memory*, 65).

177. Carr, *What Is History?*, 9–10.

178. White, *Tropics of Discourse*, 84, emphasis original. For more on the phenomenon of emplotment, see White's essay "Interpretation in History," in *Tropics of Discourse*, 51–80.

But the historian also must gauge which facts to include and which to leave out, or else all history would be understood as merely a chain of causes and effects.[179] It appears then that Carr's estimation of the historian is correct: "The historian is necessarily selective," and this means that history also contains subjectivity, just like social memory.[180]

Since memory and history are active, selective processes transmitting and interpreting information about the past, both must also stake claims about the relationship between the present and the past. Halbwachs characterized collective memory as driven solely by the interests of the present, of the living memory of social groups. Schwartz, on the other hand, argues for more continuity between the past and present, recognizing the stability of certain images or commemorative processes that have been superimposed upon—without replacing—older images, perceptions, or commemorations. Schwartz grounds this continuity in society: "The primary condition for the endurance of traditional constructions is always the endurance of the social realities they symbolize."[181] As long as social groups preserve a particular identity over time, social memory cannot be entirely untethered from its past.[182]

History and memory are intricately related. Patrick Hutton examines the crossroads of memory and history and, drawing on Frances Yates's work, refers to history as "an art of memory" that helps uncover the forgotten experiences of the past.[183] Jeffrey Barash, on the other hand, de-

---

179. White discusses this as the function and effects of "interpretation" at the heart of history and historical narrative: "On the one hand, there are always more facts in the record than the historian can possibly include in his narrative representation of a given segment of the historical process. And so the historian must 'interpret' his data by excluding certain facts from his account as irrelevant to his narrative purpose. On the other hand, in his efforts to reconstruct 'what happened' in any given period of history, the historian inevitably must include in his narrative an account of some event or complex of events for which the facts that would permit a plausible explanation of its occurrence are lacking. And this means that the historian must 'interpret' his materials by filling in the gaps in his information on inferential or speculative grounds. A historical narrative is thus necessarily a mixture of adequately and inadequately explained events" (White, *Tropics of Discourse*, 51).

180. Carr, *What Is History?*, 9.

181. Schwartz, "Social Change and Collective Memory," 233.

182. "Every society, whatever its ideological climate, requires a sense of continuity with the past, and its enduring memories maintain this continuity. If beliefs about the past failed to outlive changes in society, then society's unity and continuity would be undermined" (Schwartz, "Social Change and Collective Memory," 222; cf. Shils, *Tradition*, 327).

183. "Memory prompts our inquiries as historians, just as the search for that which has been forgotten focuses them. The past as it was experienced, not just the past as it has subsequently been used, is a moment of memory we should strive to recover"

scribes memory as "a prerequisite both for historical understanding and for tradition."[184] Assmann sees the role of memory as transformative for history, arguing that "what counts for cultural memory is not factual but remembered history. One might even say that cultural memory transforms factual into remembered history."[185] While specific conceptions of their relationship differ, both history and memory act as enterprises relating the past and the present. Through the similarities in their function, basic assumptions, and manners of inquiry, as well as a general agreement of some sort of overlap, history and memory—and by extension, historians and memory theorists—are more connected than Halbwachs's or Nora's work may make it seem. Indeed, many scholars from either side of the history/memory debate would agree with Carr that "the past is intelligible to us only in the light of the present; and we can fully understand the present only in the light of the past."[186]

Summary of Social Memory Theory

Though there are discrepancies in terminology, conceptualization, or in application of theory, there are still a number of consensus points in memory studies that are beneficial for understanding social memory theory. First, memory is an active process of reconstructing and interpreting past experience, and like de Saussure's view of language, it is an inherently socially-structured phenomenon, even at the individual level. Second, the social aspect of memory serves a constitutive role in the formation of group identity. Third, the study of memory draws on the relationship between the past and the present, between memory, history, and tradition. The past is not viewed as a historical entity that can be stripped of its varnish or removed like a kernel, but rather always exists, in some degree, in relation to the needs and interests of the present. Similarly, tradition and memory are closely related, if not interchangeable, and both experience dynamics of stability and change given the needs of the social groups that keep them alive by passing them to subsequent generations. Fourth, memory is not an objective phenomenon; the *transmission* and imbuing of *meaning* within memory is subjective and requires contextualization,

---

(Hutton, *History as an Art of Memory*, xxv).

184. Barash, *Collective Memory and the Historical Past*, 2. Le Goff also argues that history draws on memory as memory "seeks to save the past in order to serve the present and the future" (Le Goff, *History and Memory*, 99).

185. Assmann, *Cultural Memory and Early Civilization*, 38.

186. Carr, *What Is History?*, 69.

and each recontextualization of memory requires reinterpretation. Fifth, social memory allots for an element of distortion between actual events and the remembered past; in other words, memories are selective and in order to render the past intelligible to the present, they operate under a number of factors that can impact their transmission and influence the ways in which they are reconstructed and reinterpreted. Sixth, memory is context-dependent, so the meaning of a memory is susceptible to change. This again articulates the idea that the actual past is not an external entity located on a shelf that is only accessible if we reach far back enough. Finally, memory studies are not only concerned with questions of "*what actually* happened?" but also concerned with *how* and *why*, particularly concerning the preservation, persistence, and permutation of traditions.

This chapter offers a broad foundation for understanding social memory theory. The early discussion on the terminology of social memory demonstrated Olick and Robbins's characterization of the field as a "centerless enterprise" by displaying different problems, nuances, and trends in the way that social memory theory has been discussed. The brief discussion of social memory theory revealed some of the base assumptions in the theoretical conception of how social memory works. The survey of theorists provided a representative history of the theoretical underpinnings of social memory, further explaining and articulating some of the previous assumptions through the work of several prominent theorists. Finally, the chapter closed with an examination of the ways social memory theory influences our understanding of memory: through tradition, stability and change, distortion, media, and history.

Early on in this chapter, I stated that social memory was not a method, but a theory about the ways in which social groups construct, represent, and transmit memories and traditions about the past into their present circumstances. It remains to be seen what exactly this looks like and how it is done. As a theory, social memory must be applied to a field of study. In the next chapter, I survey how the tenets of social memory theory set forth in this chapter have been introduced to the field of New Testament studies, and particularly historical Jesus research, by examining scholars who follow in the wake of Halbwachs, Assmann, and Schwartz in appealing to social memory to ask questions about the transmission and reception of Jesus traditions based on the socio-cultural frameworks available at the time of the tradents.

2

Memory Theory in New Testament Research

> It will never be possible to draw a sharp line of demarcation between pious imagination and historical tradition. We have the latter only in the framework of the former. If the recollections of Jesus have been preserved for us, it is because he was preached as crucified Messiah and resurrected Lord. What *mnēmosyne* would have been able to tell about Jesus of Nazareth would have been very little indeed if Jesus had not been commemorated by those whose faith was in the Risen Lord and who broke the bread *eis anamnēsin Christou*.
> —Nils Alstrup Dahl[1]

MANY OF THE TOPICS at the core of Gospel studies—the transmission of Jesus tradition, the history and historicity of early Christianity, the role of media in shaping Jesus tradition—provide fertile ground for the introduction and application of social memory theory. However, the application of memory theory, particularly social memory theory, within New Testament studies as a whole has been surprisingly minimal until the last few decades. In this chapter I will explore the ways social memory theory has been introduced to New Testament studies and, more specifically, Gospel studies. I will outline how key discussions in the

---

1. Dahl, *Jesus in the Memory of the Early Church*, 29.

composition of the gospels and the understanding of (or "Quest for") the historical Jesus frame the arrival of memory theory. I will then examine the theoretical applications of scholars such as Jens Schröter, Alan Kirk, Anthony Le Donne, Rafael Rodríguez, Chris Keith, and Sandra Huebenthal to demonstrate how social memory theory has been applied. I will also highlight how key memory theorists, such as Jan Assmann, Barry Schwartz, and Jeffrey Olick, have provided specific insight for the field. Finally, I will examine critiques and defenses of the theory and its application in Gospel studies. In tracing social memory theory's impact on the field, I seek to answer four questions: (1) How was social memory theory introduced into New Testament/Gospel studies?; (2) How has social memory theory been used in New Testament studies?; (3) How has the application of social memory theory been received?; and (4) What does the application of social memory theory have to offer future New Testament and Gospel studies?

Introducing Social Memory Theory to New Testament Studies

Though social memory theory was articulated in the early twentieth century, its core interests—transmission of tradition, impact of commemorative activities, dynamics of media, and the relationship between the present and the past—have been felt as long as traditions of and about Jesus have been in circulation. This section looks at how New Testament studies moved from memory to social memory, examining the ways in which tradition and memory have been identified and studied from the earliest Christians to the Gospels criticism of the twentieth century.

Foundations and Forerunners

Memory and tradition have long been recognized as central to the formation of early Christianity, particularly in the self-awareness of early Christians and their role in the process of transmitting the stories about and words of Jesus.[2] Paul highlights this transmission process by using

2. My use of the category "early Christians" is fluid, dynamic, and based on their status as commemorative communities concerned with the social memory of Jesus. This category is not mutually exclusive with other cultural categories (e.g., Hellenistic/Diaspora Jews, first-century Judaeans, Romans, Greeks, Alexandrians, etc.) or representative of any single or unified overarching theological system, in the (unlikely) case

verbs like παραδίδωμι and παραλαμβάνω (1 Cor 15:3). His insistence on having transmitted the tradition without alterations (Παρέδωκα γὰρ ὑμῖν ἐν πρώτοις, ὃ καὶ παρέλαβον, "For I handed on to you first of all that which also I received") is perhaps further belabored by restating what he has supposedly already proclaimed (v. 11) to the Corinthian community. This proclamation seems to be the core of Paul's own Jesus tradition, the transmission of a series of events and memories from which Paul was largely absent: Jesus's death, burial, resurrection, and subsequent resurrection appearances (1 Cor 15:3-8).[3] The resurrection narratives in the Gospels expand this framework by offering a different view of tradition and highlighting a tradent group missing in Paul's proclamation: each resurrection narrative initially begins with women at the empty tomb who relay this information to the remaining disciples.[4] Elsewhere in the New Testament, tradition, transmission, and memory appear as foundational for communal belief (1 John 1:1-3; John 20:30-31) as well as catalysts for communal action (Rev 3:3). Later sources further emphasize the role that memory played in sustaining the written tradition. Justin Martyr conceived of the gospels as "memoirs" (ἀπομνημονεύμασιν), placing memory (μνήμη) and the acts of recollection not only at the core of their composition, but as their generic designation (*Apol.* 66.3.1; *Dialogue with Trypho* 100.4.5; 101.3.7).[5] Likewise,

---

that one ever existed (see Hurtado, "Interactive Diversity," 445-62). Instead, the category "early Christians" is meant as a pragmatic title descriptive of the function played by those who constructed, contributed to, and circulated Jesus tradition in the first three centuries CE.

3. The ordering of the resurrection appearances plays an important role in staking Paul's authority in this passage: Paul himself is the last witness to the resurrected Jesus. The question of Paul's apostolic authority looms large in his writings (Gal 1:11-12; 1 Cor 1:11-17; 3:2-9), and Paul caps the tradition by including himself with the others (perhaps also other faction leaders) proclaiming the tradition so the Corinthian community can be assured in their belief (15:11).

4. Mark and Matthew locate the resurrection's transmission as a response to the angelic command (ταχὺ πορευθεῖσαι εἴπατε τοῖς μαθηταῖς αὐτοῦ, Matt 28:7; ὑπάγετε εἴπατε τοῖς μαθηταῖς αὐτοῦ, Mark 16:7), whereas Luke's "two men" exhort the women to "remember" (μνήσθητε ὡς ἐλάλησεν ὑμῖν ἔτι ὢν ἐν τῇ Γαλιλαίᾳ, Luke 24:6) and, having recalled Jesus's words, they organically share news of the resurrection with the disciples (24:9). John employs Mary Magdalene as the central "double-tradent" of resurrection news: first, to relay to the disciples that the stone had been rolled away (20:2), and second, to document the first resurrection appearance (20:18).

5. Richard Heard argues that Justin's use of ἀπομνημόνευμα was actually dependent upon Papias's statement about the gospel tradition. See Heard, "ΑΠΟΜΝΗΜΟΝΕΥΜΑ," 122-27. More recently, Matthew D. C. Larsen's work focuses closely on the literary category of the ὑπόμνημα and sketches the implications that this genre has for our

Papias rooted the written canonical gospel tradition in memory, claiming that "whatever [Mark] remembered" of Peter's preaching, "he wrote accurately, though he did not order the things said and done by the lord" (ὅσα ἐμνημόνευσεν, ἀκριβῶς ἔγραψεν, οὐ μέντοι τάξει τὰ ὑπὸ τοῦ κυρίου ἢ λεχθέντα ἢ πραχθέντα, Eusebius, *Ecclesiastical History* 3.39.15).[6]

What can actually be gleaned from these early Christian understandings of memory? Memory, and the resulting tradition, is discussed in a variety of ways and in relation to both individual eyewitnesses as well as larger groups of disciples. Memory is seen as a generative creative act as well as a reactionary response; it allows for and is contained within the transmission of information across various media (the women's proclamation, Peter's preaching, Mark's writing, Paul's letters, the gospel genre).[7] Papias's claim that the memory at the source of the Gospel of Mark is "accurate" (ἀκριβῶς) even when unordered offers insight into concerns about and defenses of gospel reliability; however, the threshold of accuracy is not prescribed, nor are the limits of memory questioned.[8] Therefore, what these early Christian sources offer is the *recognition* of memory, an awareness of the importance of remembering and a variety of examples in which the past and the present are connected. The *dynamics* of memory—how remembering works in the formation of tradition—remained largely taken for granted until nearly two millennia later when memory theory was introduced into and applied to gospels scholarship.[9]

---

understanding of the Gospel of Mark and the Synoptic Problem. See Larsen, *Gospels Before the Book*.

6. Papias goes on to absolve Mark of any error in structuring his gospel by claiming that its order is due to the ad-hoc nature of Peter's preaching, who shaped his teaching "according to the needs [of his audiences]" rather than an attempt at "making an arranged account of the sayings of the lord" (ὃς πρὸς τὰς χρείας ἐποιεῖτο τὰς διδασκαλίας ἀλλ' οὐχ ὥσπερ σύνταξιν τῶν κυριακῶν ποιούμενος λογίων, Eusebius, *Ecclesiastical History* 3.39.15).

7. Justin Martyr briefly references the process of transmission of tradition and claims that the evangelists "handed over that which was enjoined to them" (οὕτως παρέδωκαν ἃ ἐντέταλται αὐτοῖς, Justin Martyr, *Apol.* 66.3.2), which echoes Paul's understanding of tradition.

8. Thucydides admits that his speeches are not "verbatim" replications of the past; even if they were, given the distance from the historical situation, it is unlikely that they would hold the same rhetorical sway. Still, Thucydides offers a pragmatic approach to his speech-writing that attempts to capture his (rhetorical) interpretation of historical mood and character. He is not fully probing the dynamics of memory, but neither is he ignoring the problems of handling the past. See *History of the Peloponnesian War* 1.22.1.

9. Alan Kirk highlighted this lacuna by stating that, as of 2005, "while memory

Though memory remained largely ancillary to discussions of tradition in early Christianity, there have been implicit touchpoints between the two fields of study.[10] As noted in the introduction to this chapter, many of the marquee topics of discussion in NT scholarship over the last century are also of particular interest or tangential relation to memory theory. At minimum, these topics—historical Jesus research, gospel composition, tradition studies, and media criticism—serve as useful arenas in which to trace the trajectory of memory theory's introduction into NT scholarship.[11] The following brief overview of the previous century of NT studies sketches these foundational issues pertinent to the application of memory theory today.

Questing through History, Searching for Jesus

The late nineteenth and early twentieth centuries were an abundant period for "life-of-Jesus" scholarship set up by a number of critical turning points for New Testament scholarship that took place in the preceding century.[12] Hermann Samuel Reimarus's *Apologie* set in motion the pursuit of "lives of Jesus" inquiries while scientific and philosophical advancements in the post-Enlightenment period also reshaped inquiries into the exact nature of the gospels and their Jesus traditions.[13] Where

---

studies have burgeoned in the humanities and social sciences, no comparable effect can be noticed in New Testament scholarship" (Kirk and Thatcher, *Memory, Tradition, and Text*, 1).

10. Kirk draws on the *anamnesis* passage of 1 Cor 11:23–26 as one example of the "memorializing practices of early Christian communities implicated in ritual and ethics, in issues of oral tradition and transmission, and accordingly in historical Jesus questions as well" (Kirk and Thatcher, *Memory, Tradition, and Text*, 1).

11. In the words of Chris Keith, "How one conceptualizes the transmission of the tradition can play a determinative role in how one uses it to take the further steps of historical Jesus enquiry" (Keith, "Narratives of the Gospels," 441).

12. The abundance of this period was not solely limited to historical inquiries on Jesus's life; the wider world of biblical scholarship also flourished in this era. Significant achievements in biblical studies include: Julius Wellhausen's source-critical Documentary Hypothesis of the Hebrew Bible (Wellhausen, *Prolegomena zur Geschichte Israel*); the interest in comparative religion—particularly comparing biblical traditions with contemporary religions—undertaken by Hermann Gunkel and the *Religionsgeschichtliche Schule* (Gunkel, *Schöpfung Und Chaos in Urzeit Und Endzeit*); and Bernard Pyne Grenfell and Arthur Surridge Hunt's excavation of a trove of papyri at Oxyrhynchus (Grenfell and Hunt, *Oxyrhynchus Papyri*).

13. Originally published posthumously as part of Lessing's Wolfenbüttel fragments. See Reimarus, *Apologie*.

gospel traditions had once been deemed historical in a broad sense, Reimarus pointed to incongruities and contradictions in the resurrection narratives, rewriting the historical setting and origin of earliest Christianity. Rather than an organic extension of Jesus's message, Reimarus argued that "the intention of Jesus and the intention of the disciples [were] totally at odds."[14] While Reimarus's work (published anonymously by G. E. Lessing) was initially received negatively, it served as a portent of future New Testament research, as later scholars further questioned the historicity of scripture.

If Reimarus opened the door to historical Jesus research, D. F. Strauss burst through with his *Das Leben Jesu*. Strauss expanded J. G. Eichhorn's work on biblical myth by widening his critical gaze beyond fragments of myth embedded within scripture; instead, he took a broader approach, highlighting the *mythus* of ancient cultures within the entirety of the gospel tradition. Rather than appealing to the rationalistic tendencies of his day, Strauss sought to distinguish what he deemed as "unhistorical" material in the gospel narratives, sifting out myth from history.[15] Two distinct figures emerged from Strauss's work: a Christ of faith, wrapped in ancient myth and divinity, and a Jesus of history, a man sifted from the historical remains of the gospel traditions.[16]

A major shift took place around the turn of the twentieth century sparked by the work of William Wrede and Albert Schweitzer. Writing at a time when the positivism asserted by historical Jesus scholarship brought confidence that the gospels could be utilized as historical sources, Wrede shook that confidence by questioning the line between historical fact and literary creation. Wrede argued that traditions in the Gospel of Mark,

---

14. Baird, *History of New Testament Research*, 1:170–71. It is also important to point out that Reimarus lived in an era where the historicity of miracles was of foremost importance in biblical theology and the rationalism of the Enlightenment. Though Reimarus showed an inclination at engaging scripture critically, his work preceded the larger refinement of the historical-critical method by Johann Semler, Johann David Michaelis, and others. See Baird, *History of New Testament Research*, 1:116–54.

15. Strauss, *Life of Jesus*, 86–92. Strauss also touched on the relationship between Jesus and the temple in a manner that prefigures a memory approach by attempting to reconcile (what he considered) historical traits with mythical events: "The narrative of the rending of the veil of the temple at the death of Jesus seems to have had its origin in the hostile position in which Jesus, and his church after him, sustained in relation to the Jewish temple worship. Here already we have something historical, though consisting merely of certain general features of character, position, etc.; we are thus at once brought upon the ground of the historical *mythus*" (87).

16. Baird, *History of New Testament Research*, 1:254.

particularly the motif of its "messianic secret," did not originate in the life of Jesus but rather were the products of the evangelist's theology, which was a later structure imposed on the gospel. Schweitzer's massive survey of Life of Jesus scholarship concluded on an even bleaker note for those wishing to utilize the gospels as historical. Schweitzer argued that the Jesus perpetuated by nineteenth-century scholarship "never had any existence. He is a figure designed by rationalism, endowed with life by liberalism, and clothed by modern theology in an historical garb."[17]

Martin Kähler and the Subjectivity of History

While Wrede and Schweitzer often receive the most recognition for their role in bringing an end to the "first quest" for the historical Jesus, Martin Kähler also played an important role in quietly critiquing the liberal "Lives of Jesus" scholarship that claimed to have historical insight into the moods and motivations of Jesus. Kähler took issue with contemporary scholarship's effort to separate "history" from the inherently theological gospels. Kähler was also against the theological progression that followed, namely, that faith must be founded upon whatever historical Jesus scholarship determined as scientific fact.[18] Instead, Kähler argued that any wide-reaching historical inquiry into the gospels must reckon with the difficulty of the gospels's history: "We have no sources for a biography of Jesus of Nazareth which measure up to the standards of contemporary historical science... Furthermore, these sources [the canonical Gospels] cannot be traced with certainty to eyewitnesses."[19]

Though not the immediate focus of his work, the identification of memory in the formation of the gospel tradition quickly became a consolation of Kähler's critique of overreaching historical-critical scholarship. Kähler made many points that, in retrospect, would be applauded by contemporary memory theorists. For instance, although he felt it insignificant, his locating Jesus against the backdrop of Hebrew

---

17. Schweitzer, *Quest of the Historical Jesus*, 398.

18. "If historical research is meant to 'lay the foundation'—the one and only foundation—it will soon become clear that such a foundation will provide no real support. For historical facts which first have to be established by science cannot *as such* become experiences of faith. Therefore, Christian faith and a history of Jesus repel each other like oil and water as soon as the magic spell of an enthusiastic and enrapturing description loses its power" (Kähler, *So-Called Historical Jesus*, 74).

19. Kähler, *So-Called Historical Jesus*, 48.

scriptures and traditions, which he also believed affected the "coloring of [Jesus's] life as he lived it," is more generally reminiscent of keying and framing.[20] Elsewhere, Kähler demonstrated a similar attitude to presentists in arguing that "every detail of the apostolic recollection of Jesus can be shown to have been preserved for the sake of its religious significance."[21] At the same time, however, Kähler recognized that these recollections were not fabricated wholesale; rather, he believed that apostolic memory owed its formation to the historical life of Jesus, who "engraved his image on the mind and memory of his followers with such sharp and deeply etched features that it could be neither obliterated nor distorted."[22] Tying this all together with his larger argument, Kähler summed up his critique against historical "lives of Jesus" by restating the problems of history within the gospel traditions:

> We possess no historical documents concerning those specific events in which God's revelation took place—if at all—in the form of historical facts; that is, we possess no historical documents concerning Jesus' public ministry. *What we do have is simply recollections*, which are always at the same time confessional in nature since in presupposition and intention they always witness to something which lies beyond mere historical factuality.[23]

In viewing memory as separate from history, Kähler utilized the gospels as early Christian memory, a confessional vehicle for understanding the Jesus tradition and the biblical faith built upon it.

Form Criticism and the Jesus Tradition

Form criticism followed in the wake of the Schweitzer's dismantling of "lives of Jesus" scholarship and attempted to respond to the problems raised at the end of the nineteenth century by those with backgrounds in various history of religions, historical, and source critical methodologies. Described as "a cognitive framework that controls the production

20. Kähler, *So-Called Historical Jesus*, 86. On the Hebrew Bible as the key interpretive framework for understanding Jesus's life and mission: "It is, of course, undeniable that the Old Testament and Hebrew thought-forms have conditioned Jesus' outlook on things. Yet such obvious remarks gain us almost nothing" (Kähler, *So-Called Historical Jesus*, 51).
21. Kähler, *So-Called Historical Jesus*, 93.
22. Kähler, *So-Called Historical Jesus*, 90.
23. Kähler, *So-Called Historical Jesus*, 126, emphasis added.

of knowledge in [New Testament] scholarship,"[24] form criticism not only set the trajectory for memory theory's introduction into New Testament research but also serves as the foil for its alternative epistemological framework. A critical method pioneered by Karl Ludwig Schmidt, Martin Dibelius, and Rudolf Bultmann, form criticism is aimed at analyzing the individual units of tradition ("forms") comprising the gospels "to determine the *original* form of a piece of narrative, a dominical saying, or a parable."[25] More specifically, Bultmann's goal was "discovering what the *original* units of the Synoptics were . . . to try to establish what their historical setting was, whether they belonged to a primary or secondary tradition or whether they were the product of editorial activity."[26] For Bultmann, this task picked up the thread of German Gospels scholarship from Wilhelm Wrede, Johannes Weiss, and Julius Wellhausen, "to separate the various strata in [the gospels] and to determine which belonged to the *original* historical tradition and which derived from the work of the author[s]."[27] Bultmann viewed the evangelists as compilers of tradition and editors of the gospel materials who played a formative role in structuring the material and associating passages based on content or catchword. In doing so, however, he argued that "the *original meaning of a saying is often distorted* or made unrecognizable by such editing. Further, in such an editorial process the collectors have sometimes added *intensifications and explanations*."[28] Thus, whatever "original" words of and stories about Jesus that existed have accreted layers of subsequent tradition imported from or created by a variety of situations in the life of early Christian communities. These settings, referred to as a form's *Sitz im Leben*, provide an analytical window not only into when the form was added to the tradition but also "the influences at work in the life of the community."[29] The task of the form critic, then, is to:

24. Kirk, *Memory and the Jesus Tradition*, 5.

25. Bultmann, *History of the Synoptic Tradition*, 6, emphasis added; cf. Dibelius, *Die Formgeschichte des Evangeliums*.

26. Bultmann, *History of the Synoptic Tradition*, 2–3, emphasis added. Bultmann viewed the evangelists as significantly limited to a stock of traditional forms, so this envisioned "editorial activity" is restricted mainly to compiling and arranging forms (rather than actively producing or creating oral or written traditions of their own).

27. Bultmann, *History of the Synoptic Tradition*, 1, emphasis added.

28. Bultmann, *History of the Synoptic Tradition*, 326, emphasis original.

29. Bultmann, *History of the Synoptic Tradition*, 4. "In particular [Bultmann] seemed to know in advance that the historical Jesus was an eschatological prophet who issued a radical call to repentance, so that material that reflected such a radical

a. identify and extract a form from its gospel (literary) setting;

b. determine a particular genre (e.g., apophthegms, dominical sayings, miracle stories, historical stories) of the form;

c. determine what the form's content and style reveal about its historical or sociological setting (*Sitz im Leben*); and

d. if that setting matches the "Palestinian" layer of tradition most closely associated with the life of Jesus, "extract kernels of memory from the husks of tradition in which they were now encased in the Gospels, creating a database of recollections from which the true image of Jesus could be reconstituted."[30]

Birger Gerhardsson and the Role of Memory

Birger Gerhardsson offered an alternative perspective on the formation of the Jesus tradition.[31] Gerhardsson originally situated his work as a foil to the form critical approach to gospel origins, critiquing form criticism for insufficiently addressing the actual transmission process of gospel material.[32] Whereas the form critics located the development of the Jesus tradition in the kerygma of the early church, Gerhardsson rooted the Jesus tradition in a rabbinic-like model where Jesus's disciples would have actively learned (via repetition) his teachings and transmitted them accurately.[33] Gerhardsson argued memorization and repetition played key roles in the preservation of the oral Jesus tradition

---

immanent eschatology was most likely to be authentic . . . Bultmann's judgments about the history and authenticity of the synoptic tradition were in practice seldom based on the ostensible methods of form criticism, but on his dissection of pericopae in the light of his literary and historical judgments. It is these judgments that then drove his view of tradition history and hence his deductions about the tendencies of the tradition" (Eve, *Behind the Gospels*, 27).

30. Kirk and Thatcher, *Memory, Tradition, and Text*, 29.

31. Gerhardsson set in motion a school of thought that continues to this day as represented in the work of Samuel Byrskog. See Byrskog, *Story as History*.

32. E.g., Dibelius never expounded on the idea that Christian tradition was passed on through "preaching," (other than to locate "preaching" as the *Sitz im Leben* of the gospels), and Bultmann proposed several forms (apologetics, polemics, ecclesial rule, etc.) without offering a concrete exhibition of how these forms were imparted. See Gerhardsson, *Memory and Manuscript*, 14.

33. "The material which must be known is *memorized*. It is imprinted on the memory ready formulated, and is kept alive by constant repetition" (Gerhardsson, *Memory and Manuscript*, 81, emphasis original).

prior to (or alongside) the textualization of the tradition.[34] Gerhardsson also highlights several theoretical frameworks for the transmission of (rabbinic) oral material: desire for authenticity, desire for brevity, mnemonic techniques, use of written notes, and repetition.

Gerhardsson's work prioritizes memorization over larger theoretical considerations of memory. In fact, Gerhardsson's interest in memory really stems from his work on a comparative model of disciples as learners in a hypothesized (and sometimes anachronistically retrofitted) historical context. As a teacher, "[Jesus] must have made his disciples learn certain sayings off by heart; if he taught, he must have required his disciples to memorize. This statement is not intended to be dogmatic or apologetic but is a consideration based on a comparison with the contemporary situation."[35] Furthermore, Gerhardsson argues that "when the Evangelists edited their Gospels, however, they did not take their traditions from" the uses of the gospel tradition in preaching, such as doctrinal debate, apologetics, or teaching, but rather "they worked on a basis of a fixed, distinct tradition from, and about, Jesus—a tradition which was partly memorized and partly written down in notebooks and private scrolls, but invariably isolated from the teachings of other doctrinal authorities."[36] Altogether, Gerhardsson's view of memory is fairly static, and he brushes off larger theoretical questions and concerns about the mnemonic process. For Gerhardsson, sayings are repeated and taught until, for the most part, rote memorization is achieved. The recollection of sayings ("halakic") material is thus a mechanical process with little variation, whereas narrative ("haggadic") material "is often transmitted with a somewhat wide margin of variation in wording" when compared to sayings material.[37] It would be inaccurate to say that Gerhardsson pioneered memory theory in New Testament studies, but his work certainly foreshadowed more robust treatments of memory theory and opened important conversations about the role, extent, and dynamics of memory (and orality) in early Christianity.

---

34. On the pedagogical process of memorization, Gerhardsson writes, "The material is first committed to memory, and then an attempt at understanding is undertaken" (Gerhardsson, *Memory and Manuscript*, 126).
35. Gerhardsson, *Memory and Manuscript*, 328.
36. Gerhardsson, *Memory and Manuscript*, 335.
37. Gerhardsson, *Memory and Manuscript*, 335.

Werner Kelber, James D. G. Dunn, and the Transmission of (Oral) Tradition

No two scholars played a more important role in clearing the path for social memory's introduction into New Testament studies than Werner Kelber and James D. G. Dunn. In fact, Werner Kelber is often credited as the pioneer of modern memory theory and has been recognized as the single most important scholar responsible for shaping discussions of memory and media in New Testament scholarship today.[38] Both Kelber and Dunn have left an indelible stamp on Gospels and Jesus studies, and it is not a stretch to recognize that the development and advancement of memory theories over the past two decades would look significantly different without their seminal contributions.

Kelber's *The Oral and the Written Gospel* opened the conversation about the difference in media dynamics between orality and literacy and showed the profitability of orality studies in Gospels research. Positioning himself against Bultmann and Gerhardsson, Kelber argued that "oral and written compositions come into existence under different circumstances," which necessarily impacts the ways in which the history and interpretation of the Gospels must be understood.[39] As a point of similarity to both prior and future studies of memory, Kelber argues that the approach established by Bultmann and carried on by contemporary form critics is built on a range of faulty assumptions and missteps, especially the "failure to appreciate the actuality of living speech as distinct from written texts."[40] Additionally, form criticism believed that present concerns (understood as a form's *Sitz im Leben*) were removable husks enveloping "authentic" past tradition, but Kelber, pointing to the importance of the

---

38. Alan Kirk credits Kelber for "pioneering memory approaches in Gospels scholarship" in the early 1990s (Kirk, "Ehrman, Bauckham and Bird," 88). Richard Horsley notes that Kelber has been on the forefront of several important trends in New Testament research: "Kelber was one of the first to explore Mark's Gospel as a dramatic story. He then almost single-handedly pioneered the recognition of the difference between and relation of orality and literacy and the implications for Mark and other New Testament literature. More recently he has been the first to discern the importance of studies of cultural memory in other fields and how understanding memory will further change the way we approach the composition and use of Mark and other Gospels" (Horsley, "Prophet Like Moses and Elijah," in Horsley et al., eds., *Performing the Gospel*, 166–67).

39. "A speaker addresses an audience in front of him, and its presence in turn affects the delivery of his speech . . . An author, by contrast, writes for readers who are normally absent at the time and from the place of writing" (Kelber, *Oral and the Written Gospel*, 14–15).

40. Kelber, *Oral and the Written Gospel*, 8.

present frameworks in shaping the past, argues "what lives on in memory ... is what is necessary for present life. Neither oral composition nor oral transmission can ever escape the influence of audience and social circumstances."[41] However, appreciating the oral dynamics at play within the gospel tradition does not automatically lead Kelber to a static model of transmission. Rather than adopting Gerhardsson's model of memorization, Kelber argues that "none of the canonical gospels depicts Jesus as being insistent on verbatim learning of his words. Nor is there any indication that apostles, teachers, prophets, or ordinary people were trained in what Gerhardsson considered to be a Rabbinic tradition of memorization."[42] Later, Kelber critiqued this mode of thinking even more strongly, stating "we can no longer think of the early tradition as an assembly-line production carrying inert items of information to be collected and preserved for posterity. Neither oral performances nor the early papyrological evidence permit us to opt for mechanical word processing and verbatim preservation as the primary impulse motivating the tradition."[43] For Kelber, orality studies and the early insights of memory theory "challenge biblical scholarship to rethink fundamental concepts of the Western humanistic legacy such as text and intertextuality, reading, writing and composing, memory and imagination, speech and oral/scribal interfaces, author and tradition."[44] Kelber recognized that theories of memory have the generative power to shape our understanding of the New Testament texts and traditions. According to Kelber, "consideration of the inventive role of memory suggests a judicious plugging into the web of cultural memory, retaining, collating, and adapting traditional items, reclaiming and citing

41. Kelber, *Oral and the Written Gospel*, 15.

42. Kelber, *Oral and the Written Gospel*, 21. Kelber later returned to this line of critique when considering the importance of social memory for gospel traditions: "There is no indication that the charismatic itinerant surrounded himself with a group of followers who were duty bound to preserve his exact wording of his message by repeating it over and over again" (Kelber, "Generative Force of Memory," 17).

43. Kelber, "Generative Force of Memory," 20–21.

44. Kelber, "Oral Tradition in Bible and New Testament Studies," 40. Elsewhere, Kelber ruminates on the important conversations and insights offered by the variety of memory studies, including "the enigma of the present (or representation) of the absent past, the tradition of the *ars memoriae*, the entanglements of memory and imagination, the role of image (and imaging) in the process of remembering, the problem of forgetting, the phenomenon of multiple commemorative activities, the cultivation of inwardness from Augustine to Husserl, the notion of a socially shared memory introduced in modernity by Halbwachs, crises and traumas of memories, the representation of the historical personality as an *Erinnerungsfigur*, and others" (Kelber, "Generative Force of Memory," 16).

some, responding critically and even deconstructively to others, while recontextualizing many so as to make them serviceable to the present."[45] These theoretical insights, matched with his extensive research in the communicative oral, scribal, and memorial dynamics, show how Kelber's work itself left a variety of footprints on memory's viability as a theory and product in New Testament studies.[46]

James D. G. Dunn's massive *Jesus Remembered* also prefigures the introduction of social memory theory to the English-speaking world and offers critical insights into what would later be a shifting tide on the method and approach to historical Jesus scholarship. Like Kelber, Dunn's work focuses on oral tradition and media dynamics as determinative for our understanding of Jesus. Dunn's program, however, is to investigate the gospels as they present the "impact" of Jesus. This is an important point that Dunn expounds from Kähler's earlier work; in a similar manner to both Kähler and Dahl, Dunn notes that "we do not have a 'neutral' (!) portrayal of Jesus. All we have in the NT Gospels is Jesus seen with the eye of faith. We do not have a 'historical Jesus,' only the 'historic Christ.'"[47] Taking Kähler's work a step further, Dunn argues, "The Synoptic tradition provides evidence not so much for what Jesus did or said in itself, but for what Jesus was *remembered* as doing or saying by his first disciples, or as we might say, for the *impact* of what he did and said on his first disciples."[48]

One way Dunn signaled what was to come from the memory theorists was his target of criticism. Dunn's work identifies form-critical approaches to Jesus tradition as its primary opponent and highlights the legacy that form-critical assumptions have had on historical Jesus scholarship, such as historical positivism and its claim to objectivity.[49] To counter these assumptions, Dunn argues for a more nuanced view of what exactly the goal of historical Jesus research is by defining who and what the historical Jesus is:

45. Kelber, "Case of the Gospels," 79.
46. See Kelber, *Imprints, Voiceprints & Footprints of Memory*.
47. Dunn, *Jesus Remembered*, 127.
48. Dunn, *Jesus Remembered*, 130–31, emphasis original.
49. "The Enlightenment ideal of historical objectivity also projected a false goal onto the quest of the historical Jesus. For from its inception, questers have made the assumption that behind the text of the Gospels, behind the traditions which they incorporate, there is a 'historical Jesus', an objective historical datum who will be different from the dogmatic Christ or from the Jesus of the Gospels and who will enable us to criticize the dogmatic Christ and the Jesus of the Gospels" (Dunn, *Jesus Remembered*, 125).

> The "historical Jesus" is *the Jesus constructed by historical research*. Despite that, however, the phrase is used again and again in a casual way to refer to the Jesus of Nazareth who walked the hills of Galilee, and it is that sense which predominates overall ... Again and again the one sense elides indistinguishably into the other ... The "historical Jesus" is properly speaking a nineteenth- and twentieth-century construction using the data provided by the Synoptic tradition, *not* Jesus back then and *not* a figure in history whom we can realistically use to critique the portrayal of Jesus in the Synoptic tradition.[50]

In addition, rather than promoting an approach that would strip the gospels of their theology or sift out authentic tradition from inauthentic husks, Dunn argues against the form-critical perspective: "the idea that we can see through the faith perspective of the NT writings to a Jesus who did *not* inspire faith or who inspired faith in a *different* way is an illusion."[51] Furthermore, "the idea that we can get back to an objective historical reality, which we can wholly separate and disentangle from the disciples' memories ... is simply unrealistic ... at best what we have are the teachings of Jesus as they impacted on the individuals who stored them in their memories and began the process of oral transmission."[52] Dunn argues for more "continuity between pre-Easter memory and post-Easter proclamation."[53] This continuity does not get us back to a "historical" Jesus, but as Dunn argues, it gives us a glimpse of the "remembered" Jesus, since "*a characteristic and relatively distinctive feature of the Jesus tradition is most likely to go back to the consistent and distinctive character of the impact made by Jesus himself.*"[54]

What do all these insights mean for the state of historical Jesus scholarship? Dunn sums up his work in four concluding statements:

> (1) The only realistic objective for any "quest of the historical Jesus" is Jesus *remembered*. (2) The Jesus tradition of the Gospels confirms *that* there was a concern within earliest Christianity to remember Jesus. (3) The Jesus tradition shows us *how* Jesus was

---

50. Dunn, *Jesus Remembered*, 125–26, emphasis original.

51. Dunn continues his critique more explicitly: "That we can somehow hope to strip out the theological impact which he actually made on his disciples, to uncover a different Jesus (the real Jesus!), is at best fanciful" (Dunn, *Jesus Remembered*, 126, emphasis original).

52. Dunn, *Jesus Remembered*, 130–31.

53. Dunn, *Jesus Remembered*, 133.

54. Dunn, *Jesus Remembered*, 884.

remembered; its character strongly suggests again and again a tradition given its essential shape by regular use and reuse in oral mode. (4) This suggests in turn that that essential shape was given by the original and immediate *impact made by Jesus* as that was first put into words by and among those involved as eyewitnesses of what Jesus said and did. In that key sense, the Jesus tradition *is* Jesus remembered.[55]

Though it suffers from limitations in its understanding of oral tradition and its handling of the relationship between the past and present,[56] Dunn's work is an important step for historical Jesus scholarship and set the stage for memory to burst into New Testament studies in the coming years.

Applications of Memory Theory in New Testament Research

As argued above, the application of social memory theory to Gospels research is an organic extension of the insights formed from the mid- and late-twentieth-century studies in orality, gospel origins, and historical Jesus scholarship. Kähler's dissatisfaction with the first quest produced insights that mirror the historiographical assumptions of later memory theorists. Nils Alstrup Dahl, who is included as the epigraph of this chapter, recognized the role in which the disciples's present post-Easter situation shaped their understanding of the past pre-Easter traditions. Elsewhere within the Scandinavian school, Gerhardsson's work on memory, although markedly different from social memory theory, created a dialogue encompassing Jesus tradition and memory transmission. Kelber's further research on collective and cultural memory in the 1990s and early 2000s shows how scholarly interest in one category naturally leads to the other,[57] while Dunn's work, although heavily rooted in orality studies, addresses both oral traditions and memory culture.[58] On the other hand, it is important to point out that applications of memory theory were already established by Halbwachs in the early twentieth

---

55. Dunn, *Jesus Remembered*, 882.

56. Samuel Byrskog raises both points as areas of improvement for future scholarship. See Byrskog, "New Perspective on the Jesus Tradition," 468–69.

57. See Kelber, "Case of the Gospels," 55–86.

58. Dunn later engaged more directly with social memory theory. See Dunn, "Social Memory and the Oral Jesus Tradition," in Stuckenbruck et al., eds., *Memory in the Bible and Antiquity*, 179–94.

century before these similarly related subjects gained major traction in New Testament studies. The following survey provides a representative look at scholars who engage and apply memory theory—social, collective, or cultural—in their efforts to offer an array of different theoretical insights or arguments about Jesus and the Gospels.

Maurice Halbwachs

Maurice Halbwachs was not only the first to develop the concept of social (collective) memory, but also the first to apply his fledgling theory to Christian origins. Though often classified as a work of "sociology" rather than "New Testament studies,"[59] his *La topographie légendaire des évangiles en Terre sainte* blended social history with the principles of collective memory to demonstrate how topographical traditions in the Holy Land changed based on the interests of groups across antiquity.[60] However, Halbwachs did not limit himself solely to discussing locations and the traditions that connect them to the gospels (e.g., Gethsemane, the Holy Sepulchre, the Mount of Olives); instead, he applied his insights more broadly. Halbwachs recognized that the gospels were a prime example of his theory of collective memory, and he left room for "deformations,

---

59. This distinction is somewhat arbitrary, but it serves to delineate Halbwachs as a sociologist rather than a New Testament scholar. The difficulty in determining what qualifies and separates someone as a "New Testament scholar" is an important debate within the field. However, perhaps the more relevant question in this regard is: what makes a work a piece of New Testament research? Is it engagement with NT texts? If so, Halbwachs references the gospels throughout. Is it discussion of relevant NT topics? If so, Halbwachs has devoted an entire monograph to the gospels, early Christian origins, and Jesus traditions. Is it discussion with other NT scholarship? Here, Halbwachs's interaction with the field seems to be anchored in Ernest Renan's *Vie de Jésus* (1869), but his commentary on the gospels demonstrates many tendencies of the nineteenth century "Lives of Jesus," particularly psychological conjecturing, aligning him with the influential French NT scholarship of his contemporary world. All in all, while Halbwachs may be remembered as a French sociologist, it is difficult to say that *La topographie légendaire des évangiles en Terre sainte* is not a work of NT research, and thus the first piece of NT scholarship to incorporate and apply social memory theory. For more on what the essence of NT scholarship consists of, including the excellent example of Rodney Stark and Frank Kermode as scholars from other disciplines whose work made significant ripples in the field, see Crossley, "Immodest Proposal for Biblical Studies," 153–77.

60. "Sacred places [e.g., Gethsemane, the Holy Sepulchre, the Mount of Olives] thus commemorate not facts certified by contemporary witnesses but rather beliefs born perhaps not far from these places and strengthened by taking root in this environment" (Halbwachs, *On Collective Memory*, 199).

errors, and omissions" as distortions of that memory.[61] Likewise, he saw early Christians playing an active role in the upkeep of this memory: "To the extent that [the gospel memory] grew more distant from the events, this group [of early Christians] is likely to have burnished, remodeled, and completed the image that is preserved of [the events of the gospels]."[62] The foundation of Halbwachs's theory is the understanding of memory as an active process that serves group interests in the present,[63] so it is unsurprising that he calls great attention to the same activity taking place in early Christian commemoration:

> Toward the end of the first third of the first century a group of Galilean Jews may have preserved a rather vivid recollection of somebody who had been their master and companion. They might well remember his teaching, his travels, his discussions with other Jews, and the circumstances that preceded and followed his violent death. These recollections would have remained closely linked to the personalities of the disciples and to the appearance of Galilee, Judea, and Jerusalem at the time when Jesus had lived... In order for the recollections of the life and death of Christ and of the places through which he passed to endure, they had to be made part of a doctrine: that is, of an idea that was alive for an enduring and extended group.[64]

Thus, *La topographie légendaire des évangiles en Terre sainte* sees Halbwachs import his theory of social memory into the study of the gospels. Halbwachs ends in the same place he does in his other works on social memory: all individual memory must be contextualized within larger social frameworks that are subject to change given the needs of

61. "In short, the Gospels already represent a memory or a collection of memories held in common by a group. Although a short time elapsed between the events and the moment when these memories—even before they were recorded—took a collective form, we should not expect only a minimum of deformations, errors, and omissions ... At the moment when [witnesses] report what they have seen, they are likely to exclude some details they think are of no interest to their communities" (Halbwachs, *On Collective Memory*, 194). Halbwachs's suspicion of eyewitness testimony is interesting and puts him in line (generally) with Judith Redman's more recent research on the psychology of eyewitness testimony. See Redman, "How Accurate Are Eyewitnesses?"

62. Halbwachs, *On Collective Memory*, 196.

63. "[Collective memory] retains only those events that are of a pedagogic character. The very manner in which memory distorts facts reflects the need to show that each one has a significance beyond the event itself, that it has a logical place in the complete history and that it is part of a chain of events which together culminate in an event comprising all the others" (Halbwachs, *On Collective Memory*, 223).

64. Halbwachs, *On Collective Memory*, 200.

the group. Articulating this point in light of the traditions about Jesus, Halbwachs concluded that "in each period the collective Christian memory adapts its recollections of the details of Christ's life and of the places where they occurred to the contemporary exigencies of Christianity, to its needs and aspirations."[65]

Halbwachs's tragic death—as a prisoner in the Buchenwald concentration camp—prohibited him from extending his forays into New Testament scholarship or engaging in deeper conversations with continental form critics on the development of the gospel tradition. His work remained siloed from English-speaking scholarship, NT or otherwise; it was not until decades after his death that Robert Wilken's *The Myth of Christian Beginnings* (1971) would be the first NT scholarship to engage Halbwachs's theories.[66] Though his work is foundational for the theoretical understanding of social memory and his early application of the theory should be duly noted, Halbwachs's lasting impression on the field has been far more subdued than more contemporary theorists of the late twentieth century.[67]

Alan Kirk and Tom Thatcher

Not long after Halbwachs's work appeared in English and gained a broader readership, the tides of NT interest shifted. Form criticism dominated the methodology, and more importantly the assumptions, of Gospels and Jesus scholarship for the majority of the twentieth century. From Rudolf Bultmann to John Dominic Crossan, the "New Quest" to the "Third Quest," the criteria used by John P. Meier and the consensuses of the Jesus Seminar, and even the development of redaction criticism, the Jesus scholar's *modus operandi* was to sift out the "authentic" kernels of history embedded within "inauthentic" husks of tradition to build an understanding of the "historical" Jesus. However, an underlying discontent

---

65. Halbwachs, *On Collective Memory*, 234.

66. As noted by Keith, "Social Memory Theory (Part One)," 354–55.

67. Schwartz is critical of Halbwachs's view of memory and the way in which it is employed: "Halbwachs's greatest failure is his inability to see commemoration as anything more than an elaborate delusion . . . He assumes that memory, as opposed to history, is inauthentic, manipulative, shady, something to be overcome rather than accepted in its own right . . . Bultmann's and Halbwachs's common failure is their refusal even to ask how pericopae, texts, and physical sites reflected what ordinary people of the first century believed" (Schwartz, "Christian Origins," in Kirk and Thatcher, eds., *Memory, Tradition, and Text*, 50).

with such form-critical assumptions had been brewing since the days of Martin Kähler and was articulated anew by Werner Kelber, and memory theory spurred further critique by providing a new theoretical framework for the transmission and reception of tradition. German NT scholars such as Cilliers Breytenbach and Jens Schröter fronted this wave of critique by briefly incorporating Assmann's theory of cultural memory into gospels research.[68] After highlighting how the "Third Quest" relied on the same assumptions of attestation and authenticity as the "Second Quest," Schröter invoked Assmann's use of collective memory and the "formative power" of "myth" to refigure the understanding of the Gospels:

> We should not ask for the life of Jesus in a paradigm of "original" and "interpretation" but rather put the view on "history," as far as it concerns Jesus in the early Christian writings, into sharper focus. The way to confront the difficulties created by the relationship between the "Jesus of history" and the "Christ of faith" should be to look for a model which explains the characteristic features of the early Christian writings *as interpretations of historical events* . . . It is not a hierarchy of attestation which should be aimed for, but the description of the early reception of Jesus as comprehensively and precisely as possible . . . What we get may not be a safe basis of authentic words of Jesus but rather a diversity of pictures which could not, without arbitrariness, be reduced to a single portrait.[69]

Schröter's work briefly set the stage for how memory theory could unravel contemporary claims of historicity by calling out the ease with which scholars discarded tradition as "unoriginal" or a layer of "interpretation." However, the full value of social memory theory was not felt until the first landmark study of memory theory in New Testament research: Alan Kirk and Tom Thatcher's seminal *Memory, Tradition, and Text*. Building on the momentum of German scholarship,[70] Kirk and Thatcher's work continued the critique of form-critical assumptions by

---

68. Keith, "Social Memory Theory (Part One)," 355–56. In discussing the changing scholarly attitudes toward history and historicism, Schröter names Jan Assmann's insights into cultural memory as having shaped "how the past is appropriated as history and becomes a common point of reference for a community" (Schröter, *From Jesus to the New Testament*, 1; cf. Schröter, *Erinnerung an Jesu Worte*).

69. Schröter, "Historical Jesus and the Sayings Tradition," 165, emphasis added.

70. Kirk himself highlights the work of Werner Kelber and Jens Schröter in the 1990s as predecessors to his own work. See Kirk, "Ehrman, Bauckham and Bird," 88–89; *Memory and the Jesus Tradition*, xiii; cf. Kelber, "Language, Memory, and Sense Perception," 409–50; Schröter, *Erinnerung an Jesu Worte*.

articulating the theory of social memory and avenues for its application in the field of Gospels research.

Kirk opens the work with an introduction to social memory theory and an overview of ways it has been applied to issues such as the politics of memory, tradition transmission, commemoration, identity, and culture. After establishing a theoretical foundation, Kirk and Thatcher immediately set to work applying the theory to the broad-scale understanding of the Jesus tradition. First, Kirk and Thatcher link the concept of tradition to the larger commemorative processes operative within social memory. For them, tradition is not a vessel passed casually from generation to generation, but "the indissoluble, irreducibly complex artifact of the continual negotiation and semantic interpenetration of present social realities and memorialized pasts."[71] Once such an understanding of tradition is established, it follows that the Jesus tradition operates exactly as social memory: "Jesus was represented through multiple acts of remembering that *semantically fused the present situations of the respective communities with their memory of the past as worked out in commemorative practices*, with neither factor swallowed up by, or made epiphenomenal of, the other."[72] The Jesus tradition as exemplified by—but not limited to—the written gospels is not just a static transmission of narratives about and sayings attributed to Jesus, but an active negotiation between the past and the present. Memories of Jesus were continually orienting and formatively forging communities while also being shaped in the contemporary social realities of these communities. Every recollection, reconstitution, and reconstruction of the remembered—or "salient" as Kirk puts it—past must negotiate between the events of that past and the concerns of the present. What comes out of this negotiation is a concrete example of how a community formulates its identity, orients its worldview, and creates its own sense of cultural memory, all wrapped into the category of "tradition," which serves as "an abbreviation for the countless transactions between sacralized past and actual present vital to the life of a community."[73] Though focused on "tradition" as the nexus between history and memory,[74] the thrust of Kirk's argument lays clear its larger implications: to recognize

---

71. Kirk and Thatcher, *Memory, Tradition, and Text*, 33.

72. Kirk and Thatcher, *Memory, Tradition, and Text*, 33, emphasis added.

73. Kirk and Thatcher, *Memory, Tradition, and Text*, 33.

74. "Though constitutively oriented to historical events ... the tradition serves not so much historiographical as cultural ends" (Kirk, *Memory and the Jesus Tradition*, 226).

and refer to Jesus tradition—whether the minutiae of forms or the large-scale material artifacts of gospels—is, in essence, to recognize and refer to the social memory of Jesus.[75]

Thatcher's *Why John Wrote a Gospel* puts social memory theory to the test by applying it to the Fourth Gospel in order to question the decision of the evangelist to commemorate his gospel tradition in writing. Thatcher's title is operative on at least three levels. First, *Why* serves as a shortcut to Thatcher's view on memory theory in that it should help us responsibly postulate the contexts and motivations for tradition transmission.[76] Thatcher suggests an answer to this question by contextualizing the Gospel of John within a larger theological conflict between the Johannine community and their opponents, whom he identifies as the Antichrists; "this social context may be thought of as the framework of Johannine memory, the mold in which John's image of Jesus was constantly shaped and reshaped."[77] Within this context, "John's memory of Jesus was shaped in dialogue with Christians who felt persecuted and who faced significant doctrinal divisions. Within that framework, he sought to construct a vision of the past that would unify his churches on the basis of a common image of Jesus."[78] Second, *John* anchors the tradition of Thatcher's focus in the Fourth Gospel but also situates this question within larger conversations concerning the Johannine community, a topic central to much of Thatcher's work.[79] Third, *Wrote* introduces and reflects upon important media dynamics between written and oral tradition, as well as what Thatcher highlights as the rhetorical dimension of writing: "It seems likely, then, that John *wrote* a Gospel primarily to capitalize on the potential symbolic value of writing."[80]

---

75. After offering this reconceptualization of tradition, Kirk and Thatcher point to seven areas ("seven points of intersection of social memory theory and Christian origins") where the insights offered by social memory theory may prove useful in NT scholarship: Memory as an analytical category, tradition formation and transformation, oral tradition as cultural memory, written gospels as commemorative artifacts, early Christian commemoration, the role of normative memory, and continuity and change in early Christianity. Kirk and Thatcher, *Memory, Tradition, and Text*, 40–42.

76. "John does not, in other words, think that his portrait of Jesus is equivalent to the disciples' initial empirical experiences of Jesus, and he does not treat his accounts of those experiences as raw recollections of moments from Jesus' life" (Thatcher, *Why John Wrote a Gospel*, 23).

77. Thatcher, *Why John Wrote a Gospel*, 69.

78. Thatcher, *Why John Wrote a Gospel*, 68.

79. See Le Donne and Thatcher, *Fourth Gospel in First-Century Media Culture*.

80. Thatcher, *Why John Wrote a Gospel*, 48, emphasis added.

Whereas Thatcher applied his theory of memory to the Fourth Gospel, much of Kirk's early work on social memory is heavily engaged in theory, so his investigations often grant insights on the nature of memory or signal pathways forward rather than exhibit concrete applications to the text or traditions of the New Testament.[81] Even Kirk's later work continues to treat memory theory with an eye toward theoretical foundations rather than focusing on its application to New Testament tradition(s).[82] Still, Kirk's early works offer a practical implementation of memory theory by turning toward "death of Jesus" traditions. In one of his first forays into social memory, Kirk examines the "Legs Not Broken" pericope fragment of John (19:31–37) and its parallel in the *Gospel of Peter* (4.10–14),

---

81. *Memory, Tradition, and Text* also features the standout applications of several other scholars building upon the early insights of Kirk and Thatcher's theoretical work: Richard Horsley highlights how the Mosaic Covenant and miracles/exorcisms function as two cultural frameworks of Israelite social memory which form the basis of Mark's traditions (74–77); Holly Hearon offers a methodological proposal to examine the stability and instability of pericopae to trace the contours of shared memory and contested identities and applies this to the pericope of the woman who anoints Jesus (Mark 14:3–9; Luke 7:36–50; John 12:1–8), arguing that this pericope "reflects the variety of Christologies that are emerging within and in response to the life situations of local communities" (118); Georgia Masters Keightley engages the early Christian commemorative rituals in 1 Corinthians (baptism, eucharist, and other bodily practices) as forms of Paul's understanding of Jesus (143–50); and April DeConick looks to the Gospel of Thomas as a "repository of communal memory" that "has been reworked to reformulate older apocalyptic traditions, shifting the ideology of the traditions away from an earlier eschatological emphasis to a mystical one" (211).

82. For instance, in reflecting on how memory theory has been applied to New Testament research, Kirk focuses more on broader arguments about cognition, memory distortion, the importance of reception history, and the nature of tradition: "The tradition becomes the medium, the lens, for focusing the contemporary predicaments of the tradent communities. *The Synoptic and Johannine tradent communities are not directly remembering the past, but the tradition, which mediates the normative past in symbolic forms into the present.* The tradition circulates in visual, oral, and written media, all of which have tractable properties. It can be redacted, reformulated, recontextualized, re-performed, reconfigured, consolidated, and in the course of unfolding its symbolic potential supply the resources for Christological and moral reflection and for its own elaboration. The autonomy of the tradition entails that past and present come to coexist in the tradition in ways that are not easily parsed (though the normative past is certainly the dominant factor)" (Kirk, *Memory and the Jesus Tradition*, 228, emphasis added). While this insight continues his earlier work (itself a "reformulated, recontextualized, re-performed" piece of the Kirk scholarly tradition), it is limited in how it builds toward an application of the theory of social memory or in what it actually tells us about particular instances of the Jesus tradition. In other words, much of his theoretical work offers insights rather than arguments. For an example of Kirk's later work that serves as a long-form application of his theoretical insights, see Kirk, *Q in Matthew*.

pushing against John Dominic Crossan's "cross gospel" hypothesis.[83] Instead of an early pre-Synoptic source behind this crucifixion tradition, Kirk argues, "the Passion narrative in the *Gospel of Peter* opens a window onto a group of second-century Christians negotiating their identity in their contemporaneous social and historical frameworks."[84] Among these frameworks is the "religious rivalry between the Jewish and Christian communities in the second century," a rivalry that is "co-opted to serve the *Gospel of Peter*'s generative redactional concern to portray the Jews as the agents directly responsible for Jesus's death."[85] This brief study flows nicely into his *Semeia* contribution: an investigation of Q's reference to Jesus's death (11:47–51). To counter contemporary claims of Q's disinterest with the death of Jesus, Kirk employs commemorative keying, an important analytical tool that draws tradition together with "memory scripts" embedded in larger cultural narratives:

> The oracle [Q 11:47–51] displays the hallmark operations of commemorative keying. The prophets, and the violent deaths of the prophets, held a secure place as *Erinnerungsfiguren* in the cultural memory of ancient Judaism. A memory script, that is, an iterative sacred narrative, incorporated this deaths-of-the-prophets motif, namely, the pattern according to which Israel chronically rejects the prophets God sends to call her to repentance. The oracle maps an analogy between Jesus' violent death and the deaths of the prophets, and accordingly appropriates the Deuteronomistic cultural script of sending and rejection for comprehending and interpreting this event . . . Q 11:47–51 does not merely establish the death of the righteous messengers as a term of comparison for Jesus' death; rather, it integrates the

---

83. For more on this hypothesis, see Crossan, *Birth of Christianity*; "Gospel of Peter and the Canonical Gospels," 7–51.

84. Kirk, *Memory and the Jesus Tradition*, 243 (see also 244–65).

85. Kirk, *Memory and the Jesus Tradition*, 239–40. Kirk's point is not to make a universalizing claim about the distinction between Judaism and Christianity in the second century CE, but rather to assess a localized relationship as it pertains to the *Gospel of Peter*'s tradents. The relationship between Judaism and Christianity in the first several centuries CE was, of course, far more complex than iterated in the *Gospel of Peter*, which serves only as a small snapshot. As Lori Baron, Jill Hicks-Keeton, Matthew Thiessen, and their contributors have shown, "Christianity's eventual distinction from Judaism was messy and multiform, occurring at different paces in diverse geographies with varied literary resources, theological commitments, historical happenstance, and political maneuvering" (Baron et al., *Ways That Often Parted*, 2).

death of Jesus into the sweep of that sacred narrative, in fact as its climactic episode.[86]

Kirk finds another operative script in the motif of the killing of a righteous man, which keys Jesus's death to the Israelite cultural memory of martyrs. Rather than viewing this as an inconsequential change in the shape of the tradition, Kirk views this as an intentional, "aggressive commemorative strategy responding to Jesus' degradation and death . . . to transform the horrific public stigma attach[ed] to the executed person, and by extension to the identity of the affiliated group."[87] Pulling these two threads together, Kirk argues this saying is an active example of the Q community's commemoration of Jesus's death, demonstrating the way in which the community

> invok[ed] hermeneutical frameworks from Israel's epic past—Israel's cultural memory—to give meaning to and master [Jesus's death]. Moreover, these frameworks are indicators of a political and social conflict, a struggle for control of the memory of Jesus' death, for this frameworking strategy is, in effect, an attempt to reverse the moral and social signification of Jesus' status-degrading death and to attribute culpability to that thin though powerful stratum of local elites, incorporated into the Roman order, responsible for his condemnation and execution.[88]

Though Kirk's work often prioritizes theory, his theoretical insights and their application to gospel traditions are incredibly important in exploring the potential for social memory theory in New Testament studies. Kirk and Thatcher's monumental efforts are foundational for shaping the state of social memory theory within New Testament studies today.

Barry Schwartz

Zeba Crook has referred to Kirk and Thatcher's *Semeia* volume as the work that "introduced memory theory into Biblical Studies."[89] This high praise is certainly not undeserved, but perhaps a more accurate description is that this work introduced biblical studies to Barry Schwartz.[90] Like

---

86. Kirk and Thatcher, *Memory, Tradition, and Text*, 197.
87. Kirk and Thatcher, *Memory, Tradition, and Text*, 199–200.
88. Kirk and Thatcher, *Memory, Tradition, and Text*, 204.
89. Crook, "Memory and the Historical Jesus" 196.
90. Though not the first time Kirk had referenced Schwartz's work, *Memory,*

Kirk, Schwartz's New Testament contributions are heavily theoretical, but his insights are invaluable for scholars. For instance, his depiction of the "cultural diamond" conceptualizes the relationships between (1) a creator, (2) a recipient, (3) a social world, and (4) a cultural object where each item has a significant bearing upon the others.[91] This is a pivotal matrix in which to envision the emergence of the Jesus tradition, where (1) the evangelists and (2) their communities are dealing with (4) gospels shaped by (3) socio-cultural patterns.[92] More directly, however, Schwartz applies the task of social memory theory to Gospels studies:

> The job of social memory scholarship is to assess what we know: assembling documents like the Gospels, estimating their meanings and relation to the culture of which their authors were a part, and drawing conclusions. From the social memory standpoint, then, our object of study is not the authenticity of the Gospels; it is rather the Gospels as sources of information about the popular beliefs of early Christianity. The Gospels are critical to us because they put us in touch with the way early Christians conceived Jesus' place in their world, and because without them our understanding of the social memory of this world would be more shallow. At question, then, is what popular meanings were conveyed, aspirations satisfied, fears quieted, by Jesus' invocation.[93]

Schwartz goes on to discuss the Jesus tradition as a *traditum* in which a fairly stable image of Jesus (even in the face of "inevitabl[e] changes") is handed down. Based on this, "successive generations do not create Jesus

---

Tradition, and Text brought Schwartz to the forefront of a conversation that had previously been dominated by European (predominantly German) scholarship on commemoration and cultural memory. See Kirk, "Johannine Jesus in the *Gospel of Peter*," 313–22; Schwartz et al., "Recovery of Masada," 147–64.

91. See Schwartz, "Christian Origins," in Kirk and Thatcher, eds., *Memory, Tradition, and Text*, 54.

92. "The cultural diamond's connecting links furnish the warrant for drawing inferences about memory from knowledge of social worlds and cultural objects, and for embedding changes in the memory of individuals in social change. Such must be our methodological tenet" (Schwartz, "Christian Origins," in Kirk and Thatcher, eds., *Memory, Tradition, and Text*, 55). This cultural model could also be applied to other methods of criticism, for instance, in investigating (1) a performer and (4) their performance to (2) an audience within (3) a performance arena.

93. Schwartz, "Christian Origins," in Kirk and Thatcher, eds., *Memory, Tradition, and Text*, 50.

anew but inherit most of their knowledge, which is why the image of Jesus remains identifiable across generations—and centuries."[94]

Elsewhere, Schwartz's work on keying and framing offers methodological moves for memory theorists to use in analyzing tradition. "Keying defines social memory's function, matching the past to the present as (1) a model *of* society, reflecting its needs, interests, fears, and aspirations; (2) a model *for* society, a template for thought, sentiment, morality, and conduct; and (3) a *frame* within which people find meaning for their experience."[95] These commemorative strategies assign determinative roles to the past as it shapes the way the present is *presented* ("model *of* society"), *replicated* ("model *for* society"), and *understood* ("*frame*" of meaning). For instance, Schwartz points to the Gospel of Mark as a (past) interpretation that "contributed" significantly to the (present) interpretations of the Gospels of Matthew and Luke.[96]

Schwartz's claims are not always as insightful or helpful in understanding how social memory can be mapped onto New Testament studies. His treatment of the "charisma" of Jesus in social memory, for example, stems from the messianic memory of Jesus before claiming that miracles are key to understanding Jesus's significance in his cultural world. Schwartz then considers Heinrich Paulus's Enlightment-era rationalizations of Jesus's miracles before asking, "Without miracles, however, what made Jesus distinctive to his generation?"[97] Schwartz does not offer any further historical exploration of this question, nor does he propose any alternatives to *why* Jesus might have been remembered as a miracle worker (e.g., a more in-depth keying of Jesus to Israelite prophetic tradition or competition with Greco-Roman imperial authority). The ambiguity of how social memory theory can be applied makes it difficult to gather a fuller picture of where the theoretical insights lead. Still, Schwartz is a helpful resource for understanding the theoretical foundations of social memory. Overall, he provides numerous insights from a perspective that values continuity in social memory, and although his self-recognized

---

94. Schwartz, "Christian Origins," in Kirk and Thatcher, eds., *Memory, Tradition, and Text*, 55.

95. Schwartz, "Where There's Smoke, There's Fire," in Thatcher, ed., *Memory and Identity*, 16.

96. "That 90 percent of the Gospel of Mark appears in Matthew and Luke exemplifies the relevance of path-dependency for memory and tradition" (Schwartz, "Where There's Smoke, There's Fire," in Thatcher, ed., *Memory and Identity*, 16).

97. Schwartz, "Where There's Smoke, There's Fire," in Thatcher, ed., *Memory and Identity*, 30.

"naïve optimism" is not always followed in memory approaches,[98] his influence has shaped and continues to shape the ever-evolving landscape of social memory theory within New Testament studies.

Anthony Le Donne, Rafael Rodríguez, and Chris Keith

The decade following Kirk and Thatcher's work saw a new wave of social memory studies applied to a variety of subjects within New Testament scholarship.[99] The most robust area of application was in Jesus studies, and this surge was due in part to the works of Anthony Le Donne, Rafael Rodríguez, and Chris Keith, the latter two of which were Thatcher's former students and all of whom went on to hone their craft in the UK.[100] Their combined efforts brought the concerns of social memory to the forefront of historical Jesus scholarship, ultimately turning a spotlight onto the methodological foundations of historical Jesus research that would upend questers both new and old.

Anthony Le Donne

A few months before *Memory, Tradition, and Text* appeared in print, the Fifth Durham-Tübingen Research Symposium convened "to contribute to a better understanding of the meaning and significance of memory and remembrance as constitutive elements of Jewish and Christian practice and self-definition in the early period."[101] The results of this symposium, published a few years later, offered a continental complement to Kirk and Thatcher's work expanded to include a variety of conceptions of memory

---

98. Though Schwartz's claim of "naïve optimism" is rhetorically used as a tongue-in-cheek way to cast himself against what he describes as the more "fatalistic" approaches of memory theory (i.e., presentism), his contributions to New Testament scholarship can sometimes feel far more optimistic than his work in American political history. Schwartz, "Where There's Smoke, There's Fire," in Thatcher, ed., *Memory and Identity*, 31.

99. Keith lists fourteen subjects or specific areas of application relative to early Christianity (the Apostolic Fathers, the Dead Sea Scrolls, Egyptian magical papyri, Pauline literature, etc.) that occur either in *Memory, Tradition, and Text* or in the decade following. See Keith, "Social Memory Theory (Part Two)," 518.

100. Keith points to his MA thesis and Le Donne and Rodríguez's published PhD dissertations as the first graduate and doctoral work on social memory. Keith, "Social Memory Theory (Part One)," 356n11.

101. Stuckenbruck et al., *Memory in the Bible and Antiquity*, 1.

(e.g., societies of memory, oral and written memory, historiography, etc.) in a variety of fields (Hebrew Bible, Dead Sea Scrolls, Second Temple Judaism, etc.). As a doctoral student at the time, Anthony Le Donne's contribution to the symposium highlighted several theoretical aspects of social memory and the role and nature of distortion. Le Donne preemptively addresses the negative connotations of "distortion" and notes several times that distorted memory is not synonymous with non-veracity/non-historicity. Additionally, he reminds his audience that all memory is selective. Sinister aims are not a necessary requirement of distorted memory because "distortion is, most commonly, a natural and benign function of memory selection."[102] Borrowing from Halbwachs's use of "localization" and Schudson's four categories of memory distortion,[103] Le Donne discusses the process of narrativization and how typologies play a role in articulating and distorting memory. Le Donne urges historical Jesus scholarship to consider "how narrativization influences perception"; if certain images of Jesus—as healer, law-giver, exorcist, or monarch—fit typologies accessible to Jesus's contemporaries, then it is possible that such "typological narrativization" could have occurred as a process of what Le Donne calls "informal localizations," what he defines as "those traditions of Jesus which were reminiscent of HB precedents by the first eyewitnesses."[104] Rather than dismissing this material as later additions or theological redactions by later compilers and hand-waving it away from historical Jesus scholarship,[105] Le Donne pinpoints how social memory theory should change the way scholars approach Jesus traditions:

102. Le Donne, "Theological Memory Distortion," in Stuckenbruck et al., eds., *Memory in the Bible and Antiquity*, 167.

103. Schudson discusses memory distortion in four ways: "(1) Distanciation: the tendency for memories to become vague or for details to be forgotten; (2) instrumentalization: the tendency for memories to be reinterpreted to serve the present better; (3) conventionalization: the tendency for memories to conform to socio-typical experiences; and (4) narrativization: the tendency for memories to be conventionalized through the constraints of story telling." Le Donne adds a fifth category of memory distortion: "(5) articulation: the tendency for memories to conform to language conventions" (Le Donne, "Theological Memory Distortion," in Stuckenbruck et al., eds., *Memory in the Bible and Antiquity*, 168).

104. Le Donne, "Theological Memory Distortion," in Stuckenbruck et al., eds., *Memory in the Bible and Antiquity*, 175–76.

105. This is the same critique that grounds much of Kirk's work, and it also forms the basis of Le Donne and Keith's dismantling of the criteria of authenticity, methodological criteria utilized in contemporary historical Jesus scholarship which, as Le Donne, Keith, and their contributors argue, rely on many form-critical assumptions that do not pass a more rigorous assessment of contemporary historical or literary

> Historical interpretations do not begin with the historian, but within the perceptions, memories and articulations of the first witnesses. If this is so, then the historian's task is not simply to sift through the data looking for facts (from which they will create their own interpretations), but to account for these *early* interpretations by explaining the perceptions and memories that birthed them.[106]

Le Donne expands this work in his dissertation, *The Historiographical Jesus: Memory, Typology, and the Son of David*. After swapping out the language of "distortion" for that of "memory refraction,"[107] Le Donne homes in on the particular typological presentation of Jesus as "Son of David." In terms of the use of Christological titles, Le Donne argues that this title "stands at a bridge between the initial memories of Jesus and the Jesus tradition as it was commemorated by the authors of the NT."[108] Specifically, Le Donne sees the "Son of David" title developing in a therapeutic matrix composed of Solomonic (exorcistic/healing) typology and Isaianic prophetic tradition. As for the first instantiation of "Son of David" being applied in Jesus's ministry, Le Donne argues the Beelzebul controversy (Mark 3:20-35 *par.*) explains the need to articulate Jesus as the "Son of David" because this pericope

> probably reflects the real concerns of Jesus' family and of the local religious leaders that Jesus' ministry incorporated foreign practice or sympathy. I think that this was how the historical stage was set when the title "Son of David" first entered the scene. Jesus or his disciples had need of an effective answer to these accusations. The Solomonic title "Son of David" served as a domestic

---

considerations. See Keith and Le Donne, *Jesus, Criteria, and the Demise of Authenticity*.

106. Le Donne, "Theological Memory Distortion," in Stuckenbruck et al., eds., *Memory in the Bible and Antiquity*, 165.

107. Similar to his prior work, Le Donne uses the language of memory refraction because it captures the essence of distortion without the difficult connotations. Instead of arguing that all memory is (to an extent) distorted, the language of memory refraction allows Le Donne to reframe this basic methodological point: "All perception is *bent* in the mnemonic process" (Le Donne, *Historiographical Jesus*, 13, emphasis added). Le Donne goes on to explain his method, which consists of tracing memory refraction to account for its different "trajectories" of resulting tradition: "Memory refraction (most often) is a gradual and imperceptible process that renders past perceptions intelligible to the continually shifting contexts of the present. Because of this, refraction trajectories can be charted backward and the historian can postulate the most plausible historical memories that best account for these refractions" (Le Donne, *Historiographical Jesus*, 14).

108. Le Donne, *Historiographical Jesus*, 94.

precedent by which Jesus could be "properly" interpreted: *No, Jesus is not practicing foreign "magic." He is like Solomon, the Son of David. He is therefore acting on the authority of YHWH on behalf of Israel.* Such arguments most likely found support and set in place the mnemonic framework of typology.[109]

In other words, as Jesus's reputation and memories about Jesus's deeds were being transmitted, the "Son of David" title became a convenient way for early Christians—and particularly the author of Matthew—to articulate Jesus's identity and behavior in a particular way and under a particular mnemonic rubric.[110] The "scriptural" (Isaiah) and "archetypal" (Solomonic) typologies at play in these traditions about Jesus "worked as mnemonic lenses that were commonly employed on the subconscious level of worldview."[111] The finer point for Le Donne is that "Matthew's redactional agenda has followed the mnemonic trajectory set in motion by the historical Jesus."[112] On the more methodological scale, however, Le Donne's work casts a wide net around such "mnemonic lenses" and trajectories to argue that historical memory exists as a continuum of perceptions, memory refractions, and localizations within mnemonic categories or frames[113] and that this continuum is penetrable when trajectories are mapped out and explained.

---

109. Le Donne, *Historiographical Jesus*, 181, emphasis original.

110. "Matthew understood Jesus' therapeutic ministry in light of the promises of Isaiah . . . At the same time, Matthew has associated Jesus with the most well-known (indeed the archetypal) precedent for exorcism: Solomon, the Son of David . . . There can be no doubt that this [Isaianic] framework was crucially important to Matthew; it has led him to classify Jesus' exorcism as a therapeutic act. But the fact that he specifically associated this passage with 'Son of David' (a title not taken from Isaiah) shows that Matthew had a broader notion of how to interpret Jesus' therapeutic ministry. Because exorcism was such a large part of his received tradition and because it (at least in this case) carried the negative connotation of foreign exorcistic practice, Matthew had need of a category that was in line with both royal messianism and Jewish exorcism. Solomon typology served to bridge these two mnemonic spheres for Matthew" (Le Donne, *Historiographical Jesus*, 166–68).

111. Le Donne, *Historiographical Jesus*, 136. In addition, Le Donne argues that Matthew's redactional activity—i.e., emphasizing the "Son of David" title in therapeutic contexts—fits into a larger interpretive scheme "synthesizes the evangelist's perception of Jesus with familiar Jewish categories like Isaianic therapy and Son of David" (Le Donne, *Historiographical Jesus*, 183).

112. Le Donne, *Historiographical Jesus*, 182.

113. See Le Donne, *Historiographical Jesus*, 259–68.

Rafael Rodríguez

Contemporaneously, Rafael Rodríguez set forth on a project to examine memory, tradition, and the historical Jesus. His dissertation, later published as *Structuring Early Christian Memory*, proposed an alternative manner of understanding the Jesus tradition with an eye toward memory and media studies. Though Rodríguez and Le Donne covered similar territory—both focused on exorcism narratives in the gospels and their place against the backdrop of Israel's scriptural traditions (particularly Isaiah)—there were significant differences between the way each approached their study. In terms of starting point, Le Donne probed New Criticism and historiography, whereas Rodríguez focused on the dynamics of oral tradition and performance. In terms of social memory, Le Donne was rooted in Halbwachs and Assmann, while Rodríguez also leaned heavily on Schwartz and Olick. And finally, in terms of argumentative endgames, Le Donne sought to break down dichotomies of history/interpretation and memory/typology, while Rodríguez's work urged Jesus scholarship to consider the effects of oral tradition and social memory on the formation and transmission of the gospel tradition.

Central to Rodríguez's work is media studies, particularly as it pertains to the dynamics of tradition—how tradition, like memory, is held together by stability and variability[114]—and how these dynamics play out in an oral-performative context.[115] "The gospels," Rodríguez argues, "were received as performances, instances of the tradition . . . the gospel texts are *instances* of the ambient Jesus tradition rather than *editions* or *redactions* of each other."[116] As the tradition found its instantiation in the written medium, there must have existed a measure

---

114. Contrary to any belief that textualization and orality exist on opposite sides of the spectrum of stability/variability, these dynamics are not bound to any particular medium. In Rodríguez's estimation, "Written tradition, like . . . oral tradition, is itself caught within the interacting ebb and flow of stability and malleability, each implicated in the other, so that stability is not equal to preservation and malleability is not equal to redaction. Fixity and fluidity belong together" (Rodríguez, *Structuring Early Christian Memory*, 9).

115. On the importance of performance and the similar dynamics at work in performance and social memory/commemorative activity: "Performance *actualizes* tradition, and both performer and audience enter into and perceive the performance in reference to its *ambient tradition* . . . performance takes place in the 'context of a special social event' . . . and draws together past and present, reaffirms traditional social values and understandings, and connects a group (in its present) with its traditions (its past)" (Rodríguez, *Structuring Early Christian Memory*, 85, emphasis original).

116. Rodríguez, *Structuring Early Christian Memory*, 111, emphasis original.

of continuity between the written and oral Jesus tradition.[117] Much like Schwartz's plea for the continuity perspective in social memory, Rodríguez argues that discontinuity between the oral and written media would create conflict for their audiences, who would have no reason to be persuaded by a written gospel that conflicted with preexistent oral tradition.[118] With this in mind, Rodríguez cautions against placing too much emphasis on "analysing the texts against each other—identifying the tradition's 'tendencies' or 'trajectories'—rather than in relation to the tradition of which they are but individual instances."[119] The Jesus tradition was malleable and flexible; it existed within an oral milieu as "a living, dynamic, organically unified entity capable of variable expressions for various purposes. Jesus' tradents could express differing, even conflicting images of Jesus through this tradition."[120] With such a dynamic view of oral tradition, it is unsurprising, then, that one of Rodríguez's main aims is recalibrating New Testament scholarship toward recognizing this oral milieu, which he does by preferring the language of "traditions" rather than "texts."[121] Even though texts open the door for our understanding of and mediate our access to ancient oral traditions, it is crucial to remember that the overarching tradition "transcended and contextualized our texts in dynamic and robust ways."[122]

---

117. Rodríguez stressed that these two media—written and oral traditions—are not *separate* traditions: "We do not propose oral sources *between* gospel texts but rather oral tradition and performance *enveloping* and *contextualizing* the texts themselves ... The gospels, each of them individually and all of them collectively, *are* the Jesus tradition" (Rodríguez, *Structuring Early Christian Memory*, 6, emphasis original).

118. "The more we read the written gospel traditions as subverting and challenging the oral Jesus tradition, the more we have to reckon with the question of the audience and how they so willingly accepted written texts that contradicted their already established traditions. Here, then, is another reason for presupposing continuity between the images and patterns of signification across the oral and written traditions" (Rodríguez, *Structuring Early Christian Memory*, 112).

119. Rodríguez, *Structuring Early Christian Memory*, 111.

120. Rodríguez, *Structuring Early Christian Memory*, 112–13.

121. To emphasize this point, Rodríguez employs the phrase "traditions of Israel's restoration" as a stand-in for alternative textual terms: "Implicitly throughout, and explicitly in places, we did not explain Jesus' answers in terms of *texts*, a term which continues to suggest fixed, bounded entities, but in terms of *tradition*. We emphatically stressed ... that texts in the ancient world were anything but fixed and bounded, as can be seen in the various textual traditions preserved at Qumran or by the Rabbis. When New Testament scholars speak of 'texts', however, they continue to hear (and mean) 'fixed texts'" (Rodríguez, *Structuring Early Christian Memory*, 214, emphasis original).

122. Rodríguez, *Structuring Early Christian Memory*, 214.

In addition to greater awareness of first-century media dynamics, Rodríguez also utilizes the tenets of social memory as a corrective to historical Jesus scholarship. In the same way that Kirk placed himself against form critics, Rodríguez positions himself against historical Jesus scholars who "fail to allow that the location of presentations of the past squarely in the present does not disqualify these as images *of the past*."[123] Rodríguez calls out this misstep, arguing that it leads to at least one of two assumptions that inevitably dovetail into a faulty determination about the "authenticity" of the tradition: "(a) that at least some 'authentic' traditions illustrate the past imposing itself tyrannically upon the present (e.g., Jesus' acceptance of John's baptism of repentance); and (b) that 'inauthentic' traditions illustrate the present imposing itself tyrannically on the past (e.g., Jesus' anticipation of the 'mission to the gentiles')."[124] Both perspectives miss the fact that past and present are mutually constructive and mutually informative; in Rodriguez's estimation, these scholars miss that "the Jesus tradition was *interactive*, impacting and shaping Jesus' followers *even as* they left their marks upon the content and structure of their traditions."[125] Rodríguez uses this insight to argue that historical Jesus scholarship must move away from the form critical assumptions that formed the foundation of the New Quest and Third Quest—especially the criteria of authenticity—and instead attend to the Jesus tradition as we have it. As Rodríguez puts it, rather than "conceptualizing 'historical Jesus' research as a programme of distinguishing and categorizing tradition into 'authentic' and 'inauthentic' bins, our research in the future will have to attend more closely to the gospels as we have them and *as we can reconstruct their function within their originative contexts*."[126] Rodríguez's study demonstrates this by proposing the originative contexts for Jesus's healings and exorcisms are found in both past and present. Jesus's ministry is framed against the backdrop of Israelite traditional materials, particularly those traditions focusing on Israel's restoration (e.g., Mosaic, Isaianic, and Davidic traditions, as well as the Elijah/Elisha cycles); however, this ministry cannot be understood without placing it into its contemporaneous geopolitical context as well: the Judaean world under Roman domination.[127] These contexts are mutually informing, working

---

123. Rodríguez, *Structuring Early Christian Memory*, 220.
124. Rodríguez, *Structuring Early Christian Memory*, 220.
125. Rodríguez, *Structuring Early Christian Memory*, 5, emphasis original.
126. Rodríguez, *Structuring Early Christian Memory*, 220–21, emphasis added.
127. Here Rodríguez draws on Hollanbach's socio-historical approach to the

as a two-way process in which tradition informs memory and memory reshapes/transforms tradition. Thus, for Rodríguez, historical study of the early Christian social memory of Jesus's healings and exorcisms—and the conflict and conversations they elicited—reveals "the interface between the heightened demonology of Second Temple Judaism and the concerns generated by Rome's presence over Judaean and Galilean society. Jesus and his opponents understood that interface in terms of Israelite tradition, which enabled them to orientate themselves in a difficult present, but that interface also transformed the tradition's significance."[128]

Chris Keith

Following in the wake of Le Donne and Rodríguez, Chris Keith's *Jesus' Literacy* offered a glimpse of what social memory theory, what he dubs "the Jesus-memory approach," could look like when applied to sociohistorical questions in New Testament studies. Keith's interest in literacy stems from his doctoral research on the *Pericope Adulterae* and the unique Jesus traditions in John 8:6, 8, where the term καταγράφω is applied to Jesus. Keith argues that the *Pericope* projects an intentional portrayal of a "grapho-literate" Jesus intended to draw connections to the divine writing of the Decalogue in Exod 32:15, and this interpretation suggests an apologetic origin placed in the midst of the Christological critiques of the third century.[129] In *Jesus' Literacy*, however, Keith turns the conversation toward the historical Jesus, asking, "On which side of the literacy line did Jesus fall?"[130] To suggest an answer to this question, as well as to offer an account for this answer, Keith turns to social memory theory, whose "primary task . . . is to conceptualize and explain the various manners in which cultures (and individuals as culture-members) appropriate the past in light of, in terms of, and on behalf of the present."[131]

As a theoretical model, Keith contrasts the "Jesus-memory" approach against the criteria approach to the historical Jesus, stating that

---

exorcism narratives in the gospels: "Hollanbach pointed out over twenty-five years ago that the colonial presence of Rome in first-century Galilee must have been a compelling factor in the experience of demon-possession, and thus Rome factored into any successful programme of exorcism" (Rodríguez, *Structuring Early Christian Memory*, 203).

128. Rodríguez, *Structuring Early Christian Memory*, 206.
129. See Keith, *Pericope Adulterae*.
130. Keith, *Jesus' Literacy*, 4.
131. Keith, *Jesus' Literacy*, 56.

any approach seeking to exhume "authentic" (meaning past historical information without any later interpretation or interference) is flawed from the start: "Not only are there no longer Jesus traditions that reflect solely the actual past, there never were. In other words, there is no memory, no preserved past, and no access to it, without interpretation."[132] Still, interpretation does not deny any sort of historical-critical work; on the contrary, Keith argues that Jesus scholars must "explain the existence of the Jesus-memories in the Gospels. That is, one must quest for the historical Jesus by accounting for the interpretations of the Gospels, not by dismissing them and certainly not by fragmenting them."[133] Though the criteria approach is considered flawed, Keith posits social memory as a way of advancing historical Jesus scholarship by defending the compatibility of social memory and historical hypothesizing:

> Jesus historians are warranted in asking "What actually happened?" because the actual past *happened* and some of it was preserved through social memory; Jesus historians are warranted in being cautious with their claims because the actual past happened and some of it was preserved *through social memory*. Cumulatively, then, the Jesus historian must, in light of the various claims about Jesus preserved in early Christian commemoration, posit an actual past that best explains the existence of the Jesus-memories in light of the contexts of remembrance in early Christianity . . . [Le Donne] helpfully describes the general historical task of considering what *could* have happened in the past to produce the different interpretive trajectories that exist.[134]

For Keith, the actual past is posited based on historical reconstruction, not revealed by a special method that decontextualizes fragments of tradition.[135] The historian's reconstruction is not the actual past, but an argument for what the actual past might have looked like when taking all texts and contexts into account.

---

132. Keith, *Jesus' Literacy*, 61.
133. Keith, *Jesus' Literacy*, 66.
134. Keith, *Jesus' Literacy*, 67, emphasis original.
135. Even if traditions about Jesus are considered not to reflect the historical past, Keith argues that "the proper *historical* approach to that tradition is not to ask '*Did* early Christians misremember Jesus?' and dismiss it based on the assumed affirmative answer, but rather to ask '*How* did early Christians misremember Jesus?' and proceed to explain what socio-historical conditions led to the production of that memory" (Keith, *Jesus' Literacy*, 64, emphasis original).

Keith's assessment of Jesus's literacy demonstrates this historical task by leaning heavily on socio-historical research into ancient literacy. Keith lays out an extensive coverage of literacy that examines six key features in first-century Judaean literate behavior: widespread illiteracy, widespread textuality, literacy spectrums, scribal literacy, the knowledge of religious texts, and the perception of literacy.[136] Keith's overall thrust is that literacy, however defined, was restricted to a minority, and literate education was not required for either religious devotion or the *modus operandi* of first-century agrarian life.[137] On the role of textuality, Keith notes that although there exists a variety of literary and documentary evidence, "the presence of texts in Roman Palestine [did] not require that all members of that culture were able to access them (read, write, understand, etc.) on their own."[138] This leads to discussion of the literacy spectrum and the variety of different levels and functions of literate behavior, including that of semi-literates. Keith argues the variety of literate skills and levels of literacies held by craftsmen dwarf in comparison to scribal literacy: "Despite whatever literate skills an artisan attained, however, there remained a stark difference between those skills and the literate skills of a scribal-literate teacher of the law."[139] The nuance employed here is helpful in portraying the complexity of literate behavior in the ancient world, and Keith's work presents a helpful reminder that "in light of the complex gradations of literacy in Second Temple Judaism, and particularly the presence of craftsman's literacy, one should not be so quick to identify artisanship with utter illiteracy."[140] Keith is careful to distinguish gradations of literacy and abandons the "literacy/illiteracy" dichotomy, which leads to a more nuanced treatment of how Jesus was remembered in literate and illiterate ways.

Keith then turns toward traditions that touch on Jesus's literacy. Keith examines various Synoptic (Mark 1:22; 6:3; their parallels in Matt 7:29; 13:55, respectively; and Luke 2:41–50), Johannine (John 7:15,

---

136. Keith, *Jesus' Literacy*, 71–123.

137. Keith, *Jesus' Literacy*, 81–85. For more on the conversation of ancient literacy and its place in the first-century Greco-Roman and Roman-Judaean world, see Harris, *Ancient Literacy*; Hezser, *Jewish Literacy in Roman Palestine*; Botha, "Greco-Roman Literacy," 195–215; Morgan, *Literate Education*; Thomas, *Literacy and Orality*; Youtie, "ΑΓΡΑΜΜΑΤΟΣ," 161–76; Beard, *Literacy in the Roman World*; Wise, *Language and Literacy in Roman Judaea*.

138. Keith, *Jesus' Literacy*, 86–87.

139. Keith, *Jesus' Literacy*, 113.

140. Keith, *Jesus' Literacy*, 115.

45–52; 8:6, 8), and non-canonical (the Abgar legend as it appears in Eusebius, Rufinus, Coptic, and Syriac; *Narrative of Joseph of Arimathea* 3.4; Adamantius's *Dialogue on the True Faith in God* 2.13; *Epistle of Barnabas* 12:9; and *Infancy Gospel of Thomas* 6:1–8:3; 14:1–5; 15:1–7) passages that discuss Jesus's literate status or behavior. For the Synoptics, Keith argues that the contrasting portrait of Jesus's status in the Synoptics "reveals an early Christian social memory that is corporately confused or, better, in a state of disagreement on the matter of Jesus' scribal-literate status."[141] Keith claims that the Johannine portrait, including the later reception of this portrait in the *Pericope Adulterae*, "provided sufficient fodder for [Jesus's] enemies to maintain conflicting assumptions/conclusions about his scribal-literate status."[142] Finally, later traditions display a continuation of debate over Jesus's literate status, with examples of Jesus as both an illiterate craftsman *and* participating in literate behavior, such as dictating and writing. Keith summarizes, "from the first century, the early Church remembered Jesus, sometimes vigorously, as someone who did not have scribal literacy, someone who did, and someone who was able to blur the lines between scribal literacy and scribal illiteracy."[143]

What can explain these divergent presentations of Jesus's literacy? Based on the available evidence and the ways in which Jesus was remembered, Keith postulates a historical situation where Jesus, as a first-century teacher, was embroiled in debate with Judaean religious leaders. This debate, which mirrors the situations narrated in the gospels, left those who perceived the confrontation with the impression that Jesus's literate status was equal to that of his opponents, the scribes and authorities of the Hebrew scriptural texts and traditions.[144] Keith concludes that

---

141. Keith, *Jesus' Literacy*, 146.

142. Keith, *Jesus' Literacy*, 163. Keith also traces this murky portrait to a clear demonstration of his ability to write in John 8:6–8, where "the interpolator [of the *Pericope Adulterae*] claims that Jesus is not only scribal-literate, but grapho-literate; and not only grapho-literate, but divinely so" (Keith, *Jesus' Literacy*, 156).

143. Keith, *Jesus' Literacy*, 164.

144. "One does not have to affirm the historical accuracy of each of these texts in order to affirm the likelihood of their broad claim—someone somewhere perceived Jesus to have won a public battle of wits with Pharisees, scribes, or other scribal-literate authorities. If this ever occurred, then it requires no great leap of imagination to understand that some members of Jesus' audiences could have moved from the perception that Jesus successfully responded to a challenge from scribal-literate authorities to the conclusion that he himself held such authority and was, thus, himself a scribal-literate individual" (Keith, *Jesus' Literacy*, 185).

studying the socio-historical frameworks of first-century literacy and the resulting social memory of early Christianity suggests that

> Jesus most likely did not hold scribal literacy. This alone, however, was not enough to keep some of his audiences, or members of his audiences, from concluding that he did. Although he was not a scribal-literate teacher, he was the type of teacher who was able to make people assume or conclude that he was. Therefore, within Jesus' own lifetime there likely were contradictory and confused perceptions of his scribal-literate status.[145]

The use of scripture in Jesus's challenges against the scribal elite did not require the ability to read, but the interpretive debates and perception of victory by his audience members were a catalyst for their accrediting scribal-literate status to him.[146] Keith later took this conclusion and focused on the controversy narratives between Jesus and the scribal elite, arguing, "confusion over Jesus's scribal-literate status accounts for how Jesus came to be on scribal authorities' radars initially and offers a plausible launching pad for additional hostilities, especially since the confrontations occurred publicly in an honor/shame culture."[147]

THE DEMISE OF AUTHENTICITY

One of the by-products of the early social memory approaches was the critique and overall circumvention of the criteria of authenticity. The criteria of authenticity (e.g., dissimilarity, multiple attestation, embarrassment, etc.) were paramount in the historical Jesus scholarship of the second half of the twentieth century: the Jesus Seminar used them to argue for the authenticity of particular sayings, while John Dominic Crossan, N. T. Wright, and John P. Meier, among others, used them to a programmatic and systematizing effect when building their respective historical reconstructions of Jesus's life.[148] However, the shifting attitude can be seen in the cadre of early social memory approaches: Le Donne's work appealed to the criteria selectively,[149] whereas Rodríguez and Keith

---

145. Keith, *Jesus' Literacy*, 187.
146. See Keith, *Jesus' Literacy*, 185–86.
147. Keith, *Jesus Against the Scribal Elite*, 156.
148. See Funk et al., *Five Gospels*; Crossan, *Historical Jesus*; Wright, *Jesus and the Victory of God*; Meier, *Marginal Jew*.
149. "I have made judicious use of authenticity criteria. The application of such criteria has been one step among several to postulate historical memory" (Le Donne,

jettisoned the criteria entirely.[150] Their individual works led to a larger collaborative project, *Jesus, Criteria, and the Demise of Authenticity*, focused on evaluating the pitfalls of the criteria of authenticity, especially those addressed as early as 1972 by Morna Hooker.[151]

One of the major focal points throughout the collection of essays is the dissatisfaction with form-critical assumptions embedded in the criteria approach. Le Donne suggests the criteria are the subject of controversy due to two competing notions of authenticity.[152] Keith traces the criteria of authenticity to their root as an "outgrowth" of form criticism and critiques the criteria for maintaining the same faulty dichotomy of "authentic"/"inauthentic" at the core of form criticism's sifting of the *Sitz im Leben* concept.[153] Schröter critiques the way in which emphasis on "authentic" material confuses interpretation of past events with the past itself.[154] In the same way that Kirk and Thatcher addressed form criticism

---

Historiographical Jesus, 265). Le Donne later characterizes this position as one of substitution rather than dissolution: "It is the *conventional use* of the criteria that must be replaced by a more sophisticated historiography" (Le Donne, "Rise of the Quest," in Keith and Le Donne, eds., *Jesus, Criteria, and the Demise of Authenticity*, 4–5).

150. Keith's discontent with the criteria approach is founded upon its historical connection with form criticism, particularly in the way that "the criteria approach mirrors the historian's task according to form criticism . . . [that is] that scholars proceed to connect Jesus traditions in the written Gospels to the historical Jesus *only once the criteria have removed the traditions from the interpretive framework of the Gospel narratives*" (Keith, "Memory and Authenticity," 165, emphasis original).

151. See Hooker, "On Using the Wrong Tool."

152. Le Donne contrasts European scholarship (particularly German Romanticism) against American evangelical Biblicism to discuss competing worldviews of authenticity: the former sought "originality" as the core of genius and the character of heroes from the past, whereas the latter understood "authenticity" as connected to the larger conversations about biblical authority, inerrancy, and self-revealing truths. See Le Donne, "Rise of the Quest," in Keith and Le Donne, eds., *Jesus, Criteria, and the Demise of Authenticity*, 6–11, 16–17.

153. "Irrespective of how scholars today nuance and modify the meaning of 'authentic,' the criteria of authenticity were designed upon, and assume, a definition of that word that amounts essentially to 'does not reflect the theological interpretations of the Gospel authors and their communities'" (Keith, "Indebtedness of the Criteria," in Keith and Le Donne, eds., *Jesus, Criteria, and the Demise of Authenticity*, 36, emphasis original).

154. "Critical examination of the historical material does not by itself lead to an 'authentic' picture of the past. Rather, one must take into account that a historical inquiry is always an enterprise in which the historian studies historical data to develop an idea of what might have happened. Thereby, the remains from the past must not be confused with the events themselves. Rather, the historical sources are selective and often subjective recollections and interpretations of events from which the historian attempts to recover the events themselves" (Jens Schröter, "Criteria of Authenticity," in

as a foil to the introduction of social memory work, Keith, Le Donne, and their contributors systematically demonstrate how authenticity is a problematic starting point;[155] as Rodríguez puts it, "We only ever know the past as situated and interested subjects in the present. We may come to *know about* the past; we cannot ever *recover* the past we seek to know."[156]

Included in the contributions is an interesting (re)assessment by Dale Allison.[157] Allison recounts his own initial sense of distrust in the criterion of dissimilarity, all the while documenting the ways in which he employed multiple criteria in works he produced throughout his career. Allison also reassesses the prevailing historical positivism that shaped much of his career, recognizing the siren calls of Hooker and F. Gerald Downing about how limited our knowledge of Jesus and the early Church truly are.[158] Allison then draws out three major subjects of interest that further shifted his view of historical interpretation: John the Baptist, the Q source, and the temptation narratives (Matt 4; Luke 4),[159] before noting the trajectory away from the criteria in his work on Jesus

---

Keith and Le Donne, eds., *Jesus, Criteria, and the Demise of Authenticity*, 50–51).

155. In the words of Dale Allison, "We . . . have been, *in part because of form criticism*, hypnotized by tradition histories of this isolated logion or that individual pericope, histories that are, more often than we care to admit, just guesses, however educated they may be" (Allison, *Constructing Jesus*, 16, emphasis added).

156. Rodríguez, "Embarrassing Truth About Jesus," in Keith and Le Donne, eds., *Jesus, Criteria, and the Demise of Authenticity*, 133.

157. Allison, "It Don't Come Easy," in Keith and Le Donne, eds., *Jesus, Criteria, and the Demise of Authenticity*, 186–99.

158. "One of Downing's major points was that 'we do not know enough about Jesus to allow us to construct a clear account of the primitive Church because we do not know enough about the primitive Church to allow us to construct a clear account of Jesus.' I decided that he was correct, indeed obviously correct. The upshot was the realization that my ignorance about Jesus' Judaism was akin to my ignorance of the early churches. From this it seemed to follow that we know far too little to wield the criterion of dissimilarity with any precision" (Allison, "It Don't Come Easy," in Keith and Le Donne, eds., *Jesus, Criteria, and the Demise of Authenticity*, 189).

159. Regarding Allison's insight from the temptation narratives and how supposed "inauthentic" traditions still carry historical and commemorative value: "The presumed authentic—that which goes back directly to the historical Jesus—and the supposed inauthentic—that which does not directly go back to him—can be indistinct. Yet sorting the tradition with the standard criteria presupposes that there is a clear distinction between the two, that an item is either one or the other. Moreover, and as a rule, once scholars decide that Jesus did not say X or did not do Y, they forever after ignore X or Y because, they imagine, it has nothing to do with him. I decided that this is a mistake. Maybe, I began to think, the historical Jesus can be present even in post-Easter materials" (Allison, "It Don't Come Easy," in Keith and Le Donne, eds., *Jesus, Criteria, and the Demise of Authenticity*, 191).

(*Jesus of Nazareth: Millenarian Prophet* [1998]; *Resurrecting Jesus* [2005]; *Constructing Jesus* [2010]). In this then-final entry, Allison appeals to the study of individual memory,[160] using memory as an analytical category from which to examine "recurrent attestation," that is, "that a topic or motif or type of story reappears again and again through the tradition."[161] Allison demonstrates what such a method can yield by returning to previous topics, such as the eschatology of Jesus[162] or the passion narrative of Mark.[163] Based on this approach and on his dissatisfaction with the limitations of the criteria, Allison concludes, "Not only are the arguments for or against authenticity more often than not far from decisive, but they are often not to the point, because memories of Jesus can inform sentences that he did not utter and stories that never took place."[164]

In its thoroughgoing assessment of the criteria approach, *Jesus, Criteria, and the Demise of Authenticity* presents definitive and systematic

---

160. Allison's engagement with memory, which is founded on insights from psychology and cognitive theory rather than sustained engagement with social or cultural memory, builds the case that individual memories, even eyewitness testimonies, are fallible, yet can still retain a generalized (gist) picture that reflects the historical past. See Allison, *Constructing Jesus*, 1–17.

161. Allison, *Constructing Jesus*, 20. Allison argues that "certain themes, motifs, and rhetorical strategies recur again and again throughout the primary sources; and it must be in those themes and motifs and rhetorical strategies—which, taken together, leave some distinct impressions—if it is anywhere, that we will find memory" (15).

162. "What I do maintain is that the materials gathered into the Synoptics, however stylized and otherwise distorted, descend from narratives and sayings that were in circulation and widely valued from early times, and that we may reasonably hope to find in those Gospels, above all in their repeating patterns, a faint image. Bolstering this hope is the fact that, while the Synoptic Jesus often appears to be an apocalyptic prophet, we can infer his status as such forms the foundational beliefs of the earliest churches. In other words, what we otherwise know from primitive Christianity corroborates the general impression that we gather from the Synoptics" (Allison, *Constructing Jesus*, 164).

163. Allison argues that the "recurrent attestation" of accounts of Jesus's death contrasts Crossan's "prophecy historicized" approach and Bultmann's claim that Jesus did not go willingly to his death: "Why did Paul, the tradents of the Jesus tradition, and other early Christians believe that Jesus did not shun his execution but rather, when it came, accepted it? My answer is this: they believed it because that is just what he did, and people remembered it . . . To entertain the suggestion that Jesus did not go to his death willingly requires positing either widespread conscious cover-up or a catastrophic memory failure in the early Christian sources . . . I consider it much more likely that, in this particular, our sources are not bereft of memory. Jesus' decision to die, whenever made and whatever the motivation and whatever his precise interpretation, left a vivid impression" (Allison, *Constructing Jesus*, 433).

164. Allison, "It Don't Come Easy," in Keith and Le Donne, eds., *Jesus, Criteria, and the Demise of Authenticity*, 199.

critiques against various criteria, but it also builds on the importance and strength of memory approaches to historical Jesus research. Schröter promotes memory as a "narratological approach to historiography" that

> provides the frameworks which the historian has to fill in with narrative imagination. This does not deliver historiography to arbitrariness. To the contrary, the historical narrative is the representation of events of bygone times, making them accessible and meaningful also for the present. These representations are committed to the remains of the past, which still exist in present times. But these remains are not themselves the past. They rather function as "sources" if they are used as such by historians and also provide restrictions for what historians are allowed to say about the past . . . [the form-critical approach] fails in acknowledging that doing history always means to scrutinize the sources as selective, often incomplete, remains of the past. It never means to go behind the sources to the "real" events.[165]

Rather than sifting our source material into two camps, Keith claims that the reshaping of the historiographical task "requires an initial big-picture approach to the historical Jesus by including all available sources and socio-historical factors in a given theory."[166] Based on this understanding of historical sources, Keith urges a simple proposal for historical Jesus scholarship that is an undercurrent of his "Jesus-memory" approach: for scholars to consider "how Christians came to view Jesus in particular ways."[167]

Sandra Huebenthal

Sandra Huebenthal plays an important role in bridging the gap between German and English-speaking scholarship on social and cultural memory. Rooted in the theoretical works of Jan and Aleida Assmann, Huebenthal points out important "linguistic differences between English and German terminology," carefully nuancing and distinguishing the terms "social memory" from *sozial Gedächtnis* and "cultural memory"

---

165. Schröter, "Criteria of Authenticity," in Keith and Le Donne, eds., *Jesus, Criteria, and the Demise of Authenticity*, 69–70.

166. Keith, "Fall of the Quest," in Keith and Le Donne, eds., *Jesus, Criteria, and the Demise of Authenticity*, 202.

167. Keith, "Fall of the Quest," in Keith and Le Donne, eds., *Jesus, Criteria, and the Demise of Authenticity*, 205.

from *kulturelle Gedächtnis*.[168] Perhaps most helpful is Huebenthal's diagram of social memory alongside collective memory (which comprises *kommunikatives Gedächtnis* and *kulturelle Gedächtnis*). In her theoretical rendering, Huebenthal places social memory as the most immediate and smallest form of memory ("family memory") transmitting events from the recent past in small social groups, whereas *kommunicatives Gedächtnis* occurs within larger community groups after the forty-year gap and *kulturelle Gedächtnis* takes place in larger groups as they institutionalize group identity by discussing the remote past.[169] These definitions play a key role in how Huebenthal conceptualizes the role of social and collective memory for Biblical studies. For instance, because the New Testament texts, composed in the first and second centuries CE, are looking back to events that took place thirty to one hundred years prior, Huebenthal notes that we are looking at texts dealing with the "recent past," which classifies these texts as *kommunikatives Gedächtnis*.[170]

Although Huebenthal notes the frequent application of memory theories to historical Jesus studies, she offers a methodological warning: "reading New Testament texts as *kommunikatives Gedächntis* means that one cannot presume to know exactly how the events memorialized in the texts really took place. Such a reading rather gives insight into the status of the memory group and its process of identity construction."[171] One important feature that Huebenthal highlights is the role of contested meanings in New Testament texts. These contests display "the struggle for the correct understanding of the events [they narrate] . . . The Gospels represent different attempts to understand and remember the foundational events of Christianity."[172] Huebenthal further clarifies that reading the Gospels as *kommunikatives Gedächtnis* allows scholars to see how

> four different versions of the Jesus story can be read and each of them fosters a different early Christian identity construction. In this perspective, the process of *kommunikatives Gedächtnis*, the struggle for a common past that constitutes the present and the future, is *frozen* so to speak in the New Testament texts, preserved like a snapshot. New Testament texts thus mirror details of the several *kommunikative Gedächtnisse*

---

168. Huebenthal, "Social and Cultural Memory," 177–78.
169. Huebenthal, "Social and Cultural Memory," 186–87.
170. Huebenthal, "Social and Cultural Memory," 191–92.
171. Huebenthal, "Social and Cultural Memory," 192.
172. Huebenthal, "Social and Cultural Memory," 193.

(plural) of early Christianity and reflect diverse processes of identity formation.[173]

On the other hand, if the New Testament texts are understood as *kulturelle Gedächtnis*, it "would mean discovering our own position in relation to this history and understanding it as part of our own identity."[174] Reader perspective, formalization of group identity, and construction of sometimes competing or contested tradition(s) are all important factors that ebb and flow depending on which rubric is applied to the New Testament texts, and Huebenthal's insights open further avenues to expand the Assmanns's work in biblical, and more specifically New Testament, studies.

One way that Huebenthal further explores the possibilities for memory theory in New Testament studies is her work on the Gospel of Mark as a social memory text. Huebenthal's work attempts to understand "which image of Jesus, but also which self-image, this memory text presents."[175] From this, Huebenthal does not attempt to probe the historical Jesus; her interest lies in "questions [that] touch the limits of the text but do not transgress them."[176] Instead, Huebenthal contrasts her work from that of Keith, stating that her approach changes perspective from focusing on the *object* of memory, Jesus, to the *subject* of memory, the early Christians who remembered him.[177] "When images of the particular *Jesus remembered* become visible against the background of the memory text from which they originate and these images are compared with each other, they reveal less about the *object of memory* than about those who remember it, namely the *subject of memory*."[178] What then does the Gospel of Mark, as a textualized

---

173. Huebenthal, "Social and Cultural Memory," 194, emphasis original.
174. Huebenthal, "Social and Cultural Memory," 193.
175. Huebenthal, *Reading Mark's Gospel*, 81.
176. Huebenthal, *Reading Mark's Gospel*, 82.

177. Huebenthal goes on to clarify her method as "consist[ing] of a mix of narratological and historical methods, as well as analyses of motifs and intertextual references" (*Reading Mark's Gospel*, 526). This contrasts with Keith's socio-historical approach.

178. Further contrasting her work to Keith's memory approach, Huebenthal writes, "Going beyond the limits of the text in Jesus's direction—that is, to ask who he *actually was* or *what actually happened* behind the text—must necessarily remain a speculative enterprise. The research on *Jesus remembered* has rightly recognized that the texts of the New Testament present images of particular communities of commemoration and narration. It is, however, not possible to safely draw conclusions about the events or experiences that lie behind them from these images alone. And it is likewise not possible

product of collective memory, show about its community? Huebenthal points to several features of community engagement: Christology,[179] discipleship,[180] Israelite tradition,[181] and table fellowship.[182] Huebenthal again touches on the role that the gospel events (historical or literary) play and contextualizes these features as connecting the community to their understanding of Jesus. Thus, the "connective" role that memory plays for the textualized externalization of collective memory "is less about the events themselves and more about their significance for the community of commemoration and narration."[183]

Helen Bond

Helen Bond has recently utilized social memory theory to evaluate the proposals set forth for the date of Jesus's death. After examining the dates and implications of the texts, Bond argues, "In the end, all that the evidence allows us to claim is that Jesus died some time around the Passover, perhaps a few days before the feast, any time between 29 and 34 CE."[184] This thesis is not groundbreaking; in fact, compared to the bold claims made in favor of the scholarly consensus dating of Nisan 14/April 7, 30 CE, Bond's argument swings the pendulum in the other direction. Bond's work cautions scholars to be mindful of the limitations of historicity and

---

to take the existent images from the different texts and add them together to form a historically reliable image" (Huebenthal, *Reading Mark's Gospel*, 78, emphasis original).

179. "Jesus is introduced as the character for identification and not the disciples . . . Like him, they are baptized . . . but they also experience the lack of understanding, the hostility, and the occasional need to withdraw. Just as Jesus proclaimed the Βασιλεία τοῦ θεοῦ that has arrived, they try to realize this new reality in their lives as they live in this world. In this process, they adopt Jesus's perspective and not the disciples" (Huebenthal, *Reading Mark's Gospel*, 504).

180. "Just as the character Jesus heard the voice of God and called the disciples to follow him . . . the community of commemoration also sees itself on the way to follow Jesus. They do not leave this way despite all the hostility and crises they experience" (Huebenthal, *Reading Mark's Gospel*, 505).

181. "The community of commemoration sees itself in accordance with its Jewish tradition, but with its own specific emphasis on Jesus, whom the community understands to be the Christ and the Son of God, and his authoritative proclamation of the εὐαγγέλιον τοῦ θεοῦ" (Huebenthal, *Reading Mark's Gospel*, 507).

182. "Finally, it can be said that the community of commemoration also—if not predominantly—constitutes a table fellowship" (Huebenthal, *Reading Mark's Gospel*, 509).

183. Huebenthal, *Reading Mark's Gospel*, 509.

184. Bond, "Dating the Death of Jesus," 475.

offers a portrait of how social memory theory can be applied alongside and within historical-critical approaches to temper claims of "certainty," as well as point to other considerations that get lost as blind spots in historical questioning. As Keith pointed out, rather than offering us answers to quantitative questions, like *who*, *what*, *when*, and *where*, social memory encourages scholars to probe for *how* and *why* particular traditions are remembered and transmitted the way they are. Bond's work does not ignore the historical debate; she attends to the former considerations by engaging the scholarly consensus and explaining the different considerations that scholars must make when determining a particular date. But Bond addresses the latter concerns—those central to memory studies—by zooming out and questioning the scholarly consensus: how are we to understand the priestly intention in Mark 14:2 if the arrest of Jesus ultimately *did* take place during the Passover? What does it mean for Simon of Cyrene to be coming "from the field" (ἀπ' ἀγροῦ, Mark 15:21) in the context of the Passover/Sabbath?[185] In short, Bond cautions scholars to read Mark's passion narrative as its own account, arguing that, aside from a few likely redactional passages, Mark's narrative need not take place *during* the Passover, but merely *around the time of* the Passover. This realization prompts Bond to engage social memory in explaining how and why subsequent early Christian tradition[186] remembered Jesus's death at the Passover. Examining the reception of Jesus's death displays how "stories about Jesus were indirectly stories about the earliest Christians themselves, their relationship to what was past, and what they hoped for in the future."[187] In addition, Bond argues that Israel's own social memory—that is, the traditions and "cultural texts" from Israelite history embedded in sacred scriptures and rituals—provided the fertile ground in which to key the significance for Jesus's death. She argues,

> As the earliest Christians came together to remember Jesus and to ponder the significance of his death, it would hardly be surprising if the immense weight of the Passover festival began to shape their stories: to inspire them to talk of covenants, of sacrifice, of the plan of God from long ago, and to encourage hopes that the visions of the prophets and the promises of Jesus himself were about to be realised. The reading of texts

---

185. Bond, "Dating the Death of Jesus," 468–71.

186. Bond points to early Christian texts, like Justin Martyr, *Dialogue* 16; Origen, *Against Celsus* 1.47; *Commentary on the Gospel of Matthew* 10.17.

187. Bond, "Dating the Death of Jesus," 473.

such as Isaiah 53 and Psalms 22 (21 LXX), 69 (68 LXX) in the earliest Christian liturgy could only have contributed to the sense that Jesus' death belonged in a meaningful way to the great story of Israel.[188]

Social memory theory cannot solve the quandary of a historical date for Jesus's death[189]—Bond points to often "how unreliable and fragile human recollection can be"[190]—but when applied to the Markan and Johannine passion narratives, Bond shows how the "collective theological and symbolic elaborations" embedded in early Christian traditions relate to the broader historical situation of Jesus's death around the general time of Passover.[191]

Summary

Though it is still a fledgling approach, social memory theory has been employed in a variety of ways by New Testament scholars, primarily in Jesus studies and Gospels scholarship.[192] From the theoretical musings of Kirk and Schwartz to the concrete applications and arguments set forth by Le Donne, Rodríguez, Keith, and others, memory scholars have quickly made social memory theory a viable approach for New Testament scholarship. It is not a method in and of itself, but it offers an alternative understanding for the task of the historian, highlights contextual frameworks (historical, social, literary, political, etc.) and media dynamics that undergird the transmission of tradition, and pairs with other historical, literary, and social scientific methodologies and criticisms to yield insights into the active role that early tradents played in constructing and

---

188. Bond, "Dating the Death of Jesus," 472.

189. Bond does not argue that social memory offers a pathway to a recoverable, "reliable" portrait of the historical Jesus; rather, she remains cautious of the outcome of utilizing the insights of memory theory: "The Gospels reflect the *impact* Jesus made on his earliest followers, *and to a large extent this impact is the historical Jesus, or as close as we are ever likely to get to him*. While we may be able to disentangle some of the clearly later elements in the Gospels (post-Easter theology, pastoral concerns reflecting the later church and so on), we will never be able to present an uninterpreted Jesus, completely cut free from the hopes and dreams of those who followed him" (Bond, *Historical Jesus*, 52, emphasis added).

190. Bond, *Historical Jesus*, 52.

191. Bond, "Dating the Death of Jesus," 475.

192. An important instance of social memory theory's application outside of these areas of study is Benjamin White's research on Paul. See White, *Remembering Paul*.

reconstructing the past. This survey displays the work of scholars who are amenable to and steeped in memory theory, but these scholars represent only a small fragment of Gospels and Jesus studies undertaken in the past two decades. Thus, the question remains: how has social memory theory been received by the wider audience of New Testament scholars?

The Resistance to Social Memory Theory in New Testament Studies: Three Case Studies

The previous survey of scholars utilizing memory theory demonstrates a positive trend toward its implementation to Gospel studies or Jesus studies. However, not all scholars have offered the theory or its application a warm reception. In particular, this section focuses on several critiques of memory theory and touchpoints where memory theorists have offered clarification, correction, and counsel. The section opens with Paul Foster's critique of the ways in which memory, orality, and the Gospel of John factor into historical Jesus studies. It then transitions to Zeba Crook's critical review of scholars who treat memory as "reliable" and Anthony Le Donne's response. Finally, the section concludes with F. Gerald Downing's reaction to Chris Keith's methodological considerations for historical Jesus research and Keith's response.

Paul Foster and the "Dead-end" View of Memory Theory[193]

Paul Foster offered one of the earliest assessments of memory theory in Jesus studies, arguing that memory theory, orality studies, and conversations about the historicity of the Gospel of John are "dead-ends" for historical Jesus research. In his comments on memory theory, Foster "questions the applicability" that memory theory has to historical Jesus studies, arguing that the application of memory theory to New Testament studies is based on "outmoded and largely flawed" models from other disciplines.[194] He claims that the work of memory theorists, which he

193. Foster, "Memory, Orality, and the Fourth Gospel," 191–227.

194. Foster, "Memory, Orality, and the Fourth Gospel," 226. It is important to note that Foster bases this assessment on the work of Bauckham and Allison; he skims through the work of Kirk and Thatcher and does not engage with Le Donne, Rodríguez, or Keith. In other words, he makes a broad claim about the applicability of memory by only examining a very narrow (and not fully representative) exhibition of memory theory in New Testament studies. Though they too vacillate between pointing out

remarks is stuck in the theoretical domain, "laud[s] memory as a breakthrough that allows reliable access to the historical Jesus . . . with little attempt to show how the category of memory actually allows for specific traditions to be traced back to the Jesus of history."[195] Foster instead lauds the systematic approaches of the early form-critics without addressing the significant critiques that memory theorists, even in the "theoretical domain," lodged at form-critical assumptions. He appears aware that his criticism of postmodern historiographical approaches[196] (including memory and orality studies) in effect doubles-down on an argument for

---

shortcomings of social memory theory and pinpointing weaknesses in Foster's argument, Stanley Porter and Hughston T. Ong later point out, "Foster is obviously painting the supposed findings of social-memory theory with a broad brush, one that encompasses all of its various dimensions and in which it is always found wanting" (Porter and Ong, "Memory, Orality, and the Fourth Gospel," 150–51).

195. Foster, "Memory, Orality, and the Fourth Gospel," 198. Again, Foster has not actually engaged *applications* of memory theory. Rather than the field being stuck in the "theoretical domain," it is his assessment of the field that is limited. Furthermore, he acknowledges that social memory theorists *outside the discipline* make no special claim to "implicit access to the objective reality of past events," but his characterization of the field based on the works of Bauckham and Allison misrepresents scholars like Rodríguez and Keith who bring those same insights *within the field* as well. Foster, "Memory, Orality, and the Fourth Gospel," 197.

196. Foster portrays the task of social memory theory as likened to early form criticism: "Either view of social memory as articulated by professional academics in the area of memory studies has a striking similarity to the perspectives of the early form critics. That is, any underlying historical connections have either been subsumed or heavily transformed to serve contemporary community needs. Thus the reshaping of traditions functions to create a social memory that addresses community concerns, and the task of reconstructing the historical reality behind these reformulated memories may be unachievable due to the degree of mutation that past events have undergone in the service of contemporary needs" (Foster, "Memory, Orality, and the Fourth Gospel," 197). What Foster fails to point out, however, is the difference in historiographical *perspective*; that is, the form-critics and questers who borrowed their insights and methodologies to develop the criteria approach believed they could divorce pericopae from their contexts, hypothesize its formation "behind the text," and thus have access to "authentic," uninterpreted raw historical data. On the contrary, social memory theorists recognize that the tradition is interpreted from its instantiation, that there is no process by which to strip any semblance of an "authentic" tradition from accreted layers of later interpretation, and that the tasks of such scholars are to (1) explain how and why the tradition we have continued to remain salient and transmissible for successive generations under changing social frameworks and differing media dynamics, and (2) hypothesize responsibly and make arguments for historical situations that take into consideration the social, literary, and historical contexts that might account for the tradition as we have it. In this way, social memory theory is useful in examining both the "presents" of the traditions we have as well as their reconstructed "pasts".

the value and necessity of form- and redaction-critical approaches.[197] Simply put, Foster's problems with memory theory in Jesus studies, at least as represented by the works of Bauckham and Allison, are: (a) its overly positivistic claims are too far detached from the cautious implications shown in other disciplines, (b) its results are too reminiscent of the form-critical *Sitz im leben*, and (c) it "[has] not been shown to add anything to the interpretative task."[198] Though he makes the claim in reference to Thatcher's work on the Gospel of John, Foster's general position on memory theory seems to be that "perhaps it better falls into the category of tracing the early reception history of written traditions in one specific social setting of the Jesus movement."[199]

Zeba Crook and Anthony Le Donne

Shortly after being declared a "dead-end," further conversation about the role of memory theory in historical Jesus research played out in the *Journal for the Study of the Historical Jesus* between Zeba Crook and Anthony Le Donne. Crook critiques what he perceived as a growing consensus in New Testament scholarship: the use of memory to buttress the "reliability" of gospels materials. Crook argues the approaches of scholars such as Bauckham, Keener, and McIver engender an "emerging sense of optimism concerning the inherent reliability of the Gospels as collective memory" that is simply undue when considering "the more troubling implications of memory theory, including memory distortion."[200] Pointing to the work of Hobsbawm and Ranger on invented tradition, as well as instances of "manufactured memories" like the legends about Ned Ludd during the Luddite rebellion and the Satanic ritual abuse cases reported in the 1980s, Crook pushes back against the perceived "consensus" by arguing that collective memory is susceptible to transmitting such manufactured memories. The presence and commonplace nature of such examples of manufactured memories, Crook says, raises an epistemological

---

197. "Perhaps one may critique this discussion as an ossified defence of form- and redaction-criticism. That was not the intention although it may be the outcome, since by implication this discussion suggests that *such methods, perhaps modified, are still the most appropriate tools for historical Jesus research*, and indeed that they are not fossilized" (Foster, "Memory, Orality, and the Fourth Gospel," 227, emphasis added).

198. Foster, "Memory, Orality, and the Fourth Gospel," 202.

199. Foster, "Memory, Orality, and the Fourth Gospel," 200.

200. Crook, "Collective Memory Distortion," 61–62.

quandary for the historian: "how is one to distinguish real memories from manufactured memories, when those who hold both 'memories' might not be able to recognize the difference between them?"[201] Crook returns to this point again when wrapping up his study:

> My point is most certainly not to argue stridently that collective memory is inherently unreliable. That would be unreasonable. My point is that it is equally unreasonable to suggest that the Gospels are to be trusted because they involve collective remembering, and collective memory is trustworthy. A more nuanced view would maintain . . . that memory can be reliable, but that it can also be profoundly unreliable and creative, accidentally and deliberately . . . But far more serious, as far as the historian is concerned, is that it is exceedingly difficult to distinguish between real and manufactured memory, that is memory which goes back to an actual past event and memory that does not.[202]

Crook believes the adoption and application of memory theory by the cadre of scholars he mentions is overly optimistic and does not supply the historical reliability of gospel materials. In other words, "collective memory theory . . . does not provide shelter in the reliability wars."[203]

Le Donne's response immediately critiques Crook's work for its "injudicious selectivity," its emphasis on only a small handful of Jesus scholars (Bauckham, Keener, McIver, Allison, Dunn, and Le Donne's popular introduction) and its failure to cite or engage with key voices in the conversation like Schröter, Kirk, Schwartz, Rodríguez, Keith, or even Le Donne's full-length treatment of memory and historiography (*The Historiographical Jesus*).[204] Le Donne then takes issue with Crook's misrepresentation of both the current state of memory in Jesus research—that is, Crook's overlooking "biblical scholars that emphasize the creativity, fluidity, and 'presentist' utility of memory"—as well as his over-simplification of the current state of memory theory.[205] Le Donne offers a corrective view of contemporary memory research as a spectrum between the "constructionist"/"presentist" approach and the "continuity perspective" that emphasizes a more nuanced relationship between the past-present nexus, and he plots a variety of NT scholars along this spectrum, all of

---

201. Crook, "Collective Memory Distortion," 66.
202. Crook, "Collective Memory Distortion," 75.
203. Crook, "Collective Memory Distortion," 76.
204. Le Donne, "Problem of Selectivity," 80–82.
205. Le Donne, "Problem of Selectivity," 83.

whom Crook conveniently overlooks in order to make the claim of an "emerging consensus."[206] Le Donne sums up Crook's missteps with a simple, resounding rebuttal: "We are nowhere near an 'emerging consensus' and are not in any danger of a 'full-blown consensus.'"[207] After this, Le Donne systematically rebuts Crook's other claims:

1. that the Gospel of John is ignored in memory studies: here, Le Donne points to the works of Tom Thatcher and the initial Kirk and Thatcher volume;[208]

2. that the works of Allison, McIver, and Le Donne display an "optimistic" view of the gospels's reliability: Le Donne cites a far more nuanced picture of Allison's work, contextualizes the work done by McIver, and offers a sweeping defense of his own methods to argue that Crook has misrepresented these three scholars in both summary and association;[209]

3. that the examples of the Luddite movement and Satanic ritual abuse claims display cases of manufactured memory: Le Donne takes up the example of the Luddites and points out how counter-memory—as demonstrated by historians who argue against the "historical Ned Ludd"—can be an important corrective to widespread cases of "manufactured memory";[210] and finally,

4. that no memory theorist discusses memory as a telescope: Le Donne points to the analogy used by Paul Ricœur.[211]

Le Donne's critique is detailed and sweeping, but the *JSHJ* offers Crook the last word, which he uses to once again double down on "the heart of my article": the presence of manufactured memories and what that means for historians who engage with memory theory.[212] Crook then points to gospel traditions that may demonstrate this concern, spending considerable time on Matt 27:24–25. After pointing out its troubling history of interpretation, Crook declares this tradition "a wholly manufactured memory, a memory of an event in the life of Jesus that does not

---

206. Le Donne, "Problem of Selectivity," 83–85.
207. Le Donne, "Problem of Selectivity," 87.
208. Le Donne, "Problem of Selectivity," 88–90.
209. Le Donne, "Problem of Selectivity," 90–94.
210. Le Donne, "Problem of Selectivity," 95–96.
211. Le Donne, "Problem of Selectivity," 96–97.
212. Crook, "Gratitude and Comments," 98–105.

derive from an historical event. And yet, it came to be a critical part of Christian collective memory. There is no qualitative difference between this memory and other Matthean memories that could well be more historical (e.g., Jesus' delivery of the Parable of the Mustard Seed)."[213] How Crook has made the jump from a memory to a *manufactured* memory is unclear, and perhaps continues to speak to Le Donne's critique that Crook would benefit from conversation with other NT scholars in the "presentist" camp. Crook follows Luz's argument that this pericope is a Matthean redaction rather than pre-Matthean oral tradition and reinforces this by pointing out Matthean style and vocabulary. Still, this excursus in source and redaction criticism focuses so much on the "what"—whether the pericope did or did not happen in the past[214]—that it misses the chance to explore why this tradition was remembered and how it came to be transmitted and passed on. If the Matthean redactor is manufacturing tradition here, why would the audience—especially an audience aware of the Jesus tradition and experienced with other performances and instantiations—be persuaded that this creative addition either (a) suits their needs, or (b) fits into their historical or traditional worldview? Similarly, how does this pericope fit into the needs or the worldview of the tradent?[215] Crook jettisons these questions and once again raises the point that manufactured and historical memories are nearly indistinguishable. However, if New Testament scholarship is to sufficiently treat scriptures that have been used to marginalize or, worse, justify the physical harm and genocide of communities throughout history, it should not settle for a conclusion that pinpoints where a strain of memory or tradition fits on a scale of "reliable" to "manufactured." Rather, it becomes paramount to explore the social, cultural, historical, and media frameworks that led to the continued transmission of such traditions and can impact, inform,

---

213. Crook, "Gratitude and Comments," 104.

214. Crook's conclusion still does not explain why, even if a Matthean redaction, the event did not happen. This is not to suggest that Pilate's handwashing and the crowd's cry were events that happened in the past, but merely that Crook jumps to the conclusion that this memory is manufactured rather than proving so by discussing the tradition in the same vein or with the same theoretical frameworks in mind that other memory theorists like Le Donne, Rodríguez, or Keith have done with other Jesus traditions.

215. Here I use the more media-neutral term "tradent" as it can encompass any (or all) of the different roles and dynamic ranges of a compiler, scribal copyist, editor, author, or performer.

and influence treatments in the future to be more attentive to the changed or changing nature of such frameworks.

F. Gerald Downing and Chris Keith

Writing in response to Chris Keith's *JSNT* article, "The Narratives of the Gospels," F. Gerald Downing critiques Keith's dichotomy of two "models" of historical Jesus scholarship. In Keith's initial article, he contrasts form-critical ("first model") and memory approaches ("second model") to the historical Jesus, stating:

> At the conceptual center of the first model is a past reality that is assumed to be *attainable*. Under this model, the historian attempts to get "behind" early Christian interpretations of Jesus. At the conceptual center of the second model are the narratives of the gospels, which are understood to be receptions—in all varieties of accuracy and inaccuracy—of a past reality that is assumed to be *unattainable*. Under this model, the historian may posit the historical Jesus as a by-product of attempts to explain why early Christians came to interpret Jesus in the manners that they did.[216]

Keith examines both "current" (2010s) and "prior" (1950s–1960s) debates about the value of form criticism and its methodological aims, arguing the criteria of authenticity flow directly from form criticism's foundational understanding of both the nature of the Jesus tradition and how it was transmitted.[217] Keith contrasts this approach with social memory theory, which "views the historian's task as proposing a historical narrative that explains how early Christians came to conceptualize Jesus in the ways that they did and generates theories of the historical Jesus on the basis of that process."[218] Keith argues the major epistemological differences between these models can be found in the fact that form critics view the tradition as composed of *individual* units (forms) that can be atomized and separated from their contextual frameworks (i.e., the Gospel narratives) to reach uninterpreted ("authentic") historical facts behind the tradition, whereas memory approaches see the tradition as interpreted from its first transmissions and instead offer historical hypotheses of who

---

216. Keith, "Narratives of the Gospels," 427, emphasis added.
217. Keith, "Narratives of the Gospels," 437–40.
218. Keith, "Narratives of the Gospels," 450.

the historical Jesus was on the basis of how and why the tradition (i.e., the Gospel narratives as early Christian interpretations) is as it stands. Unsurprisingly, Keith finds these models incompatible and opts for the memory approach and its historiographical methodologies as a tenable way forward in future historical Jesus studies.[219] Keith defends memory approaches and their interest in early Christian interpretation by arguing that "accounting for early Christian interpretations of Jesus sensibly does not mean ... conflating those interpretations with the historical Jesus. It means that scholarly conclusions about the historical Jesus and (in)accuracy of the gospels must arise out of this larger process of constructing how early Christianity came to be in light of our current knowledge about it."[220] Downing, in response, seems to take issue with Keith's conclusion that the memory model is the only "feasible" approach to historical Jesus research, especially when compared with the form-critical criteria of authenticity.[221] The continued use of the criteria of authenticity is not a hang-up for Downing, which also puts him at odds with Keith's rejection of the criteria.[222] Furthermore, Downing criticizes the notion that only one of the models is portrayed as going "behind" the gospel texts. Rather, Downing points to a number of interpretive questions—gospel dependency/literary relationship, historical setting, genre, provenance, culture and composition of audience—in which "any interpretative reconstruction has to 'go behind' [the text], however tentatively, and hypothetically, on these issues."[223] On this basis, Downing pushes forward a much more relative approach to Jesus research, arguing that "all such attempts start equal, *and many may be as theoretically 'feasible,' 'plausible' as each other*

---

219. "What [these models] seek and how they seek it do not align; they are doing something different" (Keith, "Narratives of the Gospels," 449).

220. Keith, "Narratives of the Gospels," 444.

221. Downing also displays discomfort with the notion of "knowledge" about the historical Jesus *or* the historical early Church: "Any result claiming current 'knowledge'—knowledge in any strong sense—of the historical early church (with its tradition[s]) is, I suggest, as unobtainable as any firm knowledge of the historical Jesus, not least if not only because the uncertainties intertwine" (Downing, "Feasible Researches," 53). For his part, Keith never claims any sort of certainty, but rather clarifies that he is interested in "the ever-evolving, contingent, and therefore imperfect, knowledge of the past within which all historians must work in order to offer their hypotheses" (Keith, "Yes and No," 63).

222. "The old criteria for inclusion and exclusion—embarrassment, coherence, plausibility—may well still be deployed, if a scholar thinks fit and explains how" (Downing, "Feasible Researches," 58).

223. Downing, "Feasible Researches," 56–57.

... They are all improvable hypotheses, whose overall plausibility will be varyingly appraised by different critical readers."[224]

Keith offers an additional rebuttal to Downing to defend his original article as well as point to missteps in Downing's response. Downing's discomfort with Keith's work stemmed from seeing a dichotomy between two models, so it is perhaps ironic that Keith's response begins by addressing additional dichotomies in Downing's work:

> Are scholars paralyzed by their utter lack of knowledge and lack of agreement or can they gain some understanding by going "behind" the text? Does Downing intend to argue that knowledge of Jesus or the early church is unobtainable or is obtainable back there "behind" the text? Stated otherwise, does he fault me for believing we can know something about the historical Jesus or fault me for rejecting the idea that we must dig "beneath" the text to know it?[225]

Turning back toward Downing's central thesis, Keith restates the centrality of "authenticity" in the scholarship from the 1950s and 1960s, why "authenticity" and "certainty" are separate,[226] and further clarifies his objection to the criteria of authenticity.[227] Keith clarifies his definition of

---

224. Downing, "Feasible Researches," 58, emphasis added.

225. Keith, "Yes and No," 64. These questions attempt to portray an unevenness to Downing's thesis, but Keith makes an additional important point about both the content and context(s) of Downing's remarks, that is, that Downing's critiques are often self-serving "opportunities to tally where he has been accepted, rejected or overlooked by other scholars" (Keith, "Yes and No," 63n1).

226. "'Authenticity' in the arguments of the scholars who developed the criteria of authenticity as a formal methodology refers not to the status of the scholar (confident regarding their judgments), but to the status of the tradition (unreflective of early Christian interpretive frameworks that otherwise taint the tradition)" (Keith, "Yes and No," 65).

227. In particular, Keith again argues the form-critical approach sought individual *uninterpreted* "Jesus tradition that had been recovered *out of* the interpretive frameworks of the written gospels" (Keith, "Yes and No," 65, emphasis original). This task is incompatible with the insights of postmodern historiography and social memory theory that Keith points out. The recognition that there are both oral interpretive frameworks that exist before the text and social interpretive frameworks that exist from the moment an event in the past is perceived and transmitted corrects the assumption that scholars can get back to an uninterpreted decontextualized tradition. There is no such thing as uninterpreted tradition, since tradition itself is a vehicle with particular frameworks and contexts. Though Downing fronts the uncertainty of scholarly knowledge due to the limitations of our source material, his patent acceptance of the criteria and their use creates a dissonance that Keith urges him to consider: "He needs to explain either (a) how the concept of an uninterpreted historical Jesus or uninterpreted Jesus tradition

"tradition" before highlighting how Downing's understanding of tradition is almost identical to the form-critical approach. Keith also argues that Downing's localization of the tradition "behind," "underneath," or "beyond" the text misses the important point that *the text is the tradition*, or is at least part of it.[228] Keith also points to important ways that Downing's work misconstrues what "going behind the text" is; in Keith's estimation, much of what Downing discusses could be considered "alongside" the gospel texts or, more simply, just "other 'texts,' whether manuscripts, monuments, rituals, customs, or other expressions of identity," all of which require interpretation and argument.[229] Finally, and most importantly for this study, Keith calls out Downing's misrepresentation of (social) memory theory as concerned with the past for the sake of preserving the past. Rather, as Keith clarifies, "social, cultural and collective memory theories are categorically not concerned with the *preservation* of the past as such; they are concerned with the *presentation* of the past in the present, whether that is the actual past, a fabricated past or something in between."[230] Keith summarizes his position and the task of social memory theory once again as "account[ing] for early Christian interpretations with theories that are necessarily contingent and will find various levels of agreement and disagreement among" other scholars.[231] Unlike Crook, Downing's critique displays a failure to fully engage memory theory and instead focuses on categorical knowledge—how can scholars know *anything* about the/a Jesus tradition?—and Keith's response in turn answers this question with the theoretical concepts at the core of social memory theory: the discarding of "authenticity," the process of tradition transmission, and the historical hypothesizing for *how* and *why* a tradition exists in the state(s) in which it (currently) exists.

---

fits within his proposal, and particularly the part of his proposal where he claims that such 'firm knowledge' of Jesus is not available to the scholar, or (b) how a methodology whose logic and utility assumes that there is such tradition can be repurposed for other means."

228. Keith, "Yes and No," 67–69.
229. Keith, "Yes and No," 69.
230. Keith, "Yes and No," 66, emphasis original.
231. Keith, "Yes and No," 71.

Summary

Social memory theory has been an easy target for those who remain suspect of memory as an analytical category in Jesus and Gospels research.[232] However, a few common threads appear from the critiques offered above. First, social memory theory as a whole is often stereotyped or misrepresented based on a limited scope of scholarship that typically includes Bauckham's work on eyewitness testimony. Second, and related to the first point, the insights of social memory theory, and particularly its historiographical insights, are not fully recognized within New Testament scholarship. In other words, many critiques point to a dichotomy where memory theory outside the discipline is far more tentative about any claims to historical knowledge, while memory studies within Jesus studies is often portrayed as a tool in which to bolster the "reliability" of certain Jesus traditions. This point of criticism misses the significant theoretical work and applications done by scholars like Le Donne, Rodríguez, Keith, Huebenthal, and Bond. Finally, each critique circles around a similar underlying question: what exactly is it that social memory theory (and other memory theories) offers scholars of the New Testament or the historical Jesus? The previous critiques offer a negative picture of its potential; on the contrary, this chapter has attempted to highlight the ways in which social memory theory has already been used fruitfully to examine memory as an analytical tool in understanding the past. The final section attempts to tease out additional remarks and insights that make social memory theory a useful approach for future New Testament scholarship.

What Does Social Memory Theory Have to Offer Future New Testament Studies?

Though still relatively new in its application to Jesus and Gospel studies, there are several important insights from social memory theory that are currently guiding the present, and can continue to guide the future, of New Testament studies.

First, there is no single "standard" memory approach. Even in attempting to produce an (inherently selective) overview of various

---

232. Kirk recently published a twenty-year retrospective that responds to and engages more recent treatments of memory theory in New Testament studies. See Kirk, "Ehrman, Bauckham, and Bird," 88–114.

memory approaches, this chapter's survey just scratches the surface of the broader field of memory scholarship or its application to New Testament studies. Just as Olick and Robbins pointed out the disjointed state of memory studies as a discipline, it is also the case that there is no unified "memory criticism" in New Testament studies. Instead, scholars who purport to take a memory approach typically (a) base their work in the sociological, psychological, and historical grounding of a host of scholars (Halbwachs, Assmann, Schwartz, Ricœur, Schudson, Schacter, Fentress and Wickham, Hobsbawm and Ranger, Kammen, etc.); (b) appeal to a variety of methods (historical-critical, social scientific, source, literary, narrative, and orality/media criticism); and (c) argue and hypothesize conclusions on different "sides" of the text, positing both historical situations and historical receptions of the past. Jeffrey Olick complicates this further by describing collective memory as "far from monolithic" and as "a highly complex process, involving numerous different people, practices, materials, and themes."[233] For Olick,

> collective memory really refers to a wide variety of mnemonic products and practices, often quite different from one another. The former (products) include stories, rituals, books, statues, presentations, speeches, images, pictures, records, historical studies, surveys, etc.; the latter (practices) include reminiscence, recall, representation, commemoration, celebration, regret, renunciation, disavowal, denial, rationalization, excuse, acknowledgment, and many others. Mnemonic practices—though occurring in an infinity of contexts and through a shifting multiplicity of media—are always simultaneously individual and social. And no matter how concrete mnemonic products may be, they gain their reality only by being used, interpreted, and reproduced or changed.[234]

In other words, there are a variety of ways to approach memory and a variety of ways in which to understand memory as a subject or an object of study.

Second, social memory theory offers a cautious historiographical approach that is self-aware of its limitations. Unlike the dominant trend in the previous century of Jesus studies, memory theorists recognize there is no understanding of Jesus—historical or remembered—without the movement of early believers who talked about him and the institutions

---

233. Olick, "Products, Processes, and Practices," 12.
234. Olick, "Products, Processes, and Practices," 12.

that followed. This insight about the nature of the Jesus tradition's transmission is not restricted to memory approaches,[235] but the epistemological understanding of distortion in memory (i.e., that there is no such thing as "undistorted" memory) and interpretation in tradition (i.e., that there is no such thing as an "uninterpreted" tradition) demonstrate points of departure in the construction of the historical Jesus between memory theorists and those continuing to employ the criteria of authenticity.[236]

Third, and related to the previous point, social memory theory still tells us *something*. Whether it is employed as a means of postulating a historical situation that accounts for the expression of the tradition (the past) or examining the social—and political, cultural, historical, and so forth—frameworks of the tradents and how they shaped the tradition (the present), social memory theory is actively engaged in historical, sociological, literary, and media methodologies to help us understand the past. Social memory theory aids New Testament scholarship in reckoning with and explaining how and why Jesus tradition was transmitted in narratological (both oral and written) forms by tradents who found, articulated, and reshaped collective identity and meaning.[237]

Fourth, memory approaches remind scholars that the Jesus tradition—as a narratological commemorative historical artifact—is steeped in cultural memory. As Richard Horsley states,

> The principal settings—Galilee, Judea, Jerusalem, the Temple—are sites laden with and bearers of Israelite cultural memory, and the principal characters come into conflict over customs, rituals, festivals, and religious and economic practices central to Israelite

---

235. For Kähler's expression of this point, see footnote 23. Morna Hooker also states this point: "All [Jesus tradition] comes to us *via* the Church, and is likely to have been coloured by the beliefs of those who have handed it on" (Hooker, "On Using the Wrong Tool," 580).

236. "All memory is, at one level or another, in continuity with the interpretive frameworks of the present; else it would be forgotten. This furthermore means that there is no way to 'get behind' those interpretive frameworks. We may speculate about what could reside behind them, even speculate with strong conviction, but we cannot access it. In short, if Halbwachs, Assmann and others are correct about the nature of 'memory' (whether historically accurate or inaccurate), both the end goal of 'authentic' tradition and the means of attaining it in the post-Bultmannians' model are methodologically and epistemologically impossible" (Keith, "Narratives of the Gospels," 442).

237. Olick asks further questions, such as, "How are representations of and activities concerning the past organized socially and culturally? When and why do they change? How can we begin to untangle the diverse processes, products, and practices through which societies confront and represent aspects of their pasts?" (Olick, "Products, Processes, and Practices," 13).

memory. Jesus is represented as acting out roles reminiscent of some of the prime heroes in Israel's history. The past that the Gospels are appropriating for purposes of present community concerns is that of Israel as well as Jesus' ministry. The latter is embedded in the former and cannot be separated from it.[238]

Put succinctly, "Jesus tradition . . . cannot possibly be understood except as rooted in Israelite social memory."[239]

Finally, we should not forget that the texts, as "products" of collective memory, carried meaning for their respective commemorative communities. As Huebenthal notes, the "Jesus-memory" approach and the "externalization of collective memory" approach differ over where they place the emphasis: either on the object of memory (the group's past) or the subject of memory (the identity-formation taking place in the group's present). An important undercurrent of memory theory, especially as articulated by Keith, is to offer an explanation for *how* the Jesus tradition held the memories it did. In other words, scholars should not be afraid to hypothesize explanations for why the texts and traditions, especially those that contrast or conflict, exist in the manners in which they do. Nonetheless, Huebenthal's approach reminds scholars that the task can be carried forward to ask about the communities of memory and *what* the texts and traditions mean to these communities.[240]

Memory theory does not have a monopoly on the future of Jesus or Gospels studies—as Keith argues, it is not *the* way forward, but only *a* way forward[241]—but it offers helpful insights, questions stale assumptions, and interacts with interrelated disciplines in a way that sets it up to be a prime force in New Testament scholarship of the future. Although it does not operate under a rigid methodology or under a set of criteria, its historiographical concerns and attentiveness to tradition

238. Horsley, "Prophet Like Moses and Elijah," 167.

239. Horsley, "Prominent Patterns in the Social Memory of Jesus and Friends," in Kirk and Thatcher, eds., *Memory, Tradition, and Text*, 70.

240. Huebenthal characterizes the "externalization of collective memory" approach as "interested in a reasonable and plausible access to the present of those who express themselves in the foundational texts of the New Testament . . . [it] has worked particularly in investigating early Christian identity constructions (and their development) on the basis of New Testament and early Christian texts when they are read as artifacts or externalizations of *collective memories*. For the later generations of Christian faithful, these texts gradually become part of their *cultural memory* and thus the predetermined counterpart of their own process of identity construction" (Huebenthal, *Reading Mark's Gospel*, 542).

241. Keith, "Narratives of the Gospels," 442.

and reception make it a dynamic and flexible approach for scholars from a variety of disciplines and sub-disciplines. Finally, its concern with frameworks and larger patterns of cultural memory allows it to integrate seamlessly with many questions at the heart of New Testament studies. In the next chapter, I investigate these frameworks by turning toward the Jerusalem temple and the complex ways in which various communities identified with the temple prior to and in the immediate aftermath of its destruction in 70 CE.

3

Jewish Attitudes Toward the Jerusalem Temple in the Second Temple Period

(540 BCE–70 CE)

> Jews lived in many different geographical locations, in social conditions which varied over time, and at differing social levels. We can expect to find an almost infinite variety in the ways they reacted to their variant milieux . . . the range and diversity of the historical evidence certainly indicate that no normative unity can be assumed.
> —John M. G. Barclay[1]

THE WORK OF COLLECTIVE memory theorists proceeds from the insight that memory is constructed upon particular frameworks. These frameworks are crucial to the formation and presentation of identity. Therefore, to further understand how and why a memory is transmitted and used by different groups, it is necessary to investigate the frameworks within which it develops. In this chapter, I will investigate the social, political, historical, literary, and cultural contexts that envelop the Jerusalem temple in the Second Temple period (540 BCE–70 CE). First,

1. Barclay, *Jews in the Mediterranean Diaspora*, 3–4.

I will examine the ways in which New Testament scholarship has constructed Jewish identity in the Second Temple period and highlight how the Jerusalem temple is a component of this identity.[2] Next, I will look at the history of the Second Temple to understand its place as a framework of Jewish cultural memory. Here we will find that while the temple was a dominant force throughout the period, different Jewish communities resisted, rejected, reconstructed, and reinterpreted the Jerusalem temple in different ways. Finally, I will review the works of Jacob Neusner, Adela Yarbro Collins, and Philip Church, who each examine a matrix of potential attitudes toward the Jerusalem temple by surveying literary and documentary evidence. These attitudes aid in answering a simple question: How did Jews in the late Second Temple period relate to the Jerusalem temple? The answers to this question serve as the underlying frameworks that make any memory of the Jerusalem temple in and after the Second Temple period possible.

Paradigms of Second Temple Judaism and Jewish Identity: Contemporary New Testament Scholarship

Much of this chapter is concerned about one particular feature of Jewish identity—the Jerusalem temple—but a number of other factors play important roles in establishing group identity on both local and global levels. The interaction of many practices, customs, thought patterns, and beliefs together result in differing expressions of Judaism in the Second Temple period. Defining what it meant to be "Jewish" or who is in view when we talk about Second Temple Judaism is complex due to the variety of cultural, ethnic, and religious considerations. The following discussion of paradigms of Second Temple Judaism draws on the work done in the latter half of the twentieth century to discuss the Judaism(s) of the Second Temple period in complex, nuanced ways.

---

2. Although my larger study is focused on early Christian memory of the audiences and tradents of the Jesus tradition, the Jerusalem temple's destruction in 70 CE puts a limited window of overlap between its standing and the earliest Christian communities. Therefore, this chapter explores Jewish identity/identities in the Second Temple period as an important analog to how the temple was understood and treated during the time in which it stood as an important physical landmark for those in Palestine and throughout the diaspora world. The relationship between Judaism and earliest Christianity is complex, but there exists considerable continuity between the two that allow for attitudes and customs predating the first century CE to be seen as relevant frameworks for early Christian memory.

Martin Hengel, E. P. Sanders, and Competing Conceptions of Palestinian Judaism

Martin Hengel noticed a trend in history-of-religions scholarship: many (German) New Testament scholars in the late-nineteenth and early-twentieth centuries drew a stark contrast between Judaism and Hellenism, treating the two as distinct entities. Hengel highlights this trend in the way in which Judaism was portrayed; for instance, the Judaism practiced in the diaspora—or at least its literary remains—was often referred to as "syncretistic," whereas Palestinian Judaism was viewed as "traditional," unaffected by Hellenism.[3] Hengel suggests this divide fails to assess how deep-rooted and diverse Hellenistic culture was in antiquity, as if "the land of 'Palestine,' or an essential part of it, 'Jewish Palestine,' was hardly influenced, if at all, by 'Hellenism.'"[4] Hengel argues such a view of Palestinian Judaism is reductive. Greek, as the defining language of Hellenism, was the *lingua franca* in and around Palestine since the third century BCE.[5] Greek culture permeated daily life: Greek names

---

3. "One fundamental presupposition of historical work on the New Testament which seems to be taken for granted is the differentiation, in terms of tradition, between 'Judaism' on the one hand and 'Hellenism' on the other. Distinctions are made between 'Jewish apocalyptic' and 'Hellenistic mysticism', between the 'Jewish, rabbinic tradition' and 'Hellenistic, oriental gnosticism', between 'Palestinian' and 'Hellenistic' Judaism, between a 'Palestinian' and a 'Hellenistic' community" (Hengel, *Judaism and Hellenism*, 1:1). Hengel reacts strongly to this trend particularly because he believed it reflected contemporary theological biases: "Because of its multiplicity and complexity the process [of Hellenism] cannot be described by a single term in the religious sphere, for example by the term 'syncretism' which is so popular a watchword among Protestant theologians" (Hengel, *Hellenization*, 1).

4. Hengel also notes that, at least geographically, a Palestine completely devoid of Hellenistic influence would be an anomaly "in complete contrast to the adjacent areas of Phoenicia, Nabataean Arabia, Syria or Egypt" (Hengel, *Hellenization*, 5).

5. "From the middle of the third century BC we can trace the influence of Greek language and culture even in Judaea" (Hengel, *Judaism and Hellenism*, 1:248). While Greek culture spread dominantly across local cultures during the Hellenistic period, Greek and ancient Near Eastern cultures mutually influenced each other in earlier antiquity. Walter Burkert identifies particular points of Near Eastern influence on Greek, arguing, "Emanating from the Near East, in connection with military expansion and growing economic activities, a cultural continuum including literacy was created by the eighth century extending over the entire Mediterranean; it involved groups of Greeks who entered into extensive exchange with the high cultures of the Semitic East" (Burkert, *Orientalizing Revolution*, 128). Burkert offers several examples of Near Eastern influence—migrating craftsmen, Phoenicia's impact on the Greek alphabet, the activity of seers and healers—but one of his most interesting arguments is that Near Eastern religious and cultic practice served as the catalyst for introducing "large altars for burnt offerings and above all the building of temples to serve as houses for divinities,

became popularized (see Jewish royals like Aristobulus and Alexander Jannaeus), coins were minted with Greek text, Greek loanwords appeared in Aramaic and Hebrew texts, and public inscriptions evidenced the presence of Greek in everyday material culture.[6] Jewish literature encountered challenges with the reception of Hellenism, which Hengel traces through the development of genres such as wisdom material (e.g., Ben Sira) and Jewish apocalyptic (e.g., 1 Enoch, Daniel).[7] Furthermore, the presentation of Judaism and Jews within the Greek world, which Hengel calls "the *interpretatio graeca*," changed in important ways during the Hellenistic period. For Hengel, gentile authors portrayed Jews as philosophers, and Jewish theology underwent universalization, rationalization, and syncretism into Greek forms.[8]

Rather than imagining Judaean life as a bastion of Israelite tradition unpenetrated by contemporary Hellenistic culture, Hengel urges scholars to consider the overarching effects of Hellenism in the land of Palestine.[9] Even when considering one of Israel's central traditions—the Torah—Hengel provocatively places "the controversy with Hellenism" as

---

represented by cult statues. There seems to be no Greek temple proper antedating the eighth century, the period of the impetus of eastern craftsmanship" (Burkert, *Orientalizing Revolution*, 20). Burkert points to Phoenician influence on the central religious architecture of Kommos (southern Crete) in the ninth century; the small shipping hub was no stranger to sailors stopping in for refuge, additional provisions, or offerings to deities, but a Phoenician shrine appears to have created a centralized sacred space for offerings. See Burkert, *Orientalizing Revolution*, 20–21.

6. Hengel, *Hellenization*, 8–11. A jar fragment with a Hebrew inscription from Sepphoris dating to the second century BCE may demonstrate the use of a Greek loanword (*epimeletes*); if so, it would provide further evidence of the interaction between Greek and Jewish life in Palestine during the Hasmonean period. See Nagy et al., *Sepphoris in Galilee*, 170. Additionally, two important inscriptions demonstrate the presence of Greek in everyday life in Jerusalem during the first century CE: the famous temple inscription that issued a warning to gentiles and a synagogue inscription founded by "Theodotus, son of Vettenus," demonstrating how even a priest (ἱερεὺς) and synagogue ruler (ἀρχισυνάγωγος) could carry Greek (and Latin) naming conventions. See Cotton et al., *Jerusalem*, 42–45, 53–56.

7. Hengel, *Judaism and Hellenism*, 1:250–52.

8. Hengel, *Judaism and Hellenism*, 1:255–67.

9. "Jewish Palestine was no hermetically sealed island in the sea of Hellenistic oriental syncretism" (Hengel, *Judaism and Hellenism*, 1:312). Hengel's emphasis on cultural convergence in Palestine is important and valid, even though his characterization of "oriental syncretism" inconveniently glosses over or disregards the complex spectrum of relationships that local cultures across the empire had with the spread of Hellenistic culture.

a focal point that "made the Torah the centre point of Judaism."[10] Hengel's work also highlights the diversity of reactions to and interactions with Hellenism within the land of Israel: "It is not possible to say that Palestinian Judaism . . . maintained a straight course through the Hellenistic period untouched by the alien civilization and completely faithful to the Old Testament tradition. Still less can it be claimed that it was completely permeated by the Hellenistic spirit and fell victim to syncretism, betraying its original task. The truth lies between the extremes."[11] For Hengel, then, once the connotations of Hellenistic influence have been removed and its place as a centuries-old cultural force is understood, "Palestinian Judaism can also be described as 'Hellenistic Judaism.'"[12]

Whereas Hengel entered the conversation to expand views on the relationship between Judaism and Hellenism, E. P. Sanders's work on Jewish identity began as a critique against those who viewed Paul outside his Jewish context. Sanders's penchant for drawing out the commonalities between various strata of Jewish practice and belief—his goal in investigating Paul and Palestinian Judaism—is emblematic of his scholarship. Sanders is perhaps best known for his use of "covenantal nomism," a pattern of Palestinian Jewish theology used to characterize undercurrents in the works of Paul, Rabbinic sources, Jewish pseudepigraphy, and the Dead Sea Scrolls. Sanders constructed covenantal nomism as a series of eight interrelated propositions:

---

10. Hengel continues, "There may have been hopeless disputes over the right interpretation of the law, but it was still the expression of the unity of the Jewish people, by which it was distinguished from all other peoples. At the same time, even in the Greek-educated circles of the [d]iaspora, the law gave a guarantee of religious and national cohesion, while its ethical monotheism provided a feeling of superiority over the Hellenistic cults" (Hengel, *Judaism and Hellenism*, 1:312).

11. Hengel, *Judaism and Hellenism*, 1:310.

12. Hengel, *Hellenization*, 53. Hengel discusses the pre-Hasmonean era as a period of "profound transformation" where the deterioration of the distinction between "Palestinian" and "Hellenistic" forms of Judaism begins, even if these categories are murky. Hengel is more forceful with his description of the Hellenistic-Roman period, where "the Judaism of the mother country must just as much be included under the heading 'Hellenistic Judaism' as that of the western [d]iaspora" based on the influence of both Greek culture and Hellenistic religious beliefs, such as "the expectation of a future realm of peace, the existence of heavenly hypostases and redeemer figures, angels, demons and spirits of the dead, the significance of astrology, manticism and magic, the forms of supernatural revelation of divine wisdom through dreams, visions, journeys through heaven and the underworld, ecstatic or inspired discourse or holy scriptures given by God" (Hengel, *Judaism and Hellenism*, 1:311–12).

The 'pattern' or 'structure' of covenantal nomism is this: (1) God has chosen Israel and (2) given the law. The law implies both (3) God's promise to maintain the election and (4) the requirement to obey. (5) God rewards obedience and punishes transgression. (6) The law provides for means of atonement, and atonement results in (7) maintenance or re-establishment of the covenantal relationship. (8) All those who are maintained in the covenant by obedience, atonement and God's mercy belong to the group which will be saved.[13]

Covenantal nomism is not an attempt to derive a unified systematic theology from his sources; Sanders rightly notes multiple points of departure and diversity of thought in his comparative study of Palestinian Jewish literature (ca. 200 BCE–200 CE). However, Sanders argues that throughout his sources, "there is agreement on the primacy of the covenant and its significance and on the need to obey the commandments. The means of atonement are not precisely identical, but there is agreement on the place of atonement within the total framework."[14] This agreement is central to Sanders's work: despite the differences among his sources, Sanders surmises that "there appears to have been more in common than just the name 'Jew.'"[15]

Sanders later grouped these commonalities into what he called "Common Judaism," or "what the priests and the people agreed on."[16] Drawing heavily from the works of Josephus, the Hebrew Bible, and occasionally Mishnaic material, Sanders described Common Judaism as consisting of a number of practices and beliefs: the observance of the Mosaic Law, contributions to tithes and taxes, celebration of annual festivals, and a shared theology. Most important for Palestinian Judaism, Sanders emphasizes the participation in temple worship, including a robust sacrificial system, as central to Common Judaism. In fact, Sanders suggests "most Jews regarded the service of the temple, including the requirements to make offerings and sacrifices, as sacred, and they respected the hereditary priesthood."[17] In addition, the temple service created a

13. Sanders, *Paul and Palestinian Judaism*, 422.
14. Sanders, *Paul and Palestinian Judaism*, 423.
15. Sanders, *Paul and Palestinian Judaism*, 423.
16. Sanders, *Judaism*, 69. Sanders again focuses on Palestinian Judaism but describes western diaspora Jews as also sharing in practices of common Judaism, specifically in participation of the temple tax. See Sanders, *Judaism*, 69n1.
17. Sanders, *Judaism*, 78–79. Sanders notes that this portrayal may rely too heavily on the positive bias of Josephus, Aristeas, and Philo—who discusses the "impoverishment

surge of industries for the people of Judaea and "directly or indirectly generated most of the city's business": masons and artisans crafted stone vessels, linens were processed and used to create priestly garments, and animal husbandry was required for the sacrificial system.[18] Drawing on Philo's account of the embassy to Caligula, Sanders even describes the temple as "the basic rallying point of Jewish loyalties."[19]

Unlike Hengel, Sanders gives little attention to Hellenism as an influential force. Instead, Sanders's depiction of Judaean life in Palestine argues that it was in direct opposition to Hellenistic culture.[20] For instance, Sanders regards the Torah as a central feature of Common Judaism and attributes this singlehandedly to the rejection of Hellenization without considering other factors.[21] Sanders argues from the tenets of Common Judaism and on the accounts of 1 and 2 Maccabees that "Jews obviously rejected a good deal of the common culture, and just as obviously they kept their own."[22]

---

of the consecrated class" (*Spec. Laws* 1.154) as a potential consequence of neglected temple worship—and points to the works of "the Qumran Sect" and the *Sibylline Oracles* as critiques against the priesthood or the temple institution. Still, Sanders concludes, "while we may grant that there were some radicals who opposed the temple service as such, it is more important to emphasize that most Jews—who believed the Bible, in which commandments about the temple figure very large—accepted the sacrificial system as a principal aspect of the true worship of God" (Sanders, *Judaism*, 80). Sanders even attributes a positive attitude to those in the diaspora, claiming "ancient authors indicate that most of the Jewish people supported all aspects of temple worship" (Sanders, *Judaism*, 77). By "ancient authors," Sanders is again referring to Philo, Josephus, the author of *The Letter of Aristeas*, and the Gospel of Luke. Though important, this cadre is hardly representative of all Jewish diaspora communities and their attitudes.

18. Sanders, *Judaism*, 206.

19. Sanders, *Judaism*, 238.

20. "One option for Israelite life—merger into the common Hellenistic culture—was decisively rejected" (Sanders, *Judaism*, 21).

21. "The rejection of Hellenization essentially meant that Jews in Palestine would live according to the law of Moses. How strictly they would follow it, and how it would be interpreted in detail, were issues that led to much continuing controversy. But the fundamental result was clear" (Sanders, *Judaism*, 30). Recently, Rebecca Wollenberg has challenged assumptions about Torah by examining ways in which rabbinic authorities displayed flexibility, and even ambivalence, toward biblical texts. As Wollenberg argues, "the recitation-heavy communal reading culture that had grown up around scripture in early rabbinic circles had already rendered the written text a secondary, even superfluous, witness to the biblical revelation in communal thought and practice" (Wollenberg, *Closed Book*, 3).

22. Sanders, *Judaism*, 238–39. In the aftermath of the Maccabean revolt, Sanders suggests that the issue of Hellenization "was settled by [the revolt]: Jews would not engage in pagan religion, and they would not accept the most blatant and publicly obvious

Hengel and Sanders share a focus on Palestinian Judaism, but they represent two opposing paradigms of Jewish identity. On the one hand, Sanders emphasizes the praxis of "common" people, the centrality of the Torah, the fundamental role of the temple in daily life, and the continuity of "biblical" Israelite traditions and beliefs in "Common Judaism," especially in opposition to Hellenization. On the other hand, Hengel focuses on Hellenism as an influential and inescapable force in and beyond the land of Palestine. Hengel argues that Hellenization—whether embraced or rejected—shaped the beliefs, behaviors, language, material artifacts, literary traditions, and culture of Second Temple Judaea.

Remnants of both paradigms exist in contemporary scholarship, even beyond the limited scope of Palestinian Judaism. The following sections examine the ways in which scholarship on Judaism, as represented by Shaye Cohen, John J. Collins, and John M. G. Barclay, has received and adapted these general paradigms to the larger ancient Mediterranean world.

Shaye J. D. Cohen and Second Temple Judaism

Shaye Cohen's *From the Maccabees to the Mishnah* represents somewhat of a middle-ground between Hengel and Sanders. Like Sanders, Cohen emphasizes the role of continuity in Second Temple Judaism and unity among different groups. Cohen attributes this unity to a sense of identity, noting that "the most potent force unifying [preexilic Israelite religion and Second Temple Judaism] is self-perception or self-definition," which Cohen finds most evident "in the relations of [d]iaspora Jewry to the land of Israel and the temple."[23] Cohen recognizes the diverse expressions of Jewish identity throughout the Second Temple period, but, like Sanders,

---

forms of Hellenization" (Sanders, *Judaism*, 30). By "most blatant and publicly obvious," Sanders is likely referring to the *gymnasium* and other Hellenistic public institutions, which he emphasized in the buildup to the revolt. Sanders acknowledges Hasmonean leadership "acted very much like other Hellenistic kings, and various aspects of Hellenistic culture continued to percolate through Palestine" (33), but he fails to address *how* Hellenism continued to influence Palestine in the aftermath of the revolt. One area that has garnered significant attention in recent years is the presence of Greek language and the possibility that some form of Greek education may have been present throughout the first century BCE to the first century CE. Such an educational system may have affected the likes of Philo, Josephus, and Paul. See Andrew W. Pitts, "Hellenistic Schools In Jerusalem And Paul's Rhetorical Education," in Porter, ed., *Paul's World*, 19–50; Koskenniemi, *Greek Writers and Philosophers*.

23. Cohen, *From the Maccabees to the Mishnah*, 12.

he argues "ancient Jews were united by a common set of practices and beliefs that characterized virtually all segments of Jewry."[24] Cohen summarizes this form of common Judaism as a set of practices and beliefs, many of which overlap with Sanders's "Common Judaism": worship (which entailed the sacrificial cult and the institution of communal prayer), ritual observances of Torah (such as circumcision, dietary restrictions, and Sabbath observance), and monotheism.[25]

The temple plays a central role in many of the practices and beliefs at the heart of Cohen's construction of Second Temple identity. Similar to Sanders, Cohen suggests that, in the eyes of both diaspora Jews and those in the land of Palestine, the Jerusalem temple "represented the unity of God and the unity of Israel."[26] The temple was fundamental not only to Jewish ideology but praxis: "the annual half-shekel contribution and the festival pilgrimages bound together the entire Jewish community of both the land of Israel and the [d]iaspora."[27] Furthermore, the temple affected social conditions; Cohen argues the temple "not only unified Jewish society; it also was the power base of the (or a) ruling class."[28] Despite the presence of rival temples in the period—Cohen dismisses the temples in Elephantine, Samaria, and Leontopolis, arguing that "none of them competed effectively with the temple in Jerusalem"—the temple was central to the praxis, perceptions, and power dynamics of Jewish society.[29]

Inasmuch as he emphasizes the role of continuity and unity, Cohen also recognizes the broad diversity within the Second Temple period, especially in the role that Hellenization played. In summarizing the social conditions of Second Temple Judaism, Cohen aligns with Hengel's views on the influence of Hellenism, writing, "'To hellenize or not to hellenize' was not a question that the Jews of antiquity had to answer. They were given no choice. The questions that confronted them were 'How?' and 'How far?' . . . Even if the majority of Jews agreed that the golden mean

---

24. Cohen, *From the Maccabees to the Mishnah*, 13.
25. Cohen, *From the Maccabees to the Mishnah*, 53–102.
26. Cohen, *From the Maccabees to the Mishnah*, 105.
27. Cohen, *From the Maccabees to the Mishnah*, 105.
28. Cohen, *From the Maccabees to the Mishnah*, 105.
29. Cohen, *From the Maccabees to the Mishnah*, 105. Cohen does not address what an effective competition to the Jerusalem temple would entail; in a simple numbers game, Cohen is right that the Jerusalem temple was likely utilized by more people. If the efficacy of a temple is judged on its viability in the community's eyes, however, these longstanding temples surely competed with Jerusalem by providing their local diaspora communities with an alternative location for priestly praxis.

was best, the diversity of their responses indicates that the precise definition of this golden mean remained elusive."[30] Cohen recognizes a far greater degree of diversity and development of praxis in relation to the Jerusalem temple than Sanders's portrait of "Common Judaism" affords. In comparing the first and Second Temples as centralized locations for worship, Cohen notes how "the Second Temple likewise claimed exclusivity but faced severe competition," not by rival temples, but "in a more benign fashion" by organizations like synagogues and schools throughout both the diaspora world and the land of Israel.[31] Furthermore, Cohen discusses the overall "democratization" of Second Temple Jewish praxis, highlighting the introduction of new customs such as *tefillin* and *mezuzot*. Cohen argues these practices, along with the increased study of scripture and the institution of synagogues, demonstrate how Judaism during this period "became a religious system that sanctified the life of each individual through the constant observance of the commandments of God. This system was incumbent not only on the religious elites but on all (male) Jews equally."[32]

In addition to these democratizing practices, Cohen also mentions sects, such as the Qumran community, who sought to disrupt the authority of the priesthood or reframe their own version of the temple community outside the Jerusalem temple's precinct.[33] While Cohen remarks "the Second Temple and its cult gained a centrality and importance that the First Temple never achieved," the history of the Second Temple was turbulent.[34] The temple was rebuilt by the authority of Cyrus under Persian rule, profaned by Antiochus IV Epiphanes, a gentile ruler, rededicated and operated under the Maccabean line of priestly authority, who abandoned the line of Zadok, profaned again when Romans entered the sacred precincts, and, finally, extravagantly embellished and run by political appointments under Herod and the Romans. This turbulent history of the Second Temple offered plenty of reason for sectarianism. Cohen summarizes the situation as such:

---

30. Cohen, *From the Maccabees to the Mishnah*, 37.
31. Cohen, *From the Maccabees to the Mishnah*, 11.
32. Cohen, *From the Maccabees to the Mishnah*, 69.
33. Sanders is not unaware of the writings of the Qumran sectarians, but downplays these writings as not representative of the "common" view of the priests and the broader Judaean society.
34. Cohen, *From the Maccabees to the Mishnah*, 130.

> Although the Second Temple emerged as the central symbol and institution of Judaism, and although the priesthood, especially the high priesthood, emerged as the new aristocracy of the Jewish polity, *both temple and priesthood, especially after the Maccabean period, had serious ideological weakness.* How could the Jews be sure that the institution and the people who claimed to mediate between them and God were really authorized to do so?[35]

Cohen's portrait of Second Temple Judaism, and particularly the role of the Second Temple, demonstrates a keen eye to both unity and diversity throughout the Mediterranean. Despite the claims of its centrality and exclusivity, Cohen's emphasis on resistance to the temple—even in subtle ways through organizations or democratizing practices—suggests a limit to the temple's unification function(s).

John M. G. Barclay and "Diaspora Judaism"

John Barclay's approach to Second Temple Judaism places the focus on Jewish communities in the diaspora. Barclay's goal is "to examine how Jews reacted to their political, social and cultural environments in the Diaspora, and . . . to view both their social and political experiences and the varied modes of accommodation or resistance which they adopted in their lives and literature."[36] Rather than import a sense of normative Jewish identity, Barclay sets forth to understand diaspora communities in Egypt, Cyrenaica, Syria, Asia, and Rome on their own accord. For Barclay, it is important not to extrapolate universal characteristics of diaspora Judaism from particular instances because "the [d]iaspora cannot be assumed to be congruent with the thought and practice of Jews in Palestine, nor can Philo be taken to represent the views of all 'Hellenistic Jews.'"[37] Barclay's case studies demonstrate the multiformity of Jewish identity in the diaspora and how "the range and diversity of the historical evidence certainly indicate that no normative unity can be assumed."[38]

To navigate the complexities of the diaspora world and the differences between various communities, Barclay develops an analytical methodology that maps Jewish identity onto three sliding scales of assimilation,

---

35. Cohen, *From the Maccabees to the Mishnah*, 131, emphasis added.
36. Barclay, *Jews in the Mediterranean Diaspora*, 9–10.
37. Barclay, *Jews in the Mediterranean Diaspora*, 8.
38. Barclay, *Jews in the Mediterranean Diaspora*, 4.

acculturation, and accommodation. Barclay uses these categories rather than alternatives like "orthodoxy," "apostasy," and "deviation" to focus on the diversity of Second Temple Judaism and how no universal norm can be assumed. Barclay notes how this model does not necessarily refute Jewish commonalities or distinction but operates on a local level to understand each Jewish community surveyed without passing judgment on the basis of presupposed norms; "this does not mean that Jewish communities in particular times and places had no common mind on the limits of acceptable behavior, but that we need to be attuned to standards of measurement that were *local, contemporary* and *commonly accepted*."³⁹

Assimilation is "the degree to which [d]iaspora Jews were integrated into, or socially aloof from, their social environments."⁴⁰ Social integration was not seamless for Jews in antiquity; Barclay mentions a set of "taboos" that impeded assimilation for many Jews in the diaspora world: "the refusal to worship non-Jewish Gods, restrictions on Jewish diet, the observance of the Sabbath and the practice of circumcision."⁴¹ This list is not exhaustive, but Barclay uses it heuristically to differentiate diaspora Jews. Those who violated these "taboos" can be defined as the most integrated into gentile society; on the other hand, Jews "whose social life was confined entirely to the Jewish community" were the least assimilated, and varying levels and gradations of assimilation existed between, from participating in gymnasium education to enjoying civic life and entertainment, to developing and maintaining relationships with non-Jewish community members.⁴²

Acculturation is a narrower form of assimilation. Barclay gives special attention here to "language, values, and intellectual traditions," particularly in tandem with Greek *paideia*, which granted Jews "access not only to certain literary resources but also to a system of values which

39. Barclay, *Jews in the Mediterranean Diaspora*, 85, emphasis original.
40. Barclay, *Jews in the Mediterranean Diaspora*, 93.
41. Barclay, *Jews in the Mediterranean Diaspora*, 94.
42. Barclay, *Jews in the Mediterranean Diaspora*, 94. Hannah Cotton's work on the Babatha archive reveals that assimilation may have continued to impact those within Roman Palestine into the early second century CE. Cotton argues that the Jewishness of the documents' authors was "expressed in nothing except their names . . . Babatha and her litigants show no awareness of an existing normative rabbinic law, but are strongly influenced by Roman law, while their diplomatics resemble those of Egyptian papyri" (Cotton, "Cancelled Marriage Contract," 64–65). Cotton examines the archive's marriage contracts (*ketubbot*) and compares Greek and Aramaic documents with how the practice was conducted in Egypt, arguing "the Halakhah was not created *in vacuo*: it reflects mixed local traditions which were later absorbed into Judaism" (85).

constituted . . . the very essence of civilization."[43] Barclay notes a few groups on this scale: those who exhibited scholarly expertise in Greek literary and philosophical traditions, those who demonstrated familiarity with such traditions, those who were aware of Hellenistic values, and those unable to maneuver in or understand Greek.[44] Whereas Hengel probed the *breadth* of Hellenistic culture in Palestinian Judaism, Barclay's acculturation approach evaluates the *depth* of Hellenistic culture in the diaspora world. Building from Hengel's thesis—that Hellenistic culture permeated the lives of Jews in both Palestine and the diaspora—Barclay's approach to acculturation measures differences in degrees of Hellenism. The presence of Greek, or "the mere ability to speak Greek . . . need not signify much at all" when compared against the spectrum of Hellenistic acculturation and other forms of cultural engagement.[45]

Barclay's final category, accommodation, measures a community's attitude toward acculturation, or "the *use to which acculturation is put*, in particular the degree to which Jewish and Hellenistic cultural traditions are merged or, alternatively, polarized."[46] On one side, accommodation can be labeled as *integrative*, which describes instances of harmonization between cultural traditions. Due to the distinctiveness of Jewish practice, this often finds the uniqueness of Jewish cultural traditions obscured by Hellenistic practices. On the other hand, an *oppositional* instance of accommodation describes cultural activity that operates to the contrary, such as antagonism toward Hellenistic culture. Barclay does not measure accommodation in degrees of integration or opposition, but rather uses this third analytical category to demonstrate how "acculturation could be used to construct either bridges or fences between Jews and their surrounding cultures."[47]

Barclay's method assesses Jewish identity in a nuanced, complex, and tentative manner. In demonstrating the limits, or "levels," of assimilation, Barclay discusses the inscriptions of two Jews at the temple of Pan Euodus in Egypt (CIJ 1537, 1538). Many questions swirl around the inscribers, Ptolemaios, son of Dionysius, the Jew and Theodotus, son of Dorion, the Jew: what is the intention of these offerings, and to whom are these diaspora Jews presenting an offering? Does their theology allow for

43. Barclay, *Jews in the Mediterranean Diaspora*, 95.
44. Barclay, *Jews in the Mediterranean Diaspora*, 95.
45. Barclay, *Jews in the Mediterranean Diaspora*, 96.
46. Barclay, *Jews in the Mediterranean Diaspora*, 96, emphasis original.
47. Barclay, *Jews in the Mediterranean Diaspora*, 98.

multiple deities or have they conflated or syncretized Pan Euodos with their God? Furthermore, did they participate in any other ritual activity or worship in the temple (e.g., prayer, sacrifice, etc.)? Assimilation, acculturation, and accommodation can be articulated and discussed as "levels" along a sliding scale, but many more questions about practice, belief, and the plasticity of identity remain unanswered.[48]

Barclay's project includes the Jerusalem temple by addressing its effect on local communities throughout the diaspora. Barclay showcases support for the temple by pointing to Josephus, Philo, Cicero, and Tacitus to note how the collection of the temple tax (derived from Exod 30:11–16) "was scrupulously undertaken by [d]iaspora communities . . . the collection and dispatch of this money caused political difficulties for the communities in Cyrenaica . . . and Asia."[49] Barclay points to the *fiscus Iudaicus* as additional supporting evidence for the widespread nature of the temple collection, noting that the Roman empire enacted this practice on the presupposition that financial contributions from diaspora communities was already a regular practice. He also notes Philo's interpretation of the temple tax as "bring[ing] physical or social 'salvation'" (*Spec Leg* 1.77–78), which, when compounded with Philo's allegorical approach to sacrifices, offers a greater understanding for why some diaspora Jews embraced the collection.[50] Barclay draws heavily on Josephus to point out contributions, gifts, and "large-scale offerings" to the temple from wealthy benefactors throughout the diaspora, further demonstrating financial support of the temple institution. Likewise, he discusses the major pilgrimage festivals as events which drew diaspora communities into the homeland or served as additional opportunities of financial support for those who could not travel. In summarizing the support for the temple in the diaspora, Barclay states, "the uniqueness for Jews of the Jerusalem temple . . . suggests that its symbolic value was powerful even when its impact on daily life was weak."[51]

---

48. Additional inscriptions at the Temple of Pan mention frequent visits of a certain Lazarus, indicating that even those with more traditional (non-Greek) Jewish names could be found frequenting the temple. See Horbury and Noy, *Jewish Inscriptions of Graeco-Roman Egypt*, 207–12.

49. Barclay, *Jews in the Mediterranean Diaspora*, 417.

50. "As the same passage [*Spec Leg* 1.77–78] makes clear, [the temple tax] also helped bind each individual contributor to the local community" (Barclay, *Jews in the Mediterranean Diaspora*, 418).

51. Barclay, *Jews in the Mediterranean Diaspora*, 419.

Barclay also, however, draws attention to points of conflict regarding the relationship between Jews in the diaspora and the Jerusalem temple. Barclay argues, "It is legitimate to enquire how deep and how universal was the 'zeal for the temple' (*Legatio* 212) in the light of the existence of an alternative temple in Leontopolis and the fact that few diaspora Jews hurried to defend Jerusalem in 70 CE."[52] Though he eventually argues against these counterpoints—the siege on Jerusalem made outside support difficult to acquire; the dearth of literary attribution suggests the Leontopolis temple may have held only a limited local significance—Barclay's inquiry opens the door for a more critical understanding of the role of and relationship with the Jerusalem temple in various diaspora communities. Ultimately, Barclay argues that the persistence of post-70 CE diaspora Judaism is telling: "That [d]iaspora Judaism survived the destruction of the temple indicates the strength of its other resources; and that it continued in most respects unchanged suggests that the temple *had always been of greater symbolic than practical significance*."[53]

John J. Collins and "Hellenistic Judaism"

John Collins discusses the conflicts, both internal and external, that diaspora Jews faced in the Hellenistic world as a result of the dissonance of Jewish tradition and Hellenistic values. Collins locates dissonance in the ways broader Hellenistic culture overlooked, refuted, or mockingly provoked Jewish traditions, origins, and practices. He also identifies ways in which Jewish tradition disengaged from or discouraged interaction with Hellenistic culture. Jews in the diaspora were caught in between these cultural and traditional poles of siloed isolation and syncretistic integration, which led to multifaceted expressions of Jewish identity where "the majority sought ways to reduce the dissonance while remaining Jewish but without rejecting Hellenistic culture."[54] Collins's survey of Hellenistic Jewish literature demonstrates "a spectrum of attempts to strike a balance between these competing factors and overcome the dissonance between them."[55]

---

52. Barclay, *Jews in the Mediterranean Diaspora*, 420.
53. Barclay, *Jews in the Mediterranean Diaspora*, 420, emphasis added.
54. Collins, *Between Athens and Jerusalem*, 14–15.
55. Collins, *Between Athens and Jerusalem*, 273.

Collins does not assume a set of common practices or beliefs that unite all Second Temple Jews, asserting, "Judaism in the Hellenistic age was not nearly as uniform as Sanders suggests."[56] Even so, Collins is wary of equating the situations in Palestine and the diaspora world to the extent of Hengel.[57] Collins argues, "Both Judea and the [d]iaspora may have been Hellenistic, but there were profound differences between them nonetheless. Hellenism was not a monolithic phenomenon. Neither was Hellenistic Judaism."[58] Still, Collins notes, "The distinctive commandments, such as Sabbath observance, circumcision, and dietary laws, were the hallmarks of Judaism which were most immediately obvious to [g]entile observers . . . The fact that Jewish identity was so closely bound up with these observances obviously created obstacles for Jews who were attracted by Hellenistic culture."[59] These observances "reinforced their identity" as Jews, but there was no particular standard for measuring such identity; "exactly which beliefs and practices were essential to the way of life were not clearly defined, however, and so people might define their Jewish identity in various ways."[60] In addition, Jewish life and practice were not necessarily mutually exclusive with Hellenistic culture; Collins points to inscriptions of synagogue dedications as evidence that "a Jew could bear a Greek name and be a loyal subject of the Ptolemy and simultaneously support his local synagogue."[61]

Within the complex matrix of Jewish identity, Collins discusses scripture as a feature common to both the diaspora and Palestinian Judaism:

---

56. Collins, *Between Athens and Jerusalem*, 22. Collins counters Sanders's use of covenantal nomism as a dominant pattern of religion by examining additional patterns at play in the Hellenistic world and proposing alternative understandings of tradition: "The Jewish tradition could also be construed as the story of a glorious past which fostered ethnic pride, with little regard for religious laws or for anything that could be called nomism . . . It could also be construed as a moral system which prized universal human values and attached little importance to distinctive laws such as circumcision" (Collins, *Between Athens and Jerusalem*, 273).

57. "While the familiar opposition of Hellenistic and Palestinian Judaism cannot be maintained and while there is a considerable gray area where we cannot be sure of the derivation of particular works, the fact remains that the main evidence for the attempt to present Judaism in Hellenistic dress derives from the [d]iaspora" (Collins, *Between Athens and Jerusalem*, 18).

58. Collins, "What Is Hellenistic Judaism?," 571.
59. Collins, *Between Athens and Jerusalem*, 13.
60. Collins, *Between Athens and Jerusalem*, 19.
61. Collins, *Between Athens and Jerusalem*, 67.

> The Torah was *the basic component in the tradition*, and those who would remain within Judaism had to relate themselves to it in some way. This did not mean that all had to conform to a single pattern. Not all the laws were necessarily binding, and the element of law was not necessarily the focal point of the tradition which was most significant for establishing Jewish identity. Rather, a number of different approaches could be taken within the bounds of the tradition.[62]

For Collins, scripture threads together similarities in identity and tradition while also allowing room for differences of interpretation. Collins points to Hellenistic Jewish authors, like Artapanus (fragments in Eusebius, *Praep. Evang.* 9.18, 23, 27), who rewrote traditions and used the past to shape an alternative expression of Jewish identity. Artapanus presents Abraham as the founder of Egyptian astrology and Moses as a culture-creator responsible for organizing Egyptian animal worship, offering a syncretistic view of Egyptian and Jewish traditions that elevates and normalizes Hellenistic Judaism within Egypt.[63] The line between interpretation and new or counter-tradition may complicate just how unifying scriptural tradition is, and Collins's focus on national identity as dependent upon the continued use of recognizable figures, landmarks, and institutions offers a few broad threads from which to weave an understanding of Jewish identity.

Collins's work also explores attitudes toward the Jerusalem temple from the perspective of the diaspora, particularly of Jews in Egypt. One of the major concerns Collins examines in the Ptolemaic era is the complicated relationship between the Oniad temple in Leontopolis and the temple in Jerusalem. Of first importance is understanding whether the rival cultic centers were as mutually exclusive as they are often presented. Collins argues, albeit from silence, the absence of Leontopolis in 2 Maccabees "may simply indicate that the temple in Egypt was never seriously considered as a rival to that of Jerusalem."[64] Collins then calls

---

62. Collins, *Between Athens and Jerusalem*, 23, emphasis added.

63. Collins defends Artapanus against claims that his expression of syncretistic Judaism minimizes the religious tradition, arguing "the very endorsement of the pagan divinities as useful for humanity shows their inferiority not only to the god of the Jews but even to Moses" (Collins, *Between Athens and Jerusalem*, 42–43).

64. Collins, *Between Athens and Jerusalem*, 81. Collins also points to later rabbinic attitudes, such as the Talmud's treatment of Leontopolis as a secondary, but sometimes acceptable, sacred space for offering sacrifice or making the Nazirite vow: "The Mishnah allows that offerings made in the temple of Onias were acceptable to God

out Josephus's characterization of Onias as a self-serving opportunist who aligned with the Ptolemies for political gain;[65] this characterization is heavily colored by comparison with Hyrcanus and the Tobiad political movement in Transjordan.[66] Collins notes that both the location of the temple and the nature of Onias's exile and status in Egypt complicate Josephus's accounts:

> Whether he intended his temple in Egypt to rival Jerusalem, however, is quite another matter . . . If Onias wanted to set up a temple that would be a center for Egyptian Jewry and rival Jerusalem, he would have had to set it up in Alexandria. A temple near Heliopolis can only have been the sanctuary of the local military colony, like the earlier temple at Elephantine. Onias was evidently a leading figure in Egyptian Judaism, and there is no record that his temple was ever a bone of contention.[67]

For the Roman period, Collins directs his attention toward 3 Maccabees and Philo as examples of how Alexandrian Jewry understood itself in relation to the Jerusalem temple. In retelling the events of the Maccabean revolt, the temple features prominently in 3 Maccabees, and "there is no doubt that the author holds the Jerusalem temple in high esteem."[68] Despite the temple's central place in the story, however, Collins teases out larger themes of the narrative like exile and loyalty to gentile rule. In this sense, the temple's deliverance is important but

---

in some circumstances, although priests who officiated there would not be acceptable in the Jerusalem temple (Menahot 13:10). The Talmud confirms this view and adds explicitly that the temple of Onias was not idolatrous" (Collins, *Between Athens and Jerusalem*, 72). See Menahot 109a–b for rabbinic conversations about how service and sacrifice in Onias's temple were perceived as interchangeable—or sometimes not interchangeable—in certain cases.

65. Collins even argues in favor of the likelihood "that the followers of Onias also dreamed of restoration of the traditional Jerusalem cult" (Collins, *Between Athens and Jerusalem*, 97).

66. Collins also critically examines Hyrcanus's temple and the Tobiad saga, arguing, "the [Tobiad] temple was for [Hyrcanus's] own convenience, since he appears to have had a self-sufficient domain in Transjordan. His continued relationship with the temple in the time of Onias III shows that he did not see any incompatibility between the two temples. Significantly, Onias III did not find the Tobiad temple objectionable either. All of this casts much light on the actions of Onias IV. While he inevitably rejected the Hasmonean priesthood, there is no reason to believe that he would have definitively rejected the Jerusalem temple" (Collins, *Between Athens and Jerusalem*, 77).

67. Collins, *Between Athens and Jerusalem*, 71.

68. Collins, *Between Athens and Jerusalem*, 130.

of secondary concern, which, Collins argues, accurately matches the pragmatic situation in Alexandria:

> [Third Maccabees] does not, however, give any indication of the actual relations of Egyptian Jews to the temple. Inevitably, the temple could not play a great role in the practical religion of the [d]iaspora, despite the sending of offerings and the pilgrimages, which were undoubtedly common . . . The practical allegiance of the Jews of Alexandria was to the law, which regulated their daily lives. Jerusalem and its temple had a less immediate role which was largely symbolic.[69]

Collins also discusses Philo's allegorical approach to scriptures and how this displays a similar understanding of the Jerusalem temple. Collins argues that Philo balances disinterest in Judaean nationalism and concern for Judaism's central symbols like the law and Jerusalem temple. While Philo recognizes that the temple plays an important role in Jewish religious life, Alexandrian citizenship and concerns about Roman rule take priority over Judaean nationalism. Regardless whether Philo visited the temple (or how frequently), Collins argues that, for Philo, "the real significance of the temple is allegorical, in its symbolism of cosmic worship. It is necessary that there be a temple as a visible sign, to convey the symbolism to the masses, but *it is not necessary that Philo, or other spiritually minded Jews, live in proximity to it or go there frequently.*"[70] Jerusalem and its temple serve an important function for the symbolic identity of Alexandrian Jews like Philo—much like capitol buildings serve an important symbolic function for nations—but the further one was from this central geographic landmark, the less likely it was to impact the concerns of daily life.[71]

Collins's work, like Barclay's, demonstrates that Jewish identity in the diaspora was multifaceted, dynamic, and expressed on a spectrum between Jewish tradition and Hellenistic culture. Even more, this spectrum of identity could differ even within localities or by social status. For Collins, examining Jewish (and early Christian) memory and literary

---

69. Collins, *Between Athens and Jerusalem*, 130.

70. Collins, *Between Athens and Jerusalem*, 137, emphasis added.

71. "The urgent needs of the religion lie elsewhere. Jerusalem and the homeland remain very much in the background of Philo's thought. They are essential to Jewish identity, but they do not normally interfere with the life of the [d]iaspora Jew in his own environment" (Collins, *Between Athens and Jerusalem*, 137).

accounts is an exercise "in strik[ing] a balance between these competing factors" in an effort to "overcome the dissonance between them."[72]

Martin Goodman, Jewish Identity, and Ancient Authority Structures

Near the end of the twentieth century, Martin Goodman offered an alternative model for understanding identity based on ancient authority structures. Goodman proposes five ways of establishing Jewish identity in the ancient world: (1) through self-identification; (2) by the definition of a central Jewish authority; (3) by inclusion into a local Jewish community; (4) local gentile community demarcation; and (5) gentile state definition.[73] Goodman explores some of these options only briefly. For central Jewish authorities, Goodman points to the Jerusalem priests and rabbinic Sages as authorities with limited geographic scope.[74] In discussion of local Jewish communities, Goodman draws on Josephus, who mentions Antioch as a site of friendly and inclusive gentile-Jewish relations. For the final category, Jewish identity in the eyes of the gentile, particularly Roman, state, Goodman draws on the *fiscus Judaicus* as a pragmatic example of the Roman state's definition of Jewish identity and highlights changes in the Roman practice of collecting the tax under Vespasian, Domitian, and Nerva. For example, Goodman points to Suetonius's account of the stripping of an elderly man to see whether he was circumcised (*Domitian* 12.2) is an extreme implementation of the *fiscus Judaicus* under Domitian, which he then contrasts with Nerva's minting coins embossed with "FISCI IUDAICI CALUMNIA SUBLATA," indicating a possible reversal of the *fiscus Judaicus*.[75]

72. Collins, *Between Athens and Jerusalem*, 273.

73. Goodman, "Identity and Authority in Ancient Judaism," 192.

74. "However autocratic they may have been within the sanctuary, those who controlled the Temple never had the capacity, outside its confines, to impose very widely their idea of who was a Jew. Those adherents of the faith who never brought an offering to the Temple would never subject their status to scrutiny. This category will have included most such adherents who lived in the diaspora and who, despite the Biblical requirement of thrice-yearly pilgrimages, never went to Jerusalem" (Goodman, "Identity and Authority in Ancient Judaism," 193).

75. Goodman, "Identity and Authority in Ancient Judaism," 197–98. On the reversal of the *fiscus Judaicus*, Goodman gestures toward the minting of coins celebrating restraint ('FISCI JUDAICI CALUMNIA SUBLATA') in 96 CE. In his later work, he examines four possibilities for the meaning of this Latin phrase, preferring a reading where "the coins may advertise a decision by the emperor to do away with the hated Jewish tax altogether . . . So long as a law existed under which Jews were required to

Elsewhere, Goodman's work relies on Josephus as a major representative of Second Temple Judaism and defines Jewish identity by drawing on Sanders's work.[76] While Goodman does recognize great variety in first-century Judaism—he argues for more nuance and variations of practice than the few categories mentioned in works by Philo, New Testament authors, or Josephus—he still points to specific instances of unity across different expressions of Jewish life.[77] In particular,

---

pay a certain tax, it was inevitable that there would be a question as to who should pay the tax and who was trying to evade payment" (Martin Goodman, "Meaning of 'FISCI IUDAICI CALUMNIA SUBLATA' on the Coinage of Nerva," in Cohen and Schwartz, eds., *Studies in Josephus and the Varieties of Ancient Judaism*, 88). Goodman argues that Nerva's change in policy may have even contributed to a larger change in defining Jewish identity as a religious category and not solely as an ethnic category. If Nerva's policy relaxed the tax burden on those who were non-practicing Jews, Goodman argues, "it may be suggested that, by a reform intended to help apostate Jews, Nerva for the first time gave Roman legal recognition to Jewish proselytes, since after AD 96 the Roman definition of a Jew depended on his or her public declaration of Judaism and acceptance of the burden of the consequent tax. Jews from now on were defined as such by their religion alone rather than their birth" (Goodman, "Nerva, the *Fiscus Judaicus* and Jewish Identity," 44). In his later work, Goodman suggests a more gradual shift in this definition, conceding that the reimposition of the *fiscus Judaicus* in 98 CE and the Romans's disapproving attitude toward the policy in the 120s CE indicate that abuses of the policy did not end with the *calumnia sublata* in 96 CE. See Goodman, "Meaning of 'FISCI IUDAICI CALUMNIA SUBLATA' on the Coinage of Nerva," in Cohen and Schwartz, eds., *Studies in Josephus and the Varieties of Ancient Judaism*, 89n29.

76. "It is possible to find at least one type of Jew from this period who was presumably pious in his own eyes but who failed to conform to most of the characteristics identified by Ed Sanders as constitutive of 'common Judaism' (most obviously the extreme allegorists attacked by Philo in *De Migratione Abrahami*), but a lowest common denominator which includes even such Jews remains: it is empirically the case that all those individuals and groups who presented themselves in this period as pious Jews worshipped the God who was worshipped in Jerusalem, and accepted that the Torah, enshrined in the Pentateuch, encapsulates a covenant between God and Israel incumbent on all Jews. Variety began with interpretation of that Torah, which could lead in very many directions. Some preoccupations, such as an interest in purity or apocalyptic, or the correct way to keep the laws of shabbat and kashrut, or the right attitude to the making of oaths, were shared by Jews of many different persuasions, but these common trends can be distinguished from the emergence of groups which defined themselves in contrast to other Jews as distinctive or superior, or (in extreme cases) cut themselves off from other Jews" (Goodman, "Religious Variety and the Temple in the Late Second Period and Its Aftermath," in Stern, ed. *Sects and Sectarianism in Jewish History*, 22; cf. *Judaism in the Roman World*, 33–46).

77. On variety, Goodman argues, "Our picture of the different types of Judaism relies wholly on the sources preserved, for religious purposes, by later Jewish and Christian traditions. Since much of the material found in each of these traditions is lacking in the other, it is obvious that both traditions have been highly selective, and it was always likely that there existed further material which was ignored by both . . .

Goodman argues against the notion that Second Temple Judaism was as fractured as often portrayed, pointing to the Jerusalem temple as a centralizing and universally accepted indicator of Jewish identity.[78] First, Goodman dispels the view that the Dead Sea Scrolls display a mutually exclusive view of community identity and temple worship.[79] Then, after noting the outlier case of "extreme allegorists" mentioned in Philo's *On the Migration of Abraham*, Goodman states, "all other Jews we should expect to have felt a duty to attend the Temple and to send offerings there, even if in practice they went infrequently because they lived too far away."[80] Finally, after examining ways in which other various groups maintained temple worship, Goodman concludes, "the strong sense of group identity among members of the Qumran *yahad*, Essene communities, *talmidei hakhamim*, and early Jewish Christians seems clear . . . but group solidarity did not require separation from the shared (and biblically mandated) institution of the Temple."[81]

Goodman's work on Jewish identity yields complex results. On the one hand, his interpretation of the Dead Sea Scrolls, his reliance on Josephus, and his emphasis on temple participation as a *de facto* identity marker for *all* Jews in the Second Temple period paints an unrealistic

---

Hence, the number of varieties of Judaism that existed at the end of the Second Temple period must be judged even greater than what emerges from simply reading Josephus" (Goodman, *Judaism in the Roman World*, 45–46).

78. "If we take seriously his emphasis on the Temple in *C. Apionem* and the importance, according to the Torah, of bringing the required offerings to the place stipulated by God, it seems wholly implausible that any of these Jewish groups could have cut themselves off from the Jerusalem Temple without this aspect of their identity being mentioned by Josephus as the primary mark of their distinctiveness, in the same way as Samaritans were distinguished, both by themselves and by Jews, as those who worshipped the God of Israel on Mt Gerizim" (Goodman, "Religious Variety and the Temple in the Late Second Temple Period and Its Aftermath," in Stern, ed., *Sects and Sectarianism in Jewish History*, 26).

79. "There are, of course, a number of references in the sectarian scrolls to a time in the past when the community fell out with a Wicked Priest, and to a time in the future when corrupt priests will suffer for their sins, and at times the community could present itself as comprising within itself an atonement for the land as 'a holy house for Israel and the foundation of the holy of holies for Aaron'. But such notions should not preclude the sectarians continuing to treat the Jerusalem Temple and its worship as central to their lives" (Goodman, "Religious Variety and the Temple in the Late Second Temple Period and Its Aftermath," in Stern, ed., *Sects and Sectarianism in Jewish History*, 28).

80. Goodman, "Religious Variety and the Temple in the Late Second Temple Period and Its Aftermath," in Stern, ed., *Sects and Sectarianism in Jewish History*, 30.

81. Goodman, "Religious Variety and the Temple in the Late Second Temple Period and Its Aftermath," in Stern, ed., *Sects and Sectarianism in Jewish History*, 35.

portrait of the period. For instance, he only mentions Leontopolis briefly as a failure of Onias to establish a rival temple—again relying on Josephus's evaluation—but offers little critical insight to how this alternative temple (or others like it) challenges his argument about Jews who withdrew from the Jerusalem temple. On the other hand, he considers important political and socio-cultural factors in how identity was constructed and utilized under Roman imperial authority. In addition, some of his work provides an important challenge to those who would define Second Temple Jewish identity by singularly focusing on Josephus's reduced categories. While later sections of this chapter will provide a more robust response to his argument on the place of the Jerusalem temple within Second Temple Judaism, they do so along the lines of Goodman's own understanding that Judaism in this period was full of variety.

David M. Miller and the Terminology and Categorization of Jewish Identity

In addition to larger questions about Jewish identity, belief, and practice, David M. Miller's work examines how Ἰουδαῖος and similar terminology (*Iudaeus*, *Yehudi* [יהודי], *Yehudai* [יהודאי]) were used as group labels for Jewish people in the ancient Mediterranean. Miller questions whether these terms were considered "outsider" classifications that ought to be distinguished from "insider" labels, as well as whether these terms inherently carried an ethnic categorization that differed from a religious designation (such as "Israel" or "Hebrews").[82] In three separate articles,

---

82. An additional focus of Miller's work is addressing the issue of modern translations of Ἰουδαῖος, weighing "Judaean" against "Jew" and surveying scholarship (e.g., Danker, Levine, Mason, Esler) on the considerations and dangers of each translation. Miller concludes his three-part work with an additional appendix about translation, arguing in favor of using the language of "Jew/Jews" based on contemporary context and continuity of group identity. Miller writes, "If we are forced to choose between 'Jew' and 'Judaean'—and we are—contemporary concerns tilt the balance in favour of 'Jew.' Although 'Judaean' might help avoid anachronism, the danger will always linger. And there are, of course, also strong lines of continuity between first-century *Ioudaioi* and contemporary Jews, just as there are lines of continuity between first-century Christ-followers and contemporary Christians, and the seventh-century believers who were members of Muhammad's community and contemporary Muslims. It is surely not wrong, at times, to focus on the continuities. Retaining the label 'Jew' does this. Translating *Ioudaios* by 'Judaean', on the other hand, has the potential effect of disenfranchising contemporary Jews from their Second Temple heritage. Leaving 'Jews' out of Bible translations may also give unsuspecting Christian readers the impression that Jesus was not a 'Jew' after all, or permit them to ignore the role that passages from the

Miller surveys scholarship on the usage of Ἰουδαῖος to better understand how this category was used in the Greco-Roman world. Miller sides with previous studies in arguing the usage of the term "Israel" was exclusive to "insiders," while "outsiders only used *Ioudaios* as a designation for the Jewish people."[83] On the other hand, the self-designation of Ἰουδαῖος complicates matters, as Miller argues that Jewish usage of the term—which he points to in Josephus (*A.J.* 20.43; *JW* 2.232, 184–98; 3.110, 113–14, 229; *Life* 113; 349)[84]—leaves open three possibilities:

1. that Ἰουδαῖος was "an ethnic label" whereas other designations like "Galilaean" or "Idumaean" were used as a "non-ethnic sub-group defined by geographical region";
2. that Ἰουδαῖος marked a larger (diaspora) ethnic category, whereas other designations marked additional ethnic sub-groups; or finally,
3. "that *Ioudaios* came to function as a religious term before the destruction of the Second Temple."[85]

Miller's subsequent articles explore contemporary scholarship on Ἰουδαῖος and demonstrate how understanding of the term has evolved into the categories of ethnicity and religion that pervade scholarship

---

New Testament have played in the tragic history of Christian anti-Semitism" (Miller, "Ethnicity, Religion and the Meaning of *Ioudaios*," 259).

83. Miller, "Meaning of *Ioudaios*," 122.

84. "Josephus seldom contrasts *Ioudaioi* and Galilaeans. The general impression one receives is of a unified group with regional distinctives, whose members shared a commitment to the Jerusalem temple and to a common way of life. This is the perspective of Josephus at the end of the first century CE. If Smith and Cohen are correct, the meaning of *Ioudaios* shifted over time, and even within the same period meant different things to different people" (Miller, "Meaning of *Ioudaios*," 121). Because Josephus uses the term *Ioudaios* in a multitude of manners inclusive of Galileans and other geographic regions and sub-groups, Miller finds the modern translation of *Ioudaios* to have more flexibility: "If insiders accepted *Ioudaios* as a self-designation, there is no need for modern scholars to switch from 'Jew' or 'Judaean' to 'Israelite,' as Elliott recommends" (Miller, "Meaning of *Ioudaios*," 122).

85. Miller, "Meaning of *Ioudaios*," 122. I tend to favor a combination of Miller's second and third possibilities, where Ἰουδαῖος is understood in an ethno-religious dimension. In this way, the term essentially functions as a cultural category that describes the shared experience of both the members of a particular (Israelite) lineage, as well as those who adhere to and associate with a set of traditions and practices (e.g., Ἰουδαϊκός, ἰουδαΐζω). This malleable, polyvalent understanding also accounts for instances of anti-Semitism around the Mediterranean where either ethnic or religious dimensions could be in view, as well as ethno-religious markers on buildings, which is attested in an early second century BCE Egyptian land survey that describes a "synagogue of the Jews" (προσευχῆς Ἰουδαίων, P. Tebt. 1.86 17a, 28b).

today.⁸⁶ Miller's surveys explore a variety of attitudes on the relationship between ethnicity and religion and whether these categories are defensible or anachronistic for the ancient world. Miller adopts a *via media*, arguing that defining such categories is still a complex and contested task in modern scholarship. For Miller, it seems best to recognize that "both ethnicity and religion are heuristic modern concepts that can inform an examination of ancient patterns of thought."⁸⁷ Miller acknowledges that "ethnicity may well be the 'best' model 'presently available' to articulate what it meant to be a *Ioudaios*," but this model is not mutually exclusive with other forms of group identity like religion, which, at least in some inchoate form, he argues "was in the process of emerging as a distinct concept during the Second Temple period."⁸⁸ Miller's work offers insights into the granular details of studying Jewish identity, particularly in a manner that is concerned with ancient self-conscious definitions, and contributes to the larger scholarly designation of "Second Temple Judaism" by raising important defining questions for Jewish identity.

Summary

In drawing these paradigms together, one might wonder whether it is fair to compare such different customs and practices of Jewish life. Can life under Persian rule in Jerusalem in the early fifth century BCE be compared with Jewish life under Ptolemaic rule in Alexandria in the early second century BCE or Roman rule in Rome during the first century CE? Are there uniting features or comparable factors? The Jerusalem temple's second iteration is an abiding presence across these examples—to what extent will be examined below—but there are a number of other points of unity and diversity between the expressions of what could variously be called Second Temple Judaism, diaspora Judaism, or

---

86. "If the object of our inquiry is ancient perceptions of 'groupness', then insights from modern scholarship on race, nationalism, ethnicity—perhaps even religion—are all welcome. Of course, one must still decide on a term for 'groupness.' In my view, 'ethnicity' remains a better alternative to 'race' or 'nation' for group labels, such as 'Egyptian' and 'Parthian,' with which *Ioudaios* is often compared. Although both 'race' and 'ethnicity' are social constructions, 'ethnicity' is a broader term that generally includes other cultural and geographical characteristics, while 'race' has tended to be more narrowly associated with a belief in common ancestry both in popular thinking as well as in scholarship" (Miller, "Ethnicity Comes of Age," 306–7).

87. Miller, "Ethnicity, Religion and the Meaning of *Ioudaios*," 254.

88. Miller, "Ethnicity, Religion and the Meaning of *Ioudaios*," 255.

Hellenistic Judaism. Ancient Jews lived in a world of multidimensional identity factors including, but not limited to, geography (diaspora vs. Palestine), social environment (urban vs. rural), culture (a spectrum of attitudes toward Hellenism demonstrated by Barclay's matrix of acculturation, accommodation, and assimilation), language (Greek, Aramaic, or a host of regional dialects and alternatives), education (a sliding scale of literate, semi-literate, and illiterate), and socioeconomic status (ranging from wealthy elite to poor). What is true of one community may not be true of others. Common or unifying traits and practices may be heuristically helpful—as in Sanders's "Common Judaism" or the continuities pointed out by Cohen—but communities, and their constituent residents, differed in praxis and thought throughout the ancient Mediterranean world. Markus Witte, Jens Schröter, and Verena Lepper highlight this variability by describing ancient Judaism as, "subject to constant processes of change, both of its self-perception and its external perception. What was deemed to be 'Judaism' or 'Jewish' was fluid and often contested with a need for constant renegotiation."[89]

Accessibility is an additional concern for understanding Second Temple Judaism. The extant literary and material evidence are useful in extracting attitudes, but these remains are typically the product of a single socio-economic group. Collins argues that Jewish expressions toward Hellenism varied significantly based on wealth and class: "Social stratification undoubtedly modified Jewish understanding of the tradition and relations with the [g]entiles. Unfortunately, the views of the lower classes are not well recorded in the literature."[90] Furthermore, some of the earliest interactions between Judaism and Hellenism exist in fragmentary remains. While Collins incorporates the writings of Demetrius, Artapanus, Eupolemos, and Greek authors like Alexander Polyhistor, the difficulty in navigating claims of authenticity, situating date and context, and the scant nature of such fragments add further complications and limitations to building a broader understanding of Jewish thought and practice in the Second Temple period. At the very least, the implication for study of Second Temple Judaism, as Stewart Moore puts it, is that "we can no longer write up an expansive list of potential Judean behaviors and measure various ancient Judeans' Judeanness by how many of those behaviors they conform to and by how many

---

89. Witte et al., *Torah, Temple, and Land*, 1.
90. Collins, *Between Athens and Jerusalem*, 23–24.

are replaced by Greek markers."⁹¹ Ethnic—and, if Miller's proposal is correct, religious—Jewish identity is not quantitatively measured by how many boxes are checked, but by careful and cautious qualitative analysis of praxis, thought, and self-definition. The process of defining identity requires room for diverse expressions; as Laurie Pearce puts it, "Identity, like 'ethnicity,' the more value-laden term it often replaces, is a two-sided mirror—reflecting the perceptions, presumptions and constructs of the viewer as well as the viewed."⁹²

What does this mean for studying the Jerusalem temple? The temple is one of many factors of Jewish identity, but it cannot be determinative on its own. This study must keep this in mind and should not contend to make normative claims about ancient Judaism or ancient Jewish communities based on a presumed set of qualifying practices or beliefs. Attitudes or behaviors that go against the grain are not disqualifying in terms of Jewish identity. Put another way, we should not expect every Jewish community to react or relate to the temple in the same way. Communities that reject the temple are of the same historical value as those that participate in regular ritual worship. It is important to be inclusive when studying these complex communities, accounting for the full variety in expressions of Judaism, as common or rare as they appear.

---

91. Moore, *Jewish Ethnic Identity*, 255. Instead, Moore argues we ought to build our understanding of "Judeanness" (which he uses as an ethnic alternative to "Jewishness") from self-understanding evident in ancient texts: "We must look for what markers are considered by Judeans and their contemporaries as essential to a Judean identity. Even one marker, if held to with sufficient social force by a group of Judeans, and recognized as such a marker by their neighbors, could be enough to anchor a Judean self-consciousness that we would otherwise be tempted to write off as wholly assimilated" (Moore, *Jewish Ethnic Identity*, 255).

92. Laurie E. Pearce, "Identifying Judeans and Judean Identity in the Babylonian Exile," in Stökl and Waerzeggers, eds., *Exile and Return*, 7. Pearce's study of the onomastics and prosopography of Judean exiles in Babylonia demonstrates levels of acculturation and ambiguity by pointing out "names that resemble known monikers but which, in reshaping through linguistic and orthographic manipulation, evolve into unique forms that enable their bearers to identify with multiple social environments . . . Did parents bestow ambiguous names on their children with the expectation that they would facilitate integration into a host society? Did individuals change their names in the hopes of the same? In their interaction with Judeans at various administrative levels, did Babylonian scribes intentionally or unintentionally transform names into ones resembling the native onomasticon?" (Pearce, "Identifying Judeans and Judean Identity in the Babylonian Exile," in Stökl and Waerzeggers, eds., *Exile and Return*, 30). By asking these important questions of acculturation, Pearce reimagines Barclay's sliding scale model into a multi-dimensional plane consisting of additional factors like motivation and agency.

With this in mind, this chapter proceeds by surveying the history of the Second Temple and examining literary and material remains of Jewish communities and their attitudes toward the temple.

The History of the Second Temple(s)

The Second Temple's stature and symbolic significance in Jewish cultural memory is intricately tied to the traditions and narratives of its past, which serve as frames of reference, source material, or patterns from which to explain, retell, or key later events. In addition, a number of different temples were erected during this period, and, although scant, the details of these alternative temple locations offer additional perspectives on the significance of the Jerusalem temple in Jewish memory. In this section, I discuss the historical, social, and cultural frameworks of the Second Temple and other temple locations throughout four periods: the Persian period (560–323 BCE), the Hellenistic period (323–166 BCE), the Hasmonean period (166–63 BCE), and the Roman period (63 BCE–70 CE).

The Persian Period (560–323 BCE)

The destruction of the first Jerusalem temple and the transportation of Judaean exiles marked the end of the Israelite monarchy and the beginning of the Babylonian Exile (587–538 BCE).[93] The Exile posed major

---

93. The narrative of the Exile and deportation of Judeans is located in different biblical accounts, which are retold in slightly different ways. Second Chronicles presents the initial deportation and deposition of Jehoiakim as limited to the monarch and temple vessels (2 Chr 36:5–8), whereas the later capture during the deposition of Zedekiah was totalizing, removing all people from the land (2 Chr 36:17–21). Similarly, 2 Kings presents two deportations under Jehoiakim and Zedekiah but, in both cases, all but the "poorest in the land" (דלת עמ-הארץ) are deported (2 Kgs 24:13–16; 25:11–12). This narrative depiction is further complicated by the cadre later assembled during Gedaliah's demise, which apparently included prominent military leaders (כל-שרי החילים) and members of the royal family (מזרע המלוכה) who had all been left in the land (2 Kgs 25:23–26). Jeremiah also mentions an additional third deportation where the sum of deportees amounted to under five thousand captives (Jer 52:30). Due to the conflicting narratives, there is not a clear portrait of the socio-economic status or scale of deportees; as Caroline Waerzeggers and Jonathan Stökl argue, "the story of the Exile and return as narrated in the biblical text is a construct that replaces a much more complex and socially contested history" (Stökl and Waerzeggers, *Exile and Return*, 1). The effect of the Exile on sixth-century BCE settlement patterns also complicate the totalizing accounts in the biblical narrative. Tero Alstola argues,

challenges that reshaped Jewish thought, practice, and daily life. As Richard Elliot Friedman summarizes, "The Babylonian destruction of Judah had brought horrors and tremendous challenges and crises to this nation. [The exiles] were forced to reformulate their picture of themselves and their relationship with their God. *They had to find a way to worship Yahweh without a Temple.* They had to find leadership without a king. They had to learn to live as a minority ethnic group in great empires."[94] Some of these challenges were signaled in earlier prophetic declarations against the people, the monarchy, and the temple. Micah 6:6–8 and Isaiah 1:11–15 demonstrate a sense of waning enthusiasm toward the sacrificial cult. Micah, ever wary of the consequences that the Assyrian domination of Israel may have on Judah (1:8–9), also warned of the destruction of the temple as a result of the corruption of Israelite leadership (3:9–12), which is later transferred to the corruption of the entire people (7:1–6). Likewise, Malachi 1:6—2:3 explicitly calls out the corruption of the priesthood and the rejection of their improper sacrifices. These prophetic attitudes tied the actions of the temple leadership to the institution of the temple, recognizing that cultic practice was not a panacea for larger injustices and corruption. Aaron Glaim discusses the prophetic debate over cultic efficacy, arguing that the focus on "Yahweh's rejection of sacrifices is a consequence of broken relations with his people, and is particular to specific moments in history."[95] Other

---

"Recent archaeological studies on Judah in the sixth century do not conform to the idea of desolate land depicted in 2 Chronicles 36, but they do not support the opposite view of strong continuity either. They show that there was a significant collapse in population, especially in the Jerusalem region, but also a continuity of settlement in the north and south of the capitol . . . A rough estimation of 10,000 deportees appears to be plausible, given the number of Judeans attested in Babylonia in the sixth century. Part of these were the Jerusalemite elite and educated professionals . . . The deportations aimed to punish Judah for rebellion, prevent future unrest, and . . . increase agricultural output and provide the state with taxes and a work force" (Alstola, *Judeans in Babylonia*, 14–15). Based on cuneiform records, Alstola concludes there was "notable diversity in the deportees' socio-economic status and level of integration into Babylonian society. The financial means and social networks of the royal merchants were quite different from those of the average Judean farmer, while some farmers were able to benefit from the structure of the land-for-service sector at the expense of their compatriots" (Alstola, *Judeans in Babylonia*, 251).

94. Friedman, *Who Wrote the Bible?*, 155, emphasis added.

95. Aaron Glaim, "'I Will Not Accept Them': Sacrifice and Reciprocity in Prophetic Literature," in Wiley and Eberhart, eds., *Sacrifice, Cult, and Atonement in Early Judaism and Christianity*, 125. Ma. Maricel S. Ibita approaches prophetic literature from a social-scientific standpoint by situating these critiques in the larger honor/shame and covenantal context, arguing, "the reason behind the cultic reproach is not about the

prophetic figures from the last days of Judah's monarchy offer similar outlooks. The entirety of Jeremiah is dedicated to the fall of Judah, which culminates in the destruction of Jerusalem, the ransacking of the temple, and the execution of the priestly hierarchy (Jer 52:12–27). The temple is also of central concern for Ezekiel, whose oracles contend with both the temple's destruction (Ezek 1–24) and its divine restoration (Ezek 40–48). As traumatic as the loss of the temple was, the prophetic attitudes in the late seventh and early sixth centuries BCE show how some in Israel had already begun to grapple with questions about Jewish identity and practice in a world without the Jerusalem temple.

The Persian triumph over the Babylonians was consequential in shaping the history of the sixth to fourth centuries BCE, especially as it set the ground for the return of Jewish exiles and the restoration of the temple. After periods of tumultuous Assyrian and Babylonian rule, Cyrus the Great became a cynosure of Jewish memory when he allowed the Jerusalem temple to be rebuilt (Ezra 1:2–4; 6:1–5; cf. Isa 41:25; 45:1).[96] The rebuilding of the temple carried on beyond Cyrus's reign. Darius and Artaxerxes I are both credited with supporting the temple's reconstruction in the late sixth and early fifth centuries BCE, but the temple's completion is dated to the reign of Darius (Ezra 6:14–15). Life in Palestine was primarily consumed with the reconstitution of the city, and while Palestinian historical record is limited, the accounts in Ezra and Nehemiah document how these two Jewish leaders, with the support of the Persians, "consolidated Judaism and adapted it to an existence within a world empire."[97]

---

sacrifice itself but the forgotten and mistaken identities of the covenant partners" (Ma. Maricel S. Ibita, "'What to Me Is the Multitude of Your Sacrifices?': Exploring the Critique of Sacrificial Cult and the Metaphors for YHWH in the Prophetic Lawsuit [Micah 6:1–8 and Isaiah 1:1–20]," in Wiley and Eberhart, eds., *Sacrifice, Cult, and Atonement in Early Judaism and Christianity*, 193).

96. Geo Widengren argues that Cyrus's messianic status in Deutero-Isaiah serves the dual purposes of Jewish theology—setting prophetic expectations for divine intervention and messianic action—as well as Jewish propaganda that undermined Nabonidus and the Babylonians. Geo Widengren, "Persian Period," in Hayes and Miller, eds., *Israelite and Judaean History*, 519.

97. Widengren, "Persian Period," in Hayes and Miller, eds., *Israelite and Judaean History*, 532. The timeline is confused and conflated in Josephus, where events are conformed to 1 Esdras rather than the MT of Ezra. For instance, Zerubbabel is mentioned as returning the temple vessels during Darius's reign, even though the Ezra account has the vessels returned under Cyrus's reign when the ornaments were originally gifted to Sheshbazzar, who returned to Jerusalem with Zerubbabel and the first wave of exile returnees (cf. Ezra 1:5–2:2; *A.J.* 11.12–18, 64–65; 1 Esd 3:3–14; 4:42–57). Much like

Though the biblical narrative focuses on the rebuilding of the Jerusalem temple, the Persian period also witnessed at least two additional temple communities develop in Samaria at Mount Gerizim and an Egyptian Judaean military colony in Elephantine.[98] Aramaic letters from Elephantine indicate that the community was already present in Egypt at the end of the seventh century BCE.[99] However, the community itself claimed to have had a longstanding temple built prior to the Persian

---

the biblical narrative of the Exile, the narrative records of exiles returning to the land in Ezra and Nehemiah have been questioned and critiqued against archaeological evidence. Against the Ezra narrative, which depicts a massive influx of immigrants, Lester Grabbe argues "the archaeology suggests a slow but gradual growth, such as would be the result of natural population increase and perhaps a small amount of immigration. This would be best explained not by large groups of immigrants returning to the land and attempting to be absorbed into the community but, rather, a trickle of people returning individually or in small groups . . . If Zerubbabel and Joshua were sent from Babylonia, as seems the case, they might have brought a number of immigrants with them: priests, bureaucrats, officials, along with some others. But these would have been a couple thousand at most, and might have been only a few hundred" (Lester Grabbe, "Reality of the Return: The Biblical Picture Versus Historical Reconstruction," in Stökl and Waerzeggers, eds., *Exile and Return*, 302). Grabbe's comments reflect the complexity of the return to the land, highlighting the potential socio-economic and ethno-cultural factors at play in the divide between the returning immigrants and those who remained in the land after the deportation.

98. Baruch Halpern argues that the centralization formula in Deuteronomy (12:14) is ambiguous and allows for two possible interpretations: (1) a singular interpretation that situates the Jerusalem's temple community as the only legitimate cultic center, or, (2) a distributive interpretation that legitimizes cultic operations at significant shrines, which exists as a means of conserving the status quo while also limiting innovation for future cultic activity. If Halpern's proposed interpretations are correct, those living in Elephantine may have still viewed their activity as within the bounds of Deut 12:14—that is, if the community was aware of Deuteronomy; John Collins points to the fact that the books of Ezra and Nehemiah present the (re)introduction of Torah, including Deuteronomy, in the later Persian period, which occurred after Elephantine's temple construction. See Halpern, "Centralization Formula in Deuteronomy," 20–38; Collins, *Invention of Judaism*, 44–53.

99. If the community pre-dated Josiah's reform, it may not be as surprising that a sacrificial cult was embraced in Elephantine. Baruch Halpern argues that Josiah and the Deuteronomistic reformists, as represented in Jer 8, instituted "the rejection of tradition in Judah," which "began with clan religion and the cult of the ancestors and culminated in the rejection of JE, Israel's sacred history" (Halpern, *From Gods to God*, 342). Although Halpern's focus is on the practice of child sacrifice at the Tophet, his emphasis on the rejection of tradition shows variant strands of ideology and practice in Judah in the seventh century BCE. Collins also contrasts the variant attitudes and understandings of Torah between Judah and Elephantine. The Elephantine community's use of its own central sacrificial system, as well as its complex relationship with other deities and its apparent absence of Torah adherence, demonstrates flexibility with tradition and practice. See Collins, *Invention of Judaism*, 50–53.

conquest, reporting that Cambyses already found the temple standing in the early sixth century BCE.[100] The temple also appears to have been public knowledge across the region; one personal letter from Lower Egypt even offers greetings to the temple ([ב שלמ]ביב יהו ית, A3.3), suggesting that acceptance of the temple may have been far-reaching for Jews in Egypt.[101] Karel van der Toorn shares a similar sentiment, noting, "it is clear the greetings are addressed to the communities that patronized these temples. But it is striking that the greetings are not to 'the Jews,' nor to 'the Babylonians,' or 'the Syrians,' but to the temples of their gods. It suggests that these communities took their identity from their religious orientation."[102]

Competition with the nearby temple of Khnum/Khnub led to local rivalry, which appears to have been a root cause for the temple's destruction.[103] A series of fifth-century BCE letters to Bagohi, the Persian

---

100. The community even claims their temple had been built by ancestors in the land of Egypt during the reign of the pharaohs (ומן יומ מלכי מצרין אבהין בגו אגורא זך ביב ב[ירתא], A4.8.12). For the Aramaic facsimiles, see Porten and Yardeni, *Textbook of Aramaic Documents from Ancient Egypt*. The language used for the temple in Elephantine is particularly interesting and variable. The term "agora" (אגורא) is used with respect to both the temple of Khnum/Khnub (חנוב) and the other Egyptian temples, as well as the temple to YHW (יהו), indicating that this term is a more neutral indicator of sacred space (A4.7, A4.8). In response to the requisition, Bagohi (בגוהי), the governor of Persian Judea, allows for the rebuilding of what he calls an "altar-house" (בית מדבחא). A personal letter from Osea to Shelomam also simply calls the temple "the House of YHW ([יט יהו[ב]) in Yeb" (A3.3). Additionally, the temple was seen to by a set of priests; a letter within the Jedaniah archive (A4.3) names Jedaniah and Uriah among "the priests of YHW the God" (כהניא זי יהו אלהא).

101. See Porten and Yardeni, *Textbook of Aramaic Documents from Ancient Egypt*, 30. Despite this record of far-reaching support, the larger question of Egyptian acceptance remains unknown. However, it is telling that Jedaniah and the priests of Elephantine felt the need to reach out to Judaean and Samarian government for financial support once their temple was destroyed. It can likely be presumed that financial support did not pour in from more local or regional Egyptian sources before the Elephantine priesthood set their sights on support from their ancestral homeland.

102. Karel van der Toorn, "Religion of the Elephantine Jews," in Witte et al., eds., *Torah, Temple, and Land*, 84.

103. In addition to the rivalry with local priests, the ruling governor of Elephantine, Vidranga, appears to be the instigator of the temple's destruction. James Lindenberger draws an interesting parallel in the community's response to Vidranga's transgressions against the temple and the Jewish response to the Babylonian destruction of the temple in Jerusalem. Even though Judaism in the Elephantine community looked vastly different than it did in the land of Palestine, Lindenberger remarks, "it is all the more striking that [the Elephantine community's] response to the loss of their temple in 410 was such a deeply traditional one. Like their ancestors in the time of Nebuchadnezzar nearly two centuries before, they fasted, they prayed and they called down God's curse on their

governor of Judah, and the sons of Sanballat, the Persian governor of Samaria, request financial assistance for the temple's reconstruction. One of the more intriguing discourses from the series of letters to Bagohi is the removal of animal sacrifices (עלותא) from the temple. In the drafts to Bagohi, Jedaniah and the priests of Elephantine request for a letter of recommendation (A4.7–A4.8), and, in an attempt to entice Bagohi's favor, the priests declare they will offer burnt offerings, meal offerings, and incense offerings in his honor upon the restored altar. However, the official record (זכרן) of Bagohi and Deliah's response (A4.9) removes animal sacrifice and only permits the reinstitution of meal offerings and incense offerings. Collins questions whether this change was imposed for pragmatic local purposes or was a result of Judaean influence, supposing that "the compromise may have been necessary to appease the priests of the ram-god Khnum, but it may also have been required by the authorities of Jerusalem."[104]

Little is known about day-to-day life in Elephantine, but the response to the Elephantine temple's destruction suggests those within the community did not view it in competition against the Jerusalem temple.[105] Rather, it seems to have served as a local alternative able to carry out cultic functions for the community.[106] Additionally, the claim that the temple dated to the "days of the kings of Egypt" hearkens back to its traditional status and role within the community. Though life may have looked vividly different in Elephantine—Lindenberger describes Elephantine as "a syncretistic, non-traditional community"—the community still referred to itself

---

enemy" (James M. Lindenberger, "What Ever Happened to Vidranga? A Jewish Liturgy of Cursing from Elephantine," in Daviau et al., eds., *World of the Aramaeans*, 3:153–54).

104. Collins, *Invention of Judaism*, 51–52; cf. Grabbe, *History of the Jews and Judaism in the Second Temple Period*, 211.

105. Noting the presence of priests at the nearby settlement of Edfu, Toorn suggests that Edfu had its own temple. For Toorn, the existence of multiple temples makes it less likely that these temples were intended to rival Jerusalem. See Toorn, "Religion of the Elephantine Jews," in Witte et al., eds., *Torah, Temple, and Land*, 81.

106. One of the draft petitions (A4.5) mentions the priests of Khnum destroying a well frequently used by garrisoned soldiers, but it is unclear if this well existed within the temple or was adjacent to the temple precincts. Given that the well's destruction took place within the context of the ransacking of the temple, it appears to have been related to the temple, which suggests there may have been frequent interactions between the priests of the Elephantine and soldiers in the fortress. At the very least, if the well was utilized frequently by those garrisoned within the walls, there was likely a not insignificant level of visibility of priestly activity within the community.

as Jews (יהודי) and took its temple worship of YHW (יהו) seriously.[107] In fact, van der Toorn goes so far as to conclude that, based on the response from Judaean and Samaritan leadership, "the diaspora community [of Elephantine] was seen as mainstream."[108]

As one distant temple was destroyed in Elephantine in the fifth century BCE, a proximate one appeared in Samaria. Josephus dates the construction of the Samaritan temple at Mount Gerizim to the last third of the fourth century BCE. In Josephus's account, Manasseh, brother of the high priest, wished to divorce the daughter of the Persian governor of Samaria, Sanballat, in order to salvage his sacerdotal position in the priestly lineage. Sanballat instead offered to build a temple in Samaria and install Manasseh as high priest. Sanballat, sensing Persian control waning, shifted allegiances to the Macedonians and petitioned Alexander for permission to build the temple at Mt. Gerizim, and Alexander's acquiescence set the stage for Samaria's own temple (*A.J.* 11.306–324).[109] Josephus's timeline, however, is confused. He mistakenly places Sanballat, who was addressed in the fifth-century Elephantine papyri, in the fourth century BCE. He also shifts the marriage of Sanballat's daughter to a member of the high priestly family—reported in Neh 13:28 during the time of Artaxerxes I—into the time of the transition in imperial power from Darius III to Alexander the Great. The anachronistic postdating may be inconsequential for Josephus, who was probably reliant on traditional narratives about the Samaritan temple's construction, but it does hint at a point Yitzhak Magen's excavations of Mt. Gerizim have revealed:

107. Lindenberger continues, "They called themselves 'Jews', but it is clear from their relaxed attitude towards the worship of other divinities, from their possession of their own local temple, and from their complete innocence of the basic tenets of the Deuteronomic reform that the word meant something rather different to them than it meant to stricter-minded contemporaries such as Ezra and Nehemiah" (Lindenberger, "What Ever Happened to Vidranga?," in Daviau et al., eds., *World of the Aramaeans*, 3:153). However, Collins draws the situations in Elephantine and Judah together, emphasizing Ezra and Nehemiah's (re)institution of the Torah and how great an influence that had on Judah in the fifth century BCE. Both the picture in Judah pre-Ezra and Nehemiah and the portrait we get from the papyri in Elephantine "show that it was possible to be 'Judean' in the fifth century without reference to the Law of Moses" (Collins, *Invention of Judaism*, 52).

108. Toorn, "Religion of the Elephantine Jews," in Witte et al., eds., *Torah, Temple, and Land*, 89.

109. Hengel also dates the founding of the Samaritan temple to this time period: "Alexander's drastic measures against Samaria, which changed the city into a Macedonian colony . . . led to the resettlement of Shechem and thus probably also to the building of the temple on Gerizim" (Hengel, *Judaism and Hellenism*, 1:13).

the Samaritan temple went through two major phases of construction, the earliest phase dating to the mid-fifth century BCE.[110] It would not be surprising, then, if Sanballat or other fifth-century BCE figures played a pivotal role in the foundation of the Samaritan temple.

Once established, the temple at Mt. Gerizim required a priesthood to operate and maintain its cultic functions. As Timothy Wardle notes, "a proper Israelite priesthood, equal in legitimacy to the priesthood ensconced in the Jerusalem temple, presided over the worship of the God of Israel at Gerizim."[111] Josephus's narrative forefronts Manasseh and how the Mt. Gerizim temple traced its foundation to the high priestly lineage, a feature it would have shared with the Jerusalem temple. Because of this shared priestly lineage, Wardle argues that tensions between Jews and Samaritans were not as high as they would later appear after the second century BCE. "Since both temples were almost certainly overseen by members of the same priestly clan, many of the continuing beliefs, practices, and traditions shared by Judeans and Samarians likely stemmed from ongoing communications between the two."[112] The longevity of the temple "meant that two temples dedicated to the God of Israel . . . were constructed around the same time and coexisted for hundreds of years."[113] Like at Elephantine, the Samaritan temple, at least throughout the Persian period, was not viewed in competition or as a rival, but as a local alternative rooted in its own Israelite traditions.[114]

---

110. Yitzhak Magen, "Dating of the First Phase of the Samaritan Temple on Mount Gerizim in Light of the Archaeological Evidence," in Lipschits et al., eds., *Judah and the Judeans in the Fourth Century BCE*, 158–60; cf. Stern and Magen, "Archaeological Evidence for the First Stage," 49–57.

111. Timothy Wardle, "Samaritans, Jews, and Christians: Multiple Partings and Multiple Ways," in Baron et al., eds., *Ways that Often Parted*, 20.

112. Wardle, "Samaritans, Jews, and Christians: Multiple Partings and Multiple Ways," in Baron et al., eds., *Ways that Often Parted*, 21. Gary Knoppers also discusses the commonalities between Jews and Samaritans during the fourth century BCE: "It is quite possible that the leaders in Samaria and Jerusalem enjoyed generally good relations during much of the Achaemenid era . . . It was precisely because there was so much overlap between the two groups that an appeal could be made from one to the other. Such unity based on shared bloodlines, shared customs, shared traditions, shared prophets, shared beliefs, a shared past, a shared land and a shared social structure could be cited to build hope for a common future" (Knoppers, "Mt. Gerizim and Mt. Zion," 327; cf. Knoppers, *Jews and Samaritans*).

113. Wardle, "Samaritans, Jews, and Christians: Multiple Partings and Multiple Ways," in Baron et al., eds., *Ways that Often Parted*, 20.

114. Several biblical traditions involve important geographic and cultural Samarian landmarks. See, e.g., Gen 12:6–7; Deut 27:11–12; Josh 8:33.

This compatibility would change during the Hasmonean period, but at least until "the close of the third century BCE, the relationship seems to have been relatively cordial, albeit with the Samaritans holding most of the cards politically."[115]

The Hellenistic Period (323–166 BCE)

Inasmuch as the Hellenistic period can be described as the dominating legacy of Alexander, it can also be characterized by political, social, and economic turbulence in Palestine. Hengel argues that Palestine during this era "was shaped by its role as a disputed buffer-state between the two great powers" of Ptolemaic Egypt and Seleucid Syria.[116] Because of its role in the middle of geopolitical conflict, Jewish support likely fell to whichever dynasty ruled over the state.[117]

The Jerusalem temple played an important role in these political, social, and economic spheres of influence. Under Ptolemaic rule, Ptolemy III Euergetes offered sacrifices of thanks at the temple after the third Syrian war, drawing favor with those in the region (*C.Ap.* 2.48). Ptolemy IV Philopator later emulated this by offering sacrifices throughout the region after the successful staving off of Antiochus III and the Seleucids in 217 BCE. Dedicatory inscriptions were set up in his honor in Joppa (SEG 20.467), Marisa, and Tyre (SEG 39.1596,b). Philopator's presence in and around Jerusalem likely indicates that he visited Jerusalem and its temple as well.[118] Decades later, the Seleucid king Antiochus III and his army marched into Ptolemaic territory and successfully occupied Palestine. As a post-war peacemaking concession, Antiochus III "promised the Jews not only his support in rebuilding the city and the temple,

---

115. Wardle, "Samaritans, Jews, and Christians: Multiple Partings and Multiple Ways," in Baron et al., eds., *Ways that Often Parted*, 29.

116. Hengel, *Judaism and Hellenism*, 1:11.

117. Jewish support was not always unanimous; multiple parties existed within Jerusalem with varying allegiances toward ruling kings. Additionally, as Barclay demonstrates around the diaspora world, there were varying attitudes toward accommodating, assimilating, and acculturating to Hellenistic practices. The diversity of political ruling opinions in Palestine likely indicates the inklings of what would later become a conflict over differing cultural beliefs resulting in the reaction of Antiochus IV and the Maccabean revolt.

118. Later Hasmonean memory would key this visit with that of Antiochus IV Epiphanes, claiming that Philopator attempted indignantly to desecrate the temple against the warnings of the entirety of the city. See 3 Macc 1:1–2:24.

but also exemption from tribute for three years and the release of Jewish prisoners."[119] The promise of peace and semi-autonomy did not last long; the last days of Antiochus III and the reign of his successor, Seleucus IV Philopator, brought another period of unrest to the region. Relations were frayed with Ptolemaic Egypt, and the Roman threat to the Seleucids resulted in military defeats and increased reparations, which trickled down to the Jewish populace. The report of Heliodorus's attempt at taking possession of the temple riches in 2 Macc 3 likely attests to both the financial burden placed on the Jews and the political tensions and resistance that was growing against the Seleucids.

Jewish sentiment toward the Seleucids, which had been positive at the beginning of the second century BCE, unraveled under Antiochus IV Epiphanes.[120] Soon after Antiochus IV took the throne, a Seleucid attack on Egypt ca. 169 BCE led him to plunder the Jerusalem temple treasury as a royal reimbursement. Antiochus also reportedly prohibited Jewish customs and instituted a series of policies that went against traditional Jewish practices, including the building of a *gymnasium* (leading to an increase in instances of epispasm), the prohibition of circumcision, the introduction of new altars and the restriction of burnt and drink offerings, the profaning of holy days, and, most notably, the sacrifice of impure animals/swine on the temple altar (1 Macc 1:11–15, 41–61). Josephus also includes the building of a Seleucid citadel overlooking the temple from the south (*A.J.* 12.252), and Diodorus reports not only the sacrifice of a swine, but the profaning of the altar and holy texts with the blood of the sacrifice, as well as the extinguishing of the undying altar flame (*Lib.* 34.1.1–5). These violations were compounded with the previous decades of financial strain, strife in the high priesthood (2 Macc 3:4–6; 4:1–17), and the frenetic nature of geopolitical conquests and changing national allegiances, setting the stage for revolt at the hands of the Maccabees.[121]

119. Hengel, *Judaism and Hellenism*, 1:10.

120. For a fuller discussion of the Seleucids, see Kosmin, *Time and Its Adversaries in the Seleucid Empire*.

121. Erich Gruen surveys several potential explanations for Antiochus IV's persecutory policies, such as conformity with Hellenistic rule across the Seleucid kingdom, pragmatic repression to enforce political and financial fealty, persecution as the product of a surprising and eccentric monarch, and as an intra-Jewish conflict driven by a Jewish Hellenizing party (led by Jason and, later, Menelaus). Gruen instead offers a two-pronged hypothesis explaining Antiochus IV's persecution: Rome's thwarting of Seleucid advancement in Egypt (Polybius 29.27.1–10) and the recent civil strife in Jerusalem (cf. 2 Macc 5). Gruen suggests that the damage done to Antiochus IV's reputation would be ameliorated by forcefully reining in Jerusalem: "The upheaval in Judaea came

Similar to the Persian period, alternative Jewish temples were founded in the tumult of the Hellenistic period. The Oniad temple is perhaps most well-known due to its mention in Josephus (*A.J.* 12.387–388; 13.69–73) and its relation to the prophecy of Isa 19:19, but the purpose of the temple and the events leading to Onias's flight to Egypt are not entirely clear.[122] According to Josephus, Onias fled Judaea in the high priestly turnover and turmoil that occurred at the start of Antiochus IV's reign and was successful in petitioning the Ptolemies to build a temple in Leontopolis (*A.J.* 13.62–68). Strikingly, Onias's petition mentions the presence of multiple Jewish temples (ἱερὰ; *A.J.* 13.66) in Egypt, but the implication is that if these are actual temple locations—Joan Taylor questions whether Josephus/Onias is referring to synagogues here—they have created issues that a centralized cult location would ameliorate.[123] This suggests that the intention for the Leontopolis temple was to serve in the same function as the Jerusalem temple: as a meeting place for Egyptian Jews in fulfillment of Isaiah's prophecy. Elsewhere, however, Josephus accuses Onias of using the Leontopolis temple as a recruiting device not only to entice Jews to emigrate to Egypt to join the fight against Antiochus IV, but also out of spite against the Jerusalem temple due to his supposed gripe in being passed over for the high priesthood (*B.J.* 7.431). Gideon Bohak, however, assesses the situation in a slightly different manner. Bohak argues Onias's arrival in Egypt was mutually beneficial for the Oniads and the Ptolemies. Pointing to the role the Oniads played in commanding the Ptolemaic army, Bohak states "it seems that the opportunity of establishing a strong and loyal military commander in Heliopolis could serve two important Ptolemaic goals: on the one hand it would defend Egypt against future invasions from the north-east, and

---

at a convenient time and offered a suitable target. The introduction of a garrison and the intimidation of the populace by state terrorism had a larger design than simply to punish the Jews. It would announce Antiochus Epiphanes' resumption of control to the diverse peoples and nations nominally under the Seleucid regime ... Antiochus would answer any potential questions about his withdrawal from Egypt by taking the offensive in Palestine" (Gruen, *Constructs of Identity in Hellenistic Judaism*, 356).

122. An additional quandary in Josephus's narratives is the identification of which Onias is responsible for the construction of the temple, as Josephus's writings offer conflicting information about whether it was Onias III (Onias the son of Simon; *B.J.* 7.423) or Onias IV (Onias the son of Onias; *A.J.* 13.62). For more on the identification, see Taylor, "Second Temple in Egypt," 297–321.

123. See Taylor, "Second Temple in Egypt," 305; Hjelm, "Cult Centralization as a Device of Control," 302.

on the other hand Onias would keep an eye on the native population."[124] Whatever the reasons that prompted it, the Leontopolis temple remained in use throughout the Hasmonean period until it was destroyed at the close of the Jewish War (*B.J.* 7.433–436).

The gravitas of the Oniad temple is often minimized when compared to Jerusalem, but it is possible that the Oniad temple had more reach in Egypt. A private letter from the first century BCE (SB VI.9564 = *CPJ* 1.141) requests aid and accommodations for a certain priest (ἱερέος*) from Tebtunis because the people of Memphis "are nauseated by Jews" (βδελύσονται Ἰουδαίους).[125] Rémondon argues convincingly that the priest is Jewish: based on onomastics, the author of the letter is likely writing to a fellow Jew(s), and a pagan priest would only need protection in the unlikely case that Memphian Jews overran the city and prevented temple worship, whereas a Jewish priest would elicit concerns for protection if Memphis had the reputation for anti-Semitism at the time, which is more likely.[126] Given the proximity of Memphis to Leontopolis, it seems far more likely that this priest served in the Oniad temple than Jerusalem. Additionally, the association with the remote town of Tebtunis (ἱερέος* τοῦ τῆς Τεβτύνεως) may indicate that the Oniad temple drew Jews from across Upper Egypt. This would reflect the widespread awareness of the Oniad temple in the same way as the Elephantine papyri (see above, A3.3). Abraham Wasserstein also notes the temple was memorialized in later rabbinic writings, arguing the rabbis believed "whatever the status of that temple may have been, it was not an idolatrous temple, and some of the sacrificial acts performed there were, under certain circumstances,

---

124. Bohak, "CPJ III, 520," 37. Bohak reads the reconstructed CPJ III, 520—a fragmentary anti-Jewish papyrus mentioning the Jews as the target of unclear destructive action(s)—as an apocalyptic text from Egyptian priests that had been displaced by Onias's temple and settlement in Heliopolis: "These disenfranchised priests and prophets, seeing their beloved Heliopolis turned into a military colony, could only gnash their teeth and beg their gods for a day of revenge" (Bohak, "CPJ III, 520," 38). Bohak also identifies traces of temple imagery in *Joseph and Aseneth*, arguing this text refers to the Oniad temple in Heliopolis. See Bohak, *Joseph and Aseneth*.

125. Although a land survey of Tebtunis does mention a synagogue (P. Tebt. 1.86), it seems odd that a Jewish author would conflate a synagogue leader (ἀρχισυνάγωγος) with a priest (ἱερεύς). To my knowledge, this confusion has not been attested before by a Jewish author and, therefore, this is not a preferred interpretation.

126. Rémondon, "Antisémites de Memphis," 256–57; cf. Bagnall and Derow, *Hellenistic Period*, 284.

to be regarded as valid."[127] Wardle also articulates the complexity of the temple's status in summarizing its legacy:

> If the lack of reference to this temple in Egyptian Jewish literature is any indication, it had little impact on Egyptian Jewry, nor was it ever considered a serious rival to the Jerusalem temple. But it did have some weighty arguments on its side. Founded by the legitimate Zadokite priest, fueled by a prophecy from Isaiah, and designed to replicate the temple in Jerusalem, the Oniad temple presented itself as an alternative to the one in Jerusalem.[128]

While the Oniad temple is perhaps the most popular temple alternative of the period, another more controversial location may have existed closer to Judaea. Josephus discusses activity in the Transjordan region by the Tobiad family, particularly Hyrcanus, who built an estate in the area that included "a strong fortress (βᾶριν ἰσχυράν)" built out of marble (*A.J.* 12.230–231). The purpose and nature of this fortress, the Qasr el-Abd, has long been questioned, and excavations in modern Jordan ('Iraq al-Amir) continue to raise questions about its classification.[129] Félicien de Saulcy's "temple hypothesis" in the mid-nineteenth century was attractive and influential for the next century of scholarship, garnering support from followers like Paul Lapp and even Martin Hengel.[130] Hengel argued in favor of the probability "that Hyrcanus wanted to make the Qasr into *a temple to compete with Jerusalem*, a parallel to the sanctuaries of Elephantine, Leontopolis and Gerizim."[131] The competition between Jerusalem and alternatives in Elephantine and Gerizim has been addressed and downplayed in the sections above, but it is possible that Hengel is attributing the competition to the overall depiction of

---

127. Wasserstein, "Notes on the Temple of Onias at Leontopolis," 125. For the complex rabbinic discussions of the temple of Onias and its legitimate status for particular sacrifices and vows, see *m. Men.* 13:10; *b. Men.* 109a–b; *b. Meg.* 10a; cf. n64.

128. Wardle, *Jerusalem Temple and Early Christian Identity*, 138–39.

129. The Qasr is one of the key indicators that 'Iraq al-Amir ought to be linked to the ancient Tobiad estate of Tyre, but there is also an inscription with the word "Tobiah" (*CIJ* II, 105 no. 868) carved over a nearby cave entrance further connecting this location to Josephus's narrative. See Lapp, *Excavations at Araq el-Emir*.

130. For more on the development of de Saulcy's temple hypothesis and its rejection of de Vogüé's palace identification, see Ernest Will, "Recent French Work at Araq el-Emir: The Qasr el-Abd Rediscovered," in Lapp, ed., *Excavations at Araq el-Emir*, 149–54.

131. Hengel, *Judaism and Hellenism*, 1:274.

Hyrcanus and the frayed relationship between Hyrcanus and the temple priesthood found in the Josephus narrative. Peter Schäfer also links the temple identification to the Qasr's inner room and the imposing statues positioned around the exterior, arguing the "installation represented a temple, possibly a rival of the Jerusalem temple."[132] However, other research based on excavations and floorplans has encouraged scholars to be doubtful of the temple hypothesis and instead argue in favor of the Qasr el-Abd as a residential palace, what Ernest Will calls "the luxurious dwelling place dreamed about by Hyrcanus."[133] Though Will argues "nothing [in the site plans] recalls a temple—at least a temple of a known type," there is no clear consensus on the purpose of the Qasr, and the temple designation remains a possibility.[134]

The Hellenistic period was a complex era characterized by periods of stability and fluctuation. Ptolemaic influence and reign held strong for around one hundred years, and the early Ptolemaic period signaled prosperous times for those in Palestine.[135] But a series of Syrian wars in the late third and early second centuries BCE resulted in a starker reality. Palestine stood in the middle of major power struggles between the Ptolemies and Seleucids, and these political, economic, and cultural power struggles had a significant impact on the future of the Jewish people and the development of Second Temple Judaism.

---

132. Peter Schäfer, "Hellenistic and Maccabean Periods," in Hayes and Miller, eds., *Israelite and Judaean History*, 550.

133. Will, "Recent French Work at Araq el-Emir," in Lapp, ed., *Excavations at Araq el-Emir*, 153. For more recent research on the Qasr, see Grabbe, *History of the Jews and Judaism*, 2:42.

134. Will, "The Recent French Work at Araq el-Emir," in Lapp, ed., *Excavations at Araq el-Emir*, 151. While the Qasr el-Abd persisted in an unfinished state through the Byzantine era, another fortress from the Byzantine period was also represented as a temple—at least in ancient literature. Procopius, in detailing the buildings attributed to the emperor Justinian in the fortress of Boreium (Cyrenaica), mentions an "ancient [Jewish] temple" (καὶ νεὼς ἦν ἀρχαῖος αὐτοῖς, *Aed.* 6.2.22) that was reportedly built by Solomon. R. G. Goodchild's notes on the excavation of Boreum understands the reference to be of a synagogue, but the use of νεώς/ναός is peculiar. See Goodchild, "Boreum of Cyrenaica," 11.

135. Peter Schäfer mentions the Zenon papyri, which include letters from Tobias in the Transjordan region to Apollonius, *dioketes* of Ptolemy II Philadelphus. These letters reference riches and gifts offered to Ptolemy and Apollonius, and Schäfer suggests that Apollonius's journey was for the "inspection and improvement of the financial administration and the betterment of economic relations between the Egyptian mother-country and its northern province" (Schäfer, "Hellenistic and Maccabean Periods," 572).

The Hasmonean Period (166–63 BCE)

For all intents and purposes, the Hasmonean period is merely a subset of the Hellenistic period. The major defining difference for the Hasmonean period was the shift to political autonomy when the Maccabean revolt eventually led to Judaean independence and political power was seated in the Hasmonean family.[136] Otherwise, the cultural, religious, and social conflicts of the third century BCE—e.g., relating to gentile authorities and neighbors, the interpretation of the law, and adapting to or rejecting Hellenistic culture—continued to be characteristic of life in the second and first centuries BCE.

The Jerusalem temple played a significant role in the lead up to and during the Hasmonean period. In particular, it was the central focus of the Maccabean revolt. At the start of the period, Antiochus IV's reign led to financial power struggles and friction between influential families within Palestine, like the Tobiads and the high-priestly Oniads.[137] However, Antiochus IV's provocation in the temple—setting up an altar to Zeus, interfering with the daily offerings, and sacrificing swine—was the tipping point that kickstarted the revolt.[138] The temple was a motivating factor for the Maccabeans. The beginning of the armed conflict, Mattathias's slaughter of a fellow countryman and royal officials (1 Macc 2:15–26), is narratively framed by his lament for the temple (1 Macc 2:7–13) and the destruction of altars in Israel (1 Macc 2:42–48), demonstrating that the temple was a central catalyst to revolution. After Mattathias's death, Judas led the reclamation and rededication of the temple, which marked perhaps the most significant victory for the revolutionaries (1 Macc 4:36–61; 2 Macc 10:1–9).

Within a few decades of the temple's rededication, the Hasmoneans transitioned from a defensive stance around the temple to an offensive stance against the Samaritan temple. Political influence played

---

136. Josephus (*A.J.* 12.265) traces Mattathias's lineage back to a Jerusalem priest Asamoneus/Asamonaios, which is likely from where the "Hasmonean" nomenclature has been derived.

137. Hengel argues that the result of this turbulence was priestly competition and turnover of the high priesthood that saw "the founding of competing sanctuaries, as under the Tobiad Hyrcanus in Transjordania or under Onias IV in Leontopolis" (*Judaism and Hellenism*, 1:12; cf. 1:304; *A.J.* 12.196–202).

138. See 2 Macc 6:5; Dan 12:11. The Gospel of Mark also keys itself to an apocalyptic act of disruption in the temple by using the same coded language about "the desolating sacrilege" (τὸ βδέλυγμα τῆς ἐρημώσεως, Mark 13:14).

an important part in the shift as the Hasmoneans gained a number of concessions from the Seleucids in the second century BCE that the Samaritans did not.[139] The rivalry between the Hasmoneans and Samaritans came to a tipping point at the turn of the first century BCE when John Hyrcanus destroyed the temple at Mount Gerizim and took control of the region. In discussing the intentions and implications of the destruction of the Samaritan temple, Wardle argues,

> It may be that [John Hyrcanus] wished to integrate those living in Samaria into the Hasmonean state and to force their allegiance to the Jerusalem temple and its priesthood. Alternatively, he may have felt threatened by the Samaritan priesthood, which had a much older and more prestigious priestly heritage than did the upstart Hasmonean family, and so decided to rid the region of any sacerdotal rivals. In any case, it is clear that the destruction of the Samaritan temple on Mount Gerizim drove a sharp wedge between Jews and Samaritans, exacerbating tensions that had likely been simmering for quite some time.[140]

Additional conflicts surrounding and within the priesthood defined the Hasmonean period, including at the very outset. In the aftermath of the Maccabean revolt, Jonathan took charge of the resistance and was appointed to, and consequently assumed, the role of high priest (1 Macc 10:21), which reshaped and formally usurped the Zadokite lineage of the priesthood. The shift in social dynamics during this period revolves heavily around priestly replacement and priestly competition, both external (Hasmoneans against former Zadokite priests) and internal (Hasmoneans against one another). Priestly feathers would have been ruffled when

---

139. Timothy Wardle points to "the title of the high priest (1 Macc 10:17-21; Josephus A.J. 13.45); three tracts of Samarian land: Aphairema, Lydda, and Ramathaim (1 Macc 11:34-36; cf. 10:30, 38); and tax exemptions that were not granted to those who sacrificed at the Gerizim temple (1 Macc 11:34)" (Wardle, "Samaritans, Jews, and Christians: Multiple Partings and Multiple Ways," in Baron et al., eds., *Ways that Often Parted*, 21-22).

140. Wardle, "Samaritans, Jews, and Christians: Multiple Partings and Multiple Ways," in Baron et al., eds., *Ways that Often Parted*, 22. Jan Dušek downplays the role of Hellenization in the divide between the Samaritans and the Hasmoneans but does note that it may have contributed to the Seleucid favor toward the Samaritans, arguing, "We do not know the degree of Hellenization among the other Yahwists in Samaria but it does not seem to affect the official cult in the sanctuary on Mt. Gerizim, in spite of the attribution of a Greek name to it. At the same time it was probably sufficient to give a reason to Antiochus IV to leave them in peace in the time of persecution of pious Jews after the suppression of Judaism in December 167 BCE" (Dušek, *Aramaic and Hebrew Inscriptions*, 115).

"the Maccabees expelled or killed many of the 'old guard' and advanced 'new men' like themselves to become a new aristocracy."[141] Likewise, the antagonism and jockeying between Hyrcanus II and Aristobulus II (*A.J.* 13.16—14.4) demonstrates that the temple institution and priestly hierarchy continued to play a central role in the political ambitions of the Hasmoneans down to the very last days of their dynasty.

The Maccabean changes to the priesthood also seem to be a catalyst for those who aligned with the Dead Sea Scrolls's disdain toward the Jerusalem establishment. The animosity against the Jerusalem priesthood is apparent in the figure of the "Wicked Priest" that appears in the *Commentary on Habakkuk* (1QpHab 9.9–12), an antagonist likely styled after the Hasmoneans.[142] Similarly, 4QMMT offers several examples of differing halakhic interpretations, demonstrating "some of the continuing disputes between those living at Qumran and the priestly establishment at Jerusalem."[143] The text punctuates these sectarian disagreements by pointing out how the authors have separated themselves from those who conduct such practices (C, 1.7–9), as well as highlighting their hopes that the proper interpretation will guide the recipients (C, 1.26–32). The attitude and approach demonstrated by 4QMMT is also evident in several other rules documents. The *Damascus Document* expounds on three "traps of Belial," grievances against the priesthood that resonate with conflicts mentioned in 4QMMT: fornication/marriage, wealth, and the defilement of the sanctuary (4.14–5.15). Separation is encouraged in 1QS (5.1–2; 8.12–13), and the Zadokite priestly lineage ("Sons of Zadok") holds an integral positive function as instructors for the community (5.2–3, 9; 6.3–4; 8.1). The community is also reimagined

---

141. Cohen, *From the Maccabees to the Mishnah*, 23.

142. Vanderkam and Flint argue the most likely referent of "the Wicked Priest" is Jonathan, "who acquired wealth through his campaigns of conquest and, though he was only a military leader at first, became the high priest despite not being from the high-priestly family . . . His death at enemy hands comes closest to matching what the *Commentary on Habbakuk* says about the Wicked Priest's terrible end" (Vanderkam and Flint, *Meaning of the Dead Sea Scrolls*, 286).

143. Wardle, *Jerusalem Temple and Early Christian Identity*, 67. Though fragmentary, these disputes seem to have included proper sexual relations/marriages, the calendrical system, the proper place of sacrifice, the purity of certain practices, and who (or, in the case of dogs, what) was permitted within the temple precincts. Wardle also argues that an additional contention the authors of 4QMMT may have had with the priesthood was financial mismanagement, drawing on Lev 15:5 and later Mishnaic usage of מעל to tease out "allegations of financial misappropriation of temple funds" (Wardle, *Jerusalem Temple and Early Christian Identity*, 69).

as a temple (8.5–6) where community association is understood in sacrificial ways (8.6–10; 9.4), even though the composition of the group is mixed between priests and laypeople (8.1). Finally, the physical temple precincts take center stage in the *Temple Scroll* (11Q19), where their proportions are expanded and additional sacrifices and holy days are divinely appointed. Although the text is less explicit about its dissatisfaction with the Jerusalem establishment, the manner in which significant differences between the dimensions of the temple (30.3–47.3) and the extrabiblical festival practices (14.9–17.4; 21.12–23.1) are directly revealed by God suggests this text "clearly stakes a claim of authority and raises the question whether this text, too, was considered scriptural at Qumran—*the* proper interpretation of the Torah."[144] In addition, the temple described by 11Q19 is attributed to divine construction (29.7–9), which adds to the notion that the text has disregarded or moved beyond its contemporary Jerusalem temple. Together, these and other texts in the Scrolls catalog demonstrate how, "in the interim period before God established a new temple, the sectarians were able to function without a temple, as usually defined, due to their belief that the community, in the present, acted as a substitute temple."[145]

The Roman Period (63 BCE–70 CE)

The Roman period—at least during the time when the temple was standing—is intricately tied to significant events in and around the temple. From the very beginning of Pompey's intervention in the civil strife between Hyrcanus II and Aristobulus II, the temple featured prominently. Josephus (*A.J.* 14.3) focuses on the temple as central to the military strategy of the conflict. Aristobulus's forces entrenched themselves within the temple fortifications, so Pompey's siege was primarily focused on the temple itself. Later Roman memory amplified Pompey's accomplishments; for instance, Dio Cassius cited the impressive fortification of the temple as if it were impenetrable, claiming that were it not for Jewish observance of the Sabbath, Pompey "could not have got possession of it" (*Hist. rom.* 37.16). Once the siege was complete, Pompey marched into the temple precincts and into the holy of holies, leaving the temple treasures untouched and instead reinstating Hyrcanus II as high priest (*A.J.*

---

144. Vanderkam and Flint, *Meaning of the Dead Sea Scrolls*, 211, emphasis original.
145. Wardle, *Jerusalem Temple and Early Christian Identity*, 162.

14.4). Similar to the Maccabean revolt, the events in the temple were a harbinger of the shift in broader political power. Once Pompey's forces took control of the temple, the siege of Jerusalem was effectively over and, as a result, so was Hasmonean autonomy in Judaea.

After claiming control of the region, the Romans installed local rulers to serve in positions of governance in return for their fealty to Rome. Herod was a major beneficiary of the transition to Roman rule, utilizing his wealth and imperial connections to gain power and prestige during an era of semi-autonomy in Judaea (*A.J.* 14.158–487). During his reign, Herod had a rocky relationship with the priesthood, often removing high priests and replacing them for political or personal reasons (*A.J.* 15.14–41, 50–56, 317–322). However, he also oversaw a period of the reinvigoration and renovation of the Jerusalem temple, turning it into even more of a spectacle for the ancient world (*B.J.* 1.401; *A.J.* 15.380).[146] Later Roman historians favorably remembered the temple long after its destruction: Tacitus (*Hist.* 5.8) doted on the impressive opulence of the temple's treasures and its strategic location, while Dio Cassius (*Hist. rom.* 37.17) admired its size and beauty. The reputation of Jerusalem's temple also brought increased attention to its practices. Josephus mentions multiple pillars that announced "the law of purity" (τὸν τῆς ἁγνείας... νόμον, *B.J.* 5.194), which limited gentiles entering into the innermost temple precincts, in both Greek and Latin. The composition of two extant Greek inscriptions—both are copies of the same inscription and only contain minor insignificant textual variants—seems to confirm that they were installed as a visible means of warning foreigners (ἀλλογενῆ) that anyone trespassing into the inner-courts would be liable for their own "following death" (διὰ τὸ ἐξακολουθεῖν θάνατον, *OGIS* 598).[147] However strictly and to whatever degree these warnings were

---

146. A Greek dedicatory pavement inscription lists a benefactor, Paris, who was either from or presently located in Rhodes. This inscription suggests that Herod's temple project benefitted from the contributions of wealthy foreigners, rather than Josephus's insistence that Herod financed the construction himself (*A.J.* 15.380). See Cotton et al., *Jerusalem*, 45–47.

147. Both temple warning inscriptions only contain Greek lettering (*contra* Josephus's description of both Greek and Roman lettering, *B.J.* 5.192) and are more robust of a warning than the brief descriptions given by Josephus, who uses other, seemingly interchangeable terms for "foreigners" (ἀλλόφυλον, *B.J.* 5.194; ἀλλοεθνῆ, *A.J.* 15.417); cf. Cotton et al., *Jerusalem*, 42–45.

adhered, these inscriptions evidence the dynamic tensions at play in the temple during the Roman period.[148]

As Jewish semi-autonomy faded, a series of conflicts with Roman rulers led to clashes over the symbolic and religious dimensions of the temple. A few decades after Archelaus was removed and Rome took direct control of Judaea, the Roman emperor Gaius Caligula attempted to install a statue of his likeness in the temple (ἐγκαθιδρύσοντα τῷ ναῷ τοὺς ἀνδριάντας αὐτοῦ, Josephus, B.J. 2.185). Philo's account of these events places Gaius's actions in the context of the emperor's other cruelties (Legat. 3–10) and pursuits of godhood (Legat. 12–15), contextualizing it as another instance of persecution against Jews. Josephus highlights the sense of nationwide resistance to this breach of law and custom (τὸν νόμον καὶ τὸ πάτριον ἔθος, B.J. 2.195) and mentions how, in order to avoid all-out war, the Roman general Petronius risked his own life by removing the army and defying Gaius's orders. However, Philo claims Gaius relented on account of Agrippa's letter, but cancelling the statue's installation was actually a ruse: initially, Gaius intended to goad defiance elsewhere, and when no such defiance occurred, he considered installing an even grander statue (Legat. 42). Whatever Gaius's long-term plans for the Jerusalem temple were, his death temporarily ameliorated the brewing outrage. However, economic, political, and religious tensions came in waves for several decades until revolt ultimately broke out in Judaea. Josephus, in hindsight, discusses some of the portents, anomalies, and warning signs that took place in the temple precincts: a mysterious shining light on the altar and the inner chamber of the temple (B.J. 6.290), the mystifying opening of the massive east gate (B.J. 6.293), and an earthquake accompanied by the sound of voices declaring "we are departing from here" (μεταβαίνομεν ἐντεῦθεν, B.J. 6.296–299). Josephus also recounts the warnings of a certain Jesus, son of Ananus, who proclaimed sustained and unwavering warnings against Jerusalem even when beaten by Roman authorities; this Jesus's prophetic woes lasted from years before the revolt until his death during the siege of Jerusalem (B.J. 6.300–309). The last clashes between Roman authority and Judaean resistance in this

---

148. Peretz Segal, pointing to rabbinic sources, argues that these warnings likely reflect legal terminology referring to the death penalty ("death at the hands of heaven", מיתה בידי שמים), which "was administered by the priestly authorities of the Temple through summary execution" as a means of maintaining purity, since "they also exercised jurisdiction over those who profaned the Temple by their trespass" (Segal, "Penalty of the Warning Inscription," 84).

period resulted in a series of wars, which led to the devastation of Jerusalem and the final destruction of the temple in 70 CE.

In the same way that the destruction of the first temple led to massive shifts in Judaism, the destruction by the Romans reignited questions about theology, authority, and praxis that would dominate several centuries of literature. As Menahem Mor states, "Palestine Jewry after the year 70 CE was forced to cope with the new realities: Jerusalem destroyed, the Temple destroyed, the cancellation of the religious worship, and the loss of the high priesthood. The extent of the crisis that the population experienced is related to the estimated importance and centrality of the city and its institutions in the consciousness of the people in the period before the suppression of the revolt in 70 CE."[149] Early post-70 CE responses questioned who was at fault and what significance the temple's destruction would have. Josephus blamed Judaean "tyrants" for coaxing the Romans into attacking the city (*B.J.* 1.10–12), while also reexamining messianic traditions and prophetic scriptures as evidence of Vespasian's divine anointing (*B.J.* 6.310–315). Fourth Ezra also exculpates the Romans by interpreting the destruction of the temple and city as divine punishment for abandoning the covenant (1:5–6, 25–35; 2:1) while also situating these actions within a larger apocalyptic context (5:1–14; 11:1—12:39).[150] Second Baruch offers a similar explanation for the temple's destruction; although it is narratively placed in the past, it places the blame on the people and their sinful behavior (1:1–5). Second Baruch also claims the destruction and diaspora of Judaeans are temporary pieces of a divine timeline, but it goes further in undermining the Second Temple's status by claiming the Jerusalem temple has never been equal to the heavenly temple (4:2–7). Still, the temple remained a prominent symbol long after its destruction. Whereas these apocalyptic writings found ways to shift focus from the Jerusalem temple, others continued to draw on hopes or the significance of the temple. For instance, during the Second Revolt of 132–135 CE, Bar Kokhba employed temple imagery as a rallying cry for his vision of Judaean independence.[151]

---

149. Mor, *Second Jewish Revolt*, 26.

150. Hindy Najman argues 4 Ezra presents a "reboot" of Jewish tradition, where the audience is encouraged to imagine an "alternative past" in which the temple is downplayed in favor of scriptural tradition, prophecy, and apocalypticism. See Najman, *Losing the Temple and Recovering the Future*.

151. Bar Kokhba's motivations regarding the temple (i.e., its reconstruction and reinstitution of the sacrificial cult) cannot be claimed with any degree of certainty; however, the Bar Kokhba coins demonstrate temple imagery, which suggests the temple

Summary

Throughout the waxing and waning of imperial forces from the sixth century BCE to the first century CE, the Jerusalem temple remained a dominant cultural, religious, and political force. The temple was intricately tied to life in Judaea and the diaspora. As Wardle puts it, "The temple and its cult created a shared religious and emotional experience that knit together Jews all around the ancient world. In a very real sense, the temple, and participation in it, fashioned both an individual and a collective Jewish identity."[152]

Despite the centrality of the Jerusalem temple, several communities throughout the Second Temple period sought to establish a cultic center outside of Judaea. Alternative temple sites in Elephantine, Leontopolis, Samaria, and potentially in the Transjordan region demonstrate the diversity and variability of how ancient Jews practiced cultic worship. The alternative temples also add nuance to our understanding of how ancient Jews thought about the Jerusalem temple. In Elephantine, Jedaniah and a cadre of priests sought cooperation with and support from the ruling authorities in Judaea for the rebuilding and reestablishment of their Egyptian cultic center, a posture that would not have been imaginable if they lived in an irreparable state of rivalry with their Judaean counterparts. If Wardle is correct, Samaritan priests demonstrate how the Zadokite lineage coexisted for centuries between two neighboring temples. Josephus's depiction of Onias oscillates between political and militaristic opportunism, devout piety for scripture and prophecy, and spite for the Jerusalem temple. Alternative temple communities are often treated as unrepresentative outliers in the overarching history of the Second Temple period, but these ancient communities offer useful insights into the variability of Jewish identity in the Second Temple period, and this opens the door for more nuance in understanding how other Jewish communities understood and related to the Jerusalem temple.

---

played some significance in the revolt. In surveying the causes of the Bar Kokhba Revolt, Mor finds that the *Fiscus Judaicus* and the destruction of the temple "forced the Jews to adapt themselves once again to new realities, and this in itself could have been a dangerous stage in the system of relations between Jews and Romans" (Mor, *Second Jewish Revolt*, 31) even prior to the advancement of the Roman military, prohibition against circumcision, and construction of the *Aelia Capitolina* and Temple of Jupiter. On the Bar Kokhba coins, see Mor, *Second Jewish Revolt*, 242–49; Goodman, *Judaism in the Roman World*, 55.

152. Wardle, *Jerusalem Temple and Early Christian Identity*, 1.

Jewish Attitudes Toward the Jerusalem Temple

The prior survey of scholarship on Jewish identity introduced the diversity of ways the temple functioned in Jewish life both in Judaea and in the diaspora. The historical overview of the Second Temple period addressed the central role of the Jerusalem temple throughout the various eras of foreign and domestic rule. It also demonstrated a brewing turbulence manifested in prophetic literature, varying levels of Hellenization, the construction of alternative temples, and polemics against Jerusalem's priesthood. This final section expands on these reactions to the Jerusalem temple by examining the schematizing works of Jacob Neusner and Philip Church.

Jacob Neusner

Jacob Neusner investigates Jewish attitudes toward the temple by surveying the community association (or genre) of four groups: apocalyptic literature, the Qumran community, "Christian Jews," and the Pharisees. For apocalyptic literature, Neusner draws on 4 Ezra and 2 Baruch and leans on a few apocalyptic tropes—wickedness as a cause of destruction, the hope of a redemptive new era—in examining the apocalyptic reaction. Neusner describes the apocalyptic response to the temple's destruction as "essentially negative" but does not dive into the implications the destruction has for the temple's restoration or reexamination in the apocalyptic age.[153] While apocalyptic literature is treated in a cursory manner, Neusner draws several connections between the remaining groups. For both the Qumran community and the early Christians (whom he calls "Christian Jews"), Neusner discusses how a growing sense of community came to replace the temple before 70 CE. In the Dead Sea sect's case, the result of the rejection of and separation from the Jerusalem (Maccabean) priesthood "was to reconstruct the Temple and to reinterpret the nature and substance of sacrifice. The *community* constituted the reconstructed Temple."[154] In this regard, "Torah and obedience to its commandments

---

153. "The response of the visionaries is, thus, essentially negative. All they had to say is that God is just and Israel has sinned, but, in the end of time, there will be redemption. What to do in the meantime? Merely wait. Not much of an answer" (Neusner, "Judaism in a Time of Crisis," 317).

154. Neusner, "Judaism in a Time of Crisis," 319, emphasis original.

formed the new sacrifice" for the Qumran community.[155] On the other hand, Neusner argues that "Christian Jews" held a less antagonistic stance toward Jerusalem as well as a reinterpreted understanding of the sacrificial cult. Neusner claims, "while the early Christians felt a solidarity with Israel the people, with Jerusalem, and with the Temple, to them the cult of the Temple was meaningless, for the forgiveness of sins had taken place once for all through the last sacrifice, which rendered the continuation of the cult a matter of indifference."[156] Finally, Neusner utilizes rabbinic literature to reconstruct a Pharisaic position on the matter.[157] Neusner claims that, prior to the temple's destruction, "the Pharisees . . . arrogated to themselves—and to all Jews equally—the status of the Temple priests and did the things which priests must do on account of that status."[158] After its destruction, Neusner points to the declaration by Rabbi Yohanan ben Zakkai that acts of kindness serve as a new form of atonement in the wake of the destruction of the temple (*Avot de Rabbi Natan* 4:5).

Neusner's survey demonstrates "several ways in which individuals and groups of Jews of that day responded to the calamity" of the temple's destruction.[159] However, references to the Dead Sea Scrolls or Pauline literature draw on texts that pre-date the destruction. In reality, then, Neusner's survey examines literature that grapples with the *loss, rejection, or replacement* of the temple, and he is far more dismissive of literature that grapples with how to understand its destruction—either the threat of destruction (as with Philo) or the actual aftermath of the Jewish War (as with 4 Ezra and 2 Baruch). Still, Neusner's survey offers a helpful spectrum of varying responses to the symbol of the temple, both pre- and post-70 CE. In his iconoclastic and provocative manner, Neusner argues, "long before 70 the Temple had been rejected by some Jewish groups. Its sanctity . . . had been arrogated by others. And for large numbers of ordinary Jews

---

155. Neusner, "Judaism in a Time of Crisis," 319.

156. Neusner, "Judaism in a Time of Crisis," 320.

157. Neusner's approach to constructing this attitude relies on imputing later rabbinic beliefs onto the earlier Pharisaic community. The earlier Pharisaic community, however, resists any conclusive characterization because of the dearth of evidence and lack of primary, contemporary sources. Neusner's method of continuity has recently been scrutinized as an unreliable manner to approach studying the Pharisees. For more on the difficulties of reconstructing the Pharisees, see Sievers and Levine, *Pharisees*.

158. Neusner, "Judaism in a Time of Crisis," 322.

159. Neusner, "Judaism in a Time of Crisis," 313.

outside of Palestine, as well as substantial numbers within, the Temple was a remote and, if holy, unimportant place."[160]

Adela Yarbro Collins

Adela Yarbro Collins's work on "hidden transcripts" of resistance examines texts "in the context of power relations, namely, the exercise of power and resistance to" the second temple's social, political, and religious dominance.[161] By reflecting on the assumption that the temple's destruction was catastrophic across all spheres of Judaism, Collins prefaces her study by cautioning, "attitudes toward the temple and its imagined or actual destruction were more complex" than often assumed.[162] She finds the dream vision of "the Animal Apocalypse" of 1 Enoch (1 En. 85–90)—a section of the apocalyptic text that retells Jewish history by replacing key figures with animals—of particular interest. Collins highlights the contrasting reception between the two temples: the First Temple is characterized positively or, at worst, neutrally (1 En. 89:50), whereas the Second Temple is described as containing polluted and impure bread (1 En. 89:72–73). Further, Collins points out the missing temple in the vision of the new Jerusalem (1 En. 90:28–36). The combination of these two factors, a negative Second Temple and no temple in the new Jerusalem, leads Collins to argue "this resistance may have come from dissident priests or from alienated scribes."[163] Elsewhere, Collins examines texts like Daniel (including Josephus's retelling of Daniel's four kingdoms motif in Josephus [*A.J.* 10.210]), *The Community Rule* (1QS), *The Damascus Document* (CD), and the Gospel of Mark to showcase different attitudes and manners of resistance toward the Second Temple.

Collins does not argue that every instance (or "hidden transcript") of critique is aimed at the imperial forces behind the Second Temple, but she does note that there are sometimes intertwining political and religious contentions or ambiguity in the critique of/resistance to the temple. For example, she finds Jesus's critique in Mark 11 more likely aimed at the authorities in charge of temple policies, while also noting the possibility that it critiques Herod's renovation of the temple and

---

160. Neusner, "Judaism in a Time of Crisis," 314.
161. Collins, "Second Temple and the Arts of Resistance," 118.
162. Collins, "Second Temple and the Arts of Resistance," 115.
163. Collins, "Second Temple and the Arts of Resistance," 116.

implicitly advocates for "the overthrow of the current political order."[164] Collins also argues the Covenanters of the Dead Sea Scrolls rejected the temple on account of its priestly administration, but notes that this critique also inherently relates to the political dimensions of the priesthood under the Hasmoneans.[165] Similarly, she highlights how "the Animal Apocalypse" critiques the failure of certain priests rather than the imperial forces that allowed for the temple's reconstruction, while also "reflecting resistance to the dominant orders of society in the second temple period up to the crisis of Hellenization."[166]

Outside of references to Josephus, Collins's work offers several ways pre-70 CE Jewish groups resisted and rejected the Second Temple, as well as the Jewish and imperial political authorities encompassing it. Collins resists the urge to lump these different instances of resistance into categories, so her treatment of each group is filled with nuance. For instance, the "Animal Apocalypse" appears to discard the temple and could be described as "anti-temple," but the first temple is not negatively portrayed. Likewise, the Dead Sea Scrolls reject the temple and the priesthood in Jerusalem, but their preference for their community as a substitute for both the temple and priesthood makes it difficult to say that they are "anti-temple." The central thread to Collins's work, therefore, is that it is valid to look for instances of "hidden transcripts" resisting the temple, and these "subtle and indirect" instances often are formed where the Jerusalem temple's political, social, and religious dominance converge.[167]

Philip Church

Unlike Neusner, Philip Church's *Hebrews and the Temple* surveys a broader swath of Jewish texts from across the Second Temple period. Rather than listing them by community or genre, Church categorizes these texts by their depiction of and relation to the Jerusalem temple, what he calls "temple symbolism."[168] Church utilizes four overarching categories of literature: those that contain a positive view of the temple ("temple affirmed"), those that reflect on the destruction of the temple

---

164. Collins, "Second Temple and the Arts of Resistance," 124–25.
165. Collins, "Second Temple and the Arts of Resistance," 119–20.
166. Collins, "Second Temple and the Arts of Resistance," 117.
167. Collins, "Second Temple and the Arts of Resistance," 115.
168. Church, *Hebrews and the Temple*, 5–10.

("temple destroyed"), those that offer dissatisfaction with the temple ("temple contested"), and a specific excursus on how the Jerusalem temple and its priesthood was an albatross for the Dead Sea Scrolls community ("temple rejected").

"Temple Affirmed"

Church's first category reviews the standard position, and his survey of literature examines how a positive attitude is demonstrated by texts like Sirach's encomium to Simon (Sir 50:1–24), the Letter of Aristeas (Let. Aris. 33–83, 83–99), the Wisdom of Solomon (9:1–18), and Philo's writings (*Legat.* 278–320; *Spec.* 1.67–78). Church also points to Book 3 of the Sibylline Oracles, which, he argues, "reflects a clear theological commitment to and a positive attitude towards Jerusalem and the temple."[169] Here, Church highlights positive mentions of the temple's beauty, divine appointment, and post-exile restoration (Sib. Or. 3.265–94), its sacrificial system compared to gentiles/"Greeks" (Sib. Or. 3.565–80), and its wealth and divine protection (Sib. Or. 3.657, 669–709, 767–95).

In light of the earlier surveys of Jewish identity and Second Temple history, Church's "temple affirmed" texts are unsurprising; there are, however, a few weak points for this particular attitude. Church's survey of "temple affirmed" texts excludes post-70 CE texts that also include a positive attitude toward the temple. The most significant bodies of literature affected by this decision are Josephus's works (especially *Antiquities* and *Jewish War*) and the Mishnah, which continue to hold a very positive, affirming view of the temple even after its destruction. In addition, Church suggests the surveyed texts have a connection with Egypt and questions whether this connection "could indicate that Jews in Egypt viewed the temple as an ideal, being too far removed from the reality to be aware of the difficulties recognized by Palestinian Jews."[170] Though his focus appears to be on nonbiblical texts, Church could potentially further this argument by including the LXX. On the other hand, material evidence and inscriptions, like the inscription at the temple of Pan Euodos or the Elephantine letters, demonstrate that Egyptian attitudes toward the temple varied. Despite these brief critiques, however,

---

169. Church, *Hebrews and the Temple*, 64.
170. Church, *Hebrews and the Temple*, 78.

Church's survey shows that the Jerusalem temple was viewed positively by many communities in the Second Temple Period.

"Temple Rejected"

Church's subtitle for his second chapter—"Temple Symbolism in the Dead Sea Scrolls"—signals the limits of this category, which focuses solely on the literature from Qumran. Church relies heavily on 4QFlorilegium, the Temple Scroll, 1QS, the War Scroll, Hodayot, and the Songs of the Sabbath Sacrifice, and also includes smaller fragments. He begins with the Qumranic framework of temple rejection, then sifts these texts into three subcategories that understand the temple as eschatological, communal, or angelic. Church argues,

> In some texts there is the expectation of an eschatological temple to be built by God in the last days. Sometimes this was juxtaposed with the notion that the community itself was an (interim) temple while they awaited the eschatological temple, with their cultic activity a substitute for temple worship in Jerusalem. Allied with this was the belief that their worship was somehow connected with the worship of angels, either in the heavenly temple or in their own liturgical practices, where angels were considered to be present with them in the Judean desert. Other texts refer to exalted individuals, considered to be already present in the heavenly temple, sometimes with a (high) priestly role and perhaps an angelomorphic identity.[171]

As seen in the historical survey of the Hasmonean period, the scrolls frequently advocate separation from the Jerusalem temple and demonstrate the rejection of its priesthood. There is also, however, a consistent emphasis on the community's status as a temple replacement and a (valid) priestly community. Fragments of 4QMMT (B, 1.27–35) even emphasize Jerusalem as a holy city. Therefore, the attitude(s) within the scrolls literature may be messier than Church's schematization allows; for instance, the above texts might skew closer to "reinterpretation" rather than outright "rejection."[172] Still, Church's survey of the DSS demon-

---

171. Church, *Hebrews and the Temple*, 80.

172. Regardless of label, it is important to note the entire temple institution or priestly hierarchy was not discarded but rather reframed. Wardle discusses this by referring to Qumran as "withdrawing" from, rather than "rejecting," the Jerusalem temple, and he groups it together with the communities in Leontopolis and Samaria that had

strates dissatisfaction with the Jerusalem temple and its priesthood, while also articulating the nuance within the Dead Sea Scrolls as a patchwork library containing a variety of attitudes.

"Temple Contested"

For Church, this category consists of "texts that reflect dissatisfaction with the Jerusalem temple."[173] Church focuses on texts that envision or advocate for a heavenly temple replacing the Jerusalem temple. These texts include 1 Enoch, Jubilees, the Testament of the Twelve Patriarchs, and the Testament of Moses. In 1 Enoch, Church points to the Book of the Watchers to make several arguments regarding the heavenly temple. Church links the language of 1 En. 1:3–4 with Mic 1:2, references "the sanctuary of heaven" in Milik's reconstruction of 1 En. 9:1, and draws on Enoch's vision of the heavenly temple/sanctuary in 12:4–15:3, which narratively and thematically reoccurs in later sections of the text (1 En. 38–40, 46–53, 71).[174] Church examines references to the sanctuary/temple (Jub 1:17; 23:21), Zion (Jub 4:26; 8:19), and Eden (Jub 3:1–35) in Jubilees. He also points to the defilement of the temple in the Testament of Levi (10:2–5; 16:1–5), which appears to be a post-70 CE Christian text explaining the destruction of the temple in relation to the death of Jesus.

Once again, Church's schematization falters, as "dissatisfaction" appears to be a matter of interpretation. For instance, Church claims "the Second Temple is overlooked in favour of the heavenly, eschatological temple" in 1 Enoch's closing chapters, even though he notices that the temple is absent in the vision of the new Jerusalem (1 En. 90:28–36).[175]

---

their own temple establishments: "The deep suspicion and distrust of the priesthood [in Judaea] did not seem to be accompanied by a withdrawal from the involvement with the temple and its cult. Critique coexisted with participation. This was not the case, however, for the three distinct communities discussed in this chapter. The Samaritan temple, the Oniad temple at Leontopolis, and the 'temple of men' at Qumran provide de facto evidence that some groups felt strongly enough about the happenings in Jerusalem that they deemed it better to strike out on their own and found alternative or rival temples" (Wardle, *Jerusalem Temple and Early Christian Identity*, 162–63).

173. Church, *Hebrews and the Temple*, 144.
174. Church, *Hebrews and the Temple*, 146–63.
175. Church, *Hebrews and the Temple*, 170. Church notes "house" language is still utilized, but "tower" language, which referred to the First and Second Temples, is absent in this passage. In order to make this text fit his categorization, Church argues, "Since God dwells within the entire city, it becomes a city-temple." Here, Church manifests an eschatological temple where the text does not and, in doing so, is able to argue this

This claim heavily relies on silence about the Jerusalem temple, which could be explained in a number of other ways; Church recognizes this overall tendency, conceding, "most of [these texts] are silent about Jerusalem and the temple, and the dissatisfaction is more implicit than explicit."[176] Furthermore, Church interprets an eschatological or heavenly referent in some cases where a physical temple could instead fit the symbolic temple language. This is especially evident in Jubilees 1:17, where Church emphasizes the divine construction of the sanctuary as evidence that an eschatological temple is in view.[177] However, if God's building of the sanctuary is envisioned as indirect or causative, as it is earlier in 1:13's reference to the diaspora, instead of a direct action, there is little reason not to interpret this as a reference to the Second Temple, especially when vv. 8-17 follow the sequence of cause and effect leading to the temple.[178] Finally, a discussion or cursory note on alternative temple sites would be interesting, especially since these contest the centrality of the Jerusalem temple.[179] In short, the language of "Temple Contested" is perhaps too strong for Church's actual aim of this chapter, which is not to survey attitudes displaying direct opposition or dispute, but rather to look at texts

---

"city-temple" is preferable to the polluted temple of 1 En 89:72 (Church, *Hebrews and the Temple*, 160).

176. Church, *Hebrews and the Temple*, 197.

177. *Contra* R. H. Charles; cf. Church, *Hebrews and the Temple*, 173; Charles, *Book of Jubilees*, 5.

178. Elsewhere, when the temple is clearly in view (49:18), Church argues it is Solomon's temple, not the Second Temple, that is intended: "the closing sections of Jubilees anticipate the wilderness tabernacle, Solomon's temple and the eschatological temple. The Second Temple is overlooked, and the references to Zion and Jerusalem in Jubilees indicate that the anticipated eschatological temple was probably conceived of as a physical structure" (Church, *Hebrews and the Temple*, 174). The difficulty with Church's position is there is no "smoking gun" pointing only to Solomon's temple, nor is there the possibility that both the First and Second Temples could be conflated.

179. Wardle highlights how Qumran, Leontopolis, and Samaria each appealed to different scriptures in an effort to legitimate itself by appealing to an authoritative source: "Moreover, appeal to the authority of Scripture greatly aided these communities in their dispute with the caretakers of the temple in Jerusalem... The Samaritan appeal to the Pentateuch to substantiate their claims for the sanctity of Mount Gerizim, Onias IV's dependence on Isaiah 19:18-20, and the Qumranian interpretation of passages such as Isaiah 40, Jeremiah 31, and Proverbs 15:8, all instilled in their community a sense of legitimacy and granted justification for their dissenting actions... In addition, the construction of each of these temples was accompanied by, and legitimated through, the presence of members of the Jerusalem priestly elite, who took part in establishing the new community" (Wardle, *Jerusalem Temple and Early Christian Identity*, 164-65).

that focus on a heavenly or eschatological temple, which is not mutually exclusive with the Jerusalem temple.

"Temple Destroyed"

Church's final category looks at texts that responded to the destruction of the Jerusalem temple. Here, Church examines the temple (implicit and explicit references) and Jerusalem/Zion in the dialogues and visions of 4 Ezra (7:26–44; 10:21), 2 Baruch (3:1–5:5), the Sibylline Oracles books 4 and 5, and, as mentioned earlier, Josephus. These texts demonstrate a small amount of variety in the manner in which the temple appears, ranging from affinity for the temple (Josephus) to rejection of a physical temple (Sib. Or. 4.6–9).[180] Overall, however, Church suggests that "the Second Temple is by and large overlooked," and emphasizes that "where these texts anticipate a restored, rebuilt temple, it is the eschatological temple."[181]

Once again, this schematization leads to further questions. The texts attributed to this attitude all share a post-70 CE date and respond in their own ways to the destruction of the temple. It creates complications, then, that the Testament of Levi is not included in this survey, particularly because Church acknowledges it is likely a second-century CE Christian document with first-century sources and also offers a brief foray into explaining the cause of the temple's destruction. Again, Church attributes silence about the Second Temple or references to Solomon's temple as dissatisfaction, suggesting, "that 4 Ezra concentrates on Solomon's temple indicates the same sort of dissatisfaction with the Second Temple that appears elsewhere in the literature. The implication is that the 'real' temple was Solomon's rather than Herod's."[182] In light of this, it is curious that Church understands "Babylon" as a cipher for Rome, but attributes several references to Solomon's temple in literal fashion here and elsewhere, rather than as a cipher for the Second Temple, particularly

---

180. Although anti-temple sentiment is characteristic of Sib. Or. 4, the fourth Sibyl also describes the Jerusalem temple's destruction (Sib. Or. 4.114–27) as one of the atrocities committed by Rome, which justifies the nation's calamitous end. This characterization complicates the rather negative depiction of God's dwelling in a temple displayed earlier in the text (οὐδὲ γὰρ οἶχον ἔχει ναῷ λίθον, Sib. Or. 4.8). For more on Sib. Or. 4, see Olivia Stewart Lester, "Four Kingdoms Motif and Sibylline Temporality in Sibylline Oracles 4," in Perrin et al., eds., *Four Kingdom Motifs*, 121–41.

181. Church, *Hebrews and the Temple*, 265–66.

182. Church, *Hebrews and the Temple*, 201.

since at times he recognizes the use of Solomon's temple in connection with the destruction of the Second Temple.[183]

Church's work is a valuable demonstration of the variety of attitudes toward the Jerusalem temple. Although his surveys is situated within the greater context of an argument on the use of temple symbolism in Hebrews, there are a few important insights that stand out from his study for those looking to understand the general contours of Jewish attitudes toward the temple. First, there is a vast catalog of literature available that references the temple either explicitly or implicitly, and that catalog expands when considering documentary and material evidence. Second, the temple is almost never an isolated topic; it can often be found in conjunction with other important issues of identity, eschatology, theology, apocalypticism, and rewritten scripture. Finally, it is difficult to draw rigid boundaries on any attitudes toward the temple. Whether texts are arranged by date, theme, or attitude, some texts defy a clear label in their relationship to the Jerusalem temple.

Summary

The works by Jacob Neusner, Adela Yarbro Collins, and Philip Church demonstrate the variety of Jewish attitudes toward the temple in and immediately after the Second Temple period. While the temple was standing, many Jews participated in temple worship (Josephus), contributed to its upkeep and preservation (Philo), and praised its opulence (Letter of Aristeas, Sibylline Oracles 3) and leadership (Sirach) as evidence of its divine and cosmic significance. Others resisted the temple, critiquing it or drawing on its symbolism and imagery as a means of reinterpreting its significance in apocalyptic or eschatological ways (1 Enoch, Dead Sea Scrolls). Its destruction also elicited a variety of responses: some Jews were distraught by the loss of the temple and reached back into traditional narratives to explain their identity without a physical temple, whether that meant holding out hope for an eschatological temple (4 Ezra, 2 Baruch), discarding the notion of a physical temple (Sibylline Oracles 4), or explaining the destruction as punishment for wickedness or a change in divine favor (Josephus). There was no singular way to be Jewish during the Second Temple period and, accordingly, there was no singular way to relate to the Jerusalem temple.

---

183. For Rome as a cipher, see Church, *Hebrews and the Temple*, 201, 265.

Conclusion

Judaism in the Second Temple period was diverse. Thought and practice differed across regions, and diverse expressions existed even within the same locality, so the best model of understanding Jewish identity is to approach it from a polythetic standpoint. One frequent and recurring component in constructions of Jewish identity, however, is a defining relationship with a temple. For many Jews in the early fifth century BCE to the late first century CE, the Jerusalem temple was a central component of their collective identity.[184] It served as the central cultic center to their God (Deut 12), it grounded a yearly calendrical system (Exod 23:14–19; Deut 16:1–17; Ezra 6:19–22), and it was supported financially through their annual contributions.[185] Sanders is reliant upon this view of the

---

184. Jonathan Trotter draws heavily on Second and Third Maccabees, Philo, and the Letter of Aristeas to determine that the temple collection and pilgrimage were viewed positively and practiced in the diaspora, even though some diaspora Jews may have felt disconnected from their ancestral homeland. Trotter argues "it is difficult to conclude that most diaspora Jews, therefore, had little concern for the Jerusalem temple or that the temple had no practical value for them ... One of the defining features of diaspora Jewish practice in the eyes of Jews and their neighbors was Jews' unique loyalty—especially when compared to others living outside their ancestral homelands—to their mother-city and its temple. The temple cult enabled many diaspora Jews to remain connected to the ancestral homeland through personal or vicarious pilgrimage and contributions, practices viewed by some as obligatory. The offerings in particular contributed to the wealth and well-being of the temple, a symbol of the wealth, greatness, and security of the Jewish nation for much of the Second Temple Period. Additionally, various diaspora Jews continued to associate the divine presence and their people's election with this sacred space" (Trotter, *Jerusalem Temple in Diaspora*, 175).

185. "Over the decades following the beginning of the half-shekel offering, it was so popular that it became a characteristic practice known to non-Jews as a defining feature of Judaism at that time. Moreover, Jews repeatedly petitioned officials in order to protect their sacred money and be allowed to send it to the Jerusalem temple. This is not to say that there was no dissent concerning the issue as the author of 4QOrdinances, and perhaps the entire Qumran community, certainly did not embrace the practice. It may be that the Qumran community had already broken away from the Hasmonean-led priesthood and temple before the institution of the half-shekel offering, which would be the case if our placement of the origin of the practice at the end of the second century BCE is correct. A group that did not support the validity of the priesthood certainly would not have been sympathetic to an ordinance requiring an annual contribution from all Jews throughout the world to support the cult and its illegitimate priesthood. Even though almost exclusively positive evidence for the practice remains from the late Second Temple period, it is likely that certain Jews or Jewish communities did not participate for various reasons. Nonetheless, the overwhelming weight of the evidence supports popular participation of diaspora Jews in making half-shekel offerings, especially during the last century before the destruction of the Second Temple" (Trotter, *Jerusalem Temple in Diaspora*, 65).

temple when defining Judaism during 63 BCE–66 CE as "Common Judaism." As seen in the surveys above, however, attitudes toward the temple were dynamic. Some revered the temple itself while critiquing corruption of its leadership. Some created local alternatives. Some reimagined the entire concept of a temple, reinterpreting it as a collective community dedicated to purity and practice.

This chapter has examined the social, political, literary, historical, and cultural frameworks that Jews and early Christians navigated when constructing, remembering, and transmitting tradition and memory about the Jerusalem temple. In addition, this chapter has discussed several significant insights about the temple. First, the temple was an important factor contributing to Jewish identity, but failure to participate in temple worship is not (and was not) a disqualifying feature of what makes one "Jewish." Jewish identity was multifactored, variable, self-ascribed, and not normative. Whether looking through the lens of "Common Judaism," "Hellenistic Judaism," "Second Temple Judaism," or other models, it is important to remember there are multiple paradigms of Jewish identity. Second, the history of the Second Temple was complex and turbulent. Military conquest and domination frequently changed the landscape of Judaea's political and religious figureheads, and the development and sustained existence of local alternatives in Leontopolis, Elephantine, and Samaria shows how Jewish life looked different depending on where and when you were. Finally, schematizing attitudes toward the temple is an exceedingly difficult task. Both Neusner and Church drew on terms such as "negative" and "positive," but these are highly nebulous terms that exist on a subjective, and often ill-defined, spectrum. Church's attempt to categorize attitudes by whether a text affirmed, rejected, contested, or responded to the temple's destruction took a further step in defining the texts thematically, but his schematization hit some snags when his interpretive decisions or implicit insights drove categorization more than the text itself. Thus, when attempting to sort texts methodically by an attitude toward the temple, it is important to define clearly what that attitude means. I will return to this discussion in the following chapter, but my own schema will rely on a functional approach: does the text presuppose utilizing the Jerusalem temple or its priesthood? Does it reinterpret aspects of the Jerusalem temple or its priesthood? Does it reject or oppose the Jerusalem temple or its priesthood? Or does it display tendencies of multiple attitudes?

In the next chapter, I will turn to the Gospel of Mark and other early Christian gospels to discuss how early Christians remembered Jesus's attitude toward the temple.

4

Jesus and the Temple

There is substantial evidence that Christian reflection upon Jerusalem and the Temple, and expectations regarding their continuing significance in the eschatological unfolding they awaited, diversified considerably at a very early date. While there is a clear core of belief that the Temple was under judgement and would be destroyed, there is less evidence of unity of vision as to the nature of the dispensation which would be established in its place.
—N. H. Taylor[1]

Attitudes toward the Jerusalem temple varied in the Second Temple period. As we saw in the previous chapter, Second Temple Jews held a complex matrix of attitudes when constructing and transmitting traditional materials about the temple or its alternatives. By extension, early Christians also felt the impact of the temple as they constructed and commemorated traditions about Jesus. The gospels, as products of early Christian memory, exist at the epicenter of colliding factors: the historical past of the first-century Judaean world, the cultural memory of Israel's scriptures, and the present concerns of the nascent Christian communities. The gospels' depictions of Jesus engaging with and responding to the Jerusalem temple—and its priesthood—serve as case studies through which to study these dynamics. This chapter, therefore, examines a simple

---

1. Taylor, "Jerusalem and the Temple," 458.

question: how did the gospel traditions, particularly the Gospel of Mark, construct and utilize the temple in their commemorations of Jesus? First, I will begin by discussing the Gospel of Mark in an effort to contextualize the "present" concerns for these early Christians. I will then survey texts where Jesus interacts with the temple and/or its attendants in the Gospel of Mark, drawing careful attention to the narrative characterization of the temple or priesthood.[2] Like other Second Temple literature that concerned the temple, I include texts that engage the temple as a cultic center (i.e., the building and ritual practices), as well as the temple as an institution (i.e., the priests, scribes, and other people associated with temple functions). I will then expand to look at how other early Christian communities treat these traditions within canonical and non-canonical gospels. Throughout this chapter, we will see that the temple is remembered in multiple ways, and the variety and complexity of the temple's characterization throughout Mark and other early gospels will set us up to ask why these memories persisted throughout the first few centuries.

The Gospel of Mark

The Gospel of Mark is our oldest extant gospel, but the exact details about the date, authorship, and location of its composition are widely debated. The earliest traditions about the Gospel of Mark link it to Peter's preaching in Rome. Papias, citing John the presbyter, claims Mark was the "interpreter" (ἑρμηνευτής) of Peter's ad hoc preaching; it was then Mark who ordered the gospel according to the traditions he recalled (ὅσα ἐμνημόνευσεν, ἀκριβῶς ἔγραψεν, *Hist. eccl.* 3.39.15). Since Mark does not appear to give special prominence to Peter and tells several stories without Peter (or any disciple) present, Markan scholarship typically downplays these early Christian traditions in favor of internal details as to its composition. For instance, the prophecy about the temple's destruction (13:1–2) is often employed in discussions of the date of the gospel, serving as fodder for those who argue this is a prophecy *ex eventu* and suggest a post-70 CE date.[3] Other scholars suggest the description of the temple's destruction, the trend of predicting the

---

2. "Since memory texts are narrative compositions, the key to understanding them lies in the field of narratology" (Huebenthal, *Reading Mark's Gospel*, 222).

3. "The discourse in Mark 13 presupposes that Jerusalem has fallen" (Moloney, *Gospel of Mark*, 13). Mark 13 "is a theologically loaded way of describing the significance of what happened in AD 70" (France, *Gospel of Mark*, 502).

destruction prior to 70 CE, the symbolic "abomination of desolation," and other factors make it more difficult to determine whether the gospel was written prior to or after 70 CE.[4] James Crossley even suggests a date as early as the late 30s or early 40s CE where the pre-Markan tradition of Jesus predicting the destruction of the temple is then attached to concerns about Caligula's intended actions in the temple.[5] Recent studies by Alfredo Delgado Gómez and Christopher Zeichmann, however, have attempted to date the gospel apart from the temple tradition by focusing on particular Markan vocabulary or social concerns, but their proposed dates still point speculatively on either side of 70 CE.[6] Perhaps the most solid grounding for the date of Mark is a general mid- to late-first-century CE setting, which places the authorship of the gospel anywhere between the 30s and 70s CE.

Even without a solid date, the general consensus is that Mark represents the first commemorative codification of the Jesus tradition into a textualized narrative form. The textualization of these traditions employs them within a broader narrative framework that is rhetorically shaped by community needs. As Huebenthal states, "when different episodes are integrated into a larger narrative frame, the different possible versions of the episode are narrowed down to a version that is subordinate to the perspective of the overall narrative."[7] However, the early textualization of the gospel was likely not a total linear transfer; "at this stage, oral and written memories coexist and interact."[8] In fact, Rodríguez reminds us that "the gospel traditions were primarily accessed as oral phenomena rather than written texts. They were primarily received in performance rather than reading; and despite all this, the distinctions between oral and written

---

4. "In view of these conflicting arguments [the description of the temple's destruction in 13:1–2 as 'not one stone upon another' and the extant remains of the temple's retaining wall], it does not seem possible to make a decision about whether Mark knows that the Temple has been demolished, or whether he merely is positive that it *will* be destroyed very soon" (Marcus, *Mark 1–8*, 38–39, emphasis original); "Most scholars have concluded that this discourse reflects some knowledge or even experience of the first Jewish war with Rome, which lasted from 66 to 74 CE. The major difference of opinion concerns whether the Gospel was written before or after the destruction of the temple, which occurred in 70 CE" (Collins, *Mark*, 11; cf. Hengel, *Studies in the Gospel of Mark*, 14–28).

5. Crossley, *Date of Mark's Gospel*, 19–43.

6. Gómez, "Mark's σπεκουλάτωρ," 79–107; Zeichmann, "Date of Mark's Gospel," 422–37.

7. Huebenthal, *Reading Mark's Gospel*, 180.

8. Huebenthal, *Reading Mark's Gospel*, 184.

traditions appear rather meaningless in a first-century setting."[9] Mark, therefore, exists at the nexus of orality and textuality, commemoration and proclamation, variability and stability. Its presentation of the Jesus tradition offers a window into the commemorative shaping of group identity in navigating the past and present, while also serving as *an* instantiation of the Jesus tradition from which other instantiations engaged. Rodríguez discusses this process of early Christian gospel traditions interacting from the perspective of media criticism and memory theory, urging attentiveness to "the possibility that the verbal similarities and differences between our gospels do not represent reactions to or modifications of other textual phenomena. Instead, wording peculiar to an expression of one traditional unit may represent an instance of the variability with which different traditions could be expressed."[10] From this perspective, then, understanding Mark's portrayal of Jesus and the temple is foundational for establishing how early Christian audiences commemorated and understood traditions about the temple, and once the Markan framework is established, we can view other gospel traditions as instantiations of variability—and stability—to understand if, and how, the memory of the temple changed throughout the first few centuries CE.

Jesus and the Temple in the Gospel of Mark

Studies of the Gospel of Mark have often been dominated by a few questions, which Christopher Skinner has succinctly summarized as: "Under what circumstances was the Gospel of Mark written? What sort of Christology do we find in the Gospel of Mark? What are we to make of Mark's secrecy motif? What, if anything, can we know of a Markan community?"[11] One area that has often been a pit stop rather than a starting point is the relationship between Jesus and the temple. The temple typically plays only a minor role in inquiry about the gospel and is not the subject of further discussion, but more recently, however, Timothy Gray's work has demonstrated that Jesus's interaction with temple is a dominant narrative thread and bears significant meaning for the gospel. Gray argues, "The temple plays a vital role in the plot of Mark's gospel and

9. Rodríguez, *Structuring Early Christian Memory*, 32.
10. Rodríguez, *Structuring Early Christian Memory*, 32.
11. Christopher W. Skinner, "Study of Characters in the Gospel of Mark: A Survey of Research from Wrede to the Performance Critics (1901 to 2014)," in Skinner and Hauge, eds., *Character Studies and the Gospel of Mark*, 4.

is deeply connected to the story of Jesus. It serves as the stage for the Markan Jesus' conflict with the Jewish authorities, and moreover it is the vital reference point for the narrative portrait of Jesus' identity, mission, and eschatological message."[12] Following Gray's work, this section will further examine the ways in which the temple, as both a location—the house of God and center of the sacrificial cult in Jerusalem—and an institution comprised of religious authorities, appears in the Gospel of Mark. If Huebenthal is correct in arguing "identity formation is due instead to engagement, that is, the acceptance and self-localization within the shared story," then investigating the characterization of Jesus's interactions with the temple shows us both *what* and *how* the Markan commemorative community utilizes their memories of Jesus in expressing their own identity.[13] In other words, the Gospel of Mark "reflects the efforts of a group to draft a *group identity* based on that group's memories of Jesus . . . the text of Mark's Gospel gives voice to a community of commemoration understanding itself to be carriers of memories about Jesus."[14]

Jesus and the Temple: What Does the Markan Jesus Say about the Temple?

David Rhoads, Joanna Dewey, and Donald Michie describe Mark as "a story of action and conflict."[15] As the narrative moves into Jerusalem, much of that conflict takes place in or is directly related to what Jesus has done and said in the temple. We can assess the Markan Jesus's relationship with the temple, then, if we examine these instances of conflict and engagement. When Jesus refers to or interacts with the temple in 2:23–28; 11:11–26; 13:1–2, 14; 14:53—15:29; and 15:38, these instances demonstrate ways in which the gospel commemorates the temple as a cultic center. As we will see, Mark presents Jesus's interaction with the temple in both positive and negative ways, which paints an ambivalent portrait of the relationship between the two.

---

12. Gray, *Temple in the Gospel of Mark*, 198.
13. Huebenthal, *Reading Mark's Gospel*, 182.
14. Huebenthal, *Reading Mark's Gospel*, 81.
15. Rhoads et al., *Mark as Story*, 46.

Mark 2:23-28

Jesus's first mention of the temple occurs early in the narrative during a Sabbath controversy between Jesus and the Pharisees (Mark 2:23-28). To defend his disciples against the questioning of the Pharisees, Jesus draws on biblical narrative as precedent for reinterpreting the framework of doing what is not permissible (τοῖς σάββασιν ὃ οὐκ ἔξεστιν, 2:24). In the narrative of First Samuel 21:1-6, David meets with the priest Ahimelech in Nob, gives a non-descript reason for his presence in Nob, then requests provisions. Ahimelech responds that he only has "holy bread" (Οὐκ εἰσὶν ἄρτοι ... ἄρτοι ἅγιοι εἰσίν, 1 Sam 21:5 LXX) on hand; then, after inquiring about David's ritual purity (and that of his companions), he offers David the bread of the presence (τοὺς ἄρτους τῆς προθέσεως, 1 Sam 21:7 LXX), which was reserved for priests to eat in a holy place (Lev 24:5-9). Jesus's retelling of this narrative, however, differs in significant ways. David's interaction with Ahimelech is jettisoned entirely. Instead, David enters into "the house of God" (τὸν οἶκον τοῦ θεοῦ, Mark 2:26) and eats the bread of the presence, distributing it to those with him, seemingly on his own accord.[16] The location also differs from the more generic location in Nob. Although the phrase "house of God" is sometimes used in conjunction with the tabernacle, as in 1 Chr 6:33 LXX (σκηνῆς οἴκου τοῦ θεοῦ), references to the tabernacle usually contain the specific term σκηνή (Exod 25:9; 26:1-37). The οἶκος τοῦ θεοῦ was likely not used as a phrase to represent the tabernacle on its own; for instance, Josh 6:24 and 9:23 use the terms בית יהוה/בית אלוהם ("house of YHWH/house of God"), but the phrase drops out in the LXX, as there is no Greek equivalent given.[17] Finally, the major change from Ahimelech to his son Abiathar skews the retelling.[18] Robert Gundry argues this priestly mix-up intentionally gives "a link with the added house of God, which for Jesus and his audience

---

16. "In contrast to the heavy role that Jesus makes David play, Ahimelech the priest not only changes to Abiathar the high priest but also becomes totally inactive, his name merely identifying the section of the OT where the story is found" (Gundry, *Mark*, 141).

17. Josephus also frequently uses ἱερόν to refer to the tabernacle compound, while distinguishing the tabernacle proper with the term ναός (A.J. 3.103, 125-30, 242-48). Even though he imports this temple language onto the tabernacle, he reserves ὁ οἶκος τοῦ θεοῦ for the Jerusalem Temple, only using the phrase sparingly (B.J. 4.163, 281; 6.104).

18. David Daube suggests the change is the circumstance of memory, although it is not clear whether he thinks it is a failure of Jesus's memory or of the Markan author. See Daube, "Responsibilities of Master and Disciples in the Gospels," 6.

stands in Jerusalem, where Abiathar officiated ... not in Nob, where Ahimelech gave bread to David."[19]

Jesus's retelling renders David as someone who went into the *temple* and ate the bread which was only stipulated for priestly consumption. Jesus uses David's action as the model example for his disciples, so his behavior is lauded while also serving analogously as justification for debating Sabbath regulations (Mark 2:28). Other than briefly dating the event to the time of Abiathar the high priest and mentioning the priests as the sole consumers of the bread of the presence, there is little discussion of the priesthood.[20] However, Jesus's mention of the "house of God" as a likely reference to the temple brings the temple institution in view of this pericope. This pericope is ultimately a set-up for the Christological point about the Son of Man driven home in 2:27–28 and another instance of Jesus's authority countering other religious leaders in Galilee. Still, Jesus's retelling of David eating the bread of the presence offers an interesting counter-debate of priestly tradition in a way that highlights and approves altering the function and use of a fundamental part of the sacrificial cult, at least for someone as significant as King David.[21] In other words, Jesus does not call for a stop to the cultic practice of the bread of the presence; instead, his retelling emphasizes a permissible exception to the rule, then expands that exception as an analogy to modify Sabbath practice. Overall, this pericope does not display an attitude that rejects the temple or make any explicit claims against the priesthood or the temple cult. Rather, Jesus engages in debate over the Sabbath and utilizes temple practices and Israelite tradition as a relevant and formative key to his understanding of the Sabbath.

---

19. Gundry, *Mark*, 141.

20. While the 1 Sam narrative occurs before the construction and institution of the Jerusalem temple under Solomon's reign, it still raises important questions about the location of the tabernacle (Nob?), the setting of the interaction between David and Ahimelech (in the tabernacle sanctuary?), and the implications of a priest willingly providing the bread to someone who was *not* a priest (does the abrogation of Levitical law make this permissible?). On this last point, it is interesting to note that Josephus has scrubbed the reference to the bread of the presence and has Ahimelech acquiesce more generally to David's request for food (*Ant.* 6.243), which demonstrates how some first-century interpreters, particularly those with ties to the priesthood, handled the difficult implications of the tradition.

21. That the bread of the presence was refreshed weekly on the Sabbath and demanded continually (תמיד, Exod 25:30) demonstrates its regular place and expected practice within the sacrificial cult.

Mark 11:11-26

Jesus's arrival in Jerusalem (Mark 11:1-10) commences the final section of the narrative. As David Rhoads, Joanna Dewey, and Donald Michie indicate, "the journeys of Jesus and the disciples around Galilee and up to Jerusalem provide the structural framework for the narrative as a whole."[22] Jesus's passion predictions (see below) reveal this framework, notifying the audience to expect his demise in Jerusalem at the hands of the chief priests, scribes, and elders (8:32; 10:32-34). The peripatetic setting of the first half of the narrative slows down once Jesus enters Jerusalem, and "the conflicts intensify as Jesus confronts the authorities with the rule of God in his actions and teaching *in the temple*."[23] From this point forward, the temple becomes a major focus of both the setting and content of the gospel.[24]

After arriving in Jerusalem, Jesus briefly enters the temple before leaving for Bethany (11:11). On his way back to the temple the next day, a hungry Jesus passes a fig tree showing signs of blooming (ἔχουσαν φύλλα, 11:13). Seeing that the tree had no fruit, since "it was not the time for figs" (ὁ γὰρ καιρὸς οὐκ ἦν σύκων, 11:13), Jesus exclaims (εἶπεν, 11:14)—later described as curses (κατηράσω, 11:21)—for no one to eat fruit from this tree ever again (11:14). Jesus then proceeds immediately into the temple, where he "casts out" (ἐκβάλλειν, 11:15) the buyers and sellers and overturns the tables of the money-changers and the seats of the dove-sellers.[25] Mark also includes the detail that Jesus would not permit anyone to carry a "vessel"

---

22. Rhoads et al., *Mark as Story*, 63.

23. Rhoads et al., *Mark as Story*, 68, emphasis added.

24. "From the moment of Jesus' entry into Jerusalem (Mark 11), the temple is almost always present in the story, whether as the location of Jesus' teaching (Mark 12), the subject of his eschatological discourse (Mark 13), or the basis of the charge at his trial (14:58) and the point of mockery on the cross, and even in the account of Jesus' death the temple seems to be ever present in Mark's story of Jesus" (Gray, *Temple in the Gospel of Mark*, 198).

25. Katherine Shaner, following Edward W. Cohen's work on Athenian banking, suggests the money-changers and temple merchants involved in this pericope would not have been present but their tables would have been maintained by enslaved peoples. There is a natural difficulty in assessing the role of women and enslaved peoples in the first-century world, especially since these marginalized characters are, at times, silent or invisible in the texts. However, the relevancy of Athenian banking for Jerusalem's temple service and the lack of any primary texts that support the presence or the role of these characters in the temple incident make it difficult to assess the historical viability of Shaner's argument. Shaner, "Danger of Singular Saviors," 139-61.

(σκεῦος) through the temple (11:16).[26] In the aftermath of this disruption, Jesus teaches in the temple, drawing on two prophetic statements (Isa 56:7; Jer 7:11) to contend that the temple ought to be "a house of prayer for all nations" (ὁ οἶκός μου οἶκος προσευχῆς κληθήσεται πᾶσιν τοῖς ἔθνεσιν), but that an unspecified "you" has made it a "den of thieves" (σπήλαιον λῃστῶν, 11:17).[27] The chief priests and scribes overhear and take offense at Jesus's teaching, which indicates they are his projected target. As he heads back into the temple the next day, Peter points out the now-withered fig tree,

26. Edmondo Lupieri argues that the prohibition from carrying a "vessel" through the temple indicates this scene took place on a Sabbath and is an example of Jesus's deferential treatment of halakhah around temple practice, putting him in line with other Jewish thought (Neh 13:15–22; Jer 17:19–27; 4Q251; 4Q265; Jubilees 2:29–30, 50:7–8). In light of this, Lupieri argues, "the prohibition of Mark 11:16 fits perfectly well in the frame of the discussion on sabbatical prohibitions against carrying. According to it, Jesus does not prohibits [sic] carrying a 'burden' per se (therefore, we should not translate 'anything'), but rather carrying a 'vessel,' that is anything belonging to the category of *kelim*, that is, objects that can contain or hold something, such as vases, for transport ... This probably means that the prohibition should be in place *always*. If this is true, then Jesus wants to implement a typically sabbatical prohibition every day in the normal life of the temple" (Edmondo Lupieri, "Jesus, Jerusalem, the Temple: Traces of His Halakhic Teaching in Defense of the Temple," in Mimouni and Painchaud, eds., *La Question*, 186–87, emphasis original). Lupieri suggests that Jesus's actions are not intended to loosen cultic practice, but are serious and deferential to the temple's sacred nature: "Jesus wanted to apply more careful and rigid rules to the life of the temple, which, in his opinion, should have been subjected to the more stringent rules of sabbatical prohibitions against carrying ... I feel comfortable saying that the Gospel narrative of the so-called 'cleansing of the temple' very probably contains the memory of some action and teaching of the 'real Jesus' and that this tradition is coherent with an aspect of his activity (a 'fragment' of his figure) which was deeply respectful of the temple, its cult and its priesthood" (189–90). Lupieri's interpretation is interesting, but still encounters issues of consistency. Lupieri concludes that Jesus's proposed sabbatical program operates differently *within* the temple than it does *outside* the walls of Jerusalem in the synagogues and open fields; however, this feels more of a matter of convenience in explaining the differing attitudes toward the Sabbath in the gospel. Jesus's argument when confronted earlier in the gospel (2:23–28) was that he had authority over the Sabbath. In this specific instance, his attitude significantly relaxed Sabbath practice. If the narrative of 11:11–26 also takes place on a Sabbath, as Lupieri argues, his initial approach of the fig tree would also indicate the relaxation of Sabbath practice, since he approached it with the intention of plucking fruit. In addition to the relaxed Sabbath attitudes elsewhere, the temple incident also makes no reference to the Sabbath in Jesus's teaching; instead, his teaching focuses on the (implied) exclusion of the Gentiles and the priesthood's responsibility for the temple's status as a "den of thieves" (11:17).

27. Oskar Skarsaune points to the emphasis on prayer to suggest tentatively that "the early believers purposefully ignored the sacrificial cult going on in the temple. To put it a little more pointedly, they treated the temple as if it were the supreme synagogue" (Skarsaune, *In the Shadow of the Temple*, 157).

and Jesus responds with a teaching on faith and prayer (11:20–26); however, Jesus later explains that the fig tree is symbolic of the apocalyptic signs he has given them (13:28–31).

When it comes to assessing Jesus's relationship with the temple, the temple incident of Mark 11 (and its parallels) is often the North Star for many scholars, the pericope that guides their overarching understanding of Jesus's view of the temple.[28] Two streams of interpretation dominate scholarly conversations regarding the intention or outcome of this pericope: those who see the action as a "cleansing" intended to rectify improper cultic practice, or those who see the action as a "demonstration" of the temple's destruction, which portends the end of the temple cult.[29] Sanders, for instance, argues for the latter, using this pericope to synthesize his apocalyptic interpretation of Jesus's historical ministry:

> Thus we conclude that Jesus publicly predicted or threatened the destruction of the temple, that the statement was shaped by his expectation of the arrival of the eschaton, that he probably also expected a new temple to be given by God from heaven, and that *he made a demonstration which prophetically symbolized the coming event* . . . Jesus predicted (or threatened) the destruction of the temple and carried out an action symbolic of its destruction by demonstrating against the performance of sacrifices. He did not wish to purify the temple, either of dishonest trading or of trading in contrast to 'pure' worship. Nor was he opposed to the temple sacrifices which God commanded to Israel. He intended, rather, to indicate that the end was at hand and that the temple would be destroyed, so that the new and perfect temple might arise.[30]

---

28. On the use of "incident" as a neutral term for the conflict, see Hooker, "Traditions About the Temple," 7–19. Jonathan Klawans also notes the thorny implications of the language used to describe this incident and instead opts for "Jesus' action in the temple." Against the often-used language of "temple cleansing," Klawans writes, "It has no basis in the New Testament texts themselves, for no explicit concerns with purity (ritual or moral) are expressed in *any* of the gospel traditions on the temple incident. The term is also inappropriate, for it implies that something practical was achieved by Jesus' act, that some filth was cleansed or some sin purged. This conclusion too is something that the all-too-brief gospel accounts simply cannot support" (Klawans, *Purity, Sacrifice, and the Temple*, 224–25).

29. David Fiensy identifies two additional interpretive streams within scholarship on the pericope: the rejection of the temple cult and the "attack" on the temple, which was intended to institute violent revolt against the Roman Empire. Fiensy, *Jesus the Galilean*, 210–13.

30. Sanders, *Jesus and Judaism*, 75, emphasis added. Sanders classifies Jesus's actions as an "attack" against the temple: "Like others, he regarded the sacrifices as commanded

Marcus agrees with Sanders about the symbolic demonstration, also reserving room for the possibility of restoration. Unlike many Second Temple texts that denigrate the presence of Gentiles in the temple (4QFlor A 1:3–6; 1 En. 89:73; 1 Macc 14:36; *Pss. Sol.* 17:22), Marcus argues, "while other eschatologically minded Jews, caught up in the horror and excitement of the war against Rome, dream of a Messiah who will purge the Temple by ridding it of foreign influences, Mark's Messiah cleanses it by expelling the (Jewish) traders who defile the Court of the Gentiles and thereby thwart the Temple's divinely intended purpose of becoming a 'house of prayer for all peoples.'"[31] Gray comes to a similar conclusion: "Jesus condemned the Jerusalem temple for failing in its vocation to be a house of prayer for all nations."[32] Jesus's actions in the temple—halting buying, selling, and money-changing for sacrifice, as well as eliminating

---

by God, he knew that they required a certain amount of trade, and he knew that making a gesture towards disrupting the trade represented an attack on the divinely ordained sacrifices. Thus I take it that the action at the very least symbolized an attack, and note that 'attack' is not far from 'destruction'" (Sanders, *Jesus and Judaism*, 70–71).

31. Marcus, *Mark 8–16*, 793. Elizabeth Struthers Malbon examines the narrative Christology on display and comes to a similar conclusion: "The Markan Jesus' deflection of attention *from* the buying and selling that were essential to the role of the temple as a center of sacrifice *to* its role as a center of prayer for all nations would likely have had a profound effect on Mark's first-century audience if, as many scholars argue, this audience had recently experienced the destruction of the temple and the loss of a sacrificial center" (Malbon, *Mark's Jesus*, 156–57).

32. Gray, *Temple in the Gospel of Mark*, 196. Gray also reads the teaching on faith (11:20–25) as a further indictment against the temple, arguing the referent of "this mountain," which is to be cast into the sea, is the temple mount, and the emphasis on prayer establishes the disciples as the new "house of prayer" in place of the rejected temple (Gray, *Temple in the Gospel of Mark*, 48–54). Gray's analysis on why 11:20–25 is a further indictment against the temple is unconvincing. Gray spends much of his argument on how "this mountain" is not idiomatic, rhetorical, or generic (as in 3:35; 4:41) but instead a definite nod to a (presumably literary) referent that will alter the meaning of the pericope in favor of the temple's rejection. However, the emphasis that Gray places on identifying "this mountain" is not equally measured with identifying "the sea," which does not have a direct reference in the pericope but instead fits more into the idiomatic, rhetorical, or generic categories that Gray has dismissed. Elizabeth Shively somewhat softens Gray's argument by suggesting Jesus's actions and teachings in the temple "extends his struggle against Satan to rescue what is held captive. Jesus has not only cast out what corrupts the human body, but now also casts out what corrupts the Temple and its worship ... The image of the Temple Mount as lifted and cast into the sea underscores Mark's portrayal of Jesus' conflict with the religious authorities as a struggle against satanic power" (Elizabeth Shively, "Characterizing the Non-Human: Satan in the Gospel of Mark," in Skinner and Hauge, eds., *Character Studies and the Gospel of Mark*, 146). In addition, the teaching on faith is narratively proximate to another castigation of the temple authorities, where the parable reveals it is not the temple/vineyard that is destroyed, but the wicked tenants/priestly opposition to Jesus.

the movement of cultic vessels—indicate the action is targeted at the temple as an institution. Sanders relies on this line of thinking, supposing that "if Jesus were a religious reformer, however, bent on correcting 'abuse' and 'present practice,' we should hear charges of immorality, dishonesty and corruption directed *against the priests*. But such charges are absent from the Gospels (except for Mark 11:17), and that is not the thrust of the action in the temple."[33] Sanders's exception is extremely important for the Markan narrative, though, as Mark 11:17–18 brings the priesthood directly in view of Jesus's actions in the temple.[34] Like Sanders, Moloney also argues Jesus's action "brings to an end the cultic activity of the Jewish temple," but he postulates that this pericope relates to the concerns of the post-70 CE Markan community's turn to prayer, noting, "symbolically, however, before the physical destruction of the temple, Jesus has already brought its practices to a close (vv. 15–16), and *indicated to the Jewish leadership that their administration of God's house had frustrated its purpose* (v. 17)."[35] Collins, on the other hand, argues Jesus's actions are not against the entire cultic institution, but rather are meant to be understood in line with Ezekiel and the *Temple Scroll* as maximizing the sacred space (*temenos*) of the temple, which was reduced by the Herodian expansion and allowed vendors and money-changers to move inside the temple precincts. "Herod's remodeling program increased the degree to which the outer court served as a profane civic center," and Collins suggests Jesus envisioned "the outer court was to be sacred space devoted to prayer and teaching, not civic space open to the general public and devoted to profane activities. Those who needed or wished to sacrifice doves could

33. Sanders, *Jesus and Judaism*, 66, emphasis original.

34. Klawans cautions against attributing too much historical validity to the thought of priestly corruption: "It must be emphasized that the gospel narratives and the prophetic verses cited therein are hardly unambiguous evidence for economic *abuse* on behalf of the priests or their cohorts. And—to add a touch of reality—it should also be noted that these evaluations of the Second Temple rarely consider whether it is reasonable to assume that whatever priestly corruption there was (if any) would have been any worse than economic oppression in general in the ancient world or any abuse carried out by tax collectors, other Roman authorities, or even members of Jerusalem's aristocracy who were not priests or not directly associated with the temple. In the end, the possibility that Jesus opposed priestly abuse in his day cannot be excluded, but it can't be proven either" (Klawans, *Purity, Sacrifice, and the Temple*, 228).

35. Moloney, *Gospel of Mark*, 224–26, emphasis added. Moloney's suggestion of the end of the temple cult is interesting, but the celebration of the Passover meal (14:12) likely indicates that the sacrificial cult was still active during the narrative. Under Moloney's interpretation, then, Jesus's actions are then a temporary halt, rather than a permanent stop, for the sacrificial cult.

purchase them outside the temple mount."³⁶ Within this framework, Collins argues that Jesus's actions "place the honor and dignity of God above human convenience. Or perhaps it would be better to say that he placed the honor of God above the architectural pretensions of Herod and the convenience of the chief priests."³⁷ Collins's focus on placing Jesus's actions within his overall message is shared by Jonathan Klawans, who suggests this incident indicates Jesus's concern for "the moral issues at the nexus between sacrifice and purity."³⁸ Klawans connects Jesus's actions in relation to the effects of the temple's economic system—which, like Sanders, he understands as a necessary and common piece of a sacrificial cult—on the poor, who would have suffered financially and socially from certain economic practices. Klawans suggests,

> The common denominator here is that both of these types of traders would have a marked impact on poor pilgrims in particular. The money changers have their impact on the impoverished because only the poor would feel pinched by the small surcharge assessed at the temple (again, following rabbinic sources). The pigeon sellers have their impact on the destitute because the birds are the cheapest of the animal sacrifices, and presumably it's the poor who are buying pigeons, as opposed to more expensive animals such as lambs or goats . . . both the selling of pigeons and the money changers' surcharge are practical and reasonable. But that doesn't mean they are entirely unobjectionable, especially to a group or movement that has different ideas about how one should relate to the poor. It could be argued that *any* given tax or fee is practical and reasonable; but surely practically every tax or charge has had its opponents. In my view, Jesus opposed those aspects of the temple system—the temple tax and the pigeon sellers—that required exacting money or goods from the poor.³⁹

---

36. Collins, *Mark*, 528; cf. "Jesus' Action in Herod's Temple," in Collins and Mitchell, eds., *Antiquity and Humanity*, 45–61.

37. Collins, *Mark*, 529.

38. Klawans, *Purity, Sacrifice, and the Temple*, 237.

39. Klawans, *Purity, Sacrifice, and the Temple*, 237. Klawans does not completely dismiss the notion that the temple incident may carry a critique against the priesthood, but he cautions against using this particular pericope to then extrapolate the priesthood as economically corrupt and wicked; while these may have been points of criticism lobbied at the priesthood, Klawans cautions there is not enough evidence for this to fit a historical argument of the first-century priesthood. It is interesting, however, that Klawans's interpretation of the temple incident as a comment on the effect of temple practice on poor and marginalized people resonates with a narrative reading of Mark

Whether Jesus's actions are viewed as a demonstration of the temple's destruction or an act of reformation, the actions in the temple are not unilateral, as Jesus sequentially moves from acting against the practices in the temple to castigating temple leadership.

A significant feature of this narrative is its rhetorical use of intercalation, where a central story is sandwiched within another, and the central story provides a foundation through which to understand the entire story sequence, including the outside framing narrative.[40] The sequential relationship between narratives, as Tom Shepherd argues, reveals dramatic irony and sharpens the Christology of the gospel.[41] For Shepherd, the intercalation draws out the irony between "the demise of the temple" and the role of the authorities: "Jesus is a threat to their religious authority, hence they desire to remove this hindrance to their power. However, it is this plan of theirs which actually brings the destruction of the temple."[42] Similar to Marcus, Shepherd's reading walks the line between the intention of "cleansing," while also dealing with the effects of foretold destruction.[43] While Shepherd, Edwards, and others focus on the A-B-A sequential nature of Markan intercalations, this narrative can actually be extended if 11:27–12:12 are considered, creating an A-B-A-B pattern.[44] This pericope will be treated below, but the effect of rhetorically placing Jesus in conflict with the chief priests, scribes, and elders, and employing a parable about their destruction and replacement (12:9) again demonstrates the common thread of Jesus's opposition to the priesthood rather than the temple cult.[45]

12:38–44, in which the scribes are critiqued for the economic effects of their practices, demonstrated by the extraction of all wealth from a poor widow.

40. See Shepherd, "Narrative Function of Markan Intercalation," 522–40; Edwards, "Markan Sandwiches," 193–216; Downing, "Markan Intercalation," 118–32.

41. Shepherd, "Narrative Function of Markan Intercalation," 538–40. Shepherd's emphasis on the literary aspect of intercalation (dramatic irony) is a bit more generalized and oriented toward Christology compared to Edwards's argument that the function was theologically pointed to "emphasize the major motifs of the Gospel, especially the meaning of faith, discipleship, bearing witness, and the dangers of apostasy" (Edwards, "Markan Sandwiches," 196).

42. Shepherd, "Narrative Function of Markan Intercalation," 536.

43. "The cleansing of the temple becomes a curse as the religious leaders plot the death of the purifying Messiah. The end of the temple is not the end of prayer, there will be a new praying community" (Shepherd, "Narrative Function of Markan Intercalation," 539).

44. Downing, "Markan Intercalation," 121.

45. Nicole Duran suggests the pericope "becomes an allegory in which the fig tree

In addition to the narrative intratextual "sandwich" features, this pericope draws on intertexts with scriptural traditions in explicit and implicit manners. The prophetic traditions of Isa 56:7 and Jer 7:11 are brought together, placing emphasis on the ones who have prevented the temple from serving its purpose with an emphatic "but you" (ὑμεῖς δὲ, 11:17). Nicole Duran points to the intertextual relationship between Mark 11 and Jeremiah 7, which centers on a prophetic critique of Israel's persistent improper behavior as denigrating the temple cult (Jer 7:9–10). Duran argues, "Jesus thus uses the Jeremiah allusion to portray the temple as both abandoned by its rightful caretakers and used, exploited by others ... The prophet does not see temple worship in and of itself as inadequate or wrong-headed. Rather, the effectiveness of temple sacrifice and the divine presence there seem to be conditional upon the people's righteousness."[46] While Duran is correct that the immediate reference to Jer 7:11 is not expressly against the temple, the following verses offer an explicit condemnation of the people that results in God threatening to destroy the temple and expel the people (Jer 7:12–15), which aligns with the "demonstration" attitude of Sanders, Moloney, and Marcus.[47] Furthermore, the intertextual passage later delegitimizes the sacrificial cult (and especially child sacrifice, Jer 7:23–34).[48] The attitude from Jeremiah 7 is held in tension with the larger context of Isaiah 56, which the Markan Jesus cites in relation to the temple's purpose as "a house of prayer for all nations/Gentiles" (Mark 11:17; Isa 56:7). Given the tension, some

---

does not represent the temple itself. Rather, it stands for a leader or group of leaders who have chosen to wield power over others, like a king, rather than to produce the good fruits that they were created to bear" (Nicole Wilkinson Duran, "'Not One Stone Will Be Left on Another': The Destruction of the Temple and the Crucifixion of Jesus in Mark's Gospel," in Wiley and Eberhart, eds., *Sacrifice, Cult, and Atonement in Early Judaism and Christianity*, 321).

46. Duran, "Not One Stone Will Be Left on Another," in Wiley and Eberhart, eds., *Sacrifice, Cult, and Atonement in Early Judaism and Christianity*, 318.

47. Morna Hooker instead sees the reference to Jeremiah 7 as evidence that Jesus's actions are intended to be a "cleansing," focusing on the call for repentance and acts of justice in vv. 5–7. "So what was Jesus doing when he entered the temple and overthrew the money-changers' tables? Was he, perhaps, after all, *cleansing* the temple rather than destroying it? Was he, in other words, protesting against those who worshipped there while failing to love God with all their heart and soul and mind and strength? ... Are not his actions more appropriate against such false worship than as a symbol of coming destruction?" (Hooker, "Traditions About the Temple," 18).

48. On the passing of children through the fire in the ancient Near East, see Heth and Kelley, "Isaac and Iphigenia," 481–502; Heth, "Stripping of the Bulls," 583–606, esp. 593–94.

interpretations view Jesus's action as a permanent interruption to sacrifice; Shaner summarizes this view: "Jesus's actions theologically mark the end of God's acceptance of cultic sacrifice in Jerusalem."[49] In its Isaianic context, it is not merely prayer that is intended for the temple, but the legitimation and inclusion of burnt offerings (ὁλοκαυτώματα) and sacrifices (θυσίαι) made by "the foreigners who join themselves to the Lord to minister to him and love the name of the Lord, and to be his servants" (τοῖς ἀλλογενέσι τοῖς προσκειμένοις κυρίῳ δουλεύειν αὐτῷ καὶ ἀγαπᾶν τὸ ὄνομα κυρίου τοῦ εἶναι αὐτῷ εἰς δούλους, Isa 56:6). Gray also draws on the resonances to another prophetic tradition, examining Jesus's actions in the temple as framed by Malachi 3. Gray highlights how "Malachi warns about the Lord's coming to the temple (Mal 3:2) as he will come in judgment (3:5f), a judgment particularly focused upon the priests (3:3). The charge against them is that they are robbing God (Mal 3:8-9), a charge that resonates with the accusations Jesus will make against the temple authorities."[50] That the chief priests and scribes react negatively (11:18) suggests they are the intended target of Jesus's words.[51] However, Gray again moves the target from the priesthood to the temple itself, arguing, "Mark's framing of the temple demonstration with the condemnation of the fig tree makes it evident, whatever the ambiguity of Jesus' actions, that Jesus is giving a prophetic condemnation of the temple."[52]

In Jesus's first major physical encounter with the Jerusalem temple, his actions upend temple practices. These actions have a certain sense of ambiguity to them and, therefore, result in interpretations ranging from anti-imperial, anti-temple, prophetic enactment, or apocalyptic demonstration. When combined with his teaching, however, these actions fit within an overall critique of the failure of the temple leadership to ensure the temple fulfills its purpose. The intertextual resonances of prophetic critique against the improper behavior of the priests and the

---

49. Shaner, "Danger of Singular Saviors," 143. Shaner rightly notes the major risk of this view is that it may devolve into, or be used to justify, a form of Christian supersessionism.

50. Gray, *Temple in the Gospel of Mark*, 44.

51. Gray suggests the temple leadership is symbiotic with the temple, where the pronouncement against one leads to the end of the other: "Too often, because of the culpability of the temple establishment, interpreters focus on the Jewish leadership and miss the thrust of the narrative—the corruption and self-serving leadership is poignantly judged by bringing the temple institution to an end" (Gray, *Temple in the Gospel of Mark*, 34).

52. Gray, *Temple in the Gospel of Mark*, 44.

people of Israel further suggest Jesus is not rejecting the temple outright, which still has a purpose (Isaiah 56), although the allusion to Jeremiah 7 draws on the complexity of attitudes against the temple and sacrificial cult in the prophetic tradition (cf. Ezek 24:21; Mal 1:6–10; Mic 3:12). Still, Jesus's continued presence in the temple (11:27–12:44; 14:49) hints at the temple still having some sort of legitimate role, and his continued interaction with the chief priests, scribes, and elders further demonstrates his rejection of the contemporary priesthood without directly rejecting the temple.

Mark 13:1–2, 14

The most explicit statement by Jesus about the temple's destruction comes in Mark 13's apocalyptic/eschatological discourse.[53] As Jesus and the disciples leave Jerusalem, one of the disciples draws attention to the stones and the buildings. Jesus responds to this statement by predicting "there will not be left here stone upon stone which will not be destroyed" (οὐ μὴ ἀφεθῇ ὧδε λίθος ἐπὶ λίθον ὃς οὐ μὴ καταλυθῇ, 13:2). Later, when he is sitting directly opposite the temple (κατέναντι τοῦ ἱεροῦ, 13:3), a small cadre of disciples asks when this destruction will take place. Jesus responds with a lengthy discourse on the eschatological signs (the "beginning of the birth pangs"; ἀρχὴ ὠδίνων, 13:8) prefiguring the temple's destruction. Among these signs are war, the appearance of false messiahs and false prophets, and the "abomination of desolation standing where he ought not to be" (τὸ βδέλυγμα τῆς ἐρημώσεως ἑστηκότα ὅπου οὐ δεῖ, 13:14), which signals those in Judaea to flee to the mountains. The Markan Jesus appeals to the apocalyptic traditions in Daniel to assure the disciples that, after these events, the Son of Man will appear and send his angels to gather together the elect (ἐπισυνάξει τοὺς ἐκλεκτοὺς, 13:27) from their widespread dwellings. Jesus refers back to the fig tree as a lesson in understanding the signs, suggests the timing of the events is near, then urges awareness since no one, including the angels in heaven and the son, knows the day or hour (13:32).

---

53. The distinction between apocalypticism and eschatology is notoriously difficult. Mark 13 does not draw on all the features of Jewish apocalyptic (e.g., a heavenly intermediary revealing divine words), but in its eschatological presentation it does reference apocalyptic literature like Daniel. For more on Jewish apocalyptic, see Collins, *Early Christian Apocalypticism*; Collins, *Apocalypse*; "Genre Apocalypse Reconsidered," 21–40.

The reference to "the abomination of desolation" draws on the imagery of Dan 9:27, 11:31, and 12:11, which describe the profanation of the temple by a foreign ruler. Many scholars suppose Mark utilizes this imagery to reference the events of 66–70 CE.[54] Gray suggests Mark understands these three passages together and proposes they be read in light of one another: "In Daniel, the 'desolating sacrilege' marks the imminent destruction of the temple, accompanied by a time of 'tribulation' that will last until the 'end.' That Mark is familiar with Daniel's use of this expression is quite clear, which confirms that, at the heart of the discourse, the temple is undoubtedly in his mind."[55] However, the "end" of the temple is not clearly spelled out in Dan 11:30–45 or 12:1–13 but only foretold in 9:26–27. If Mark's audience has in mind the context of Antiochus and the Maccabeans (1 Macc 1:54), which Gray also suggests, the audience would be aware that the "desolating sacrilege" did not lead to the temple's destruction but, after a period of revolt, its restoration.[56] It is possible, as in Josephus (*Ant.* 10.203–210), that the Markan audience connected the Danielic references to Roman activity.[57] James Crossley posits "the best first-century Roman parallel to the actions of Antiochus IV and the establishment of something idolatrous in the Temple is Caligula's attempt to erect his statue in the Jerusalem Temple."[58] Crossley mentions echoes and parallels between the Caligula crisis and the despair of the Maccabean Revolt in Josephus and Philo, including the possibility of widespread rebellion, martyrdom, and the "manic" nature of the

---

54. Marcus, "Jewish War and the *Sitz im Leben* of Mark," 441–62; Wardle, "Mark, the Jerusalem Temple," 60–78; Moloney, *Mark*, 259–60; Kloppenborg, "*Evocatio Deorum*," 419–50. Collins also dates the composition of the gospel to this general time but argues "[Mark] wrote not primarily to portray present or past events as prophecy after the fact but to place in the mouth of Jesus a prophecy of the turning point in the war which was still future from his perspective" (Collins, *Mark*, 611).

55. Gray, *Temple in the Gospel of Mark*, 130.

56. See Theissen, *Gospels in Context*, 158; Crossley, *Date of Mark's Gospel*, 27–29.

57. Collins, on the other hand, cautions attributing similar interpretive strategies to a first-century audience: "It is important for us twenty-first-century readers to remember that Jews and Christians in Mark's time did not understand Daniel as an apocalyptic interpretation of the crisis created by the persecution of Antiochus Epiphanes. Rather, they understood Daniel as a prophecy of the eschatological kingdom of God, which was about to be inaugurated, perhaps during their own lifetimes. Thus, for Mark, the passages in Daniel about the 'desolating sacrilege' did not refer to the profanation of the altar in the second century BCE, but to an event of the future that would precede the establishment of the rule of God through the Son of Man who was about to come" (Collins, *Mark*, 13).

58. Crossley, *Date of Mark's Gospel*, 29–30; cf. Marcus, *Mark 8–16*, 865–66.

foreign rulers's decisions. Crossley also suggests Mark's instruction to "flee to the mountains" (13:14) may echo 1 Macc 2:28, and he argues the Caligula statue helps explain the grammatical construction of the masculine participle ἑστηκότα.[59] Setting this possible interpretation within the mnemonic framework of first-century audiences, Crossley writes,

> These suggestions alone do not of course mean that Mark or Mark 13 was necessarily written during the Caligula crisis. Moreover, it is entirely plausible to suggest that a prophecy could be reinterpreted in ancient Judaism and Christianity. In the present case even if Mark 13 originated during the Caligula crisis it would not follow from an analysis of this chapter alone that it could not be re-applied (say) during the Jewish–Roman war of 66–70.[60]

The apocalyptic imagery of Mark 13 can be seen within several social and historical frameworks in the first century CE. Whether the "abomination of desolation" is understood as a reference to the Caligula crisis of the 40s CE, the outbreak of the Jewish War in 66–70 CE, or some other coming crisis, the Markan community would have been able to attach the symbolic imagery and warnings to different salient events in the community's history.[61] While the priesthood is absent from this eschatological discourse, Marcus suggests "the prophecy of Temple destruction in the present context is probably also meant to be understood as a judgment on Israel's leaders, especially the Temple hierarchy, for their rejection of Jesus."[62]

Mark 14:53–15:29

Jesus's trial combines the oppositional force of the priesthood (see below) and conflict surrounding the temple, which has been building

---

59. Crossley, *Date of Mark's Gospel*, 30; cf. Taylor, "Palestinian Christianity I," 101–23; "Palestinian Christianity II," 13–40; Günther Zuntz, "Wann wurde das Evangelium Marci geschrieben?," in Cancik, ed., *Markus-Philologie*, 47–71.

60. Crossley, *Date of Mark's Gospel*, 30.

61. Hengel proposes the historical context in the aftermath of the reign of Nero, suggesting Nero's persecution of the Christian community and the political turmoil of the three short-lived successors stoked apocalyptic concerns and fears of an antichrist figure who would take control of the temple and increase the suffering of the Christian community. Hengel, *Studies in the Gospel of Mark*, 27–28.

62. Marcus, *Mark 8–16*, 873. Hooker also links it to the narrative's greater "theme of eschatological judgment for Israel" (Hooker, "Traditions About the Temple," 10).

throughout the narrative. The temple serves as the catalyst and central focus of the trial. After Jesus's arrest, the council are greeted with charges against Jesus regarding what he has supposedly said about the temple: that he would destroy the handmade temple and rebuild another, non-handmade temple in three days. The narrator reveals that these charges are false (ψευδομαρτυρέω, 14:56, but see the reception of this tradition in John 2 below); in addition, the testimony brought against him is contradictory (14:56, 59).[63] Jesus silently offers no response to these charges, but he does respond to the high priest's question about his identity as messiah and son of the Blessed One (ὁ χριστὸς ὁ υἱὸς τοῦ εὐλογητοῦ, 14:61), at which point the trial shifts in focus to the conflict surrounding Jesus's messianic identity, which the high priest deems as blasphemous and the council subsequently condemns him to death.

Though the charges against Jesus are labelled false, many scholars suggest there is a note of truth in what Jesus is reported to have said. Collins remarks these statements are "in some tension with 13:2, where Jesus is portrayed as predicting the destruction of the temple."[64] R. T. France suggests the impact of the charges was significant since "it was [the temple charge] rather than his alleged blasphemy which was remembered by the bystanders at the cross" in 15:29.[65] Donald Juel suggests "the charge in 14:58 can be 'false testimony' (Jesus never threatened to destroy the temple) and 'prophetic' (as a result of his death the old religious order symbolized by the temple comes to an end)."[66] Gray connects the witnesses' claims with the parable of the wicked tenants; for him, what makes the charges false are Jesus's direct involvement

---

63. While the narrator plays an important role in shaping the falsehood of the claim, Rodríguez also notes the constraint of the narrator's aside: "If, however, the Gospels were written after the temple's destruction, [the lack of narrative interjections about Titus having fulfilled Jesus's destruction prophecy] is an example of tradents resisting the pressure to reshape or re-interpret the tradition in light of present exigencies" (Rodríguez, "Text as Tradition," 127).

64. Collins, *Mark*, 701. Le Donne also mentions this tension, as well as some implied ambiguity, but notes how Mark is not directly trying to link Jesus to the saying: "Notice that in Mark's narrative these 'false' witnesses accuse Jesus of claiming the ability to destroy the temple. Mark does not call them liars; he only states that they were 'inconsistent.' Given what Jesus says in Mark 13:1-2, the author would have a difficult time denying the accusation outright. However, Mark does aim to distance Jesus from this accusation" (Le Donne, *Historical Jesus*, 127).

65. France, *Gospel of Mark*, 604.

66. See Juel, *Messiah and Temple*, 206.

in the temple's destruction, but that does not negate the truth of the overall impetus of these claims:

> Many elements in the charge are correct . . . Mark wants the reader to see that Jesus is innocent of the charge that he will destroy the temple. Rather, he stands as the last one in a line of prophets sent to warn of the temple's judgment. Thus, the charge is correct in that the temple will be destroyed and that another will take its place, but it reflects a fundamental misunderstanding as to how and through whom this will take place.[67]

Jesus has spoken indirectly about the temple's "destruction" (the passive use of καταλύω in 13:2) and the Son of Man being raised "after three days" (μετὰ τρεῖς ἡμέρας in 8:31, 10:34; compare to διὰ τριῶν ἡμερῶν in 14:58), but these brief connections do not offer the fuller sense that Jesus would destroy the temple. In addition, outside of Jesus's reference to his status as "cornerstone" (κεφαλὴν γωνίας, 12:10), there are no narrative grounds for the rebuilding of the temple either.[68] As discussed in the previous chapter, some groups in the Second Temple period looked forward to a time when God would build an everlasting, eschatological temple (cf. 11Q19 29:7–10, *Jubilees* 1:17, 27). Israelite tradition also depicted God building or setting a dwelling place among the people (Ezek 37:26–28; Exod 15:17).[69] Within the historical context, then, the false testimony is not outlandish: there *were* Second Temple Jews who believed the temple would be destroyed (*B.J.* 6.300–309), and there were those who believed God would build an eschatological temple. Since the attitude displayed in the false witness fits a first-century context, Gray reads the charge in line with other instances of irony throughout the end of the gospel, arguing "it is consistent with Mark's style to show that the testimony regarding Jesus' comments about the temple is false on one level, but nevertheless true in a way that escapes the grasp and the intentions of Jesus' perjurers: the old temple is to be destroyed and replaced by another."[70] While Gray is correct to note the irony present in Jesus's passion, it is not ironic that

---

67. Gray, *Temple in the Gospel of Mark*, 173. On the parable of the wicked tenants, see below.

68. The building of the tower in the parable of the wicked tenants (ᾠκοδόμησεν πύργον, 12:1) offers perhaps the closest example of Jesus discussing the construction of the temple, but it still does not provide grounding for the saying that will be falsely attributed to him in his trial.

69. VanderKam, *Jubilees 1–21*, 155.

70. Gray, *Temple in the Gospel of Mark*, 174.

false testimony against Jesus claimed he would destroy the temple and rebuild it when he merely hinted at its destruction; rather, it is ironic that the charge is still attributed to Jesus by those passing by his crucifixion (15:29) when the audience knows it is false.[71] Even more ironic is that the truth of what these false witnesses say is not about the temple, but what the audience has been told about Jesus's impending fate (8:31; 10:33–34). The false witness at his trial represents another instance of misunderstanding, a persistent theme within the narrative, that moves the audience toward a Christological, not eschatological, understanding.

Mark 15:38

The temple appears for the final time in the narrative at Jesus's death. At the moment of Jesus's last exhalation, the veil (καταπέτασμα) of the temple is torn (ἐσχίσθη) from top to bottom (15:38). Wardle connects this pericope with the temple incident, arguing,

> Mark has woven into the fabric of his narrative an anti-temple and anti-priestly polemic. In Mark's first mention of the temple, Jesus shuts down all activity in it (11:16) and denounces its leadership (11:17). In Mark's final mention of the Jerusalem temple, the temple veil is ripped apart (15:38). These two thoroughly negative references to the Jerusalem temple bookend Mark's presentation of Jesus vis-á-vis the temple.[72]

Mark's first mention of Jesus entering the temple is slightly earlier and less dramatic (11:11) than Wardle states, and Mark's first mention of the temple itself is in 2:26. Pedantry aside, however, Wardle's characterization of these two scenes as "thoroughly negative" demonstrates Collins's emphasis on the ambiguity of this pericope: "The interpretation of v. 38 as part of the Gospel of Mark as a whole depends on what other passage or passages the interpreter considers to be key to its significance."[73] Similar to Wardle, Gray suggests "by tying together the death of Jesus and

---

71. Marcus follows Brown in arguing, "later in the narrative Jesus is mocked both as Messiah and as the destroyer and rebuilder of the Temple, and there is no indication that one charge is completely true while the other is entirely false" (Marcus, *Mark 8–16*, 1014). However, this misses the irony inherent in the mockery by the chief priests and scribes: for Mark, it is precisely *because of* his messianic identity that Jesus is being crucified (8:29–31; 10:33, 45). Therefore, both instances of mockery are reversed.

72. Wardle, "Mark, the Jerusalem Temple," 70.

73. Collins, *Mark*, 761.

the rending of the temple veil, Mark shows in the starkest terms possible that the fate of Jesus and the temple are intertwined."[74] Gray then draws on the use of ναός as evidence of Mark linking Jesus's trial, the mocking at the crucifixion, and this scene, which "helps the reader to see dramatic reversal brought about through the tearing of the 'temple' (ναός) veil and the vindication it brings to Jesus."[75] While Gray is correct that these three instances are the only times the term ναός are used in the narrative, Mark also uses a wide range of terms (οἶκος, ἱερόν, πύργον) to refer semantically to Jesus's interactions with and discussions of the temple. Focusing solely on ναός offers a direct connection point to destruction (καταλύω) in the two earliest instances (14:58; 15:29), but the claims of destruction in these pericopae are delegitimized by the Markan narrator's insistence that the original claim is false witness against Jesus. In addition, the shift from "thrown down/destroyed" (καταλύω) to "torn" (σχίζω) is significant. Marcus ties the tearing of the veil to "divine mourning," as enacted by the high priest rending his garments during the trial (14:53).[76] Marcus also emphasizes the revelatory nature this scene has when compared with the baptism (1:10).[77] Collins argues likewise: "The similarities between 1:10 and 15:38 in vocabulary and in the themes in each of their contexts strongly suggest that v. 38, in the context of Mark as a whole, should be read not as a sign of the destruction of the temple but as another nontraditional theophany."[78] The tearing of the veil is not unambiguously negative, nor is it symbolic of the foretold apocalyptic destruction removal of "stone upon stone" (λίθος ἐπὶ λίθον, 13:2). Instead, in the same way that the baptism demonstrated God's spirit moving and Jesus's identity as Son of God being revealed, 15:38-39 reaffirms this Christological identity, even in the midst of the

---

74. Gray, *Temple in the Gospel of Mark*, 186. Gray again draws on the parable of the wicked tenants to argue "Jesus' death is not simply that of another prophet or martyr but that of the Son (12:6), and now the owner of the vineyard responds as never before by punishing the wicked tenants and vindicating his Son (12:9)" (Gray, *Temple in the Gospel of Mark*, 187). If we follow Gray in using the parable of the wicked tenants as a lens through which to understand the tearing of the veil, it is a punishment against the priesthood, the target of divine action in 12:9. However, it is not made clear how the priesthood (as "tenants") is then destroyed, or how the vineyard is given to others.

75. Gray, *Temple in the Gospel of Mark*, 187.

76. Marcus, *Mark 8-16*, 1066.

77. Marcus, *Mark 8-16*, 1067.

78. Collins, *Mark*, 763-64.

darkness of Jesus's death. Thus, this pericope says less about the temple and more about who Jesus is for the gospel's audience.

Jesus and the Priests: What Does the Markan Jesus Say about the Priesthood?

While innovative religious authorities and interpretive practices impacted what Judaism looked like in the Second Temple period (e.g., synagogues, *mikva'ot*, Pharisees, allegorical interpretation of scripture, and the covenanters of the DSS), the temple still maintained its influence as an important cultic center steeped in Israelite tradition. The priesthood was responsible for the maintenance and administration of the temple, so their position is synonymous with temple rulership.[79] In light of this, I will regard references to the priesthood in the Gospel of Mark as a synecdoche with the entire temple institution. Thus, when the Markan Jesus speaks of the priesthood in 1:40–45; 8:31; 10:32; 11:18–12:12; 14:53–63; and 15:25–32, these instances offer a further characterization about the institution of the temple. In other words, the Markan Jesus's attitude toward the priesthood, which is often portrayed in conflict, offers further insight into his ambivalent relationship with the temple.

Mark 1:40–45

The first encounter between the Jesus movement and the institution of the Jerusalem temple occurs early in the narrative while Jesus is still establishing his ministry. As Jesus's reputation for exorcism, healing, and teaching grows in Capernaum, he decides to withdraw from the town and travel to neighboring villages (εἰς τὰς ἐχομένας κωμοπόλεις, 1:38) throughout Galilee. During this Galilean synagogue tour (1:39), Jesus is met by a man with a skin affliction (λεπρὸς, 1:41).[80] The manuscript

---

79. "The immediate narrative stage for the establishment of God's rule is the nation Israel under the military control of the Roman Empire. Herod Antipas is the Roman-appointed king in Galilee, and Pilate is the Roman procurator over Judea and Jerusalem. The Judean authorities in Jerusalem include the high priest Caiaphas—appointed by Rome and accountable to Rome—along with the high priests, the elders, and the rest of the national 'Sanhedrin' council. They govern Judea and Jerusalem directly and administer the temple—for as long as they keep order and provide tribute for their Roman overlords" (Rhoads et al., *Mark as Story*, 65).

80. Though traditionally translated as "leper," the ancient understanding of *lepra* (λέπρα) could refer to a variety of skin conditions that do not necessarily indicate

tradition varies on whether 1:41 has Jesus respond out of compassion (σπλαγχνίζομαι) or anger (ὀργίζω), but the end result remains the same: the man is cleansed.[81] In the aftermath of the healing, Jesus tells the man to "go, show yourself to the priest, and offer concerning your cleansing what Moses commanded as a witness to them" (ὕπαγε σεαυτὸν δεῖξον τῷ ἱερεῖ καὶ προσένεγκε περὶ τοῦ καθαρισμοῦ σου ἃ προσέταξεν Μωϋσῆς εἰς μαρτύριον αὐτοῖς, 1:44).[82] Instead, the man defies Jesus's order for secrecy as "he began to preach openly and spread the word" (ἤρξατο κηρύσσειν πολλὰ καὶ διαφημίζειν τὸν λόγον, 1:45).

The fact that Jesus points the man in the direction of the Jerusalem priesthood seemingly indicates a tacit approval of the temple's sacrificial cult. Joel Marcus notes, "By this instruction Jesus seems to acknowledge the authority of the priestly establishment," which serves a narrative function as Jesus's growing ministry will later lead to conflict

---

Hansen's Disease. See Marcus, *Mark 1–8*, 205. For more on the use of λέπρα in the LXX and ancient medical texts, see Shellberg, *Cleansed Lepers, Cleansed Hearts*, 29–94. Recently, Myrick C. Shinall Jr. has argued social stigmatization of lepers was not as systematic as often assumed, pointing to the various levels of integration and socialization displayed in HB and NT texts, while also recognizing the exclusionary—although not necessarily universally prescriptive—comments made by Josephus and the DSS. See Shinall Jr., "Social Condition of Lepers in the Gospels," 915–34. Matthew Thiessen also examines *lepra* within the context of ritual impurity, arguing it is not leprosy but rather a minor skin condition that was thought to convey ritual impurity, thus demonstrating Jesus's concern for purifying those afflicted. See Thiessen, *Jesus and the Forces of Death*, 43–68.

81. The healing by the "angry" Jesus is in itself a fascinating case study in early Christian memory. The textual variants offer two completely different ways of understanding the healing of 1:40–45. The traditional reading of "moved with compassion" (σπλαγχνισθείς) is self-explanatory as a lead into the healing, especially in context to the man's supplication of "If you wish, you can heal me" (ἐὰν θέλῃς). The commentary tradition, however, more recently leans into the reading of "anger" (ὀργισθείς), and scholars present a wide variety of reasons for why Jesus is portrayed as angry: France argues that Jesus is angry on account of the physical and social suffering; Moloney argues that Jesus's anger is directed at the exclusionary effects of ritual purity; Marcus, following Hooker, argues that the anger is aimed at the demonic forces causing the disease. France, *Gospel of Mark*, 117; Moloney, *Gospel of Mark*, 58; Marcus, *Mark 1–8*, 209. For a larger discussion on the text-critical issue in recent scholarship, see Williams, "Examination of Ehrman's Case," 1–12.

82. In attempting to keep his reading consistent with Jesus's anger, Moloney is too passive here: "[The leper] is permitted to make the offering required so that he may rejoin the holy people from which his disease has separated him" (Moloney, *Gospel of Mark*, 58). Moloney's interpretation does not capture the force of this passage; Jesus does not "permit," but commands (ὕπαγε, δεῖξον, προσένεγκε, 1:44) the man to follow the Levitical practice.

with the same religious authorities.[83] France also recognizes Jesus's adherence to purity regulations: "Despite Jesus' own lack of concern for ritual purity in v. 41, he here insists on the correct observance of the OT regulations."[84] Others, however, minimize the role of the sacrificial cult in Jesus's response; for example, Adela Yarbro Collins claims, "The healing is to demonstrate to the authorities that Jesus has the power to heal and therefore is God's agent."[85] Elizabeth Struthers Malbon even places this healing within the larger narrative characterization of Jesus, arguing, "the Markan Jesus wishes to *deflect* the attention given to him, especially as healer, to the true source of the healing, God."[86] On the other hand, Simon Joseph highlights Jesus's sending the man with the sacrificial requirements "as a witness to them" (εἰς μαρτύριον αὐτοῖς, 1:44), which Joseph reads in the oppositional sense of *"against* them." Within this framework, Joseph argues "Jesus is not deferring to priestly authority nor should we assume that Jesus was trying to facilitate the leper's official re-admission into polite Israelite society. On the contrary, the Markan Jesus is issuing a challenge to priestly authority."[87]

The cleansing (περὶ τοῦ καθαρισμοῦ σου) Jesus refers to is the Levitical law for purifying skin diseases (ὁ νόμος τοῦ λεπροῦ [המצרע], ᾗ ἂν ἡμέρᾳ καθαρισθῇ, Lev 14:2 LXX). This law requires animal sacrifice—the quantity of animals depended on the wealth of the one being cleansed (Lev 14:10–32)—at the temple. While we are not told anything specific about the man's condition, the description used for the man (λεπρός) indicates an active skin condition that presumably would not have rendered him clean under priestly consideration (cf. Lev 13:1–59). Since Jesus's healing is effective (καθαρίζω, Mark 1:41–42), the man can now be deemed clean by the priests (Lev 14:3).[88] This pericope, then, displays Jesus healing the man's affliction and, by referring to the priest for ritual purification, also upholding and supporting the function of the temple and priesthood.

---

83. Marcus, *Mark 1–8*, 210.
84. France, *Gospel of Mark*, 119.
85. Collins, *Mark*, 179.
86. Malbon, *Mark's Jesus*, 135, emphasis original.
87. Joseph, *Jesus and the Temple*, 118–19.
88. Gaston notes the oddity of the verb καθαρίζω here, suggesting the cleansing would have made the leper's trip to the priests a redundancy. See Gaston, *No Stone on Another*, 90.

Mark 8:31, 10:32

About midway through the narrative (8:31), Jesus offers the first in a series of predictions foretelling his death.[89] Between the oscillating characterization of Peter identifying Jesus as Messiah (8:27) and subsequently being rebuked by Jesus (8:33) is the gospel's first passion prediction.[90] In this prediction, Jesus offers a brief summary of what to expect for the Son of Man: excessive suffering (πολλὰ παθεῖν),[91] rejection by the "elders, chief priests, and the scribes" (ἀποδοκιμασθῆναι ὑπὸ τῶν πρεσβυτέρων καὶ τῶν ἀρχιερέων καὶ τῶν γραμματέων), being killed (ἀποκτανθῆναι), and raised (ἀναστῆναι) on the third day (8:31). Jesus later follows up this prediction with a second, less detailed prediction (9:30–32; cf. v. 12) that adheres to the general structure of betrayal, death, and resurrection. The third prediction, however, echoes the first in listing out the specific religious authorities and explicating the suffering the Son of Man will endure (10:32–34). In this final prediction, Jesus tells the Twelve that the Son of Man "will be handed over to the chief priests and the scribes" (παραδοθήσεται τοῖς ἀρχιερεῦσιν καὶ τοῖς γραμματεῦσιν). Unlike the first prediction, in which the religious authorities reject (ἀποδοκιμάζω, 8:31) Jesus but otherwise remain fairly passive, the chief priests and scribes are more active in the final prediction: "they will condemn him to death and hand him over to the Gentiles" (κατακρινοῦσιν αὐτὸν θανάτῳ καὶ παραδώσουσιν αὐτὸν τοῖς ἔθνεσιν, 10:33).

The cadre of authorities grouped together against Jesus offers a significant shift from how the temple priesthood appeared earlier in the

---

89. Gregg Morrison calls this section (broadly 8:22–10:52; specifically 8:27–9:13) the "turning point" of the gospel since it links Jesus's identity from the first half of the narrative together with the impending journey to Jerusalem and his ultimate fate. See Morrison, *Turning Point in the Gospel of Mark*.

90. Peter's identification of Jesus as ὁ χριστός (8:29) links back to the gospel's opening line, where Jesus is introduced in the same way. The text-critical debate about the opening line's inclusion of υἱοῦ θεοῦ leans heavily on Codex Sinaiticus as an early witness against the conjoined titles. The scribal redactor of Sinaiticus, however, does include the nomina sacra in superscript. Even more, the original scribal hand of Sinaiticus has Peter identify Jesus as ὁ χρίστος ὁ υἱὸς τοῦ θεοῦ (8:29), pairing the titles together in the crux of Markan Christology.

91. Rodney Decker argues πολλὰ should be read as an accusative direct object ("many things") rather than adverbially ("greatly") and points to 10:34 as unpacking the "many things" (ἐμπαίξουσιν αὐτῷ καὶ ἐμπτύσουσιν αὐτῷ καὶ μαστιγώσουσιν αὐτόν). Conversely, the same argument could be made for the adverbial case, where 10:34 demonstrates the exorbitant extremes involved in his suffering. See Decker, *Mark 1–8*, 222–23.

narrative. Whereas he previously referred the λεπρὸς to the priest (1:44), now he predicts the priesthood's active role in his own death. Marcus argues this sudden turn may also play a role in Peter's response to Jesus's first passion prediction:

> Another possibly scandalous aspect of Jesus' prophecy is the schism that it describes between the Messiah and the other leaders of Israel, including the chief priests. As opposed to this scenario, many Jews cherished scripturally rooted hopes for an eschatological alliance of the Messiah *with* the high priest ... Peter would have good reasons, therefore, for rejecting the idea of a Messiah at loggerheads with Israel's leadership and delivered to death.[92]

While Jesus has encountered resistance, questioning, and conflict with the Galilean Pharisees and Jerusalem scribes throughout the first half of the narrative, the passion predictions alter or preemptively reframe the audience's perception to the Jerusalem authorities.[93] Malbon draws attention to how these predictions link together new characters with the established opponents of the first half of the narrative, as well as heightens the extent of the conflict in a way that stands out from other conflicts within the narrative. "First, the Pharisees, Herodians, chief priests, scribes, elders, and Sadducees are united as characters by their active opposition to the Marcan Jesus. This active opposition begins with questioning Jesus, progresses to plotting against him and accusing him, and culminates in condemning him to death. This kind of opposition is unique among the Marcan characters."[94] As the narrative approaches Jerusalem and what Malbon calls a "spatial shift ... from synagogue to Temple," the audience is primed to suspect the positions of authority that will play a significant

---

92. Marcus, *Mark 8–16*, 614.

93. Malbon draws out the spatial dynamics of the gospel and their connection to the characterization of Jesus's opponents. That this final prediction takes place while they are on their way to Jerusalem (ἦσαν δὲ ἐν τῇ ὁδῷ ἀναβαίνοντες εἰς Ἱεροσόλυμα, 10:32) underlines Malbon's argument that "Galilee—not Jerusalem—bears the positive connotations within the pair of spatial terms. In these two ways, the traditional (Jewish) valuation of Galilee and Jerusalem is reversed in the Marcan narrative ... The second half of the story is a narrative escalation of the first half, as both its patterns of spatial settings and its patterns of characterization show" (Malbon, "Jewish Leaders in the Gospel of Mark," 273–74).

94. Malbon, "Jewish Leaders in the Gospel of Mark," 270. In terms of opposition characters, Malbon points to "the Roman political establishment (Herod, Pilate, soldiers) and nonhuman foes (unclean spirits, demons, Satan)" (277).

role in the gospel's final third.[95] The exact reason why the priesthood would be after Jesus is not revealed in this prediction; "that Jesus' fate 'is necessary' [δεῖ] makes it a matter of God's plan as well as Jesus' foreknowledge ... now *all* the sting is removed."[96] Therefore, unless the audience already had a preconceived notion of the priesthood and council of elders/Sanhedrin as negative—and the mention of the priests in 1:44 and 2:26 do not seem to give any such reason—the passion predictions demand the audience be attuned to an amplified conflict with and characterization of the priesthood in Jerusalem that will come as a stark departure from the typical relationship with Judaean priests.

MARK 11:18, 27—12:12

After Jesus's arrival in Jerusalem and entry into the temple (see above), he is drawn into a series of conflicts with the authorities: the chief priests, scribes, and elders, the Pharisees and Herodians, the Sadducees, and a scribe all make an appearance between 11:27—12:44. The chief priests and scribes perceive Jesus's action and teaching in the temple as a threat, immediately seeking to kill him (11:18), which actualizes the animosity Jesus predicted while on the way to Jerusalem (10:32-34). Their motivation to kill him stems from their fear of the influence and impact of his teaching about the temple—the whole crowd is "shocked" (ἐκπλήσσομαι) at his teaching. Elsewhere in the narrative, characters have responded with this reaction in a variety of ways. In 1:22, the crowd is in awe at his teaching and authority to exorcise demons. In 6:2, his hometown crowd are struck at his teaching, but become "scandalized" (ἐσκανδαλίζοντο, 6:3) as they identify him by his trade and his family. In 7:37, the crowd responds in supreme amazement (ὑπερπερισσῶς ἐξεπλήσσοντο) to his healing of the deaf man with a speech issue. Finally, in response to his teaching about the impossibility of the rich entering the kingdom of God, the disciples are utterly mystified (περισσῶς ἐξεπλήσσοντο) and question among themselves about the implications of Jesus's teaching. The variety of responses and outcomes that accompany ἐκπλήσσομαι in Mark leaves the crowd's response partly ambiguous, although the crowd's continued presence in the temple

95. "For the traditional Jew this movement (like that from Galilee to Jerusalem) represents an increase in holiness, but for the Marcan Jesus it brings an escalation of conflict" (Malbon, "Jewish Leaders in the Gospel of Mark," 273).

96. Gundry, *Mark*, 428.

with Jesus serves as the source of his opposition's fear (11:32; 12:12), indicating that the crowd is receptive to his teaching.

The same oppositional group remains in view when Jesus again returns to the temple in 11:27.[97] The chief priests, scribes, and elders question Jesus over his authority (ἐξουσίᾳ) "to do these things" (ταῦτα ποιεῖς, 11:28), which is likely a reference back to the previous activity in the temple rather than questioning his authorization to walk about in the temple (ἐν τῷ ἱερῷ περιπατοῦντος αὐτοῦ, 11:27).[98] Questioning Jesus's authority links back to a common oppositional refrain throughout the gospel (1:27; 2:10; 3:15; 6:7).[99] As Rhoads, Dewey, and Michie remark, "From the first mention of legal experts as ones who teach without authority, the narrator paints the authorities in a consistently negative light."[100] In addition to the comparison between Jesus and the scribes and the passion predictions, the negative characterization is actualized in Jesus's first interaction with this particular group of authorities.[101] Jesus conditions his response first with an alternative question about John the Baptist's source of authority, to which the authorities feign ignorance.[102] Since they offer no answer, Jesus refuses to answer their question.

---

97. Although the elders are absent in 11:18, Malbon argues "the actions of the two-part subgroup (chief priests and scribes) do not differ significantly from the actions of the tripartite group (chief priests, scribes, and elders)" (Malbon, "Jewish Leaders in the Gospel of Mark," 268).

98. Many scholars discuss the source-critical implications of the intercalation (11:12–14, 20–25) and posit that "these things" may be evidence for an underlying tradition in which Jesus entered Jerusalem, caused havoc in the temple, and then was immediately questioned by the authorities. See Marcus, *Mark 8–16*, 798; Collins, *Mark*, 538–39; France, *Gospel of Mark*, 454.

99. Gray connects the questioning of Jesus's authority with his earlier response in 2:10 and highlights how the intertextual background to these controversies is Dan 7:13–14 (LXX), where the Son of Man is given an everlasting authority (ἐξουσία αἰώνιος) over all nations. Drawing on Daniel clarifies Jesus's authority for the audience: "Jesus' condemnation of the temple is the beginning of the eschatological judgment foretold in Daniel 7" (Gray, *Temple in the Gospel of Mark*, 59).

100. Rhoads et al., *Mark as Story*, 116.

101. "What the authorities *say* involves questions that imply accusations or aim at trapping Jesus. What they *do* shows their efforts to plot the destruction of Jesus. The narrator's inside views of their thoughts and feelings distance the reader from the authorities, showing them as unreliable characters. The authorities are 'flat' characters with consistent and predictable traits that are a direct contrast to the values of the rule of God. They are the opposite of Jesus, and they illuminate his character through contrast" (Rhoads et al., *Mark as Story*, 117).

102. John's influence on the Jesus movement is a common thread for those who study the temple in Jesus's ministry. Rodríguez argues Jesus's appeal to John's authority

In response to their failure to answer his question, Jesus tells the chief priests, scribes, and elders a parable about a vineyard whose tenants refuse to pay the landowner's share of the harvest and go to the extreme measure of killing the landowner's son to retain control of the vineyard (12:1-9). The parable of the vineyard tenants draws on Israel's traditional imagery to offer a cryptic yet pointed critique of the chief priests, elders, and scribes, who grasp their identification as the negatively characterized tenants and are angered by the implications of the parable (12:12). The opening of the parable uses the imagery of Isa 5:1-7—a vineyard (ἀμπελών), a hedge (φραγμός), a wine press (ὑπολήνιον), and a tower (πύργος)[103]—which recalls the divine judgment and destruction of Jerusalem, including the temple.[104] When Jesus asks for the expected outcome for the wicked tenants, those following the Isaian allusion would infer that the destruction of the vineyard (Jerusalem, including the temple) is in view. Unlike the outcome in Isa 5, however, it is not the *vineyard* that is destroyed, but the *tenants* (12:9).[105] For this reason, Gray argues "the overall purpose of this parable is to

---

in Mark 11 may reflect the Baptist's critique of the temple: "The Markan John's message of repentance and immersion in the wilderness, apart from the temple, can be read as a critique of Jerusalem's temple" (Rodríguez, "Text as Tradition," 128). Nicholas Perrin also links Jesus's behavior and attitude to John. Perrin argues John's group, like the community behind the *Psalms of Solomon* and the covenanters at Qumran, were critical of the temple, forming a counter-temple community that moved atonement (via ritual washing) and prayer out of the temple locus. Perrin argues that this influenced Jesus's understanding of his ministry as a new temple, the embodiment of the eschatological temple. See Perrin, *Jesus the Temple*.

103. The image of the temple as a tower is prevalent in other Second Temple literature, like 1 En 89:50, 73 and 4Q500. "4Q500, therefore, almost certainly uses the Isaiah 5 vineyard material in interpretative association with a description of the temple, either heavenly, or, more probably, earthly, which is the suitable place for the people (Isaiah's own interpretation) to bless God (possibly the genre of 4Q500)" (Brooke, "4Q500 1 and the Use of Scripture," 272).

104. On the evangelists' use of the Septuagint in Jesus's teaching and in the narrative portrayals of Jesus enacting scriptural traditions (e.g., Mark 11:1-10), Rodríguez writes, "We would be foolish to deny the formative role of the Septuagint in early Christian memory of Jesus; they recalled the past, perceived the present, and hoped for the future in terms and images provided by the Septuagint. We would be equally foolish, however, to embrace an atemporal conception of the Jesus tradition, according to which the early Christians mined the Scriptures for sayings and events of the historical Jesus. If the Evangelists could paint Jesus in scriptural hues, it is because his life and teachings already evoked, for them, themes and scenes from Israel's biblical traditions. If he didn't, no one would have thought to connect Jesus to the stories of Abraham, Moses, David, Isaiah, and other figures from the biblical past" (Rodríguez, "What is History?," 44).

105. See Collins, *Mark*, 547; France, *Gospel of Mark*, 461.

demonstrate the prophetic judgment the leaders of Israel have brought upon themselves by turning the temple into a den of thieves and by refusing the summons of John to repent and prepare for the eschatological coming of the kingdom."[106] Marcus supposes that the Jewish War colored the way in which audiences received the parable: "Christian readers of the Markan parable probably knew of or could foresee the effects of the Jewish War of 66–73 CE, in which not only the leaders but also the people suffered, and in which Jerusalem was leveled, its inhabitants slaughtered or deported to slavery, and the land of at least some Judaean Jews confiscated."[107] The "others," however, are not specified to be other nations (e.g., the Romans). Instead, as Collins argues, "the focus is not on the destruction of Jerusalem, let alone the rejection of Israel as a whole. Rather it is on the removal from power of the leaders who oppose Jesus . . . Giving the vineyard to others implies that a new leadership will emerge among those who accept Jesus as the messiah."[108] Following this line of thought, the parable is aimed at the priesthood—or at least the current priesthood—without being expressly against the temple cult. The reference to vindication in Psalm 118 that follows in 12:10–11 is often interpreted as Jesus subtly hinting at his role in the construction of a new temple.[109] Still, this pericope does not depict Jesus actively advocating for the destruction of the temple, nor is it explicit in stating that Jesus is a *temple* replacement; Gundry argues it further explicates the transfer of power from the religious authorities to Jesus and "refers to rulership after resurrection."[110] Throughout this pericope, Jesus's conflict with the

---

106. However, Gray also reads the parable as demonstrative of the demise of the temple: "The parable of the wicked tenants functions as a hinge for Mark's narrative, joining the previous topic of eschatological judgment upon the old temple to the vindication of the rejected stone that will be a new temple" (Gray, *Temple in the Gospel of Mark*, 61–62; cf. Moloney, *Gospel of Mark*, 234).

107. Marcus, *Mark 8–16*, 813.

108. Collins, *Mark*, 547; cf. Gundry, *Mark*, 663.

109. "By quoting Psalm 118 in the temple, therefore, the Markan Jesus is claiming to be the new cornerstone of the eschatological temple" (Gray, *Temple in the Gospel of Mark*, 76; cf. Collins, *Mark*, 548; Marcus, *Mark 8–16*, 814). It should also be noted that by quoting two verses of the psalm, Jesus seems to offer an answer to the initial conflict over his authority. If 11:27–12:12 is read as an intercalation, the psalm is meant to bookend the controversy over authority, rather than interpret the parable. In doing so, it responds to both questions asked by the chief priests, scribes, and elders: Jesus has authority because he is the cornerstone (12:10), and his authority comes from God, who is at work behind his actions (12:11).

110. Gundry, *Mark*, 663.

elite over authority—which builds on the reputation (1:27) and conflicts (8:31; 10:33) he has had throughout the narrative—and his telling of the parable of the tenants continues to delegitimize the priestly authorities. For the Markan Jesus, temple leadership will be, or has been, replaced by Jesus and his followers. The temple, at this point in the narrative, is still expected to have its own function (11:17; see below).

Mark 14:53–63

After the parable, the chief priests, scribes, and elders leave Jesus with the deliberate goal to arrest him (κρατῆσαι, 12:12). Their next appearance in the narrative—other than a brief reminder that the chief priests and scribes were looking for a way to arrest and kill him (14:1)—is the climactic showdown in front of the entire council (ὅλον τὸ συνέδριον, 14:55). The office of the high priest is also involved in the council, and the entire pericope takes place within the high priest's confines (14:53, 54). Once again, the predictions in 8:31 and 10:33, as well as the opposition's aims in 11:18 and 12:12, shape the characterization of this group: this is not an impartial council, but a collection of hostile groups against Jesus. This is confirmed by the actions of the high priest, who considers false witness (ἐψευδομαρτύρουν, 14:56–57), especially non-corroborative statements (14:56, 59), as legitimate grounds to question Jesus (14:60). Jesus's silence to the false witness complicates the trial.[111] Moloney contends the "Jewish legal tradition supports his innocence," so his silence is a statement in protest of the charges made against him.[112] The high priest's attempt to have Jesus respond to the non-coherent testimony has failed, so he asks more directly about the possible implications of the false claims about destroying the temple. In response, Jesus acknowledges his messianic status, which is a confirmation of what the narrative has proclaimed throughout (1:1; 8:29, 31; 9:31; 10:33–34). The high priest's reaction, however, goes against what the audience has been told and, presumably, agrees with at

---

111. Collins suggests Jesus's silence fits the image of the suffering of David (Pss 37, 26 LXX), as well as narratively distances him from the false testimony. Collins, *Mark*, 703. Others, however, see Jesus's silence as an implication or admission of guilt. Marcus connects his silence to Isa 53, but conjectures that it is "partly perhaps because the Temple charge is in a way true: God will, within a generation, destroy the present Temple" (Marcus, *Mark 8–16*, 1015).

112. Moloney, *Gospel of Mark*, 303–4.

this point, which further demonstrates and underlines the oppositional role of the priesthood.

Mark 15:25–32

In their final appearance, the chief priests and scribes continue to act as the main oppositional force against Jesus. At the crucifixion, they join a cohort of those chastising Jesus, including some passing by and reiterating the false witness from the trial (15:29), as well as those also being crucified (15:32). In particular, the chief priests and scribes mock (ἐμπαίζω) Jesus by exclaiming "he saved others; he is not able to save himself" (ἄλλους ἔσωσεν, ἑαυτὸν οὐ δύναται σῶσαι, 15:31).[113] Their mockery is an instance of dramatic irony in the narrative for two major reasons. First, Jesus foretold the opposition he would face by these characters (8:31; 10:34), so their behavior throughout the narrative (11:18–19; 12:12; 14:1) is understood as a confirmation of his passion predictions. In particular, ἐμπαίζω is used in both 10:34 and 15:31, which displays their mockery as an enactment of his final passion prediction. Second, the narrative has prefigured Jesus's death in ways that undermine their mockery; for instance, Jesus is criticized for not being able to save himself, but his first passion prediction dovetails with the interpretive frame of the apothegm "whoever wishes to save their life will lose it" (ὃς γὰρ ἐὰν θέλῃ τὴν ψυχὴν αὐτοῦ σῶσαι ἀπολέσει αὐτήν, 8:35). Additionally, after his final passion prediction and the request by the sons of Zebedee, Mark further frames Jesus's death for the audience: Jesus, as Son of Man, came "to give his life as a ransom for many" (δοῦναι τὴν ψυχὴν αὐτοῦ λύτρον ἀντὶ πολλῶν, 10:45). The mockery of the chief priests and scribes fits their predicted behavior and demonstrates their misunderstanding of his death, at least compared to the understanding the audience has been guided toward. The characterization of this group has been and continues to remain overwhelmingly negative.

---

113. Though I have not included him in with the rest of the temple institution, Joseph of Arimathea is described as an honorable council member (εὐσχήμων βουλευτής), which places him in connection to the Sanhedrin who were gathered at the trial. Unlike the rest of the temple establishment, however, Joseph is described positively as "awaiting the kingdom of God" (προσδεχόμενος τὴν βασιλείαν τοῦ θεοῦ, 15:43), and his actions in requesting Jesus's body for burial (15:42–47) are admirable.

Summary

The previous survey has addressed the question of *what* was remembered about Jesus and the temple in the Gospel of Mark, as well as *how* it was remembered. Although Gray and Wardle argue for a seamlessly negative narrative portrait of the temple, the Gospel of Mark displays tension and ambivalence in discussing the function and status of the temple and its priesthood. The temple is treated as a legitimate institution that fulfills Levitical law (1:40–45), houses the divine (2:23–28), has a divine purpose as a universal house of prayer (11:17), and bases Jesus's Jerusalem ministry (11:27—12:44). Mark also delegitimizes the claim that Jesus would enact the temple's destruction and restoration (14:55–59). However, Jesus does prophesy the destruction of the temple (13:2), critique and contend with the priesthood—especially the conglomerated group of chief priests, scribes, and, when included, elders—for their role in turning the temple into a "den of thieves" (11:17–18), foretell of the priesthood's role in his own death (8:31; 10:32–34; 11:6–8), and insinuate that the priesthood will be destroyed and transferred to others (12:9–12).

The prediction of the temple's destruction is perhaps more ambiguous than the negative characterizations often attributed to it, and it is unclear whether it is intended to signal an ultimate end, particularly given that the gospel preserves the (false) memory of Jesus destroying the current temple and constructing a new temple. Nicole Wilkinson Duran suggests the temple's destruction mirrors Jesus's death, arguing, "[the temple's] destruction becomes akin to his own. The connection between Jesus's body and the temple is not that Jesus will replace the temple, but that the two will suffer the same fate."[114] Jesus's death, then, becomes a lens through which the temple's destruction may be understood for the Markan audience in the same way that the temple's destruction later (re)shapes the understanding of Jesus's death.[115] Whether the temple is already destroyed (post-70 CE), under direct threat of destruction (66–70 CE), or at a heightened sense of instability (40s CE), the temple for the

---

114. Duran, "Not One Stone Will Be Left on Another," 319.

115. "Thus the prediction of the destruction of the temple in 13:1–2, when combined with 11:13–21, 27–34; 12:1–12; 13:5–37; and 15:33, 37–39, becomes part of a historiographic narrative with a dual focus: the fate of Jesus and the fate of the temple, in which Jesus' death, at the instigation of the officials of the temple (12:1–12), is directly connected to the eventual destruction of the temple . . . In this way Mark creates a narrative in which the fate of Jesus is correlated with the destruction of the temple" (Kloppenborg, "*Evocatio Deorum*," 449).

Markan audience may have been analogous to Jesus's body, which was destroyed and, though not reappearing in the narrative (16:8), has given the community hope for its restoration.

The temple has an important role to play for Mark's commemorative community, even if that role is not currently being fulfilled. The Markan community commemorated Jesus's life and activity within the temple, treating his teaching in the temple as significant and his presence as salient. However, they also remembered and transmitted traditions of conflict against the priesthood which depicted the chief priests, scribes, and elders as corrupt, negligent, and in line for divine usurpation and reallocation. Even more, they commemorated Jesus's activity in light of prophetic traditions in Israel's scriptures. The Markan Jesus quotes from Isaiah, Jeremiah, and Daniel, and his actions can be keyed to the traditions in Jeremiah, Micah, and Malachi. Mark 13 also remembers Jesus engaging in apocalyptic or eschatological prophetic activity by proclaiming the temple would be destroyed. The fact that the Jerusalem temple's destruction did not eliminate every "stone upon stone" suggests that this prophecy was not created *ex eventu* but could have been transmitted prior to 70 CE. Furthermore, the number of historical referents for the "abomination of desolation" in 13:14—e.g., the Caligula crisis, the siege by Zealots in the late 60s CE, or the destruction by Titus in 70 CE, which is itself commemorated by the Arch of Titus in Rome—demonstrates the salience and multivalence the phrase could possess for audiences in different generations.[116] When placed in the broader context of Second Temple period attitudes toward the temple, the complex portrait of Jesus and the temple in the Gospel of Mark proves Crossley's overarching point: "the first Markan readers [and hearers] would have seen Jesus through Jewish eyes as someone directly involved in the Jewish debates of his day."[117]

Jesus and the Temple in Early Christian Gospels

As the earliest gospel, the Gospel of Mark represents the first full-scale written iteration of the Jesus tradition. It modeled the ways in which early

---

116. In addition to the disturbances in the temple after Jesus's death (including a Passover revolt instigated by Roman forces [*Ant.* 20.105–112]), Josephus also tells of events during Jesus's lifetime, such as the riot and ransacking of the temple by Sabinus during the instability of Archelaus's reign (*B.J.* 2.39–54).

117. Crossley, *Date of Mark's Gospel*, 209.

Christian communities engaged with and reconstructed that tradition to accord with their own social frameworks and salient pasts. When examining later gospels, rather than focus solely on the literary nature of redaction, a social memory perspective can gauge the ways traditions about Jesus and the temple were formed and re-formed throughout the first few centuries CE. In this way, we can say later gospel traditions "[have] not *redacted* Mark so much as [they have] *retold* Mark. [They have] internalized the gospel tradition, made it [their] own, retold it and developed it in various ways, ways which [they] did not (apparently) perceive in tension with [their] sources but which [they] nevertheless preferred to them."[118]

The following section will survey early Christian gospels from the first three centuries CE to demonstrate further how memories of Jesus and the temple were expressed in earliest Christianity. For the sake of this survey, I follow the conventional dating of the canonical gospels to sometime in the late first century CE. I am not concerned here with the compositional order of the canonical gospels; rather, I want to investigate the ways in which they characterize Jesus's attitude toward the temple. I have also included gospels and gospel fragments that may be dated to the second through fourth centuries CE: Gospel of Thomas, Gospel of Peter, Gospel of Philip, Gospel of Judas, P.Oxy. 840. These non-canonical and apocryphal gospels will further demonstrate how early Christian commemorative processes characterized the temple in a post-70 CE temple-less world. Schröter emphasizes the ability of these non-canonical gospels to "take up important aspects of the earlier Gospels and elaborate them in specific ways," so their inclusion is an important step in broadening Jesus memories and the reception of Jesus tradition in early Christianity.[119] As this survey will demonstrate, the earliest Christian memories of the temple wrestle with ambiguity and multivalence, following the pattern established in the Gospel of Mark. As communities became further removed from the temple both temporally and spatially, however, their views of the temple flattened and even became allegories for Christian practice.

---

118. Rodríguez, *Structuring Early Christian Memory*, 149, emphasis original.
119. Schröter, "Contribution of Non-Canonical Gospels," 445.

The Gospel of Matthew

Matthew's Gospel expands, reshapes, and reconstructs the memory of Jesus in a way that explicitly connects Jesus and his ministry to the fulfillment of Israel's scriptures.[120] In fulfilling these scriptures, Jesus variously fits multiple typologies: he is the new Moses and the Davidic Messiah who also performs miracles, pronounces judgment, and recalls Israel's prophets.[121] In this broader Christological narrative, Matthew's Jesus is portrayed in consonance and conflict with the temple, retaining elements of the ambiguous, multivalent attitudes found in Mark, while including new traditions that further express his relationship with the temple.

The first appearance of the temple in the Gospel of Matthew is in the testing narrative (Matt 4:1-11). After Jesus's baptism, he is led (ἀνήχθη, 4:1) by the spirit into the wilderness where he is tested by the devil (διάβολος, 4:1; ὁ πειράζων, 4:2; Σατανᾶ, 4:10). As the second of three tests moving spatially from lowest to highest altitude, the devil takes him to "the holy city" (τὴν ἁγίαν πόλιν) and the highest point of the temple (τὸ πτερύγιον τοῦ ἱεροῦ, 4:5). While the focus of this narrative is Christological in asserting Jesus's authority, Ulrich Luz notes there is an element of foreshadowing in this pericope, since Jesus's next return to the temple is accompanied with much more fanfare (21:1-17), and he declines the same authority to call on the angels in his arrest (26:53-54) and crucifixion (27:40). For Luz, "what takes place in the second temptation episode looks ahead to the obedience of the Son of God in his life and especially during his passion."[122] Still, the testing narrative preserves an interesting memory of the Matthean community's view of Jesus in conflict in the temple with the suggestion that the devil was able to enter into the sacred space of the *temenos*.[123]

Another non-Markan tradition that Matthew contains is the conversation around the half-shekel/two drachma temple tax of Exod

---

120. Matt 1:22-23; 2:15, 17-18, 23; 4:13-16; 8:17; 13:14-15; 21:4-5; 27:9-10.

121. See Allison, *New Moses*; Le Donne, *Historiographical Jesus*, 93-258.

122. Luz, *Matthew 1-7*, 153.

123. Luz argues the location, which is often the subject of debate, is "unimportant for the narrative" and instead meant as a reference "in a nontechnical sense as the outermost or the highest point in the temple" (Luz, *Matthew 1-7*, 152n37). Davies and Allison, on the other hand, suggest "the pinnacle of the στοὰ βασιλική, south of the outer court" as a possible referent, which draws attention to whether this pericope is supposed to take place inside the temple (Davies and Allison, *Gospel According to Saint Matthew*, 1:365).

30:12–16 (τὰ δίδραχμα, Matt 17:24–27).[124] Tax collectors in Capernaum question Peter about Jesus's payment of the tax, to which Peter reactively responds favorably. Once they have entered the house—a Markan storytelling device (εἰς τὴν οἰκίαν)—Jesus initiates a conversation with Peter by asking an analogous question about rulers collecting tribute (17:25). Peter's response ("from others") and Jesus's reply ("therefore the children are free," ἄρα γε ἐλεύθεροί εἰσιν οἱ υἱοί, 17:26) imply that perhaps the temple tax is not necessary to pay or that Jesus (and the community) are exempt. However, Jesus ultimately relents and guides Peter to a fish that miraculously contains payment for the both of them "so that we might not scandalize them" (ἵνα δὲ μὴ σκανδαλίσωμεν αὐτούς, 17:27). Luz suggests Jesus, in keeping with his wider social program, urged for the voluntary nature of the contribution and advocated "for the poor of Galilee the freedom from this obligation to contribute annually a large amount of money to the distant temple in Jerusalem."[125] The development of this line of thinking leads Luz to contend "a Jesus community that still understood itself to be part of Israel paid the temple tax to keep peace."[126] W. D. Davies and Dale Allison argue similarly at the level of Jesus, noting his conciliatory stance is apologetic; "voluntary payment should be made in order to prevent others from inferring that Peter or Jesus has rejected the temple cult."[127] However, the nature of this pericope and Jesus's response do seem to fit into a larger conversation about the half-shekel tax in the late Second Temple period and how Jews related to the Jerusalem temple. Jonathan Trotter also points to 4Q159 2.6–7, which maintains the tax should only be paid once rather than annually, in arguing "that there was a diversity of perspective on the issue, at least in Palestine, which impacted how and if certain people participated."[128] While this pericope

---

124. On the temple tax, see Klawans, *Purity, Sacrifice, and the Temple*, 196–98; Trotter, *Jerusalem Temple in Diaspora*, 52–64.

125. Luz, *Matthew 8–20*, 418.

126. Luz, *Matthew 8–20*, 418. Hugh Montefiore argued that this pericope was adapted throughout various strata of the early Jewish-Christian community's life, addressing pre-70 CE questions of whether Jewish-Christians should pay the temple tax and post-70 CE questions of whether this same community should continue payment to the *fiscus Iudaicus*. Montefiore, "Jesus and the Temple Tax," 60–71.

127. Davies and Allison, *Gospel According to Saint Matthew*, 2:746.

128. Trotter, *Jerusalem Temple in Diaspora*, 55–56. Klawans also points to *b. Menahot* 65a, which recalls disputes and disagreements between the positions of the Saducees and the sages. Klawans, *Purity, Sacrifice, and the Temple*, 196.

does not discard the importance of the temple, it does add complexity to the relationship between Jesus and the temple.

Matthew also expands on Markan pericopae that portray Jesus and the temple, often escalating conflict in the relationship between the two. In the Sabbath controversy over plucking grain, Jesus highlights the fact that priests break the Sabbath and remain "blameless" (ἀναίτιοί, 12:5). In addition, he claims something "greater than the temple is here" (τοῦ ἱεροῦ μεῖζόν ἐστιν ὧδε, 12:6) and references Hos 6:6, which gives a prophetic critique of Israel's behavior by elevating acts of justice over the sacrificial cult. Davies and Allison identify Jesus as that which is greater than the temple, whereas Luz sees this as a reference to mercy: "Matthew's entire argument is in its depth very Jewish, but it has a new foundation. It is based on the reality that through the *Son of Man* Jesus the biblical command of mercy becomes the greatest command—greater than the temple."[129] In either case, the temple's status is subdued in favor of something or someone else. In the temple incident (21:12-17), Matthew keeps the same allusions to Isa 56:7 and Jer 7:11 but removes "for all nations" (πᾶσιν τοῖς ἔθνεσιν, Mark 11:17). Additionally, Matthew includes additional healings in the temple that lead to the conflict between Jesus and the temple elites (21:14-16). In the parable of the wicked tenants (21:33-45), the priests ironically condemn and usurp themselves by noting the new owners "will give him the produce at the harvest time" (οἵτινες ἀποδώσουσιν αὐτῷ τοὺς καρποὺς ἐν τοῖς καιροῖς αὐτῶν, 21:41). Jesus then spells out their self-pronouncement by exclaiming "the Kingdom of God will be taken from you and will be given to a people who produces its fruits" (ἀρθήσεται ἀφ' ὑμῶν ἡ βασιλεία τοῦ θεοῦ καὶ δοθήσεται ἔθνει ποιοῦντι τοὺς καρποὺς αὐτῆς, 21:43).[130] Prior to the destruction prophecy (24:2) and warning about the abomination of desolation (24:15), Jesus utters a proclamation against Jerusalem (23:37-39), stating "Behold, your house is left to you desolate" (ἰδοὺ ἀφίεται ὑμῖν ὁ οἶκος ὑμῶν ἔρημος, 23:38). Luz draws on the parallels between this pronouncement and other Jewish literature that describes the divine presence leaving the temple (Ezek 10:18-19; 2 Bar. 8:2; *B.J.* 6.299), and Davies and Allison include additional prophetic allusions (Isa 64:10-11; Jer 12:7; 22:5; Hag 1:9) and Second Temple literature (Tob 14:4; 1 En. 89:56; T. Levi 15:1;

---

129. Luz, *Matthew 8-20*, 183; Davies and Allison, *Gospel According to Saint Matthew*, 2:314-15.

130. This departs from the traditional Matthean use of the phrase "Kingdom of Heaven" (ἡ βασιλεία τῶν οὐρανῶν).

4QFlor 1.5-6) to argue that this pronouncement fits well within popular memory and traditional imagery surrounding Israel's judgment.[131] Finally, while Matthew also recognizes false witnesses in the trial against Jesus, two witnesses give corroborating, seemingly legitimate testimony about Jesus's ability to destroy the temple (26:60-61). The Matthean version of this temple destruction saying is also significantly changed. First, the chief priests and whole council are described as looking specifically for *false* witness (ἐζήτουν ψευδομαρτυρίαν, 26:59), sharpening the critique against the nature of this trial. Second, the reference to a temple built with hands/not built with hands (χειροποίητον, ἀχειροποίητον) has been removed and is instead referred to as "the temple of God" (τὸν ναὸν τοῦ θεοῦ), which, unlike Mark, seemingly implies the rebuilding of the same temple rather than a temple of another kind.[132] Third, and most crucially, the claim is specifically that Jesus *is able* (δύναμαι, 26:61) to destroy the temple, not that he *will* (ἐγὼ καταλύσω, Mark 14:58). Luz links this to his earlier statement about being able to call for angelic support during his arrest (26:53), arguing "the assumption is that although Jesus could do it, in obedience to God he does not do it . . . As the law-abiding Messiah Jesus had nothing against the temple; his task is neither to destroy it nor to rebuild it."[133]

Matthew's story, like Mark, combines complex attitudes about the temple. On the one hand, the Matthean Jesus refers the healed leper to fulfill the requirements of Lev 14 (8:2-4), participates in the half-shekel tax (17:24-27), and teaches (21:23-23:39) and conducts his healing ministry in the temple (21:14), which validate the temple's significance and salience. On the other hand, Jesus claims there is something greater than the temple (12:6), seemingly relativizes the biblically mandated half-shekel tax (17:26-27), makes a major pronouncement against Jerusalem (23:37-39) before predicting the temple's destruction (24:1-2), and is plausibly accused of claiming to be able to destroy the temple (26:61). In addition, the narrative depicts the devil in, at, or on the temple during the testing of Jesus (4:5) and formally locates the founding of the church

---

131. Luz, *Matthew 21-28*, 162; Davies and Allison, *Gospel According to Saint Matthew*, 3:321-23.

132. Davies and Allison note "there is a good redactional motive for omission" of the ἀχειροποίητον temple: "A temple 'not made with hands' readily refers to the church, and so one might think of Jesus founding that institution only after Easter (or even after the destruction in AD 70). But in Matthew Jesus founds the church during his ministry" (Davies and Allison, *Gospel According to Saint Matthew*, 3:526).

133. Luz, *Matthew 21-28*, 427.

in the ministry of Jesus (16:17–20). While Matthew still holds the temple as an important piece of Jesus's ministry, including his presence at and engagement in the temple, he also enhances the portrait of Jesus engaging in prophetic critique of the temple, foretelling its destruction, and relativizing the temple's status.[134]

The Gospel of Luke and Acts[135]

Similarly to Matthew, Luke and Acts construct the Jesus tradition in a way that expands Mark. Luke's narrative forefronts the importance of Gentiles, focuses on socioeconomic reversal, and traces a narrative progression from Galilee to Jerusalem to Rome. Within this framework, Luke develops an extended portrait of the temple that fits into his "orderly account" (ἀκριβῶς καθεξῆς, Luke 1:3).

After the prologue, Luke opens with an extended infancy narrative that demonstrates the significance of the temple in the early life of Jesus and John the Baptist. Both John and Jesus are identified as coming from priestly families (1:5, 36), and John's father, Zechariah, encounters an angel of the Lord while in the temple sanctuary (1:8–20). After Jesus's birth, Mary and Joseph take him to the temple for his dedication, as well as Mary's purification (2:22–24). While in the temple, the family is visited by Simeon (1:25–32) and Anna (1:36–38), who both prophesy about the newborn Jesus. Finally, the childhood of Jesus closes with a pericope about the young Jesus being brought to Jerusalem during a Passover (which his family reportedly regularly attended) and staying behind in the temple and "sitting among the teachers" (καθεζόμενον ἐν μέσῳ τῶν διδασκάλων, 2:46) in deep discussion. The emphasis on the temple in this early part of the gospel demonstrates that, for Luke, "the Messiah will emerge from within a family and social world deeply enmeshed in the traditions of Israel, a pious and expectant 'people of God.' His parents

---

134. Michael Barber's work argues, on the basis of Matthean memory, that the historical Jesus was affirmative of the temple's status and that this made a significant impact on how early Jewish-Christians constructed group identity and self-expression. See Barber, *Historical Jesus and the Temple*.

135. Though the works are claimed to come from the same author and be a continuous narrative of the life and ministry of Jesus and the early church, I have opted to refer to the works separately as Luke and Acts. On the question of how unified Luke and Acts are, see Parsons and Pervo, *Rethinking the Unity of Luke and Acts*; Walters, *Assumed Authorial Unity of Luke and Acts*; Gregory and Rowe, *Rethinking the Unity and Reception of Luke-Acts*; Tannehill, *Narrative Unity of Luke-Acts*; O'Toole, *Unity of Luke's Theology*.

observe the laws regarding circumcision, purification, and presentation of the first born as dedicated to the Lord, and do so within the symbolic heart of the people, Jerusalem and its Temple."[136]

In material Luke shares with the other Synoptics, negative characterizations of the temple are often downplayed or neutralized. For example, the temple incident (19:45–48) is drastically reduced. Jesus expels only "the ones selling" (τοὺς πωλοῦντας, 19:45) and, like Matthew, makes an abbreviated allusion to Isa 56:7 that removes the "for all nations."[137] In Luke's version of the parable of the wicked tenants (20:9–16), the vineyard does not include the additional tower (πύργος) that is present in the other Synoptic parallels. While the parable still highlights the corruption of Israel's leaders in their rejection of the son, Johnson notes how "in Luke's story, the present leadership over Israel of the chief priests, scribes and elders will be replaced by that of the Twelve, a development we will observe in the narrative of Acts."[138] Jesus's sorrowful proclamation over Jerusalem (19:45–48) predicts "they will not leave stone upon stone within you" (19:44), but does not mention the temple in this destruction. The Lukan Jesus does still lament over Jerusalem (13:35; cf. Matt 23:37) and prophesies the destruction of the temple (21:6), but the temple—and the reference to the "abomination of desolation"—is removed from the apocalyptic signs. Instead, Luke signals warning of destruction at the sign of "Jerusalem surrounded by military encampments" (ὅταν δὲ ἴδητε κυκλουμένην ὑπὸ στρατοπέδων Ἰερουσαλήμ, 21:20).[139] In addition to these changes, Luke also repeatedly emphasizes Jesus's active teaching ministry that takes place in the temple (19:47; 20:1; 21:37; 22:53). The most significant difference in this narrative, however, is the temple charge missing in Jesus's trial before the council (21:66–71). By removing the false witnesses and the charge about destroying the temple, Johnson argues the narrative focuses on how "the rejection of the Prophet is not the work of

136. Johnson, *Gospel of Luke*, 56. Bovon, on the other hand, suggests "a devaluation of the temple occurs in the temple itself, for the holy, God's presence, shifts from the building to the person of Jesus" (Bovon, *Commentary on the Gospel of Luke*, 1:99). Later, in the pericope of the young Jesus in the temple, Bovon claims "the account is neither pro- nor anti-Jewish" (1:110).

137. "The elimination of this phrase is important for grasping Luke's view of the Temple. It has a significant role for Judaism and for the first Jerusalem community, but not an enduring role for the Gentiles" (Johnson, *Gospel of Luke*, 300).

138. Johnson, *Gospel of Luke*, 309.

139. "The Lukan text strictly maintains the historical character of the fate of Jerusalem" (Bovon, *Commentary on the Gospel of Luke*, 3:114).

the whole people (*laos*); they are sympathetic to him. But neither is it the work of the chief priest alone. The leadership that consistently opposed Jesus is involved as a whole in his final rejection."[140]

The temple continues to play a significant role in the opening chapters of Acts. The ministry of Jesus's followers remains in Jerusalem, and, just like Jesus, the disciples regularly continue teaching (Acts 2:46; 3:11–26; 5:21, 42) and performing miracles in the temple (3:1–10). Anthony Le Donne argues the punishment of Ananias and Sapphira is a sign of an improper offering, demonstrating the continued presence of God in the temple. Le Donne suggests "the agenda to demonstrate the presence of God's Holy Spirit at Solomon's Portico fits well with Luke's election ethic: *The Lord's presence has extended from the Holy of Holies to include those on the periphery, including those who congregate in the Court of the Gentiles* ... the key message of Acts 4:32—5:12 is that, without a doubt, the Lord's presence resides within his temple."[141] The centrality of the temple is even more pronounced in Stephen's narrative arc. Whereas the temple destruction saying was absent in Jesus's trial in Luke 22, it is a catalyst and ground for Stephen's trial before the council (6:11–15). False witnesses (μάρτυρας ψευδεῖς) frame Stephen by claiming he "never stops saying things against the holy place" (οὐ παύεται λαλῶν ῥήματα κατὰ τοῦ τόπου τοῦ ἁγίου, 6:13). They also accuse him of invoking Jesus as a destructive agent against the temple: "For we heard him saying 'This Jesus the Nazarene will destroy this place" (ἀκηκόαμεν γὰρ αὐτοῦ λέγοντος ὅτι Ἰησοῦς ὁ Ναζωραῖος οὗτος καταλύσει τὸν τόπον τοῦτον, 6:14). Like the Markan version, Jesus is the agent of destruction, and these charges are remembered as false, which delegitimizes this position for the Lukan commemorative community. Interestingly, the most significant difference between this saying and the Markan version is the removal of the rebuilding of the temple (whether it is another temple, like in Mark, or the same temple, as in Matthew). While the Lukan commemorative community may have held a positive view of the temple during Jesus's life and the early Jerusalem ministry, Stephen's response to these charges complicates matters. Stephen offers a winding retelling of Israel's history (7:2–43) before responding to the specific claims against him (7:44–53). In his response, Stephen claims "the Most High does not dwell in handmade things" (ἀλλ' οὐχ ὁ ὕψιστος ἐν χειροποιήτοις κατοικεῖ, 7:48). He also quotes Isa 66:1, which, like Jeremiah

---

140. Johnson, *Gospel of Luke*, 363.
141. Le Donne, "Improper Temple Offering," 362, emphasis original.

7, fits into a broader category of prophetic (likely post-Exilic) traditions critiquing the sacrificial cult, but also may have been used to justify the early church's movement away from the Jerusalem temple or reckon with its destruction in the post-70 CE world.[142]

Luke and Acts offer another complex portrait of the temple in the life and ministry of Jesus and his followers. In addition to the pericope of Jesus healing the leper (Luke 5:12–16), the temple's sacrificial cult is central to the infancy and early life of Jesus (Luke 1:5—2:52). The temple is the setting of much of Jesus's Jerusalem ministry (Luke 19:47; 20:1; 21:37; 22:53), and it serves as the kerygmatic center of the ministry of Jesus's followers (Acts 1–5), including Paul's ministry and mission (Acts 21:26—22:21). Traditions remembering Jesus in conflict with the temple or the priesthood remain in Luke's Gospel (19:45–48; 20:9–16) and, even though they are false, they also associate Jesus as antagonistic toward the temple in Acts (6:13–14). Additionally, Jesus does predict the divine abandonment (13:35) and destruction (21:6) of the temple, as well as laments over Jerusalem's fate for rejecting the prophet (19:45–48). Stephen's speech offers the harshest critique yet, claiming the divine does not dwell in "handmade things," likely alluding to the temple, which is further spelled out by his reference to Isa 66:1 (Acts 7:48–50). The depiction of the temple in Luke and Acts varies, then, from a largely positive, important piece of Jesus's upbringing and a center stage for his Jerusalem ministry and that of his followers to an institution of a corrupt priesthood awaiting reckoning for its rejection of Jesus.

The Gospel of John

John's Gospel constructs and remembers Jesus's relationship with the temple in a different way than in the Synoptics. Unlike the Synoptics, the Johannine Jesus travels to Jerusalem multiple times throughout his ministry, making the temple a recurrent setting of the gospel (John 2:13; 5:1; 7:14; 10:22; 12:12). John also transposes Jesus's opposition

---

142. C. K. Barrett suggests "the precise force of Stephen's words depends on the meaning assigned to the OT quotation with which it is supported." Barrett also points to the discontinuity between a total rejection of the temple, the previous ministry of Acts 1–5, and Paul's attitude in 21:26, arguing, "There must in fact have been in the first few decades a swing away from the Temple, and the Diaspora Judaism which seems to be represented in the speech attributed to Stephen may well have contributed to it" (Barrett, *Acts*, 1:374).

onto "the Jews," which variously represent Judaean leadership or those "who have made up their mind about Jesus."[143] The most significant difference, however, is the temple incident occurring at the beginning of his ministry (2:13–21) rather than toward the end. In the Johannine account, Jesus forcefully expels the animals being sold in the temple and disrupts the money-changers (2:15). His message to those selling doves seems to be a proxy for all the economic activity in this pericope: "Take these things from here, do not make my Father's house a house of trade!" (ἄρατε ταῦτα ἐντεῦθεν, μὴ ποιεῖτε τὸν οἶκον τοῦ πατρός μου οἶκον ἐμπορίου, 2:16).[144] His activity is reflective of prophetic tradition (Zech 14:21) but is framed within the disciples' memory of Israelite tradition by the allusion to Ps 69:9. When confronted by temple leadership (οἱ Ἰουδαῖοι, 2:18, 20), Jesus is remembered as directly speaking the saying about the temple's destruction (albeit not as the agent of destruction himself): "Destroy this temple and I will rebuild it in three days" (λύσατε τὸν ναὸν τοῦτον καὶ ἐν τρισὶν ἡμέραις ἐγερῶ αὐτόν, 2:19). This saying is remarkable in a number of ways. First, Jesus speaks the saying; it is no longer spoken by witnesses in his trial. In fact, Jesus's trial (18:19–24) is radically expedited and generalized in John. He is briefly questioned vaguely about his disciples and his teaching (περὶ τῶν μαθητῶν αὐτοῦ καὶ περὶ τῆς διδαχῆς αὐτοῦ, 18:19), but because the claim of destroying the temple cannot be used without immediately incriminating Jesus, it is absent from the scene.[145] Second, unlike Mark and Matthew, the agent of destruction is shifted from Jesus to others through the use of an imperative ("[you] destroy," λύσατε). Third, similarly to Matthew and against Mark, there is no differentiation between the destroyed or rebuilt temples; the destruction and rebuilding occur to the same "temple," but

143. Moloney, *Gospel of John*, 10. On "the Jews" in the Gospel of John, see Reinhartz, *Cast Out of the Covenant*; Fredriksen and Reinhartz, *Jesus, Judaism, and Christian Anti-Judaism*; Alicia D. Myers, "Just Opponents? Ambiguity, Empathy, and the Jews in the Gospel of John," in Brown and Skinner, ed., *Johannine Ethics*, 159–76.

144. "While Jesus challenges Israel's abuse of the Temple, he looks beyond himself for motivation of such a challenge. Israel relates to God through its Temple but Jesus tells his listeners that their Temple belongs to him in a special way; it is the house of his Father. The *hieron* has degenerated into an *oikos emporiou*, but the sent one of the Father has reclaimed is as *ton oikon tou patros mou*" (Moloney, *Gospel of John*, 77). In Moloney's reading, then, the temple has been reclaimed and should function, but Jesus's words of destruction (2:19) and relativization (4:23) complicate or, at the very least, temporally restrict this understanding.

145. On the other hand, Andrew Lincoln argues that Jesus's trial is actually extended throughout the gospel. See Lincoln, *Truth on Trial*.

the "temple" that is being referenced—Jesus's body—is not clear until 2:21. Fourth, and finally, the gospel offers an interpretive lens for its audience by drawing on the disciples' memory, offering an example of how the early Jesus community negotiated their past traditions and present concerns. Unlike other gospels, this saying is explicitly reframed as a commentary on Jesus's death and resurrection and is enabled by the memory of the disciples. Marianna Meye Thompson connects this to the gospel's overarching hermeneutic, arguing, "this Gospel's particular understanding of Jesus is lodged in the corporate, communal memory and interpretation of those who continued to follow him . . . Comprehension of Jesus' action in the temple does not come simply by observing what Jesus did, but from reading the Scriptures in light of the resurrection and the new understanding of Jesus that comes with it."[146]

The Johannine Jesus's attitude toward the Jerusalem temple is further revealed in the pericope with the Samaritan woman (4:1–42). In the midst of their back-and-forth repartee, the Samaritan woman responds to Jesus's insight about her personal life by identifying him as a prophet (4:19). She then states the conflict between Jews and Samaritans over sacred space and ritual practice on Mount Gerizim versus Jerusalem. Jesus's reaction treats her statement as a question or accusation, to which he "owns his origins among the Jewish people by using the plural 'we,' as he criticizes the Samaritan people and their traditions with the use of the plural 'you.'"[147] With his Jewish identity in view, however, Jesus does not reaffirm the Jewish position of the Jerusalem temple's superiority which has been imposed by the Samaritan woman, but offers an alternative to both sites of worship that transcends the aforementioned notions of sacred space (4:23). Jesus's words suggest "God is not a mountain, a place, or a sanctuary. God is spirit (v. 4:24a), an all-pervading personal presence to the believer."[148] Jesus's earlier interpretation of the temple as "my Father's house" and his initial reaction of worshipping what "we" know (4:22) asserts "a primacy to Israel, its temple, worship, Messiah, and God: it is from Israel that salvation comes. But even as the temple in Jerusalem serves as a figure of the temple that is the risen Jesus (2:21), so true worship will soon be localized

---

146. Thompson continues, "One cannot dispense with the events of the past—here, the temple action itself—but the mere events cannot and do not lead to full perception of their significance" (Thompson, *John*, 74).

147. Moloney, *Gospel of John*, 128.

148. Moloney, *Gospel of John*, 129.

in *that* temple, located neither on Gerizim nor Zion; the salvation that comes from Israel will flow beyond its borders."[149]

The understanding of the temple in the Gospel of John has been radically transformed. Jesus is frequently present and active in Jerusalem and the temple, and his actions in the temple (2:13–17) are presented as intimately tied to Israel's Davidic (Ps 69:9) and prophetic (Zech 14:10) tradition. However, Jesus's proclamation about destroying the temple (2:19) is (re)interpreted by explicitly associating the temple with Jesus's body (2:21–22), removing focus from the Jerusalem temple and onto Jesus. Jesus again transcends the Jerusalem temple's importance in his conversation with the Samaritan woman (4:23), removing focus and legitimacy from the Jerusalem temple. These traditions demonstrate the temple's relativization, at best, in the Johannine community; at worst, they display an anti-temple attitude akin to other instances of anti-Judaism in the gospel. Adele Reinhartz discusses John's the use of the temple as the gospel's attempt at "disaffiliation" with Judaism, where key components of Judaism are rhetorically expropriated.[150] In fact, the concern for the wellbeing of the Jerusalem temple escapes Jesus's ministry and falls on the Jewish leadership, who worry about the Romans destroying the temple (τὸν τόπον, 11:48). In addition, the gospel's rhetorical reframing of temple imagery make these concerns ironic: whether one maps this saying onto the community's social world prior to or after 70 CE, Jesus will, ultimately, be crucified by the Romans, and the temple will, ultimately, be destroyed by the Roman siege.

The Gospel of Thomas

There is perhaps no better example of the variability and stability of early Christian thought than the Gospel of Thomas. Variously described as a text displaying Gnostic, wisdom, ascetic/encratic, mystical, or Platonic thought, *Thomas* remembers and re-presents Jesus through 114 logia without an explicit narrative framework and largely disconnected from Israel's scriptures. In addition, its tradition history, provenance, date, and relationship to the canonical gospels are as frequently debated as its cryptic content.[151] With so much variety and division of scholarly opinion

---

149. Thompson, *John*, 104.
150. Reinhartz, *Cast Out of the Covenant*, 51–66.
151. Recent scholarship on *Thomas* has argued convincingly that it is dependent

on *Thomas*, it may seem faulty to engage its memories of Jesus for this study. Goodacre notes, "Given its genre (sayings gospel in which narratives about the temple are absent) and theological proclivity (the relative lack of so-called apocalyptic eschatology), one might not expect to see references in *Thomas* to the destruction of the temple."[152] However, *Thomas*, full of surprises, gives further characterization of the temple for early Christian memory in the first two centuries CE.

The only potential mention of the temple in the *Gospel of Thomas* is logion 71, extant only in the Coptic manuscript.[153] This logion is a hotly debated saying due to the significant amount of reconstruction required from a large lacuna in the bottom corner of the page. The logion comprises the entirety of the final two lines of the page, so the lacuna produces two significant missing portions of the text:

NHC II.45.34-35 Coptic	Logion 71 Greek Retroversion[154]
ⲡⲉϫⲉ ⲓⲥ ϫⲉ ϯⲛⲁϣⲟⲣ[ϣⲣ ⲙⲡⲉⲉ] ⲓⲏⲉⲓ ⲁⲩⲱ ⲙⲛ ⲗⲁⲁⲩ ⲛⲁϣⲕⲟⲧϥ ⲛ̄[ ]	Λέγει Ἰησοῦς καταλύσω [τοῦτον τὸν] οἶκον καὶ οὐδεὶς δυνήσεται οἰκοδομῆσαι αὐτόν [ ]

---

on or at least demonstrates familiarity with Synoptic traditions; see Goodacre, *Thomas and the Gospels*; Gathercole, *Composition of the Gospel of Thomas*; Meier, "Is Luke's Version of the Parable?," 528-47; Meier, "Parable of the Wheat and the Weeds," 715-32; "Parable of the Wicked Tenants in the Vineyard: Is the Gospel of Thomas Independent of the Synoptics?," in Skinner and Iverson, ed., *Unity and Diversity in the Gospels and Paul*, 129-45. Schröter's work should also be recognized for its contribution to scholarship on the *Gospel of Thomas*. While his brief comments do not provide the full groundwork for literary dependence—at least not to the scale or effect of Mark Goodacre, Simon Gathercole, or John P. Meier—Schröter presents an early critique against the popular notion of an independent *Gospel of Thomas*, arguing instead that it has been "influenced" by the synoptic tradition. Schröter, "Historical Jesus and the Sayings tradition," 151-68.

152. Goodacre, *Thomas and the Gospels*, 167.

153. Logion 65 contains a parable about a vineyard owner that parallels Mark 12:1-12, but told without a narrative setting (i.e., no audience or opponents mentioned as the intended target of the parable), stripped of the imagery alluding to Isa 5, and without the final proclamation of judgment against the tenant farmers. However, the following logion (Gos. Thom. 66) contains the Thomasine version of the cornerstone saying, which is paired together with the parable of the vineyard in the Synoptics as a critique against the priesthood. In addition, if the cornerstone language is symbolic of the temple, this could be another logion addressing the construction/destruction of the Jerusalem temple.

154. See Plisch, *Gospel of Thomas*, 170.

The first missing portion has fairly widespread agreement in its reconstruction, rendering the saying as "Jesus said 'I will destroy this house and no one will be able to build it.'" The final missing portion is more debated, with reconstructions ranging from "again" (N̄KECOΠ) to "except me" (N̄CABĀΛΛAI).[155] However the saying is reconstructed, DeConick is correct in cautioning that "it is impossible to know exactly how the sentence ended. This makes any interpretation of the saying tentative at best."[156]

Some scholars have argued against the temple as the referent of the "house" (IHEI). Gregory Riley argues the logion refers to the body of Jesus and is spoken against the notion of resurrection, a point of contention between the Thomasine and Johannine communities.[157] Stephen J. Patterson instead suggests "the reference may be to some ruling house—perhaps the House of Herod, or the House of David—or simply to the household and the social relationships this entailed."[158] Uwe-Karsten Plisch also offers the "House of David" as a possible interpretation, proposing, "The 'destruction' of the 'house' (of David) would then have to be understood as a rejection of a certain political messianic expectation . . . The 'rebuilding' would refer to a new interpretation of the Davidic messianic expectation in the sense that Jesus is proclaimed the messiah."[159] The obvious weakness to Plisch and Patterson's argument is the lack of concern for messianic expectations elsewhere in Thomas: Jesus is not referred to as the messiah or Son of David in any other logion. While the Thomasine community may have been aware of those Jesus-typologies and traditions—as Goodacre, Gathercole, and Meier argue, *Thomas* seems to be familiar with the Synoptic tradition— these images of Jesus were not salient enough to recall for the *Thomas* community's own sense of group identity.

Other scholars opt for interpreting this saying as a reference to the Jerusalem temple. Simon Gathercole sees the saying as representative of the post-Bar Kokhba period, arguing:

---

155. DeConick, *Original Gospel of Thomas in Translation*, 226. Plisch prefers the latter option, which follows Schenke and "puts the saying closer to the New Testament parallels" (Plisch, *Gospel of Thomas*, 171; Schenke, "Bemerkungen zu #71," 120–26).

156. DeConick, *Original Gospel of Thomas in Translation*, 226.

157. See Riley, *Resurrection Reconsidered*.

158. Patterson, "Apocalypticism or Prophecy," 813; cf. *Gospel of Thomas*.

159. Plisch, *Gospel of Thomas*, 172.

> The likelihood here is that *Thomas* is referring to the temple of Jerusalem ... with this saying probably part of the anti-Jewish emphasis in *Thomas* (cf. GTh 39; 43; 52–53). In sum, GTh 71 attributes destruction of the temple to Jesus himself, and even more strikingly, and in obvious contrast to the numerous expressions of Jewish expectation of a rebuilt temple, Jesus announces its perpetual desolation.[160]

Mark Goodacre also places the saying in the mid- to early-second century CE, contending, "The matter of special interest in Thomas's formulation is this latter clause, which hints at a date after Bar Kokhba's rebellion, placing Thomas after 135 CE."[161] Both Gathercole and Goodacre emphasize that this logion decries any future attempts to rebuild the temple in the aftermath of Bar Kokhba's failed revolt, indicating that the destruction is final.[162] Ismo Dunderberg teases out the further implications of the destruction, arguing that not only is this logion anti-Jewish, but it is anti-eschatological as well. Dunderberg claims,

> If there were, as seems likely, Christians whose eschatological hopes were connected with the destruction of the temple, the sentence "no one will rebuild it" can be understood in terms of an anti-eschatological polemic that comes to expression also in Gos. Thom. 3 and 113. Moreover, if Gos. Thom. 71 refers to the temple and its destruction, it would be in accordance with the anti-Jewish bias of the gospel. Thomasine Christians might have had their reasons, either religious or political, to welcome the destruction of the temple, but it is also not surprising that they did not link any eschatological hopes with this event.[163]

---

160. Gathercole, *Gospel of Thomas*, 479.

161. Goodacre, *Thomas and the Gospels*, 168. DeConick, who places this logion into the earliest layer of her "kernel gospel" in the 40s CE, suggests "it is certainly possible that this saying came to be understood by the later community to prove that the earthly Temple is unnecessary. Instead God was known to be present in the heavenly Temple where the mystic now must journey in order to worship him" (DeConick, *Original Gospel of Thomas in Translation*, 227).

162. Did Christians or Jews widely hold that the temple would be rebuilt after its destruction by the Romans? Gathercole and Goodacre's arguments of a post-135 CE date hinge upon assuming the affirmative. But while Bar Kokhba's revolt is one example of attempting to rebuild and reinstitute the temple, it is not required that *Thomas*'s bleak view has to have been after 135 CE. Other texts like 2 Baruch and 4 Ezra also wrestled with the finality of losing the temple during the late-first and early-second century CE.

163. Ismo Dunderberg, "*Thomas*' I-Sayings and the Gospel of John," in Uro, ed., *Thomas at the Crossroads*, 58.

While the saying's context, content, date, and meaning are all cryptic and heavily limited by the reconstruction of the final lacuna, the saying has too many parallels to the canonical gospels for it not to refer to the Jerusalem temple or at least recall that tradition for the Thomasine commemorative community. Tentatively, then, Gos. Thom. 71 is another example of an early Christian community commemorating Jesus's complex relationship with the temple. In *Thomas*'s case, the temple, like other Jewish practices, symbols, and institutions, is obsolete in their likely post-70 CE contemporary world.[164] Rather than promoting particular Jewish practices, *Thomas*'s incipit claims wisdom is the salvific key, as it grants the proper interpretation to the sayings and leads the interpreter of the sayings to a life without death.

The Gospel of Peter

The Gospel of Peter was recognized by ancient church fathers like Origen and Eusebius, although the extant papyri are fragmentary and rely heavily on the late Akhmimic text.[165] Still, Peter offers a vivid example of the growth and expansion of Jesus tradition in early Christian memory. As Raymond E. Brown described it over a generation ago, and many scholars would still agree, "it is another window into popular Christianity of the first half of the second century."[166] In fact, even before his work on social memory theory, Kirk explored the frameworks of Peter's memory, arguing its "narrative is due to the religious viewpoints of the circles in which it took shape. These narrative interests exerted their own coercion upon the materials at their disposal."[167] Within these interests, the temple appears again to play some kind of role for the commemorative community.

In retelling the events of Jesus's crucifixion and resurrection, the Gospel of Peter mentions the temple several times. Like the Synoptics, the Gospel of Peter recalls the tradition of the temple veil—specified as "the temple of Jerusalem"—being torn in two (διεράγη τό καταπέτασμα τοῦ ναοῦ τῆς Ἰερουσαλὴμ εἰς δύο, Gos. Pet. 5.20). In the aftermath of Jesus's

---

164. *Thomas* displays a tendency to discount or argue against Jewish practices; for elements of anti-Judaism in *Thomas*, see Gos. Thom. 53 (against circumcision); 6, 14 (against prayer, fasting, almsgiving, and diet); and 104 (against prayer and fasting).

165. For a summary of recent discussions surrounding possible P.Oxy. fragments of Gos. Pet., see Foster, "Gospel of Peter," 319–26.

166. Brown, "*Gospel of Peter* and Canonical Gospel Priority," 339.

167. Kirk, "Examining Priorities," 595.

death, "the Jews" rejoiced (ἐχάρησαν δὲ οἱ Ἰουδαῖοι, 6.23), but this group is later amalgamated with other Jewish oppositional characters that offer a very different response to Jesus's death and connect it to the destruction of Jerusalem.[168] The Gospel of Peter 7.25 has "the Jews, the elders, and the priests" (οἱ Ἰουδαῖοι καὶ οἱ πρεσβύτεροι καὶ οἱ ἱερεῖς) cry out in despair that "the judgment and end of Jerusalem has approached" (ἤγγισεν ἡ κρίσις καὶ τὸ τέλος Ἱερουσαλήμ, Gos. Pet. 7.25) on account of their own actions.[169] Peter seemingly refers to this group again when talking about the disciples in hiding on account of their supposed anti-temple reputation: "For we were being sought by them [the Jews, elders, and priests?] as evildoers and as ones wishing to burn the temple" (ἐζητούμεθα γὰρ ὑπ' αὐτῶν ὡς κακοῦργοι καὶ ὡς τὸν ναὸν θέλοντες ἐμπρῆσαι, Gos. Pet. 7.26). This reputation is not explained—perhaps the earlier missing portion of the gospel clarifies why the disciples would be sought for this—but is presumably false, since there seems to be a parallelism between "evildoers" and temple-burning. It is interesting how this tradition echoes Stephen's trial in Acts 6, but rather than blame the disciples for Jesus's attitude, however, the Gospel of Peter has transferred the anti-temple sentiment to the disciples. In addition, the method of the temple's destruction is more specific than the canonical gospels: the Gospel of Peter uses ἐμπίμπρημι as opposed to the canonical gospels' καταλύω. Perhaps this change can be explained by the memory of the temple's destruction in a post-70 CE context since it parallels the historical events of the destructive fire that demolished the temple in 70 CE (*B.J.* 6.220–270).

168. Marcus also notes the ambiguity and alternating usage of the term: "Indeed, the referent of the term 'the Jews' fluctuates oddly throughout the document. At the very beginning (1.1) and near the end (12.50, 52) it refers to the hostile leaders, but by 2.5 the people have become associated with the leaders' hostility, so that, when we read in 6.23 that 'the Jews rejoiced' that the sun had returned, and that they turned Jesus' corpse over to Joseph, we are probably meant to understand the term to include both leaders and people. But two verses later, in 7.25, 'the Jews' seem to be distinguished from the elders and priests, and therefore to denote the sympathetic populace... In any case, 'the Jews' in the Gospel of Peter are sometimes the leaders, sometimes the people, and sometimes both combined, and while the term is usually hostile, it is not always so. This fluidity in denotation perhaps suggests a fluidity in conception: it is not clear in the author's environment who speaks for 'the Jews', the hostile leaders or the sympathetic people... the image of the Ἰουδαῖοι in the work is inconsistent, and not always negative, and the author's wrath is directed primarily at the leaders rather than the people" (Marcus, "Gospel of Peter as a Jewish Christian Document," 477).

169. Marcus employs this mournful attitude as evidence that the gospel was written in a Jewish-Christian community that oscillated between philo- and anti-Judaic attitudes. See Marcus, "Gospel of Peter as a Jewish Christian Document," 482–85.

The Gospel of Peter's memory of the temple is limited but reveals a similar tension as in the canonical gospels, particularly in relation to who is responsible for the temple's demise. The Gospel of Peter recalls an anti-temple reputation being attributed to the disciples, even though it pins the destruction of Jerusalem on an amalgamated Jewish oppositional group. In the recollection and commemoration of the Jesus tradition, then, Schröter argues the Gospel of Peter is "a creative *'recreation'* of the Jesus story . . . from a second-century perspective," where

> [early Jesus] traditions or narratives are reinterpreted from a new perspective. Thereby, the political and religious milieu of the passion events is still recognisable, even if it becomes blurred compared to older presentations of these events. However, Gos. Peter can be regarded as an autonomous version of the passion narrative, *demonstrating that these events were regarded as a constitutive part of the Jesus story and therefore presented in a way that makes them meaningful for Christians in a later situation.*[170]

P.Oxy. 840

First published in Grenfell and Hunt's massive trove of papyri from Oxyrhynchus, P.Oxy. 840 is a small fragment that offers Jesus tradition not found in any other gospel. The context and date of the fragment are debated. François Bovon argues the text belongs to second- and third-century CE Gnostic or Manichaean debates over baptism, and while Harald Buchinger and Elisabeth Hernitscheck agree with Bovon's interpretation, they shift the date back to the fourth century CE based on the baptismal liturgy and practice envisioned in the text.[171] On the other hand, Michael Kruger argues the fragment is a composite collection of early Jesus traditions that resembles other second-century apocryphal works, while also reflecting first-century traditions and familiarity with canonical gospels.[172] Pamela Shellberg treats the fragment similarly, reading it as intimately connected with Johannine tradition and as a reflection of Johannine intra-Jewish "replacement theology" regarding the practice of the *miqva'ot*, tentatively suggesting a date that coheres with either

---

170. Schröter, "Contribution of Non-Canonical Gospels," 452, emphasis added.

171. Bovon, "Fragment Oxyrhynchus 840," 705–28; Buchinger and Hernitscheck, "P. Oxy. 840 and the Rites of Christian Initiation," 117–24.

172. See Kruger, *Gospel of the Savior*.

the first- or second-century CE.¹⁷³ Despite the contested dating, *Sitz im Leben*, and meaning, this papyrus offers an additional window into how early Christians remembered Jesus and the temple.

The papyrus narrates an incident between Jesus, his disciples, and a member of the temple authorities over a dispute about aspects of ritual purity. After a short opening discourse, ll. 9-10 portray Jesus "walking in the temple" (περιεπάτει ἐν τῷ ἱερῷ) when he is approached by Levi, "a certain Pharisee [and] chief priest" (φαρισαῖός τις ἀρχιερεὺς Λευ[εὶς]). Levi questions Jesus about how he was able to enter the temple without ritual washing: "Who allowed you to tread this place of purification and see these holy vessels?" (τίς ἐπέτρεψέν σοι πατ[εῖν] τοῦτο τὸ ἁγνευτήριον καὶ ἰδεῖν [ταῦ]τα τὰ ἅγια σκεύη, ll. 12-14). Levi restates his discontent with Jesus and the disciples arriving unwashed: "but defiled you tread this temple, which is a clean place" (ἀλλὰ μεμολυ[μμένος] ἐπάτησας τοῦτο τὸ ἱερὸν τ[όπον ὄν]τα καθαρόν, ll. 16-18). Jesus turns the question back on Levi, asking "since you're here in the temple, are you clean?" (σὺ οὖν ἐνταῦθα ὢν ἐν τῷ ἱερῷ καθαρεύεις, ll. 23-24). Levi answers affirmatively and points to the practices of ritual washing and wearing white garments. Jesus's response in ll. 30-44 devalues the purificatory power of the ritual pool (λίμνη), distinguishes between external and internal purity (which seems to shift the debate from ritual to moral purity), and answers Levi's initial question by claiming "we have been dipped in living water of eternity" ([βεβά]μμεθα ἐν ὕδασι ζω[ῆς αἰωνίου] ll. 43-44).¹⁷⁴

The fragmentary nature of P.Oxy. 840 means any conclusions about its message, date, or the commemorative community must remain

---

173. Pamela Shellberg, "Johannine Reading of Oxyrhynchus Papyrus 840," in Evans and Zacharias, eds., *Jewish and Christian Scripture as Artifact and Canon*, 176-91. Lorne Zelyck critiques Shellberg's conclusion, arguing "there is enough evidence to question the claim that this work was composed in the first half of the second century CE because it depicts an 'intimate awareness of pre-70 temple practices'; it could also depict a superficial knowledge of Israelite synagogues and practices from the first through the fourth century CE. Jewish synagogues are already identified as 'temples' in the first century CE; a Samaritan high-priest named Levi may have reigned in the latter half of the second century CE; there is archaeological evidence for water installations and *miqva'ot* adjacent to Jewish and Samaritan synagogues from the first through fourth century CE; Jews and Samaritans may have worn white garments in the synagogues during the third century CE; two Jewish and two Samaritan synagogues from the third and fourth centuries CE contain depictions of the holy vessels with a curtain pulled back to reveal the holy ark within a temple" (Zelyck, "Recontextualizing Papyrus Oxyrhynchus 840," 195-96).

174. On ritual and moral purity and impurity, see Klawans, *Purity, Sacrifice, and the Temple*, 55-56.

tentative. However, there are a few things this fragment can tell us about early Christian commemorations of Jesus and the temple. First, early Christians continued to receive and transmit traditions about Jesus in conflict in the temple with temple authorities. Second, regardless of arguments surrounding the "authenticity" of the papyrus's tradition history or the historical plausibility of the narrative, the concerns about purity fit within the context of the Jerusalem temple, which demanded ritual purity for sacrificial practice. In other words, this community has constructed an image of the past that is, at least on some level, consonant with traditions about the temple and purity. Finally, and perhaps most importantly, the temple and its ritual purity are not denigrated in this fragment. Rather, the priest and his form of ritual washing are the target of Jesus's critique; Jesus's "dipping in living waters of eternity" is meant to satisfy the temple's purity requirements, whereas the priest's ritual washing is not. Whatever context this fragment was originally situated within—ritual purity/impurity, proper *mikva'ot* practice, validity/invalidity of baptism, etc.—the temple is not at fault but is instead utilized rhetorically to emphasize Jesus's proper practice over his opponent in whichever way these positions confronted each other within the social world of the commemorative community.

The Gospel of Philip

The Gospel of Philip, another text from the Nag Hammadi corpus dated as widely as the second century to the fourth century CE, offers quite a different insight on the temple.[175] Madeleine Scopello introduces the Gospel of Philip as "a collection of sayings and meditations belonging to different genres . . . that have not been organized in a logical fashion."[176] However, within these disparate sayings, the temple is symbolically invoked as a means of understanding the *Gospel of Philip*'s form of early Christian sacramentalism.

The temple is alluded to when the Gospel of Philip discusses the three locations for sacrifice in Jerusalem: "There were three places for sacrifice in Jerusalem" (ⲚⲈⲨⲚ̄ ϢⲞⲘⲦ Ⲛ̄ⲎⲈⲒ Ⲙ̄ⲘⲀ Ⲛ̄ⲦⲠⲢⲞⲤⲪⲞⲢⲀ ϨⲚ̄

---

175. Scopello dates it to "the second half of the second century or first decades of the third" (Meyer, *Nag Hammadi Scriptures*, 160; cf. King, "Place of the *Gospel of Philip*," 570). Isenberg dates it into "the second half of the third century AD" due to its Gnostic parallels. Layton, *Nag Hammadi Codex II,2–7*, 134–35.

176. Meyer, *Nag Hammadi Scriptures*, 158.

ⲐⲒⲈⲢⲞⲤⲞⲖⲨⲘⲀ, 69.14–15). These three "places" of sacrifice, which already draws on the terminology of the temple (ⲘⲘⲀ), are described in 69.22–25 as "the holy" (ⲈⲦⲞⲨⲀⲀⲂ), "the holy of holy" (ⲠⲈⲦⲞⲨⲀⲀⲂ ⲘⲠⲈⲦⲞⲨⲀⲀⲂ), and the "holy of holies" (ⲠⲈⲦ[ⲞⲨⲀ]ⲀⲂ ⲚⲚⲈⲦⲞⲨⲀⲀⲂ), which are then attributed to baptism (ⲠⲂⲀⲠⲦⲒⲤⲘⲀ), redemption (ⲠⲤⲰⲦⲈ), and the bridal chamber (ⲠⲚⲨⲘⲪⲰⲚ).[177] That the Jerusalem temple is in view is further made clear with the reference to the tradition to the tearing of the temple curtain ([ⲠⲔⲀ]ⲦⲀⲠⲈⲦⲀⲤⲘⲀ ⲠⲰϨ, 69.35), which echoes the Synoptics in that it was "torn from top to bottom" (ⲈⲦ[Ⲃ]Ⲉ [Ⲡ]ⲀⲈⲒ ⲀⲠⲈϤⲔⲀⲦⲀⲠⲈⲦⲀⲤⲘⲀ ⲠⲰ[Ϩ] ⲜⲒⲘ ⲠⲤⲀ ⲚⲦⲠⲈ ϢⲀ ⲠⲤⲀ ⲘⲠⲒⲦⲚ, 70.1–3). The torn temple curtain is also referenced in 84.27–29 and is explicitly connected to the destruction of the temple.[178] The language echoes Matt 23:38 and Luke 13:35 in discussing the temple as both a "house" (ⲎⲈⲒ) and "desolate" (ⲈⲢⲎⲘⲞⲤ), but with the wrinkle that it "will be destroyed" (ⲤⲈⲚⲀⲢⲔⲀⲦⲀ[ⲖⲨⲈ]). As a consequence of the destruction of the temple, "the whole godhead will flee" (ⲦⲘⲚⲦⲚⲞⲨⲦⲈ ⲆⲈ ⲐⲎⲢⲤ ⲤⲀⲠⲰⲦ, 84.29); it will not enter the holy of holies, but instead remains "under the wings of the cross" (ⲤⲚⲀϢⲰⲠⲈ ϨⲀ ⲚⲦⲚϨ ⲘⲠⲤⲢⲞⲤ, 84.33).

Matthew Twigg highlights the ways in which the temple is connected to Christian sacraments and mysteries.[179] Twigg suggests the Gospel of Philip "is not primarily concerned with either spatiality or historicity in this instance, but rather with how the temple's imagined layout articulates the deeper spiritual reality within the rites of initiation."[180] In other

---

177. The bridal chamber is particularly emphasized; as Karen King argues, "the Gospel of Philip presents Jesus' virginal birth, incarnation, and baptism (among other events) as symbolic paradigms for the ritual of the bridal chamber in which the individual initiate is reunited with his/her spiritual double through practices of baptism, anointing, kissing, and a Eucharist meal. By receiving spiritual rebirth as a child of the bridal chamber and becoming a Christ, the initiate realizes his/her incarnate role as a member of the Church, which is the pre-existent body of Christ. The bridal chamber ritual thus undoes the believer's separation from God (figured in the separation of Eve from Adam) and effects salvation by the spiritual union of the believer with his/her double (figured by analogy to heterosexual marriage)" (King, "Place of the *Gospel of Philip*," 576).

178. "When the curtain is torn and what is inside is revealed, this house will be left desolate, or rather will be destroyed," ⲈϤϢⲀⲠⲰϨ ⲆⲈ ⲚϬⲒ ⲠⲔⲀⲦⲀⲠⲈⲦⲀⲤ[Ⲙ]Ⲁ ⲀⲨⲰ ⲚⲦⲈ ⲚⲀ ⲠⲤⲀ ⲚϨⲞⲨⲚ ⲞⲨⲰⲚϨ [ⲈⲂⲞⲖ] ⲤⲈⲚⲀⲔⲰ ⲆⲈ ⲘⲠⲈⲈⲒⲎⲈⲒ ⲚⲤⲰⲞⲨ [ⲈϤⲞ] ⲚⲈⲢⲎⲘⲞⲤ ⲘⲀⲖⲖⲞⲚ ⲆⲈ ⲤⲈⲚⲀⲢⲔⲀⲦⲀ[ⲖⲨⲈ] ⲘⲘⲞϤ.

179. Twigg, "Esoteric Discourse and the Jerusalem Temple," 47–80.

180. Twigg, "Esoteric Discourse and the Jerusalem Temple," 60.

words, the Gospel of Philip's commemorative community is not necessarily making a comment on the historical temple but instead forging group identity and using a "site of memory" to encapsulate their ideology in a way that fits their present circumstances. Twigg maps out the rites of initiation as concentric along the lines of the "three structures for sacrifice in Jerusalem" (Gos. Phi. 69.14). At the heart is the bridal chamber, transposed onto the Holy of Holies, which is surrounded by redemption, the "Holy of the Holy," and all of this is located within baptism—and, as Twigg argues, chrismation—which is understood as the Holy.[181] Twigg then argues the Gospel of Philip contrasts this sacramental organization against the Jewish sacrificial cult, pointing to its polemic against the temple, which, in 54.31—55.5 and 62.35—63.4, denigrates animal sacrifice and elevates the human sacrifice of Christ.[182] Furthermore, Twigg argues the polemic in the Gospel of Philip is not solely aimed at Jews, but rather directed against any Christians whose initiation and sacramental practice deviates from the community's standard. As Twigg puts it,

> Far more important for *Gos. Phil.* is the problem of those Christians who remain mired in their Jewish origins by virtue of not having been initiated properly into Christianity . . . Inspired by the esoteric themes associated with the Jerusalem temple as an earthly centre for the revelation of divine secrets to an elect minority, *Gos. Phil.* adopts the concept of the temple as an expression of ideal Christian initiation, while polemically distinguishing it from the Jewish institution itself, the legacy of which both Jews and certain Christians are still mired within.[183]

Philip's portrait of the temple is a fascinating foil to other gospel traditions. While there is not a clear relationship between Jesus and the temple, the *Gospel of Philip* draws on some of the same images, particularly the torn

---

181. "The temple metaphor in 69.14–70.4 does not indicate any kind of spatial relationship between the sacraments, but rather a conceptual, or causal, relationship. Baptism *qua* baptism-chrismation *causes* redemption and resurrection, which in turn constitute the duplicate bridal chamber as a ritual anticipation of the final union in the bridal chamber of the heavenly temple. This is *Gos. Phil.*'s understanding of ideal Christian initiation" (Twigg, "Esoteric Discourse and the Jerusalem Temple," 61).

182. "In the worldly cult of Judaism, the sacrificed animals remain on the cosmic level, eventually being quite literally consumed by the earth; but in the perfect cult of Christianity, the sacrificed living Christ is consumed by God and Truth. Therefore, anyone initiated into the earthly mysteries of Truth, depicted as a superior version of the Jerusalem temple, likewise receives eternal life" (Twigg, "Esoteric Discourse and the Jerusalem Temple," 63).

183. Twigg, "Esoteric Discourse and the Jerusalem Temple," 63–65.

curtain (70.4; 85.1–21; cf. Mark 15:38), and, as Twigg argues, appropriates temple language in service of critiquing Jews and other Christians.[184]

The Gospel of Judas

Irenaeus attested the presence of a document in the late-second century CE (*Haer.* 1.31.1), but it was not until the early 2000s that the reconstruction of fragments of Codex Tchacos offered a text to evaluate and understand the traditions of the *Gospel of Judas*.[185] This gospel, which retells the final days of the gospel narrative through a Gnostic lens, focuses on Jesus's particular relationship with Judas in the buildup to his betrayal and singles Judas out in a series of intimate dialogues with Jesus. In fact, from its very incipit, the *Gospel of Judas* claims the tradition of Judas comes from a revelatory discourse of Jesus (33.1–6).

Within the gospel's discourse, Jesus and the disciples touch on the subject of the temple. Unlike the canonical gospels, which place Jesus within the temple during his last week, the discussion about the temple comes in part because the disciples have a vision where they see a "house" (ⲚⲎ[Ⲓ], 38.2) with a "great altar" ([ⲞⲨⲚ]Ⲟ6 ⲚⲈⲨ[ⲤⲒ]ⲀⲤⲦⲎⲢ[ⲒⲞⲚ], 38.2–3) and sacrifices. These images—including the presence of "priests" (ⲚⲞⲨⲎⲎⲂ, 38.9)—indicate they are referring to the Jerusalem temple. However, they are disturbed by the "sin and lawlessness" (ⲚⲚⲞⲂⲈ ⲀⲨⲰ ⲀⲚⲞⲘⲒⲀ, 38.23) they perceive running rampant within the temple.[186] Jesus responds to their concern claiming all the priests before the altar in their vision "call upon my name" (ⲈⲠⲒ ⲔⲀⲖⲈ[Ⲓ] ⲘⲠⲀⲢⲀⲚ, 39.10–11). Jesus then reveals that the disciples' vision of the temple and priests reflects themselves and their activity (39.18–21), which reframes the Jerusalem temple as an analog of the early Christian church. After summarizing

---

184. DeConick also examines the sacramentalism of *Philip* by comparing it with Jewish mysticism and the turn to the heavenly temple in the post-70 CE world. DeConick, "True Mysteries," 225–61.

185. Even after the publication team made their translation widely available, other scholars, particularly April DeConick, offered corrections and emendations, especially regarding whether the evaluation of Judas was positive (Meyer) or negative (DeConick); cf. April DeConick, "Mystery of Betrayal: What Does the *Gospel of Judas* Really Say?," in Scopello, ed., *Gospel of Judas in Context*, 239–64.

186. "Fasting, cultic sacrifice and abasement—all prescribed in Leviticus—are here associated with the worst of iniquities (from the point of view of the author of the *Gospel of Judas*): sacrifices, homosexuality, murder, and all these in Jesus' name (38,24–26)" (Louis Painchaud, "Polemical Aspects of the *Gospel of Judas*," in Scopello, ed., *Gospel of Judas in Context*, 176).

his attitude toward the disciples' vision, Jesus tells them to "cease sacrificing" (ⲡⲉϫⲁϥ [ⲛⲁⲩ ⲛ̄]ϭⲓ ⲓⲏⲥ ϫⲉ ϩⲱ ⲉⲣⲱ ⲧⲛ̄ ⲛ̄ⲑⲩ[ⲥⲓⲁⲥⲉ ...], 41.1–2) before the damaged manuscript's missing lines leaves the rest of Jesus's response unrecoverable.

The anti-Jewish attitude toward sacrifice and the polemical attack on the priests are reinterpreted as attacks on early Christian practice in defense of Judas's heterodox Gnosticism. As Gathercole argues, "our author shows no sympathy for traditional Christian piety: having rejected the eucharist at the beginning of the document, Jesus appears in his interpretation of this temple vision to have no truck with the common Jewish and Christian practice of fasting, and in a postscript to his interpretation of the disciples' vision, reiterates his condemnation of the eucharist."[187] The Gospel of Judas, then, utilizes temple symbolism (priesthood, sacrifice, ritual practice) in a negative way to attack other early Christians. Louis Painchaud emphasizes the polemic against sacrifice: "the identification of the apostles with these priests and with their sacrificial activity shows that the target of the *Gospel of Judas*' criticism is neither traditional Greco-Roman cultic sacrifice, nor the sacrificial liturgy of the Jerusalem temple, but rather the sacrificial interpretation of Christianity, what one might call the theology or ideology of sacrifice seen as the perpetuation of the temple cult."[188] The Judas community no longer commemorates a Jesus who engaged with the temple. Rather, their understanding of Jesus bypasses the temple entirely in favor of critiquing the hierarchical and sacramental elements of the early church, which Gathercole argues places *Judas*'s "polemic against the emerging Church establishment in the second" or third century CE.[189]

Summary

The foregoing survey examined the ways in which early Christians continued to remember Jesus and the temple after the foundational account offered by the Gospel of Mark. Matthew's inclusion of the half-shekel tax pericope shows the community wrestling with their identity and relationship to the Gentile, Jewish, and Jewish-Christian worlds. Luke's infancy

---

187. Gathercole, *Gospel of Judas*, 77.

188. Painchaud, "Polemical Aspects of the *Gospel of Judas*," in Scopello, ed., *Gospel of Judas in Context*, 177.

189. Gathercole, *Gospel of Judas*, 140.

narrative puts Jesus's life squarely into its Jewish context by portraying his childhood and ministry as steeped in the temple, his Father's house. That depiction is echoed by his early followers and their activity in the temple. Stephen's speech retells biblical narrative and participates in prophetic critique against the temple, while also echoing Jesus's death as one who suffers righteously. John applies a memory hermeneutic to reinterpret Jesus's words in light of his passion, and, in doing so, presents the temple of Jesus's body in a way that transcends previously established patterns of worship. Within the cryptic sayings and hidden meanings of the *Gospel of Thomas*, Jesus is remembered as the one who unequivocally *will* destroy the house that no one can rebuild. The *Gospel of Peter* demonstrates tension between the Jewish leadership mourning over their actions, which have provoked the destruction of Jerusalem (including its temple), while also pursuing the disciples based on their (presumably false) reputation as "wishing to burn the temple." P.Oxy. 840, on the other hand, portrays Jesus in conflict with a member of the authorities, and while particular purity practices are critiqued, Jesus's reinterpretation of the source of ritual purity elevates and reframes his ministry over temple leadership, while maintaining a positive (or, at worst, neutral) view of the temple. Finally, the *Gospel of Philip* and the *Gospel of Judas* employ temple imagery to discuss proper and improper Christian practice, particularly as it pertains to sacralization and ritual. The Gospel of Philip keys the torn veil of the temple to its present context, making meaning out of an important gospel tradition, whereas the *Gospel of Judas* sees the temple as a negative model of the early Christian church and rejects Christian rituals ("sacrifices").[190] Many of these gospels also hold the totality of the relationship between Jesus and the temple in tension; there are pericopae where Jesus is active and teaching in the temple, and there are pericopae where he pronounces its judgment, abandonment, and destruction. In addition, like Mark, these texts recollect Jesus in conflict with authorities, particularly the chief priests, scribes, and other elites (e.g., Levi the Pharisee in P.Oxy. 840); they also demonstrate how Jesus's ministry is connected to the setting of the Jerusalem temple and draw significance from the temple as a symbol that speaks meaning to their own communities.

---

190. Stephen Emmel summarizes the message of Judas as "above all avoid the senseless cult of the body of Jesus that is mainline Christianity" (Emmel, "Presuppositions and the Purpose of the *Gospel of Judas*," in Scopello, ed., *Gospel of Judas in Context*, 39).

Conclusion

This chapter examined the ways traditions about Jesus and the temple were constructed, transmitted, and transformed throughout the first four centuries CE. In essence, the two surveys in this chapter have addressed the question of *what* was remembered about Jesus and the temple, as well as *how* the temple was remembered within the earliest instantiations of the Jesus tradition. The Gospel of Mark, as the earliest presentation of the Jesus tradition, presents the temple as ambiguous and portrayed in multivalent ways. Later gospel traditions embrace and expand this ambiguity. Some gospels, like Matthew, Luke, and the Gospel of Peter add additional narratives that depict the temple in positive or functioning ways while also enhancing the foretelling of Jerusalem's destruction. Other gospels, like John, the Gospel of Judas, and the Gospel of Philip, apply interpretive hermeneutics that appropriate temple imagery as substitutive of something else; for John, the temple is Jesus's body, whereas for Judas and Philip the temple is associated (both negatively and positively, respectively) with early Christian sacramental imagery.[191] Finally, P.Oxy. 840 involves the temple as the setting of a conflict narrative about purity and ritual washing. The patterns demonstrated by these Jesus memories show that early Christians found meaning in the temple in a multitude of ways. This study has attempted to steer clear of textualized redactional concerns because of the variability in which the temple was remembered; as Rodríguez cautions, "instead of 'original' and 'secondary,' Jesus traditions are capable of multiple and multiform expression."[192] Exactly *why* they found salience and transmitted these traditions will be investigated in the concluding chapter.

---

191. Even though John applies a post-Easter interpretive lens on the temple saying, the temple does still play a significant role in the narrative as a base for Jesus's teaching. See Lieu, "Temple and Synagogue in John," 51–69.

192. Rodríguez, *Structuring Early Christian Memory*, 35.

5

Jesus, the Temple, and Early Christian Memory

> Thus our question is not simply, did Jesus turn to the Isaianic tradition to communicate his own significance? . . . Rather, we ask, what about the Isaianic tradition enabled Jesus' followers to perceive and interpret (and communicate) his significance and to properly order their behaviour? . . . If both non-Christian Jewish groups and the early Jesus movements understood and oriented themselves to the present in terms of the Isaianic tradition, it becomes all the more likely that Jesus understood his milieu (and his role therein) in Isaianic terms.
> —Rafael Rodríguez[1]

FOLLOWING FROM THE SURVEY of early Christian attitudes toward the Jerusalem temple in the previous chapter, I will set forth an explanation for why early Christians commemorated Jesus and the temple in the ways in which they did. Like others in the Second Temple period, early Christians lived in a complex world in which religious symbols, authorities, and traditions were in flux. We will see that the contrasting depictions of the temple—as well as the complicated matrix of relationships to the temple—demonstrate the tension between tradition and innovation, past and present. While many interpretive frameworks could explain the

---

1. Rodríguez, *Structuring Early Christian Memory*, 164–65.

memory of Jesus in relation to the temple, I suggest two possibilities, particularly for the Gospel of Mark: temple turmoil in the social world of the Markan community or prophetic typology in line with Israel's scriptures. The tensions early Christians faced were not necessarily different in kind than those faced by Second Temple Jews, but their response and their memories of Jesus played a significant role in how they would later define themselves with respect to the temple.

Finding the Frame for Markan Memory

Each community of early Christians commemorated traditions about Jesus's life in various ways and constructed their memories in light of present concerns and past constraints. As we saw in chapter 1, memories are actively constructed, subjectively transmitted, and naturally experience distortion. Memory, as tradition or commemorative artifact, is not static or unaffected by the past; rather, Olick and Robbins argue, "memory is a process, not a thing, and it works differently at different points in time."[2] The relationship between these "points in time," particularly the environment of the present commemoration and the past which it commemorates, was not only the starting point for Halbwachs, Schwartz, and Assmann, but also for Kirk and Thatcher's critique of the early form-critics and their sifting of Jesus tradition. As Schwartz's work has shown, the past and present are mutually informative and mutually constitutive: the past offers symbols and artifacts of memory, while the present generates and selectively imbues meaning and motivation to these symbols.[3] The resulting depictions of Jesus's relationship with the Jerusalem temple demonstrate communities navigating the Jesus tradition via coherence and complexity, variability and stability, and expansion and reconstruction. For instance, the tradition of the temple destruction saying differs significantly between gospels (variability) and at times seems incongruent with Jesus's attitude(s) toward the temple (complexity), but the tradition is recurrent across differing communities

---

2. Olick and Robbins, "Social Memory Studies," 122.

3. "The object of commemoration is usually to be found in the *past*, the issue which motivates its selection and shaping is always to be found among the concerns of the *present*" (Schwartz, "Social Context of Commemoration," 395, emphasis added). In chapter 1, we also saw how Erll, Le Goff, and Assmann discussed the ways shifts in media can impact the practice and dynamics of commemoration, and it is important to remember the shift from oral to written tradition was an ongoing factor of tradition transmission as both forms of media persisted throughout the first three centuries CE.

(stability) and plays an important role in actualizing the tradition for the community's concerns (reconstruction).

In the same way that social memory theory examines the ways past and present interact, the previous chapter analyzed the nexus between narrative characterization and memories of Jesus and the temple. The discussion of history in the works of White and Carr in chapter 1 offered important insights for memory theory: memory, like history, is emplotted, narrativized, and made coherent within contemporary frameworks. Memory influences characterization, and characterization represents commemorative activities. Therefore, any study of the memories of Jesus, as expressed in the characterization of Jesus and the temple in the gospels, particularly in the Gospel of Mark, must "account for the gospels as coherent, culturally conditioned and relevant portrayals of Jesus."[4]

That the Markan commemorative community recalls the supposed antagonism between Jesus and the temple (14:58; 15:29) demonstrates the salience of the tradition—the constraint of remembering Jesus as cloaked in controversy surrounding the temple—but does not specify *why* this recollection would be formative or important for the community's present needs. Perhaps the intent is apologetic in response to some sort of past conflict with the temple officials, regardless of whether the altercation(s) was physical (Mark 11) or verbal (Mark 12). On the other hand, perhaps conflict in the community's present necessitated a critique of the temple. Judith Lieu discusses the role that contested space, particularly sacred space, plays in the formation of group identity and compares early Christians to the covenanters of the Dead Sea Scrolls:

> Such anticipations of the future shape of "place" could become a means of articulating present conflicts of power and claims to authentic identity. Just as the actual control of the Jerusalem Temple had more than political implications, so claims to know the pattern of the future Temple among the Dead Sea Community seek to legitimate a contested identity (e.g., 11QT), while attacks against its present state may bespeak the sense of marginalization felt by a group for whom it none the less remains determinative.[5]

From the surveys above, there are two dominant threads that pinpoint ways in which the gospels express the salience of Jesus's ministry and

---

4. Rodríguez, *Structuring Early Christian Memory*, 224.
5. Lieu, *Christian Identity in the Jewish and Graeco-Roman World*, 219.

actions to Israel's traditional narratives and contemporary history: the instability of the temple and priesthood in the Second Temple period, and the prophetic tradition.

As seen in chapter 3, attitudes toward the Jerusalem temple were complex in the Second Temple period. For a majority of Second Temple Jews, the Jerusalem temple, as a center of sacrifice, prayer, and ritual offering, was a routine part of life; in Klawans's description, "the temple was the location of political, judicial, and religious decision-making, serving as an assembly, court, school, and, perhaps, library."[6] Luke's infancy narrative (1:5–2:52), Jesus's teaching, and the disciples' early ministry in the temple all commemorate activity in the temple as a normal setting in first-century life (Mark 11:27–12:44; 14:49; Luke 19:47; 20:1; 21:37; 22:53; Acts 2:46; 3:11–26; 5:21, 42; P.Oxy. 840). However, attitudes toward the temple were not uniform. Alternative temple sites in Elephantine, Leontopolis, and Samaria demonstrate variability in how and where Jews participated in the temple cult, as well as differing interpretations of biblical traditions about the establishment of God's presence. Each of these temple communities had their own relationship to Jerusalem, as well. For instance, the Elephantine community sought support and approval from Judaea and Samaria when facing external communal threats. In addition to alternative temples, political turmoil and changing Ptolemaic, Seleucid, and Roman imperial regimes made life in Judaea during the Second Temple period socially, economically, and politically turbulent: in a seventy-year span, Judaea went from reveling in the approach of Antiochus III to reviling the policies of Antiochus IV to replenishing the power of Antiochus VII.[7] Cultural debate over the adoption of certain Hellenistic practices also dominated late Second Temple thought and influenced the outbreak of the Maccabean Revolt, one of the many salient temple incidents mapped into communal memory for Second Temple Jews and early Christians.[8] Changes in the priesthood during the Maccabean Revolt also resulted in growing dissatisfaction with the temple institution, seen in Onias's flight to Egypt, the "polluted" temple and table of 1 En. 89:72, the temple built by God (Jub. 1:17, 27), and the Dead Sea community's institution of their own community rules, calendar, and vision of the temple (1QS, CD, 1QHa, 4QCalDoc A, 4QFlor, 4QMMTa, 4QShirShabba, 11QTa, 11QNJ).

6. Klawans, *Purity, Sacrifice, and the Temple*, 104.

7. On the reign and operation of the Seleucids, see Kosmin, *Land of the Elephant Kings*.

8. See Dan 9:27; 11:31; 12:11; Mark 13:14.

Dissatisfaction and criticism did not mean the entire rejection of the temple, either; as the debates around the half-shekel tax in Matt 17:24–27 and 4Q159 2.6–7 show, some Jewish and early Christian communities felt the tax or its biblical principle could be interpreted in another way that allowed dissatisfaction with a particular aspect of temple practice to evolve into reformed practice or thought.[9]

It is within this larger multivalent matrix of temple attitudes that the Gospel of Mark presents Jesus and the temple. Gray concludes Jesus's mission is "to usher in judgment for the temple's failure to fulfill its eschtolgoical [sic] mission to restore Israel and gather the nations."[10] Mark's portrayal, however, is slightly more complicated and ambiguous. First, Jesus refers the leper (1:40–45) to be active in the temple's sacrificial cult. Whether the leper acquiesces does not change that in his first instance talking about the temple cult, Jesus gives an unequivocal approval and recommendation of sacrifice. Second, Jesus retells biblical tradition about David eating the bread of the presence (2:23–28) and places the tradition in the "house of God." This is the start of a narrative typology that will continue to portray Jesus as the royal messiah (11:1–11) who subverts expectations (8:31–33). Third, Jesus's conflict with the authorities intensifies and is revealed in his passion predictions. Jesus's death is presented to be, on the one hand, at the hands of chief priests, scribes, and elders (8:31; 10:32–34), and, on the other hand, as a model of suffering, service, and atonement (8:34–38; 10:41–45). Fourth, Mark's temple incident seems to critique temple practices, but, when read along with the intertextual allusions offered for his motivation, the temple is not the target, or at least not the *only* target; instead, the chief priests and scribes who oppose Jesus are judged by *their* failure to recognize and listen to the prophets, and as such, they will be removed from their position (12:10–12). However, what this usurpation looks like is not fully spelled out because, finally, Jesus predicts the end of temple (13:2, 14). Crucially, however, Mark does not have Jesus claim to destroy and rebuild the temple himself (14:56–58); this statement is given by false witnesses at his trial. Unless Jesus and the temple are read analogously, as Duran does, the gospel ends with a

---

9. Klawans categorizes Second Temple period critiques of the temple as falling into categories of "morally defiled," "ritually defiled," "ritually inadequate," and "structurally inadequate," and further divides Qumran critiques that propose a replacement temple into sacrificial and non-sacrificial (community) replacement temples. Klawans, *Purity, Sacrifice, and the Temple*, 145–74.

10. Gray, *Temple in the Gospel of Mark*, 198.

generalized description of the temple's destruction, no clear depiction or promise of temple restoration, and no explicit guidance on how temple practices will transition to a post-temple world.

In the Gospel of Mark, then, the temple is both affirmed and condemned. It is (1) functioning, (2) functioning improperly (or at least it is when Jesus proclaims its purpose in 11:17), and (3) will no longer be functioning once its destruction takes place. The characterization of the temple elites is more consistent throughout the narrative—they fulfill Jesus's passion predictions, repeatedly are characterized with the intent to kill him, and have been condemned by the parable of the wicked tenants—but the temple is more ambivalent and ambiguous. If placed within the larger matrix of temple attitudes in the Second Temple period, the complex nature of the gospel's attitude toward the temple may not be consistent, but it does reflect the real turmoil that some Jews and Jewish-Christians had in constructing their identity vis-à-vis the temple in light of contemporary events. As Second Temple Jews and early Christians witnessed calamity after calamity, they would have connected these events in an attempt to make meaning out of their contemporary world. Antiochus's desecration, Pompey's entrance to the sanctuary, Caligula's disregard for Jewish piety, the Zealots' siege of the temple, and, if post-70 CE, Titus's triumph over Jerusalem could all have been the historical and social frameworks of the Markan community's memory. Even earlier instances like Jeremiah's condemnation of the temple and the Babylonians' destruction of the first temple continued to resonate in the cultural memory of Jews and early Christians. Their understanding of the temple could not be fully formulated in a historically detached manner; instead, they processed their understanding of the temple in light of salient contemporary and past events. Mark's community lived in a world in which the temple—the sacred house of God, the center of the sacrificial cult, and a pivotal component of Jewish practice and identity—had been defiled, threatened, and relativized. Mark's mixed attitudes toward the temple may have come from continuity with the historical Jesus, who, as a first-century CE Galilean Jew, existed within the matrix of attitudes mapped in chapter 3. If Jesus criticized the temple or its priesthood, those points of criticism, whatever they may have been, could have been remembered against the backdrop of the temple's instability. If he vaguely projected or prophesied the temple's destruction, as in Mark 13:1–2, early Christians may have again remembered this during particular points of turbulence. Whether the attitude came from continuity with Jesus or in response to contemporary events, early Christians

240   JESUS, THE TEMPLE, AND EARLY CHRISTIAN MEMORY

remembered and transmitted reverence for, criticism of, and projection beyond the temple in the performance of the Jesus tradition that shaped their collective group identity.[11]

An additional, perhaps simpler, way to explain the Gospel of Mark's stance is to locate it within Israel's prophetic tradition of critiquing the temple, priesthood, and people. Klawans investigates the prophetic critiques of sacrifice in the HB, arguing "many of the prophetic oppositions to sacrifice [and the temple cult] can be understood as a reflection of their social and economic message."[12] In particular, Klawans emphasizes the concerns of economic malpractice, particularly theft; "the prophets' rejections of sacrifice are connected to their belief that economic transgressions render sacrificial offerings not just invalid but offensive."[13] Klawans also discusses the role of "symbolic actions" in the prophetic tradition, where Israel's prophets conducted actions that symbolized points of their critique against the people or temple cult.[14] With this in mind, early Christians likely interpreted Jesus's actions and teachings within the framework of Israel's scriptures, drawing heavily on the example of the prophets.[15] Jesus's actions and teachings in Mark are, at

---

11. In describing the gospels as oral-derived texts, Rodríguez discusses the communicative transmission process as multiple instantiations, or performances, of the Jesus tradition: "The traditions contained within our texts (including the temple incident) developed and were expressed and transmitted in various performative events, from informal conversations about past events to ritualized communal performances of an increasingly sacred tradition. The earliest Christian tradents were mostly anonymous (i.e., the identities of nearly all of the oral-traditional performers have been lost to *us*; obviously, they were not anonymous to their original audiences). *The Gospels bear some relation to the earliest Christian oral expressions of the Jesus tradition*" (Rafael Rodríguez, "Zeal that Consumed: Memory of Jerusalem's Temple and Jesus's Body in the Gospel of John," in Hatina, ed., *Gospel of John*, 204).

12. Klawans, *Purity, Sacrifice, and the Temple*, 98.

13. Klawans, *Purity, Sacrifice, and the Temple*, 91.

14. "If indeed sacrifice in particular, and ritual in general, can be understood as symbolic action . . . then it becomes all the more interesting to note that many thematic discussions of prophecy in biblical Israel point out that prophets were wont to perform 'symbolic acts' in order to dramatize and illustrate their message to the Israelite people. Hosea marrying a prostitute to symbolize Israel's infidelity (Hos 1:2); Isaiah walking barefoot and naked to symbolize Egypt's impending doom (Isa 20:1–6); Jeremiah wearing a yoke to symbolize God's desire for the nations to submit to Babylon (Jer 27:1–15)" (Klawans, *Purity, Sacrifice, and the Temple*, 81).

15. As Rodríguez notes, the portrait of Jesus displayed in the gospel needs to have "resonated with Israelite tradition and communicated something of Jesus' significance in an early first-century Galilean context" (Rodríguez, *Structuring Early Christian Memory*, 214).

times, already framed by direct allusions to the prophets and traditions of Israel (11:9–10, 17; 12:1, 10, 36; 13:14, 24–25; 14:27) or framed as enacting prophetic tradition.[16] The temple incident, in particular, is shaped by combining the prophetic traditions of Isaiah 56 and Jeremiah 7, as well as drawing on Malachi 3 and Zechariah 9–14. If understood as a prophetic symbolic action, Jesus's temple incident is not an end to the sacrificial cult or even a rejection of the Jerusalem temple.[17] Instead, it acts out the exact critique he alludes to from the scriptures: the commerce in the temple restricts and excludes πᾶς τό ἔθνος from participating in the temple. In response, and perhaps as an instance of prophetic "hyperbole," Jesus excludes the merchants.[18] As hyperbole, this action does not have to be understood as Jesus against the entire economic system that allowed the temple to function.[19] Following this action, Jesus enters into a series of conflicts with religious leadership, especially the climactic parable of the wicked tenants, where the vineyard is projected to be transferred to the control of others. Here, Mark tweaks prophetic tradition; Jesus does not repeat the prophetic critique against Jerusalem, as in Isa 5, but sharpens the critique against the leadership, which fits into the larger critique building throughout the narrative of economic and social critiques against their attitudes toward property and social vulnerability (Mark 7:9–12; 12:38–44).

As the epigraph at the beginning of this chapter implies, understanding Jesus's actions and teachings as a reflection of Israel's prophetic tradition is important because it recognizes and utilizes a framework of memory already present in the first-century world. Reading the Markan Jesus within the scriptures and traditions of Israel places the teachings and actions that the early Christian community found salient in direct connection to his identity as a Galilean Jew living in Roman Palestine reflecting on centuries of political, social, and cultural instability. It also takes seriously the theological framework that Jews and early Christians used to understand the world around them, even as that framework was changing

---

16. This framing becomes an explicit key feature in Matthew with the fulfillment motif. Jesus is also even recognized as a prophet in Matthew (21:11) and John (4:19).

17. See Joseph, *Jesus and the Temple*, 118–19.

18. "There is one factor that still cannot be overlooked: prophets were prone to hyperbole. What seems like a categorical rejection can probably be better understood as a prioritization" (Klawans, *Purity, Sacrifice, and the Temple*, 81).

19. See Sanders, *Jesus and Judaism*, 70–75.

and developing.[20] Finally, it treats conflict from an intra-Jewish standpoint. As Klawans summarizes, "conflicts between disparate parties—priests and prophets in any age—can only be fully understood when the different positions' motivations are evaluated and appreciated. By doing so, we can avoid the problematic but still frequent tendency to place Jesus *against* ancient Judaism instead of within ancient Jewish disputes on matters cultic and moral."[21] In this way, Mark's memory of Jesus in conflict with the authorities is a community forging their own group identity in relation to others with shared characteristics. The mnemonic processes of commemoration and transmission of the Jesus tradition, at least the instantiation iterated in the Gospel of Mark, must be understood as expressions of Judaism within the diverse Second Temple world.

What might a social memory approach investigating these frameworks tell us of first-century history? Keith, Le Donne, and Rodríguez have utilized social memory theory to demonstrate that its central tenets can be used in constructive ways to explore and tentatively propose reconstructions of the historical Jesus. Each gospel portrays Jesus in conflict with temple authorities and remembers a significant event in the temple, and the Gospel of John offers a clear-cut example of the early Christian commemorative community mnemonically framing the event within the narrative of the gospel by interpreting in light of Jesus's resurrection. Whether that leads to the conclusion "Jesus said this" (or something like it) and "Jesus did this" (or something like it) is one possible reason to explain the appearance of these traditions in early Christian memory. I find it likely that the historical Jesus was remembered in conflict with the temple and temple authorities due to some action or teaching. Keith argues Jesus's literacy was remembered due in part to the conflicts he successfully negotiated during his life: "Jesus became a problem that demanded attention from the Jewish leadership not just because he set himself up as a scribal-literate interpreter of texts, *but because he did so, in some times and at some places, successfully*."[22] If these conflicts were centered in the temple—the seat of power for these elites—it is within reason that early Christians could and would have framed these conflicts within Israel's prophetic tradition in a way that amplified critique against the temple

---

20. For example, see the responses to the destruction of the Jerusalem temple in 4 Ezra, 2 Baruch, and the Sibylline Oracles as ways to understand contemporary events within larger theological frameworks.

21. Klawans, *Purity, Sacrifice, and the Temple*, 223, emphasis original.

22. Keith, *Jesus' Literacy*, 192, emphasis added.

as a part of understanding Jesus's message. The temple would have been a subject of critique, but it was not invalidated as null and void; rather, Jesus's words and actions in relation to the temple were consequential for, and indirectly aimed at, those early Christians who participated in it. For instance, if his teaching or ministry was conveyed as an authority that rivaled the temple authorities, as Mark 1 presents, then his actions and teachings in the temple may have also been seen to rival temple practices, or at least participate in Jewish debates on practice and interpretation of the Torah. On the other hand, if he envisioned the destruction of the temple, whether by means of an eschatological or apocalyptic event or by contemplating past and present events surrounding the temple, he may have uttered some sort of general, vague prediction of destruction. This potential prediction constrained early Christians to remember Jesus in connection with the destruction of the temple, but their understanding of this connection varied from embracing the prediction, distancing Jesus from the destructive actions, and reinterpreting the words as allegorical. However they commemorated it, early Christians continued to be constrained to remember Jesus in conflict in and with the temple throughout the first three centuries, even once the temple was destroyed and Jerusalem's populace was radically reshaped by Roman force.

On the other hand, the ambiguity and ambivalence toward the temple displayed throughout the Gospel of Mark—and the other early Christian gospels in the previous chapter—may also be reflective of the complex attitudes reflected in the broader Second Temple world and even within Israel's prophetic traditions. Whatever actions Jesus did or words Jesus spoke, early Christians did not only remember him in conflict with the temple but also remembered and transmitted traditions that saw him in continuity with regular participation in temple practices. Both the historical Jesus and the early Christian communities who commemorated him navigated a Second Temple world where the temple's status was contested, security was vulnerable, and leadership was changing. They, like others in the Second Temple period, had to hold dissonant attitudes toward the temple.[23] For these early Christian commemorations of Jesus's life, the communities recognized that Jesus

---

23. "If we read New Testament texts as collective memory, we thereby gain no insight into the question of what the events remembered in these texts actually looked like. They are better understood as carrying information about a particular phase of identity formation of the community of commemoration connected with this text" (Huebenthal, *Reading Mark's Gospel*, 174).

participated in and was frequently present in the temple; it was a significant part of his life, and the early Christian community retold its own origin story as intertwined with the temple. However, whether they were constructing, recalling, and performing their traditions in the 40s, 60s, or after the 70s CE, they recognized that the events of Second Temple history—e.g., the actions and visitations by Antiochus IV and Pompey— meant the temple was vulnerable. When recalling traditions about Jesus and the temple, they may not have understood it immediately within critique of the priesthood and people, but instead an undermining of the temple institution, as a dramatic end to the temple, and catalyst for an apocalyptic or eschatological age. Furthermore, as these communities came into contact with and were eventually comprised of others around the diaspora world who may not have held as strong of a connection to the temple as those in Judaea did, their memories of Jesus and the temple reflected this ambivalence and reframed it in ways that instilled group identity. The effect(s) of that group identity varied, as some were oriented toward a vision of the temple as still functioning for a time until its destruction, some viewed it as replaced by the community or an eschatological temple, an important symbol through which to understand the early Church, and some found it entirely secondary to their Christology. In short, early Christians, especially those prior to 70 CE, wrestled with what to make of the temple not only because of the turbulence in their contemporary worlds, but because Jesus also likely held complex, dissonant attitudes like many other Second Temple Jews.

Conclusion

What, then, has memory offered for this study? Like the image of two wrestlers used in chapter 1, memory theory enables us to see the interlocking dynamics of the past and the present, to ask questions of how the past constrains and enables commemoration in the present, and to recognize how the present shapes and reconstructs images of the past. Not only this, but social memory theory emphasizes the role that interpretive frameworks play in the recollection and transmission of memory. "If history is always events appropriated through interpretation," Schröter writes, "then this is especially true for events that radically call previous convictions into question. In order to preserve these in their ambivalence and unwieldiness and to appropriate them productively at the same time, special interpretative efforts are necessary."[24]

Throughout this study I have argued the attitudes toward the temple in the Gospel of Mark, as well as in other early Christian texts, are complex and reflective of the broader attitudes in the Second Temple period. I set my study within the epistemological frameworks of social memory theory, which I investigated in my first chapter. In chapter 1, I argued proponents of social memory theory emphasize memory as an active process of constructing and negotiating the relationship between the past and the present according to social frameworks that shape group identity. I surveyed important memory theorists like Maurice Halbwachs, Jan Assmann, and Barry Schwartz, and I analyzed the way social memory works through concepts like tradition, stability and change, distortion, media, and history. My second chapter looked at the ways in which memory theory has been employed in New Testament studies. In chapter 2, I sketched the introduction of memory theory into New Testament scholarship and particularly historical Jesus scholarship. I surveyed applications of memory theory by looking at the works of Alan Kirk and Tom Thatcher, Barry Schwartz, Anthony Le Donne, Rafael Rodríguez, Chris Keith, and Sandra Huebenthal, and mapped out specific points these applications of social memory theory have to offer the future of New Testament scholarship. In chapter 3, I turned toward examining the social, cultural, historical, political, and theological frameworks underpinning the Jerusalem temple in the Second Temple period. I examined several paradigms of identity and points of unity and diversity across Second Temple Judaism, suggesting Jewish identity was fluid, negotiable, and multifactorial; though it could play an important role, one's relationship to the Jerusalem temple was not *the* deciding factor of Jewish identity. I traced the history of the Second Temple period and examined points of conflict, including alternative temple locations and differing attitudes toward the temple within Second Temple Judaism. With these attitudes in mind, chapter 4 surveyed the Gospel of Mark and other early Christian gospels from the second to the fourth century CE to see how early Christians remembered Jesus's relationship with the temple. I argued the gospels, particularly the Gospel of Mark, display ambiguity and ambivalence in their presentations of the Jerusalem temple. Early Christians wrestled with their memories of Jesus and

---

24. Schröter, *Jesus of Nazareth*, 180.

the temple. On the one hand, they remembered Jesus and his ministry as actively engaged and present in the temple, encouraging ritual washing, and participating in the sacrificial cult through the celebration of the Passover (τὸ πάσχα, Mark 14:12–16). On the other hand, they also commemorated Jesus in frequent conflict with temple authorities and predicting the temple's destruction, signaling an end—or the end—to the temple cult. In addition, memories diverged over Jesus's claim to destroy and rebuild the temple.[25] Some early Christians discounted the saying linking Jesus to the destruction and rebuilding of the temple as patently false. Some reinterpreted or recontextualized the saying to make theological claims about Jesus's body or God's dwelling. Some even embraced the saying as authentic. In each case, early Christians recalled and commemorated Jesus as having a reputation of conflict with the temple. This final chapter offers two potential frameworks for understanding the early Christian actualizations of their individual traditions: the instability of the temple in the Second Temple world and Israel's prophetic tradition. Though these may not be the only possible lenses through which to understand the early Christian attitude to the Jerusalem temple, they account for *why* the temple traditions were characterized and remembered by early Christians in various and dissonant ways. Furthermore, both frameworks are plausible for the life of the historical Jesus, which offers a past constraint on later Christian memory.

Second Temple Jews had a complex, multivalent relationship in commemorating and practicing at the Jerusalem temple. Jews in the first century CE lived in an even more turbulent time under Roman occupation in the aftermath of decades and centuries of significant changes in the economic, political, and religious factors impacting the temple. It is unsurprising, then, that early Christian commemorations of Jesus also displayed the same complex, ambivalent attitudes toward the temple as elsewhere in the Second Temple world. The Jerusalem temple was a significant factor in determining group identity, whether that identity was oriented toward or away from the temple. As the field of biblical studies continues to encounter texts, traditions, and material evidence from the ancient world, perhaps investigations of social, collective, and

25. On the relationship between gospels and the variant memories of Jesus they provide, Rodríguez writes, "In the early communities of Jesus' followers, Jesus tradition was actualized in events that were in some senses constrained by previous performances but in other senses were each autonomous events . . . the written texts themselves appear as actualizations of that tradition rather than reactions to or editions of each other" (Rodríguez, *Structuring Early Christian Memory*, 224).

cultural memory can empower scholars to recognize ambivalence and understand dissonance in constructive ways that remember the limits of historical inquiry and difficulty of meaning-making.

Jesus's relationship to the temple, at all levels, exists within a Jewish context of a Jewish man's understanding of a Jewish concept. Jewish identity was multiform in the Second Temple period, and the multivalent attitudes toward the temple do not constitute what makes one Jewish; we must keep in mind that the remembrances of Jesus's attitudes toward the temple come from intra-Jewish theological debates and reflect the same attitudes found within the Second Temple period. Perceptions and memories of Jesus critiquing Jewish practices should not be weaponized by removing him from his context, and those interested in the supposed conflict between Jesus (and early Christians) and the temple—whatever that conflict may have been—should keep in mind the variant attitudes in broader Second Temple Judaism and the epistemological and methodological gains that memory studies can offer to New Testament criticism.

Bibliography

Alstola, Tero. *Judeans in Babylonia: A Study of Deportees in the Sixth and Fifth Centuries BCE*. CHANE 109. Leiden: Brill, 2020.
Asad, Talal. *Formations of the Secular: Christianity, Islam, Modernity*. Stanford: Stanford University Press, 2003.
Assmann, Aleida. *Cultural Memory and Western Civilization*. New York: Cambridge University Press, 2011.
Assmann, Jan. "Collective Memory and Cultural Identity." Translated by John Czaplicka. *New German Critique* 65 (1995) 125–33.
———. *Cultural Memory and Early Civilization: Writing, Remembrance, and Political Imagination*. Cambridge: Cambridge University Press, 2011.
———. *Moses the Egyptian: The Memory of Egypt in Western Monotheism*. Cambridge: Harvard University Press, 1998.
———. *Religion and Cultural Memory: Ten Studies*. Translated by Rodney Livingston. Stanford: Stanford University Press, 2006.
Bagnall, Roger S., and Peter Derow, eds. *The Hellenistic Period: Sources in Translation*. Malden, MA: Blackwell, 2004.
Baird, William. *History of New Testament Research*. 3 vols. Minneapolis: Fortress, 1992, 2003, 2013.
Barash, Jeffrey. *Collective Memory and the Historical Past*. Chicago: University of Chicago Press, 2017.
Barber, Michael Patrick. *The Historical Jesus and the Temple: Memory, Methodology, and the Gospel of Matthew*. Cambridge: Cambridge University Press, 2023.
Barclay, John M. G. *Jews in the Mediterranean Diaspora: From Alexander to Trajan (323 BCE–117 CE)*. Berkeley: University of California Press, 1996.
Baron, Lori, et al., eds. *The Ways That Often Parted: Essays in Honor of Joel Marcus*. ECL 24. Atlanta: Society of Biblical Literature, 2018.
Barrett, C. K. *Acts*. 2 vols. ICC. Edinburgh: T. & T. Clark, 1994–1998.
Bauckham, Richard. *Jesus and the Eyewitnesses*. Grand Rapids: Eerdmans, 2006.
Beard, Charles A. Review of *Alexander Hamilton, An Essay on the American Union*. *American Bar Association Journal* 12 (1926) 852–53.
Beard, Mary. *Literacy in the Roman World*. JRASup 3. Ann Arbor: Journal of Roman Archaeology, 1991.
Bergson, Henri. *Matter and Memory*. New York: Zone, 1988.

Bloch, Marc. *The Historian's Craft*. Translated by Peter Putnam. New York: Vintage, 1953.

Bohak, Gideon. "CPJ III, 520: The Egyptian Reaction to Onias' Temple." *JSJ* 26 (1995) 32–41.

———. *Joseph and Aseneth and the Jewish Temple in Heliopolis*. ECL 10. Atlanta: Scholars, 1996.

Bond, Helen. "Dating the Death of Jesus: Memory and the Religious Imagination." *NTS* 59 (2013) 461–75.

———. *The Historical Jesus: A Guide for the Perplexed*. Guides for the Perplexed. London: T. & T. Clark, 2012.

Botha, Pieter J. J. "Greco-Roman Literacy as Setting for New Testament Writings." *Neot* 26 (1992) 195–215.

Bovon, François. *A Commentary on the Gospel of Luke*. 3 vols. Translated by Christine M. Thomas, Donald S. Deer, and James Crouch. Hermeneia. Minneapolis: Fortress, 2002, 2012, 2013.

———. "Fragment Oxyrhynchus 840, Fragment of a Lost Gospel, Witness of an Early Christian Controversy over Purity." *JBL* 119 (2000) 705–28.

Boyer, Pascal, and James V. Wertsch, eds. *Memory in Mind and Culture*. Cambridge: Cambridge University Press, 2009.

Brainerd, C. J., and V. F. Reyna. *The Science of False Memory*. Oxford Psychology Series 38. Oxford: Oxford University Press, 2005.

Brooke, George J. "4Q500 1 and the Use of Scripture in the Parable of the Vineyard." *DSD* 2 (1995) 268–94.

Brown, Raymond E. "The *Gospel of Peter* and Canonical Gospel Priority." *NTS* 33 (1987) 321–43.

Brown, Sherri, and Christopher W. Skinner, eds. *Johannine Ethics: The Moral World of the Gospel and Epistles of John*. Minneapolis: Fortress, 2017.

Buchinger, Harald, and Elisabeth Hernitscheck. "P. Oxy. 840 and the Rites of Christian Initiation: Dating a Piece of Alleged Anti-sacramentalistic Polemics." *EC* 5 (2014) 117–24.

Bultmann, Rudolf. *The History of the Synoptic Tradition*. Translated by John Marsh. Rev. ed. 1968. Reprint, Peabody, MA: Hendrickson, 1994.

Burkert, Walter. *The Orientalizing Revolution: Near Eastern Influence on Greek Culture in the Early Archaic Age*. Translated by Margaret Pinder and Walter Burkert. Revealing Antiquity 5. Cambridge: Harvard University Press, 1992.

Byrskog, Samuel. "A New Perspective on the Jesus Tradition: Reflections on James D. G. Dunn's *Jesus Remembered*." *JSNT* 26 (2004) 459–71.

Cancik, Hubert, ed. *Markus-Philologie: Historische, literargeschichtliche und stilistische Untersuchungen zum zweiten Evangelium*. WUNT 33. Tübingen: Mohr Siebeck, 1984.

Charles, R. H. *The Book of Jubilees: Or the Little Genesis*. 1902. Ancient Texts and Translations. Reprint, Eugene, OR: Wipf & Stock, 2001.

Chernow, Ron. *Alexander Hamilton*. New York: Penguin, 2004.

Cohen, Shaye J. D. *From the Maccabees to the Mishnah*. 3rd ed. Louisville: Westminster John Knox, 2014.

Cohen, Shaye J. D., and Joshua J. Schwartz, eds. *Studies in Josephus and the Varieties of Ancient Judaism: Louis H. Feldman Jubilee Volume*. Ancient Judaism and Early Christianity 67. Leiden: Brill, 2007.

Collins, Adela Yarbro, ed. *Early Christian Apocalypticism: Genre and Social Setting*. Semeia 36. Atlanta: Society of Biblical Literature, 1986.

———. *Mark: A Commentary*. Hermeneia. Minneapolis: Fortress, 2007.

———. "The Second Temple and the Arts of Resistance." In *From Judaism to Christianity: Tradition and Transition. A Festschrift for Thomas H. Tobin, SJ, on the Occasion of His Sixty-Fifth Birthday*, edited by Patricia Walters, 115–29. Novum Testamentum Supplements 136. Leiden: Brill, 2010.

Collins, Adela Yarbro, and Margaret M. Mitchell, eds. *Antiquity and Humanity: Essays on Ancient Religion and Philosophy, Presented to Hans Dieter Betz on His 70th Birthday*. Tübingen: Mohr Siebeck, 2001.

Collins, John J., ed. *Apocalypse: The Morphology of a Genre*. Semeia 14. Atlanta: Society of Biblical Literature, 1979.

———. *Between Athens and Jerusalem: Jewish Identity in the Hellenistic Diaspora*. 2nd ed. Grand Rapids: Eerdmans, 2000.

———. "The Genre Apocalypse Reconsidered." *ZAC* 20 (2016) 21–40.

———. *The Invention of Judaism: Torah and Jewish Identity from Deuteronomy to Paul*. Oakland: University of California Press, 2017.

———. "What Is Hellenistic Judaism?" *JSJ* 53 (2022) 567–76.

Connerton, Paul. *How Societies Remember*. Themes in the Social Sciences. Cambridge: Cambridge University Press, 1989.

Cotton, Hannah. "A Cancelled Marriage Contract from the Judaean Desert." *JRS* 84 (1994) 64–86.

Cotton, Hannah M., et al., eds. *Jerusalem*. Vol. 1 of *Corpus Inscriptionum Iudaeae/Palaestinae: A Multi-lingual Corpus of the Inscriptions from Alexander to Muhammad*. Berlin: de Gruyter, 2010.

Crook, Zeba. "Collective Memory Distortion and the Quest for the Historical Jesus." *JSHJ* 11 (2013) 53–76.

———. "Gratitude and Comments to Le Donne." *JSHJ* 11 (2013) 98–105.

———. "Memory and the Historical Jesus." *BTB* 42 (2012) 196–203.

Crossan, John Dominic. *The Birth of Christianity: Discovering What Happened in the Years Immediately after the Execution of Jesus*. San Francisco: HarperSanFrancisco, 1998.

———. "The Gospel of Peter and the Canonical Gospels: Independence, Dependence, or Both?" *Forum* 1 (1998) 7–51.

———. *The Historical Jesus: The Life of a Mediterranean Jewish Peasant*. San Francisco: HarperSanFrancisco, 1991.

Crossley, James. *The Date of Mark's Gospel: Insight from the Law in Earliest Christianity*. JSNTSup 266. London: T. & T. Clark, 2004.

———. "An Immodest Proposal for Biblical Studies." *Relegere* 2 (2012) 153–77.

Dahl, Nils Alstrup. *Jesus in the Memory of the Early Church*. Minneapolis: Augsburg, 1976.

Daube, David. "Responsibilities of Master and Disciples in the Gospels." *NTS* 19 (1972) 1–15.

Daviau, P. M. Michèle, et al., eds. *The World of the Aramaeans III: Studies in Language and Literature in Honour of Paul-Eugène Dion*. JSOTSup 326. Sheffield: Sheffield Academic, 2001.

Davies, W. D., and Dale C. Allison. *A Critical and Exegetical Commentary on the Gospel According to Matthew*. 3 vols. ICC. Edinburgh: T. & T. Clark, 1988–1997.

Decker, Rodney. *Mark 1–8: A Handbook on the Greek Text.* BHGNT. Waco, TX: Baylor University Press, 2014.

———. *Mark 9–16: A Handbook on the Greek Text.* BHGNT. Waco, TX: Baylor University Press, 2014.

DeConick, April D. *The Original Gospel of Thomas in Translation: With a Commentary and New English Translation of the Complete Gospel.* LNTS 287. London: T. & T. Clark, 2006.

———. "The True Mysteries: Sacramentalism in the 'Gospel of Philip.'" *VC* 55 (2001) 225–61.

Delgado Gómez, Alfredo. "Mark's σπεκουλάτωρ and the Origin of His Gospel." *JSNT* 46 (2023) 79–107.

Downing, F. Gerald. *Doing Things with Words in the First Christian Century.* JSNTSup 200. Sheffield: Sheffield Academic, 2000.

———. "Feasible Researches in Historical Jesus Tradition: A Critical Response to Chris Keith." *JSNT* 40 (2017) 51–61.

Dubischar-Krivec, Anna M., et al. "Calendar Calculating in Savants with Autism and Healthy Calendar Calculators." *Psychological Medicine* (2008) 1355–63.

Dunn, James D. G. *Jesus Remembered.* Christianity in the Making 1. Grand Rapids: Eerdmans, 2003.

Duran, Nicole Wilkinson. "'Not One Stone Will Be Left on Another.' The Destruction of the Temple and the Crucifixion in Mark's Gospel." In *Sacrifice, Cult, and Atonement in Early Judaism and Christianity: Constituents and Critique*, edited by Henrietta L. Wiley and Christian A. Eberhart, 311–26. RBS 85. Atlanta: Society of Biblical Literature, 2017.

Dušek, Jan. *Aramaic and Hebrew Inscriptions from Mt. Gerizim and Samaria Between Antiochus III and Antiochus IV Epiphanes.* CHANE 54. Leiden: Brill, 2012.

Edwards, James R. "Markan Sandwiches the Significance of Interpolations in Markan Narratives." *NovT* 31 (1989) 193–216.

Erll, Astrid. *Memory in Culture.* Translated by Sara B. Young. Palgrave Macmillan Memory Studies. New York: Palgrave Macmillan, 2011.

Evans, Craig A., and H. Daniel Zacharias, eds. *Jewish and Christian Scripture as Artifact and Canon.* SSEJC 70. London: T. & T. Clark, 2009.

Eve, Eric. *Behind the Gospels: Understanding the Oral Tradition.* Minneapolis: Fortress, 2013.

Fentress, James, and Chris Wickham. *Social Memory.* New Perspectives on the Past. Oxford: Blackwell, 1992.

Fortna, Robert T., and Tom Thatcher, eds. *Jesus in Johannine Tradition.* Louisville: Westminster Knox, 2001.

Foster, Paul. "The Gospel of Peter: Directions and Issues in Contemporary Research." *CurBR* 9 (2011) 310–38.

———. "Memory, Orality, and the Fourth Gospel: Three Dead-Ends in Historical Jesus Research." *JSHJ* 10 (2012) 191–227.

France, R. T. *The Gospel of Mark: A Commentary on the Greek Text.* NIGTC. Grand Rapids: Eerdmans, 2002.

France, R. T., and David Wenham, eds. *Gospel Perspectives: Studies of History and Tradition in the Four Gospels.* Vol. 1. Sheffield: JSOT, 1980.

Fredriksen, Paula, and Adele Reinhartz, eds. *Jesus, Judaism, and Christian Anti-Judaism: Reading the New Testament After the Holocaust.* Louisville: Westminster John Knox, 2002.

Friedman, Richard Elliot. *Who Wrote the Bible?* New York: HarperOne, 1987.

Freud, Sigmund. *Psychopathology of Everyday Life.* Translated by A. A. Brill. New York: Macmillan, 1914.

Funk, Robert W., et al. *The Five Gospels: The Search for the Authentic Words of Jesus.* New York: Macmillan, 1993.

Gaston, Lloyd. *No Stone on Another: Studies in the Significance of the Fall of Jerusalem in the Synoptic Gospels.* Novum Testamentum Supplements 23. Leiden: Brill, 1970.

Gathercole, Simon. *The Composition of the Gospel of Thomas: Original Language and Influences.* SNTSMS 151. Cambridge: Cambridge University Press, 2012.

———. *The Gospel of Judas: Rewriting Early Christianity.* Oxford: Oxford University Press, 2007.

———. *The Gospel of Thomas: Introduction and Commentary.* TENTS 11. Leiden: Brill, 2014.

Gedi, Noa, and Yigal Elam. "Collective Memory—What Is It?" *History and Memory* 8 (1996) 30–50.

Geertz, Clifford. *The Interpretation of Cultures.* New York: Basic, 1973.

Gerhardsson, Birger. *Memory and Manuscript.* Grand Rapids: Eerdmans, 1998.

Gilbey, Ryan. "Toy Story 3: How Pixar Changed Animation." *Guardian*, June 30, 2010. https://www.theguardian.com/film/2010/jun/30/toy-story-3-pixar-animation.

Goodacre, Mark. *Thomas and the Gospels: The Case for Thomas's Familiarity with the Synoptics.* Grand Rapids: Eerdmans, 2012.

Goodchild, R. G. "Boreum of Cyrenaica." *JRS* 41 (1951) 11–16.

Goodman, Martin. "Identity and Authority in Ancient Judaism." *Judaism* 39 (1990) 192–201.

———. *Judaism in the Roman World: Collected Essays.* Ancient Judaism and Early Christianity 66. Leiden: Brill, 2007.

———. "Nerva, the *Fiscus Judaicus* and Jewish Identity." *JRS* 79 (1989) 40–44.

Grabbe, Lester L. *A History of the Jews and Judaism in the Second Temple Period.* 4 vols. London: T. & T. Clark, 2006–2021.

Gray, Timothy C. *The Temple in the Gospel of Mark: A Study in Its Narrative Role.* Grand Rapids: Baker Academic, 2010.

Grenfell, Bernard P., and Arthur S. Hunt. *Fragment of an Uncanonical Gospel from Oxyrhynchus.* Published for the Egypt Exploration Fund by Henry Frowde. London: Oxford University Press, 1908.

———. *The Oxyrhynchus Papyri.* Vol. 5. London: Egypt Exploration Society with the Support of the Arts and Humanities Research Council and the British Academy, 1908.

Green, Joel B. *The Theology of the Gospel of Luke.* New Testament Theology. Cambridge: Cambridge University Press, 1995.

Gregory, Andrew F., and C. Kavin Rowe, eds. *Rethinking the Unity and Reception of Luke and Acts.* Columbia: University of South Carolina Press, 2010.

Gruen, Erich S. *Constructs of Identity in Hellenistic Judaism: Essays on Early Jewish Literature and History.* DCLS 29. Berlin: de Gruyter, 2016.

Gunkel, Hermann. *Creation and Chaos in the Primeval Era and the Eschaton: A Religio-historical Study of Genesis 1 and Revelation 12*. Translated by K. William Whitney Jr. Biblical Resources Series. Grand Rapids: Eerdmans, 2006.

———. *Schöpfung und Chaos in Urzeit und Endzeit: Eine Religionsgeschichtliche Untersuchung über Gen 1 und Ap Joh 12*. Göttingen: Vandenhoeck & Ruprecht, 1895.

Halbwachs, Maurice. *The Collective Memory*. Translated by Francis J. Ditter Jr. and Vida Yazdi Ditter. New York: HarperColophon, 1980.

———. *On Collective Memory*. Edited and translated by Lewis A. Coser. Heritage of Sociology. Chicago: University of Chicago Press, 1992.

Halpern, Baruch. "The Centralization Formula in Deuteronomy." *VT* 31 (1981) 20–38.

———. *From Gods to God: The Dynamics of Iron Age Cosmologies*. Edited by M. J. Adams. Forschungen zum Alten Testament 63. Tübingen: Mohr Siebeck, 2009.

Harris, William V. *Ancient Literacy*. Cambridge: Harvard University Press, 1989.

Hatina, Thomas R., ed. *The Gospel of John*. Vol. 4 of *Biblical Interpretation in Early Christian Gospels*. LNTS. London: T. & T. Clark, 2020.

Hayes, John H., and J. Maxwell Miller, eds. *Israelite and Judaean History*. London: SCM, 1977.

Heard, Richard. "The ΑΠΟΜΝΗΜΟΝΕΥΜΑ in Papias, Justin, and Irenaeus." *NTS* 1 (1954) 122–27.

Hemingway, Ernest. "The Art of the Short Story." *The Paris Review* 79 (1981) 85–102.

Hempel, Charlotte, and Judith Lieu, eds. *Biblical Traditions in Transmission: Essays in Honor of Michael A. Knibb*. JSJSup 111. Leiden: Brill, 2006.

Hengel, Martin. *Judaism and Hellenism*. Translated by John Bowden. 2 vols. 1974. Reprint, Eugene, OR: Wip & Stock, 2003.

———. *The "Hellenization" of Judaea in the First Century after Christ*. Translated by John Bowden. 1989. Reprint, Eugene, OR: Wip & Stock, 2003.

Heth, Raleigh C. "The Stripping of the Bulls: A Reexamination of the Role of Ahaz in Deuteronomistic Historiography." *VT* 73 (2023) 583–606.

Heth, Raleigh, and T. E. Kelley. "Isaac and Iphigenia: Portrayals of Child Sacrifice in Israelite and Greek Literature." *Bib* 102 (2021) 481–502.

Hezser, Catherine. *Jewish Literacy in Roman Palestine*. TSAJ 81. Tübingen: Mohr Siebeck, 2001.

Hjelm, Ingrid. "Cult Centralization as a Device of Control." *SJOT* 13 (1999) 302.

Hobsbawm, Eric. "The Social Function of the Past: Some Questions." *Past & Present* 55 (1972) 3–17.

Hobsbawm, Eric, and Terence Ranger, eds. *The Invention of Tradition*. Past and Present Publications. Cambridge: Cambridge University Press, 1983.

Hoerl, Christoph. "Episodic Memory, Autobiographical Memory, Narrative: On Three Key Notions in Current Approaches to Memory Development." *Philosophical Psychology* 20 (2007) 621–40.

Hooker, Morna. "On Using the Wrong Tool." *Theology* 75 (1972) 570–81.

———. "Traditions About the Temple in the Sayings of Jesus." *BJRL* 70 (1988) 7–19.

Horbury, William, and David Noy. *Jewish Inscriptions of Graeco-Roman Egypt*. Cambridge: Cambridge University Press, 1992.

Horsley, Richard A., et al., eds. *Performing the Gospel: Orality, Memory, and Mark*. Minneapolis: Fortress, 2006.

Huebenthal, Sandra. *Reading Mark's Gospel as a Text from Collective Memory*. Grand Rapids: Eerdmans, 2020.

———. "Social and Cultural Memory in Biblical Exegesis: The Quest for an Adequate Application." In *Cultural Memory in Biblical Exegesis*, edited by Pernille Carstens et al., 177–99. Piscataway: Gorgias, 2012.
Hurtado, Larry. "Interactive Diversity: A Proposed Model of Christian Origins." *JTS* 64 (2013) 445–62.
Hutton, Patrick H. *History as an Art of Memory*. Hanover, NH: University Press of New England, 1993.
Johnson, Luke Timothy. *The Gospel of Luke*. Sacra Pagina 3. Collegeville, MN: Liturgical, 1991.
Joseph, Simon J. *Jesus and the Temple: The Crucifixion in Its Jewish Context*. SNTSMS 165. Cambridge: Cambridge University Press, 2016.
Juel, Donald. *Messiah and Temple: The Trial of Jesus in the Gospel of Mark*. SBLDS 31. Missoula: Scholars, 1977.
Kähler, Martin. *The So-Called Historical Jesus and the Historic Biblical Christ*. Edited and translated by Carl E. Braaten. Seminar Editions. Philadelphia: Fortress, 1964.
Keith, Chris. *Jesus' Literacy: Scribal Culture and the Teacher from Galilee*. LHJS 8. LNTS 413. London: Bloomsbury, 2011.
———. "Memory and Authenticity: Jesus Tradition and What Really Happened." *ZNW* 102 (2011) 155–77.
———. "The Narratives of the Gospels and the Historical Jesus: Current Debates, Prior Debates and the Goal of Historical Jesus Research." *JSNT* 38 (2016) 426–55.
———. *The Pericope Adulterae, the Gospel of John, and the Literacy of Jesus*. New Testament Tools, Studies and Documents 38. Leiden: Brill, 2009.
———. "Social Memory Theory and Gospels Research: The First Decade (Part One)" *EC* 6 (2015) 354–76.
———. "Social Memory Theory and Gospels Research: The First Decade (Part Two)" *EC* 6 (2015) 517–42.
———. "Yes and No: A Critical Response to F. Gerald Downing." *JSNT* 40 (2017) 62–72.
Keith, Chris, and Anthony Le Donne, eds. *Jesus, Criteria, and the Demise of Authenticity*. London: T. & T. Clark, 2012.
Kelber, Werner. "The Case of the Gospels: Memory's Desire and the Limits of Historical Criticism." *Oral Tradition* 17 (2002) 55–86.
———. "The Generative Force of Memory: Early Christian Traditions as Processes of Memory." *BTB* 36 (2006) 15–22.
———. *Imprints, Voiceprints, & Footprints of Memory: Collected Essays of Werner Kelber*. RBS 74. Atlanta: Society of Biblical Literature, 2013.
———. "Language, Memory, and Sense Perception in the Religious and Technological Culture of Antiquity and the Middle Ages." *Oral Tradition* 10 (1995) 409–50.
———. *The Oral and the Written Gospel: The Hermeneutics of Speaking and Writing in the Synoptic Tradition, Mark, Paul, and Q*. Philadelphia: Fortress, 1983.
———. "Oral Tradition in Bible and New Testament Studies." *Oral Tradition* 18 (2003) 40–42.
King, Karen L. "The Place of the *Gospel of Philip* in the Context of Early Christian Claims about Jesus' Marital Status." *NTS* 59 (2013) 565–87.
Kirk, Alan. "Ehrman, Bauckham and Bird on Memory and the Jesus Tradition." *JSHJ* 15 (2017) 88–114.

———. "Examining Priorities: Another Look at The *Gospel of Peter*'s Relationship to the New Testament." *NTS* 40 (1994) 572–95.

———. *Memory and the Jesus Tradition. The Reception of Jesus in the First Three Centuries 2*. London: Bloomsbury T. & T. Clark, 2018.

———. *Q in Matthew: Ancient Media, Memory, and Early Scribal Transmission of the Jesus Tradition*. London: Bloomsbury T. & T. Clark, 2016.

Kirk, Alan, and Tom Thatcher, eds. *Memory, Tradition, and Text: Uses of the Past in Early Christianity*. SemeiaSt 52. Atlanta: Society of Biblical Literature, 2005.

Kloppenborg, John. "*Evocatio Deorum* and the Date of Mark." *JBL* 124 (2005) 419–50.

Knoppers, Gary. *Jews and Samaritans: The Origins and History of Their Early Relations*. New York: Oxford University Press, 2013.

———. "Mt. Gerizim and Mt. Zion: A Study in the Early History of the Samaritans and Jews." *SR* 34 (2005) 309–37.

Kosmin, Paul J. *The Land of the Elephant Kinds: Space, Territory, and Ideology in the Seleucid Empire*. Cambridge: Harvard University Press, 2014.

———. *Time and Its Adversaries in the Seleucid Empire*. Cambridge: Belknap, 2020.

Koskenniemi, Erkki. *Greek Writers and Philosophers in Philo and Josephus: A Study of Their Secular Education and Educational Ideals*. Studies in Philo of Alexandria 9. Leiden: Brill, 2019.

Lapp, Nancy L., ed. *The Excavations at Araq el-Emir*. Vol. 1. AASOR 47. Winona Lake, IN: Eisenbrauns, 1983.

Larsen, Matthew D. C. *Gospels Before the Book*. New York: Oxford University Press, 2018.

Layton, Bentley, ed. *Nag Hammadi Codex II,2–7 Together with XIII,2*, Brit. Lib. Or. 4926(1), and P. Oxy. 1, 654, 655*. 2 vols. Nag Hammadi Studies 20–21. Leiden: Brill, 1989.

Le Donne, Anthony. *The Historical Jesus: What Can We Know and How Can We Know It?* Grand Rapids: Eerdmans, 2011.

———. *The Historiographical Jesus: Memory, Typology, and the Son of David*. Grand Rapids: Eerdmans, 2009.

———. "The Improper Temple Offering of Ananias and Sapphira." *NTS* 59 (2013) 346–64.

———. "The Problem of Selectivity in Memory Research: A Response to Zeba Crook." *JSHJ* 11 (2013) 77–97.

Le Donne, Anthony, and Tom Thatcher, eds. *The Fourth Gospel in First-Century Media Culture*. New York: T. & T. Clark, 2011.

Le Goff, Jacques. *History and Memory*. Translated by Steven Rendall and Elizabeth Claman. New York: Columbia University Press, 1992.

Lieu, Judith. *Christian Identity in the Jewish and Graeco-Roman World*. Oxford: Oxford University Press, 2004.

———. "Temple and Synagogue in John." *NTS* 45 (1999) 51–69.

Lincoln, Andrew T. *Truth on Trial: The Lawsuit Motif in the Fourth Gospel*. Peabody, MA: Hendrickson, 2000.

Lipschits, Oded, et al., eds. *Judah and the Judeans in the Fourth Century BCE*. Winona Lake, IN: Eisenbrauns, 2007.

Luz, Ulrich. *Matthew 1–7: A Commentary*. Translated by James E. Crouch. Hermeneia. Minneapolis: Fortress, 2007.

———. *Matthew 8-20: A Commentary.* Translated by James E. Crouch. Hermeneia. Minneapolis: Fortress, 2001.

———. *Matthew 21-28: A Commentary.* Translated by James E. Crouch. Hermeneia. Minneapolis: Fortress, 2005.

Malbon, Elizabeth Struthers. "The Jewish Leaders in the Gospel of Mark: A Literary Study of Marcan Characterization." *JBL* 108 (1989) 259–81.

———. *Mark's Jesus: Characterization as Narrative Christology.* Waco, TX: Baylor University Press, 2009.

Malkki, Liisa. *Purity and Exile: Violence, Memory, and National Cosmology among Hutu Refugees in Tanzania.* Chicago: University of Chicago Press, 1995.

Marcus, Joel. "The Gospel of Peter as a Jewish Christian Document." *NTS* 64 (2018) 473–94.

———. "The Jewish War and the *Sitz im Leben* of Mark." *JBL* 111 (1992) 441–62.

———. *Mark 1-8.* AB 27. New Haven: Yale University Press, 2000.

———. *Mark 8-16.* AB 27A. New Haven: Yale University Press, 2009.

Meier, John Paul. "Is Luke's Version of the Parable of the Rich Fool Reflected in the Coptic Gospel of Thomas?" *CBQ* 74 (2012) 528–47.

———. *A Marginal Jew: Rethinking the Historical Jesus.* Vol. 1. New York: Doubleday, 1991.

———. "The Parable of the Wheat and the Weeds (Matthew 13:24–30) Is Thomas's version (Logion 57) Independent?" *JBL* 131 (2012) 715–32.

Miller, David M. "Ethnicity Comes of Age: An Overview of Twentieth-Century Terms for *Ioudaios*." *CurBR* 10 (2012) 293–311.

———. "Ethnicity, Religion and the Meaning of *Ioudaios* in Ancient 'Judaism.'" *CurBR* 12 (2014) 216–65.

———. "The Meaning of *Ioudaios* and its Relationship to Other Group Labels in Ancient 'Judaism.'" *CurBR* 9 (2010) 98–126.

Mimouni, Simon C., and Louis Painchaud, eds. *La Question De La Sacerdotalisation Dans Le Judaïsme Synagogal, Le Christianisme et Le Rabbinisme: Colloque International Université Labal, Québec, Canada 18 au 20 Septembre 2014.* Turnhout: Brepols, 2018.

Moloney, Francis J. *The Gospel of John.* Sacra Pagina 4. Collegeville, MN: Liturgical, 1998.

———. *The Gospel of Mark: A Commentary.* Grand Rapids: Baker Academic, 2002.

Montefiore, Hugh. "Jesus and the Temple Tax." *NTS* 11 (1964) 60–71.

Moore, Stewart. *Jewish Ethnic Identity and Relations in Hellenistic Egypt: With Walls of Iron?* JSJSup 171. Leiden: Brill, 2015.

Mor, Menahem. *The Second Jewish Revolt: The Bar Kokhba War, 132-136 CE.* BRLA 50. Leiden: Brill, 2016.

Morgan, Teresa. *Literate Education in the Hellenistic and Roman Worlds.* Cambridge Classical Studies. Cambridge: Cambridge University Press, 1998.

Morrison, Gregg S. *The Turning Point in the Gospel of Mark: A Study in Markan Christology.* Cambridge: James Clarke, 2015.

Nagy, Rebecca Martin, et al., eds. *Sepphoris in Galilee: Crosscurrents of Culture.* Winona Lake, IN: Eisenbrauns, North Carolina Museum of Art, 1996.

Najman, Hindy. *Losing the Temple and Recovering the Future: An Analysis of 4 Ezra.* Cambridge: Cambridge University Press, 2014.

Neumann, Nicola, et al. "The Mind of the Mnemonists: An MEG and Neuropsychological Study of Autistic Memory Savants." *Behavioural Brain Research* 215 (2010) 114–21.

Neusner, Jacob. "Judaism in a Time of Crisis: Four Responses to the Destruction of the Second Temple." *Judaism* 21 (1972) 313–27.

Nora, Pierre. *Realms of Memory: Rethinking the French Past*. Edited by Lawrence D. Kritzman. Translated by Arthur Goldhammer. 3 vols. New York: Columbia University Press, 1996.

Olick, Jeffrey. "Collective Memory: The Two Cultures." *Sociological Theory* 17 (1999) 333–48.

———. "Products, Processes, and Practices: A Non-Reificatory Approach to Collective Memory." *BTB* 36 (2006) 5–14.

O'Toole, Robert F. *The Unity of Luke's Theology: An Analysis of Luke–Acts*. Wilmington, DE: Glazier, 1984.

Parsons, Mikeal C., and Richard I. Pervo. *Rethinking the Unity of Luke and Acts*. Minneapolis: Fortress, 2007.

Patterson, Stephen J. "Apocalypticism or Prophecy and the Problem of Polyvalence: Lessons from the *Gospel of Thomas*." *JBL* 130 (2011) 795–817.

———. *The Gospel of Thomas and Jesus*. Foundations & Facets Reference Series. Sonoma, CA: Polebridge, 1993.

Perrin, Andrew B., et al., eds. *Four Kingdom Motifs Before and Beyond the Book of Daniel*. TBN 28. Leiden: Brill, 2021.

Perrin, Nicholas. *Jesus the Temple*. Grand Rapids: Baker Academic, 2010.

Plisch, Uwe-Karsten. *The Gospel of Thomas: Original Text with Commentary*. Translated by Gesine Schenke Robinson. Stuttgart: Deustche Bibelgesellschaft, 2008.

Porten, Bezalel, and Ada Yardeni. *Textbook of Aramaic Documents from Ancient Egypt: 1. Letters*. Winona Lake, IN: Eisenbraun's, 1986.

Porter, Stanley E., ed. *Paul's World*. Pauline Studies 4. Leiden: Brill, 2008.

Porter, Stanley E., and Hughston T. Ong. "Memory, Orality, and the Fourth Gospel: A Response to Paul Foster with Further Comments for Future Discussion." *JSHJ* 12 (2014) 143–64.

Redman, Judith C. S. "How Accurate Are Eyewitnesses? Bauckham and the Eyewitnesses in the Light of Psychological Research." *JBL* 129 (2010) 177–97.

Reimarus, Hermann Samuel. *Apologie oder Schutzschrift für die vernünftigen Verehrer Gottes*. Edited by Günter Gawlick. 2 vols. Veröffentlichung der Joachim Jungius-Gesellschaft der Wissenschaften Hamburg 79. Göttingen: Vandenhoeck & Ruprecht, 1972.

Reinhartz, Adele. *Cast Out of the Covenant: Jews and Anti-Judaism in the Gospel of John*. Lanham, MD: Lexington, 2018.

Rémondon, Roger. "Les Antisémites de Memphis (P. IFAO inv. 104 = CPJ 141)." *Chronique d'Égypte* 35 (1960) 244–61.

Rhoads, David, et al. *Mark as Story: An Introduction to the Narrative of a Gospel*. 2nd ed. Minneapolis: Fortress, 1999.

Riley, Gregory J. *Resurrection Reconsidered: Thomas and John in Controversy*. Minneapolis: Fortress, 1995.

Rodríguez, Rafael. *Structuring Early Christian Memory: Jesus in Tradition, Performance, and Text*. LNTS 407. London: T. & T. Clark, 2010.

———. "Text as Tradition—Tradition as Text: Early Christian Memory and Jesus' Threat Against the Temple." *STK* 99 (2023) 115–33.

———. "What Is History? Reading John 1 as Historical Representation." *JSHJ* 16 (2018) 31–51.
Romano, Renee Christine, and Claire Bond Potter, eds. *Historians on Hamilton: How a Blockbuster Musical Is Restaging America's Past*. New Brunswick, NJ: Rutgers University Press, 2018.
Sanders, E. P. *Judaism: Practice and Belief 63 BCE–66 CE*. 1992. Reprint, Minneapolis: Fortress, 2016.
———. *Paul and Palestinian Judaism*. 1977. Reprint, Minneapolis: Fortress, 2017.
Saussure, Ferdinand de. *Course in General Linguistics*. Edited by Charles Bally and Albert Sechehaye. Translated by Wade Baskin. New York: McGraw-Hill, 1959.
Schacter, Daniel L., ed. *Memory Distortion: How Minds, Brains, and Societies Reconstruct the Past*. Cambridge: Harvard University Press, 1995.
———. *The Seven Sins of Memory: How the Mind Forgets and Remembers*. Boston: Houghton Mifflin, 2001.
Schacter, Daniel L., et al. "Memory Distortion: An Adaptive Perspective." *Trends in Cognitive Science* 15 (2011) 467–74.
Schenke, Hans-Martin. "Bemerkungen zu #71 des Thomas-Evangeliums." *Enchoria: Zeitschrift für Demostistik und Koptologie* 27 (2001) 120–26.
Schröter, Jens. *Erinnerung an Jesu Worte: Studien zur Rezeption der Logienüberlieferung in Markus, Q, und Thomas*. WMANT 76. Neukirchen-Vluyn: Neukirchener, 1997.
Schröter, Jens. "The Contribution of Non-Canonical Gospels to the Memory of Jesus: The Gospel of Thomas and the Gospel of Peter as Test Cases." *NTS* 64 (2018) 435–54.
———. *From Jesus to the New Testament*. Translated by Wayne Coppins. Waco, TX: Baylor University Press, 2013.
———. "The Historical Jesus and the Sayings Tradition: Comments on Current Research." *Neot* 30 (1996) 151–68.
———. *Jesus of Nazareth: Jew from Galilee, Savior of the World*. Translated by Wayne Coppins and S. Brian Pounds. Waco, TX: Baylor University Press, 2014.
Schwartz, Barry. *Abraham Lincoln and the Forge of National Memory*. Chicago: University of Chicago Press, 2000.
———. "Social Change and Collective Memory: The Democratization of George Washington." *American Sociological Review* 56 (1991) 221–36.
———. "The Social Context of Commemoration: A Study in Collective Memory." *Social Forces* 61 (1982) 374–402.
Schwartz, Barry, et al. "The Recovery of Masada: A Study in Collective Memory." *Sociological Quarterly* 27 (1986) 147–64.
Schweitzer, Albert. *The Quest of the Historical Jesus: A Critical Study of Its Progress from Reimarus to Wrede*. Translated by W. Montgomery. New York: Macmillan, 1968.
Scopello, Madeleine, ed. *The Gospel of Judas in Context: Proceedings of the First International Conference on the Gospel of Judas, Paris, Sorbonne, October 27th–28th 2006*. Nag Hammadi and Manichaean Studies 62. Leiden: Brill, 2008.
Segal, Peretz. "The Penalty of the Warning Inscription from the Temple of Jerusalem." *IEJ* 39 (1989) 79–84.
Shaner, Katherine A. "The Danger of Singular Saviors: Vulnerability, Political Power, and Jesus's Disturbance in the Temple (Mark 11:15–19)." *JBL* 140 (2021) 139–61.
Shellberg, Pamela. *Cleansed Lepers, Cleansed Hearts: Purity and Healing in Luke-Acts*. Minneapolis: Fortress, 2015.
Shepherd, Tom. "The Narrative Function of Markan Intercalation." *NTS* 41 (1995) 522–40.

Shils, Edward. *Tradition*. Chicago: University of Chicago Press, 1981.
Shinall, Myrick C., Jr. "The Social Condition of Lepers in the Gospels." *JBL* 137 (2018) 915–34.
Sievers, Joseph, and Amy-Jill Levine, eds. *The Pharisees*. Grand Rapids: Eerdmans, 2021.
Skinner, Christopher W. *What Are They Saying About the Gospel of Thomas?* New York: Paulist, 2011.
Skinner, Christopher W., and Matthew Ryan Hauge, eds. *Character Studies and the Gospel of Mark*. LNTS 483. London: Bloomsbury T. & T. Clark, 2014.
Skinner, Christopher W., and Kelly R. Iverson, eds. *Unity and Diversity in the Gospels and Paul: Essays in Honor of Frank J. Matera*. ECL 7. Atlanta: Society of Biblical Literature, 2012.
Southern Poverty Law Center. "Whose Heritage? Public Symbols of the Confederacy." Southern Poverty Law Center, February 1, 2019. https://www.splcenter.org/20190201/whose-heritage-public-symbols-confederacy.
Stern, Ephraim, and Yitzhak Magen. "Archaeological Evidence for the First Stage of the Samaritan Temple on Mount Gerizim." *IEJ* 52 (2002) 49–57.
Stern, Sacha, ed. *Sects and Sectarianism in Jewish History*. IJS Studies in Judaica 12. Leiden: Brill, 2011.
Stewart-Sykes, Alistair. "Bathed in Living Waters: Papyrus Oxyrhynchus 840 and Christian Baptism Reconsidered." *ZNW* 100 (2009) 278–86.
Stökl, Jonathan, and Caroline Waerzeggers, eds. *Exile and Return: The Babylonian Context*. BZAW 478. Berlin: de Gruyter, 2015.
Stuckenbruck, Loren T., et al., eds. *Memory in the Bible and Antiquity*. WUNT 212. Tübingen: Mohr Siebeck, 2007.
Tannehill, Robert C. *The Narrative Unity of Luke-Acts: A Literary Interpretation*. 2 vols. Foundations and Facets. Philadelphia: Fortress, 1986.
Taylor, Joan E. "A Second Temple in Egypt: The Evidence for the Zadokite Temple of Onias." *JSJ* 29 (1998) 297–321.
Taylor, N. H. "Jerusalem and the Temple in Early Christian Life and Teaching." *Neot* 33 (1999) 445–61.
———. "Palestinian Christianity and the Caligula Crisis. Part I. Social and Historical Reconstruction." *JSNT* 61 (1996) 101–24.
———. "Palestinian Christianity and the Caligula Crisis. Part II. The Markan Eschatological Discourse." *JSNT* 61 (1996) 13–40.
———. "Stephen, the Temple, and Early Christian Eschatology." *RB* 110 (2003) 62–85.
Thatcher, Tom, ed. *Memory and Identity in Ancient Judaism and Early Christianity: A Conversation with Barry Schwartz*. Semeia Studies Series 78. Atlanta: Society of Biblical Literature, 2014.
———. *Why John Wrote a Gospel: Jesus—Memory—History*. Louisville: Westminster John Knox, 2006.
Theissen, Gerd. *The Gospels in Context: Social and Political History in the Synoptic Tradition*. Translated by Linda M. Maloney. Minneapolis: Fortress, 1992.
Thiessen, Matthew. *Jesus and the Forces of Death: The Gospels' Portrayal of Ritual Impurity Within First-Century Judaism*. Grand Rapids: Baker Academic, 2020.
Thomas, Rosalind. *Literacy and Orality in Ancient Greece*. Key Themes in Ancient History. Cambridge: Cambridge University Press, 1992.
Thompson, Marianne Meye. *John: A Commentary*. NTL. Louisville: Westminster John Knox, 2015.

Trotter, Jonathan. *The Jerusalem Temple in Diaspora Jewish Practice and Thought During the Second Temple Period*. JSJSup 192. Leiden: Brill, 2019.

Twigg, Matthew. "Esoteric Discourse and the Jerusalem Temple in the *Gospel of Philip*." *Aries—Journal for the Study of Western Esotericism* 15 (2015) 47–80.

Uro, Risto, ed. *Thomas at the Crossroads: Essays on the Gospel of Thomas*. Studies of the New Testament and Its World. Edinburgh: T. & T. Clark, 1998.

VanderKam, James C. *Jubilees 1–21*. Hermeneia. Minneapolis: Fortress, 2018.

Walters, Patricia. *The Assumed Authorial Unity of Luke and Acts: A Reassessment of the Evidence*. SNTSMS 145. Cambridge: Cambridge University Press, 2009.

———, ed. *From Judaism to Christianity: Tradition and Transition. A Festschrift for Thomas H. Tobin, SJ, on the Occasion of His Sixty-Fifth Birthday*. Novum Testamentum Supplements 136. Leiden: Brill, 2010.

Wardle, Timothy. *The Jerusalem Temple and Early Christian Identity*. WUNT 2/291. Tübingen: Mohr Siebeck, 2010.

———. "Mark, the Jerusalem Temple and Jewish Sectarianism: Why Geographical Proximity Matters in Determining the Provenance of Mark." *NTS* 62 (2016) 60–78.

Wasserstein, Abraham. "Notes on the Temple of Onias at Leontopolis." *Illinois Classical Studies* 18 (1993) 119–29.

Wellhausen, Julius. *Prolegomena to the History of Israel*. Scholars Press Reprints and Translations Series. Atlanta: Scholars, 1994.

———. *Prolegomena zur Geschichte Israel*. Berlin: Reimer, 1883.

Wexler, Bruce E. *Brain and Culture: Neurobiology, Ideology, and Social Change*. Cambridge: MIT Press, 2006.

White, Benjamin L. *Remembering Paul: Ancient and Modern Contests over the Image of the Apostle*. Oxford: Oxford University Press, 2015.

Wiley, Henrietta L., and Christian A. Eberhart, eds. *Sacrifice, Cult, and Atonement in Early Judaism and Christianity: Constituents and Critique*. RBS 85. Atlanta: Society of Biblical Literature, 2017.

Williams, Peter J. "An Examination of Ehrman's Case for ὀργισθείς in Mark 1:41." *NovT* 54 (2012) 1–12.

Wilson, Jonathan. *Inverting the Pyramid: The History of Football Tactics*. London: Orion, 2008.

Wise, Michael Owen. *Language and Literacy in Roman Judaea: A Study of the Bar Kokhba Documents*. Anchor Yale Bible Reference Library. New Haven: Yale University Press, 2015.

Witte, Markus, et al., eds. *Torah, Temple, and Land: Constructions of Judaism in Antiquity*. TSAJ 184. Tübingen: Mohr Siebeck, 2021.

Wollenberg, Rebecca Scharbach. *The Closed Book: How the Rabbis Taught the Jews (Not) to Read the Bible*. Princeton: Princeton University Press, 2023.

Wright, N. T. *Jesus and the Victory of God*. Christian Origins and the Question of God 2. Minneapolis: Fortress, 1996.

Yates, Frances. *The Art of Memory*. London: Ark Paperbacks, 1984.

Youtie, Herbert C. "ΑΓΡΑΜΜΑΤΟΣ: An Aspect of Greek Society in Egypt." *Harvard Studies in Classical Philology* 75 (1973) 161–76.

Zeichmann, Christopher B. "The Date of Mark's Gospel apart from the Temple and Rumors of War: The Taxation Episode (12:13–17) as Evidence." *CBQ* 79 (2017) 422–37.

Zelyck, Lorne R. "Recontextualizing Papyrus Oxyrhynchus 840." *EC* 5 (2014) 178–97.

www.ingramcontent.com/pod-product-compliance
Lightning Source LLC
Chambersburg PA
CBHW071246230426
43668CB00011B/1611